D1544021

Serializing Fiction in the Victorian Press

Serializing Fiction in the Victorian Press

Graham Law
Waseda University
Tokyo

palgrave

First published 2000 by
PALGRAVE
Houndmills, Basingstoke, Hampshire RG21 6XS and
175 Fifth Avenue, New York, N. Y. 10010
Companies and representatives throughout the world

PALGRAVE is the new global academic imprint of
St. Martin's Press LLC Scholarly and Reference Division and
Palgrave Publishers Ltd (formerly Macmillan Press Ltd).

Outside North America
ISBN 0–333–76019–0

In North America
ISBN 0–312–23574–7

This book is printed on paper suitable for recycling and made from fully managed and sustained forest sources.

A catalogue record for this book is available from the British Library.

Library of Congress Cataloging-in-Publication Data
Law, Graham.
    Serializing fiction in the Victorian press / Graham Law.
        p. cm.
    Includes bibliographical references and index.
    ISBN 0–312–23574–7
    1. Serialized fiction—Great Britain—History and criticism. 2. English fiction—19th century—History and criticism. 3. Serial publication of books—History—19th century. 4. Authors and readers—Great Britain—History—19th century. 5. Authors and publishers—Great Britain—History—19th century. 6. Literature publishing—Great Britain—History—19th century. I. Title.
    PR878.P78 L39 2000
    823'.809—dc21
                                                            00–031124

10 9 8 7 6 5 4 3 2 1
09 08 07 06 05 04 03 02 01 00

Printed and bound in Great Britain by
Antony Rowe Ltd, Chippenham, Wiltshire

Dedicated to the Memory
of
My Father and Mother

*

Fred Law 1920–90
Anna Law, née Kean, 1925–97

Contents

List of Plates

List of Figure and Tables

Preface

> Even imagination is the slave of stolid circumstance; and
> the unending flow of inventiveness which finds expression
> in the literature of Fiction is no exception to the general law.
>
> Thomas Hardy 'Candour in Fiction' *New Review*
> (January 1890)

Despite the name, almost from its beginnings, the newspaper has
contained material other than news. Perhaps unsurprisingly given
the insatiable Victorian appetite for stories in instalments, increasingly often in the second half of the nineteenth century, that 'other'
material was serial fiction. However, the significance of this trend
has been largely overlooked in conventional literary history.

Although only a handful of his fictional works appear in the British
Library Catalogue, the Scottish writer David Pae (1828–84; Plate 5)
was probably one of the most widely read novelists in mid-Victorian
Britain. Around 50 of his melodramas were serialized repeatedly in
a wide range of cheap weekly newspapers in Scotland and the English
provinces from the mid-1850s (see Table A.1). Often heralded as
the 'Queen of the Circulating Libraries' (see Walbank, 9–18), Mary
Elizabeth Braddon (1837–1915; Plate 6) could with equal justification have been proclaimed as the 'Queen of the Provincial Weeklies'.
A larger number and wider social range of readers probably encountered her work in the latter form, as at least 25 of her novels
from the mid-1870s first appeared in serial in syndicates of up to a
dozen such newspapers whose combined circulations covered virtually the whole of the United Kingdom (see Table A.4). Walter
Besant (1836–1901; Plate 8), an astute analyst of the changing fiction
market towards the end of the nineteenth century, also occasionally served the provincial syndicates, but by 1890 was selling serial
rights mainly to illustrated London newspapers through the agent
A.P. Watt (see Table A.6).

Although on a less regular basis than such committed 'newspaper
novelists' as Pae, Braddon and Besant, by around 1880 even more
distinguished writers were attracted to the newspapers by the size
of the potential audience or by the remuneration they offered. Fading

stars, like Harrison Ainsworth, Anthony Trollope and Charles Reade, sold late novels to the syndicators. All seven of the full-length novels produced during the last decade of Wilkie Collins's life appeared in popular weekly newspapers (see Plate 7 and Table A.5). Even George Meredith made an isolated and unwitting serial appearance in the *Glasgow Weekly Herald* at the end of the 1870s with *The Egoist* (Collie, 43–4). The readers of the rival *Glasgow Weekly Mail* enjoyed gala years in 1885–86, when, in addition to stories by Collins and Braddon, there appeared new tales by George MacDonald, William Black, Margaret Oliphant, Joseph Hatton, 'Hugh Conway', Rhoda Broughton and Thomas Hardy. Each of these writers issued a number of other works in the provincial journals. Normally in these cases, as in those of Braddon, Collins and Besant, serialization in British newspapers was followed almost immediately by similar appearances in journals in the United States and the colonies. Although the new literary lights of the 1890s, notably Stevenson, Haggard, Doyle and Kipling, were more attracted by the large sums then being offered by American popular magazines and newspaper syndicates, they also tended to show up subsequently in British newspapers, both provincial and metropolitan.

How and by what agencies were these newspaper appearances effected? What was the nature of the newspapers involved? Why did the market for serial fiction in British newspapers emerge so suddenly and grow so rapidly in the second half of the nineteenth century? Why did the dominant mode of newspaper publication, as represented by the instances of Pae, Braddon and Besant, change more than once within that period? What were the consequences for readership, authorship and literary form? These are the questions that the later chapters of this volume try to answer with some precision. But before embarking on that project in detail, in order to provide an adequate context for it, I attempt in the opening chapter, in much more rapid, broad and inevitably rather crude strokes, a general sketch of the history of the serial publication of fiction in Britain. This demonstrates the importance of the shift from the predominance of monthly to that of weekly instalments around the 1860s. Such an undertaking requires making a beginning well before the accession of Queen Victoria and considering the issue of novels in magazines and in independent parts as well as in newspapers. It also involves discussing such serialization both in relation to the development of the book trade in fiction and in comparison with the situation in other societies similarly undergoing rapid industrialization. This initial survey naturally relies heavily on secondary sources.

The remainder of this study, which makes a good deal of use of primary materials, is divided into two sections, both composed of three chapters. The first section tells the story of the who, what, where and how of newspaper serialization and syndication, while the second analyses causes, consequences and implications. The most important single source of information has been the extensive surviving records of Tillotsons's Fiction Bureau, most now being housed at either the Bodleian Library, Oxford or the Central Library, Bolton. With the exception of two volumes of agreements (MS.Eng.Misc.f.395/ 1–2) purchased from a bookseller, all the Tillotsons's records now held on deposit at the Bodleian Library were placed there in the mid-1960s by Mr Taylor of Newspaper Features Ltd, who bought the syndication business from Tillotsons in 1935, for the use of Mr Michael L. Turner, then as now on the staff of the library, while the latter was preparing his BLitt dissertation on the Fiction Bureau. The materials now held in the *Bolton Evening News* Archive at Bolton Central Library seem to have been mislaid for a time around the 1960s (see Turner, 'Tillotson's', 352), and were housed at the John Rylands Library, University of Manchester, for a period during the 1980s (see Jones, 'Tillotson's'). Other major sources include surviving business records and correspondence held in archives in civic and university libraries in Britain (mainly at Aberdeen, Cambridge, Dundee, and Sheffield) and in the USA (notably in the Berg Collection of the New York Public Library, at the Newberry Library, Chicago, and at the Wilson Library, University of North Carolina), plus the comprehensive collection of Victorian press directories held at the British Library Newspaper Library at Colindale. In the many cases where direct evidence of the activities of the syndicating agencies is unobtainable, I have been obliged to draw inferences and establish hypotheses based on my own *ad hoc* database recording the appearances of specific novels in specific newspapers. This was produced by rapidly scanning runs of many Victorian newspapers held in volume or on microfilm at Colindale and elsewhere, with the informal cooperation of other scholars in the field. Where appropriate, sections from this database appear in the Appendix.

As will be readily apparent, although this study can be broadly and fairly characterized as 'cultural materialist', in that it seeks to demonstrate the impact of nineteenth-century publishing patterns on the development of the Victorian novel, it resists the full-blown political teleology, economic determinism, and theoretical rigour characteristic of many neo-Marxist approaches. While I have learned a good deal from, in particular, the work of N.N. Feltes in his *Modes of Production of Victorian Novels*, with its theoretical underpinnings in Althusser, Poulantzas and Eagleton, in the end this book remains more closely attached to the tradition of empirical study of the development of the publishing industry, the reading public, and popular fiction, as represented by scholars such as Graham Pollard, Richard Altick and Louis James. There are a number of specific, local explanations for this which are perhaps worth outlining.

One concerns the reasons why the topic of fiction syndication has so far been largely overlooked, which are both practical and ideological. In practical terms, as already suggested, it has proved remarkably difficult to establish with any degree of certainty the precise nature of the operations of many of the syndicating agencies in question. Few of the business records of the Victorian fiction syndicators, as indeed of Victorian provincial newspaper publishers in general, appear to have survived. The newspapers themselves obviously form a vast and unwieldy mass of material, which is still largely uncharted and may well prove to be unchartable in any comprehensive sense. Due mainly to wartime bombing and the physical deterioration of the bound volumes of later Victorian newspapers which has often outpaced the resources of the microfilm programme, there are significant lacunae in many of the runs of the provincial weekly journals at Colindale. These can be filled only partially, and at great expense in time and labour, by consultation in numerous local collections, particularly those held in the civic libraries. The otherwise comprehensive bibliographies of later Victorian novelists as different as Hardy and Henty understandably tend to stop short when it comes to precise details of weekly serialization (see Purdy and Newbolt); specialist works on Victorian serial novels, such as those of Vann or Hughes and Lund, hardly scratch the surface of newspaper publication; and the available indexes to Victorian periodicals, notably the *Wellesley* and the University of Queensland Victorian Fiction Research Guides, show a strong preference for the literary monthlies. I have therefore been particularly conscious of my debt to those empirical scholars, both Victorian and modern, whose research has been presented in such a form as to make it easy to access their original sources of information. At the same time, the weekly news-miscellanies, whether provincial or metropolitan, have generally been treated as derivative, trivial or ephemeral by mainstream newspaper history where political coverage in the daily has generally been given priority, just as the thrillers and romances that began to dominate their entertainment pages by the end of the nineteenth century have, for most of the twentieth century, been generally disregarded by literary historians. In the end, Feltes's method in *Modes of Production* cannot entirely escape the charge of producing a materialist equivalent of Leavis's 'Great Tradition', centring as it does on the process of production of novels by Dickens, Thackeray, Eliot, Hardy and Forster. In contrast, scholars like Pollard, Altick and James, given the prevailing assumptions in literary studies at the time when they were carrying out their research, remained remarkably generous and eclectic in defining the field of publications worthy of their attention.

Another reason is the difficulty of providing a theoretically rigorous distinction between the terms 'magazine' and 'newspaper', which might be seen as fundamental to this project. This remains a problem even if we limit our focus to the second half of the nineteenth century which is the primary interest of this volume, rather than the much longer time-span that is rapidly traversed in Chapter 1. Towards the beginning of this period the term 'news' was sometimes held to include any original narrative, including prose fiction. Here I have employed the rule-of-thumb that a newspaper is a periodical of frequent appearance of which a significant proportion is devoted to information concerning recent public occurrences. This formulation roughly corresponds to the definition used for tax purposes at the beginning of the Victorian period. Though, as Victorian tax-collectors and taxpayers also realized, this leaves room for a substantial grey zone, it does permit a reasonably clear division between, say, weekly news-miscellanies like the Dundee *People's Journal* or the Saturday edition of the *Sheffield Daily Telegraph*, and weekly literary miscellanies like Dickens's *All the Year Round* or the *Family Herald*, all of which carried regular serial fiction in the 1860s. However, even that liberal definition is sometimes stretched in the pages that follow, largely because periodicals change in time and regularly outlive their editors and proprietors, themselves historical entities. Where consistency would make the telling of the story more difficult, I have cheerfully ignored the rule. I have, however, attempted throughout to use the term 'periodical' as a generic term to cover the inevitably overlapping categories of the 'newspaper' and 'magazine'.

I have thus opted for what I think of as intermediate theory, by analogy with the concept of intermediate technology in the field of development economics, that is, the minimum level of analytical apparatus necessary to carry out the job in hand. The changing fashions in high academic theory often resemble the rhythm of late-capitalist consumption patterns, and certainly produce a high level of disposability in scholarly discourse. In the same 'green' spirit in which we are now encouraged to put glass and plastic bottles into distinct recycle bins, I have attempted to present the 'hard' information on which this study is based as much as possible in discrete form in tables, notes and appendices, so that it can be more easily reused by other scholars who will doubtless disagree with the stories told and the conclusions drawn here.

GRAHAM LAW
Tanashi City, Tokyo

Acknowledgements

Without the assistance of a large number of individuals and institutions in the United Kingdom and North America, Australia and Japan, this volume could not have been completed. I would like here to take the opportunity to thank as many as possible of those to whom I have incurred obligations during the process of research, composition, and publication.

First, I would like to express my thanks to my colleagues in the School of Law, Waseda University, for allowing me to take a year's study leave from April 1997 to March 1998 to carry out the principal research for this project; also to the University authorities for granting leave of absence and a generous overseas research allowance; and, at the same, to the staff of the School of English and American Studies, Exeter University, where I studied as an undergraduate in the mid-1970s, and where I was warmly welcomed back as Honorary Research Fellow during my sabbatical year, and generously provided a base for my studies.

I am also grateful to the staff of the following libraries and archives, whose kindness and expertise was of immeasurable assistance: the Archives and Local Studies Section, Bolton Central Library; the Archives Section, Sheffield Central Library; the Berg Collection, New York Public Library; the Bodleian Library, Oxford; the British Library Newspaper Library, Colindale; the British Library, St Pancras; the Department of Special Collections and Archives, University of Aberdeen Library; the Devon and Exeter Institute Library; the Exeter University Library; the Harry Ransom Humanities Research Center, University of Texas at Austin; Kendal Municipal Library, Westmoreland; the Faculty of Law, Faculty of Politics and Economics, Takata Memorial, and Central Libraries, Waseda University; the Local Studies Department, Dundee Central Library; Manuscripts Department, the Wilson Library, the University of North Carolina at Chapel Hill; Pembroke College Library, Cambridge; Plymouth Civic Library; Princeton University Library, New Jersey; Special Collections, Newberry Library, Chicago; and Tokyo University Library.

I should especially like to record the kindness of the following individuals: Doreen Jarratt of the *Bolton Evening News* who kindly allowed me to view the W.F. Tillotson papers held in Newspaper

House; Jo Ellen Dickie of the Newberry Library, who did such a marvellous job locating documents among the voluminous Lawson papers; Kenneth Geoffrey March, who wrote to me about his research into the Leng family in the 1960s; Maggi Oxley of the *Sheffield Telegraph*, who searched long but in vain for any Victorian business records surviving at the Sheffield offices today; Michael J. Palmer, who provided information concerning the research into railway periodicals carried out by his father, John Palmer, deceased, formerly of ESTC, the British Library; Richard Taylor, of Carnforth, Lancashire, who provided information about his uncle Ernest E. Taylor, and Michael Farthing who put me into contact with him; Judith Cooke of Dundee, who talked to me of the history of the Pae family; and Pam Judd, Assistant Librarian of Pembroke College Library, who allowed me to work over the lunch break when time was so tight.

The following scholars have generously offered assistance and shared information in a variety of forms: Alexis Weedon; Andrew Gasson; Catherine Peters; Charles Johanningsmeier; Chris Baggs; Chris Brooks; Eddie Cass; Elaine Zinkhan; Elizabeth Morrison; Jennifer Carnell; John Stock Clarke; Lillian Nayder; Lucy Sussex; Mary Ann Gillies; Michael Turner; Paul Lewis; Peter Darling; Simon Eliot; Steve Farmer; Toni Johnson-Woods; and William Baker. Kimberly D. Lutz of New York University and Linda Sellars of the University of North Carolina were both efficient and resourceful in carrying out research tasks on my behalf. I would also like to make special mention of the assistance and stimulus I have received from the numerous members of the VICTORIA and SHARP-L electronic forums, under listowner Patrick Leary, of the History Department, Indiana University, who maintains both with great expertise and generosity. Julian Honer, Charmian Hearne and Eleanor Birne, commissioning editors at Macmillan, have been consistently encouraging and supportive. George Hughes and Adrian J. Pinnington both read through the completed manuscript and offered wise advice. The errors and infelicities which remain are, of course, entirely my own responsibility.

The author and publishers wish to thank the following individuals and institutions who have granted permission to make citations from unpublished materials: Special Collections, Newberry Library, Chicago, concerning the Victor Lawson papers; John B. Waters, Managing Director of the *Bolton Evening News*, and Barry Mills of the Local Studies Section, Bolton Central Library, concerning the

Bolton Evening News Archive; Faith Clarke, heir of Wilkie Collins, and The Library of Pembroke College, Cambridge, concerning the Collins–Watt correspondence; Michael L. Turner, Head of Conservation, Bodleian Library, concerning the Tillotsons's papers in his care; Judith Cooke, of Dundee, heir of David Pae, concerning the unpublished records of the Pae Family in her possession; Wayne Furman, Office of Special Collections, New York Public Library, Astor, Lenox and Tilden Foundations, concerning the A.P. Watt Archive in the Berg Collection of English and American Literature; and the proprietors of the *Aberdeen Journal*, and Jane Pirie of the Department of Special Collections and Archives, University of Aberdeen Library, concerning the Aberdeen Journals Records. With the exception of the unpublished papers of David Pae and Wilkie Collins, according to the institutions or individuals owning physical rights to the documents in question, no claims appear to have been made to copyright by heirs to the deceased writers involved, and thus it has not been possible to trace copyright-holders if any. Should any copyright holders make themselves known after publication, suitable acknowledgement will be made in subsequent editions.

Grateful acknowledgment is made to the following for permission to reprint or adapt material from previously published articles by the author: *Media History* for 'The Newspaper Novel: Towards an International History' (with Norimasa Morita, June 2000; *Victorian Periodicals Review* (Research Society for Victorian Periodicals) for 'Wilkie in the Weeklies: the Serialization and Syndication of Collins's Late Novels' (Autumn 1997), and 'Before Tillotsons: Novels in British Provincial Newspapers, 1855–1873' (Spring 1999); *Wilkie Collins Society Journal* for 'Last Things: Materials Relating to Collins in the Watt Collection at Chapel Hill' (1998) and '"Belt-and-Braces" Serialization: the Case of *Heart and Science*' (with Steve Farmer, 1999); *Humanitas* (Waseda University Law Society) for '"Engaged to Messrs. Tillotson and Son": Letters from John Maxwell, 1882–8,' (1999), and 'The Newspaper Novel: International Perspectives' (2000); SUNY Press for '"Our Author": Braddon in the Provincial Weeklies' (with Jennifer Carnell) in *Beyond Sensation: Mary Elizabeth Braddon in Context* by Marlene Tromp, Pamela K. Gilbert and Aeron Haynie, eds (© 2000, State University of New York Press, All Rights Reserved). Jennifer Carnell, Norimasa Morita and Steve Farmer have all kindly given permission for the author to adapt and reprint material from articles published jointly.

Acknowledgement is also made with gratitude to the following

for permission to reprint photographs of material in their posses-
sion: Waseda University Library for Plates 1 & 3, reproduced from
Progress of British Newspapers in the Nineteenth Century, Illustrated.
London: Simpkin, Marshall, Hamilton, Kent, [1901]; *The Courier*,
Dundee, for Plates 2 & 5; the Harry Ransom Humanities Research
Center, University of Texas at Austin, for Plates 4 & 6, from mate-
rial in the Wolff Collection; the British Library for Plates 9–15,
reproduced from original newspapers at the Newspaper Library,
Colindale, with respective shelfmarks S102, 2075, 400, 64, 3418,
1467 and 912; and the Southern Historical Collection, Wilson Library, The University of North Carolina at Chapel Hill for Plate 16.
Plates 7 & 8 are reproduced from the frontispieces of, respectively,
The Works of Wilkie Collins, vol. 1, New York: Peter Fenelon Collier,
[1900], and Walter Besant and James Rice *The Golden Butterfly*, London: Chatto and Windus, 1899, both in the possession of the author.

Finally, I must express my gratitude to the members of my family,
Noriko, Matthew and Simon, for allowing me far more than my
fair share of time and space at home in both Exeter and Tokyo to
be able to concentrate on newspaper novels over the last few years.

List of Abbreviations

AJR   Aberdeen Journals Records (MS 2770), Department of Special Collections and Archives, University of Aberdeen Library.

ALS(s)   Autograph letter(s) signed.

BERG   A.P. Watt Archive, Berg Collection, New York Public Library.

BODLEIAN   Tillotsons's Fiction Bureau Agreement Books, 1880–87 & 1890–94 (MS.Eng.Misc.f.395/1–2), Bodleian Library, Oxford.

Deacon's   *Deacon's Newspaper Handbook* (1877–94).

DLB   *Dictionary of Literary Biography*, 201 vols, Farmington Mills, MI: Gale Research, 1978–99.

DNB   *Dictionary of National Biography*, eds L. Stephen and S. Lee, 22 vols, plus supplements. London: Smith, Elder, 1882–1909.

May's   *May's British and Irish Press Guide* (1871–; *Willing's* from 1890).

MITCHELL   Letters from Wilkie Collins to William Tindell (#891117), Mitchell Library, Glasgow.

NCBEL   *New Cambridge Bibliography of English Literature*, ed. George Watson, 5 vols. Cambridge: Cambridge University Press, 1969–77.

NPD   Mitchell's *Newspaper Press Directory* (1846–; *Benn's* from 1978).

PAE   Records of the Pae Family of Newport on Tay, in the possession of Mr and Mrs A.J. Cooke, c/o Archive and Record Centre, Dundee.

PARRISH   Morris L. Parrish Collection, Princeton University Library.

PEMBROKE   Letters from Wilkie Collins to A.P. Watt, 1881–89 (LCII 2840–2), Pembroke College Library, Cambridge.

RN37–50   *A Return of the Number of Newspaper Stamps, 1837–50*. House of Commons Papers, 28:42, 1852.

RN51–53   *A Return of the Number of Newspaper Stamps, 1851–3*. House of Commons Papers, 39:117, 1854.

RN54   *A Return of the Number of Newspaper Stamps, 1854*. House of Commons Papers, 40:497, 1855.

RSC51   *Report from the Select Committee on Newspaper Stamps*. House of Commons Papers, 17:558, 1851.

Sell's   *Sell's Dictionary of the World's Press* (1884–1921).
TLS(s)   Typed letter(s) signed.
TURNER   Tillotsons's Fiction Bureau Records in the care of Michael
                L. Turner, Head of Conservation, Bodleian Library, Oxford.
VFL   Victor Fremont Lawson papers, Newberry Library, Chicago.
VFRG   *Victorian Fiction Research Guides*. Victorian Fiction Research
                Unit, Department of English, University of Queensland.
WFT   W.F. Tillotson Papers, held in the *Bolton Evening News*
                Offices, Newspaper House, Churchgate, Bolton, Greater
                Manchester.
WILSON   A.P. Watt and Company Records (#11036), General and
                Literary Manuscripts, Southern Historical Collection,
                Wilson Library, The University of North Carolina at Chapel
                Hill.
WOLFF   Wolff Collection, Harry Ransom Humanities Research
                Center, University of Texas at Austin.
ZBEN   *Bolton Evening News* Archive (ZBEN), Bolton Central Library,
                Greater Manchester.

Part I:
Context

1
Serial Fiction

1.1 The eighteenth-century serial market

Serial fiction was not a Victorian invention. As R.M. Wiles has shown, already by the second quarter of the eighteenth century 'number books, independently issued in weekly or monthly parts, wrapped in blue paper covers, had become a common commodity in the publishing business' (*Serial*, 75). In his short-title catalogue of such works, Wiles even lists a few scattered experiments of a similar type dating back to the 1670s. By 1750 works thus published in fascicles already totalled several hundred and were occasionally issued in editions of as many as two or three thousand copies. Among them were both original and reprinted works, translated texts as well as those in the vernacular, and, among a wide variety of other genres, a number of examples of prose fiction, including Cervantes, Defoe, and imitations of Richardson such as *Pamela in High Life*. Apparently the motivation was simply economic. In this way, publishers could spread the cost of production, and subscribers the cost of purchase, painlessly over the period of consumption, while the nationwide distribution network for periodical publications was already more highly developed than that for works in volume form. The practice thus substantially increased the market for books when the extent of the reading public was still limited. After the boom in the 1730s and 1740s, Wiles suggests, though the works in question were often of inferior quality, instalment publication of both fiction and non-fiction continued to be commonplace throughout the century. A 1774 House of Lords' decision (in *Donaldson* v. *Beckett*) to uphold the 28-year limit to copyright duration stated in the Act of 1709 – against the claims under common law to perpetual copyright by the established booksellers of the Stationer's Company – opened the way for cheap and legal reprints of classic works.[1] Thus novels in numbers had a history of at least a hundred years before Dickens's *Pickwick Papers* began to appear in April 1836.

By the second half of the eighteenth century, with the stimulus to novel reading and writing provided by the emergence of Richardson, Fielding and Smollett, the fiction market had expanded considerably, but by then serial stories in magazines offered serious competition to the numbers trade. In *The English Novel in the Magazines 1714–1815*, which also includes a comprehensive catalogue of magazine novels and novelettes, Robert D. Mayo (chs 2–3) has shown that scattered examples of shorter serial fiction can be found before 1850. These occur not only in weekly essay-serials in the tradition of Addison and Steele's *Tatler* and *Spectator*, but also in monthly 'historical miscellanies' of current affairs, most notably Edward Cave's *The Gentleman's Magazine* (1731–1907) – probably the first periodical to use the word 'magazine' in its title. However, longer instalment fiction does not become a regular feature in the magazines until the emergence after the mid-century of the 'common miscellanies', concerned more with pleasure than knowledge and appealing to a less discriminating audience. Mayo (chs 4–5) shows that there was a brief period around 1860 when the most talented novelists of the day wrote original fiction for their own short-lived miscellanies, notably Smollett in the *British Magazine*, but with little popular success. They thus soon:

> deserted the field for others more promising, leaving it largely in the hands of extractors, abridgers, and translators, professional and semi-professional writers of less than mediocre talent, and callow amateurs endowed only with a desire to see their writings in print.
>
> (Mayo, 274)

By 1790 there were nearly 30 common miscellanies in circulation, the most long running and successful being the *Town and Country Magazine* (1769–96), and *Lady's Magazine* (1770–1837). Both were heavily dependent on sentimental serial fiction and, in their heyday, may have attracted more than 10 000 monthly subscribers (Altick, *English*, 47n). Following the *Donaldson v. Beckett* decision, there also began to appear a number of weekly periodicals specializing in reprinted instalment fiction (see Mayo, App. II), whether collections of classics like those in John Harrison's *Novelist's Magazine* (1780–89) or versions of Gothic romances as in Thomas Tegg's *Marvellous Magazine* (1802–4). Thus there was already a lengthy tradition in magazine novels before periodicals like *Blackwood's Edinburgh Magazine* and *Bentley's Miscellany* started to carry serials in the 1820s and 1830s.

More importantly for our purposes, as Wiles again has shown (*Serial*, ch. 2; *Freshest*, ch. 7), the practice of publishing material – including prose fiction – by instalments in newspapers, had grown up before the flourishing of the common miscellanies in the 1770s and even before the boom in number books of the 1730s. Wiles states that by then 'instalment printing had become a regular thing in the less distinguished areas of the newspaper world', whether metropolitan or provincial (*Serial*, 41).[2] Both the rise and demise of this practice in the eighteenth century can be attributed to a large extent to the legislation enacted to tax newspaper production, which, throughout its history from 1712 to the mid-nineteenth century, was designed by government to control dissent as much as to collect revenue. The first London news-pamphlets, like the *Mercurius Britannicus*, can be traced back to the 1620s, and the first government-controlled newspapers, like the *London Gazette*, to the 1660s. However, it is not until after the lapse in 1695 of the 1662 Printing Act, which had generally restricted commercial licences to print to a handful of London houses, that there appeared newspapers with any degree of independence in the metropolis or any newspapers at all in the provinces (Feather, *Provincial*, ch. 1; Cranfield, *Development*, chs 1–2). Just 17 years later, as Table 1.1 shows, Parliament again moved to curb the expansion of newspapers by imposing a shilling tax on each advertisement in journals published weekly or more frequently, and a newspaper stamp of a halfpenny on a half-sheet (two-pages) and a penny on a full sheet (four-pages), the two formats then current. The effect was to double the price of most existing papers, and some of the less well-established simply ceased publication. However, despite official disapproval, a number of enterprising proprietors promptly shifted to printing six-page papers of a sheet and a half, which were not specified in the 1712 Act and thus subject to much less onerous taxation as pamhlets. The extra space created was generally filled with a variety of reprinted matter in instalments, including serial fiction, thus creating a form of news-miscellany. The *Original London Post; or, Heathcote's Intelligence*, and Andrew Brice's Exeter *Post-Master; or, the Loyal Mercury*, both of which reprinted novels by Defoe around 1720, are notable examples, although at best only a few scattered copies of most journals of this type have survived.

The miscellaneous instalment material must soon have become popular with subscribers, since there are quite a number of surviving examples of stamped newspapers, with serial fiction featured prominently, from the period *after* this legal loophole was closed in 1725. Wiles thus suggests that fiction 'was probably more acceptable in serial form than any other kind of prose' (*Freshest*, 334).[3] Nevertheless, Wiles also argues that the tightening of the Stamp Act in 1725 did affect the news-miscellanies significantly in both the short and long term. Some immediately ceased publication, while most quickly cut down their miscellaneous material and reduced their size to half a large sheet. The eighteenth-century newspaper stamp legislation also created uncertainty in a number of other areas. Since enforcement was left to the understaffed Commissioners of Her or His Majesty's Revenue, evasion was rife, especially in the first half of the century. Some rebellious papers evaded the tax openly – like the farthing half-sheet *All-Alive and Merry* (1739–43) which, among other serials, reprinted both *Robinson Crusoe* and *Joseph Andrews* – until they were vigorously repressed by legislation in 1743. This offered a substantial reward to any person seizing a hawker of unstamped newspapers, who in turn became subject to a lengthy gaol sentence (Andrews, 1:153). In addition, the various Stamp Acts failed to provide a transparent definition of what constituted 'news'. The authorities thus made various attempts to impose the newspaper stamp on monthly historical miscellanies like Cave's *The Gentleman's Magazine*, on account of the 'intelligence' that they contained (Andrews, 1:149–50), while on other occasions 'news' seems to have been interpreted to mean 'anything original or of immediate interest', thus even including the first appearance of a novel (Pollard, 'Serial', 256–7). The most significant long-term trends in serial publication were thus an increasing reliance on reprinted matter, and a shifting of instalment material out of the stamped newspaper itself into unstamped supplements. These tended either to develop into independent magazines or, more commonly, to become indistinguishable from the number books themselves.[4] The combination in the second half of the eighteenth century of a series of steep rises in the stamp and advertisement taxes,[5] of the ambiguity concerning the application of the law, and of the boom in the common miscellanies, seems finally to have driven novels out of newspapers to a very large extent for many decades.

Clearly then the publication of fiction in instalments, whether as independent numbers or in magazines and newspapers, was by no means new to the Victorian era. Nevertheless, in marked contrast to the typical Victorian serial novel, continuous stories in the eighteenth-century generally tended:

- to be reprinted, abridged, or translated works;
- when original, to be written by amateurs or undistinguished authors;
- to be broken into incomplete units and indifferent to the art of serialization;
- to be shorter than novel-length;
- to belong to the general genre of narrative (history) rather than to the specific one of the novel; and
- to be unillustrated.

While there were many exceptions to these tendencies individually, there was perhaps only one on all these counts – Smollett's *Sir Lancelot Greaves*, which ran originally in monthly parts in his *British Magazine* from January 1760 to December 1761, with a series of large octavo plates, and which in many ways prefigures the art of serialization as it was to develop in the nineteenth century (Mayo, 276–88). For, by the mid-Victorian decades, the presence of the novel in parts was far more pervasive and the motivation no longer a matter of simple economics, thus suggesting that 'something in the culture of the time made it especially receptive to the serial' (Hughes and Lund, 4).

1.2 Transition and the book market

We should remember that the expansion in the eighteenth-century reading public, which in part produced and was in part produced by the developments summarized above, was still largely limited to the commercial middle classes (Altick, *English*, ch. 2). The half-century or so before the accession of Victoria, from the first rumblings of the French Revolution, through the Napoleonic Wars, to the aftermath of the First Reform Bill, was a period of extreme political agitation and rapid social change in Britain. The economic transformation that now goes by the name of the Industrial Revolution ensured that, by around 1840, the majority of the population in England and Wales were living in urban areas, and the proportion of the employed population engaged in commerce, trade and manufacturing was more than double that engaged in agriculture. The population of England and Wales as a whole doubled in the first half of the nineteenth century, with the decade from 1810 exhibiting the highest rate of growth (Porter, 3). Moreover, though no reliable figures are available, it seems likely that the reading public expanded significantly during this period, not only in absolute terms but also as a percentage of the total population. Physical conditions both in the home and at work could hardly have been more unfavourable to the growth of reading as a leisure activity among manual labourers, whether in the mushrooming industrial towns or in the declining agricultural communities. However, as Altick again has shown (*English*, 83), it was chiefly 'from among skilled workers, small shopkeepers, clerks, and the better grade of domestic servants that the new mass audience for printed matter was recruited during the first half of the century', since these were the principle groups whose occupations required literacy.[6]

The uncoordinated and indeed frequently antagonistic efforts of different groups of evangelicals or radicals, such as the Sunday School or 'corresponding society' movements of the 1790s, were the main institutional stimuli to the growth of basic reading skills among the lower classes in general and the fractions mentioned above in particular. The evangelicals and radicals were also among the first groups to exploit the possibilities of the mass production and distribution of reading matter. Key examples from the same period would be the sale of over a million copies of cheap editions of Tom Paine's *Rights of Man* with the aid of the London Constitutional Society, or the hawking of several million of Hannah Moore's Cheap Repository Tracts with the support of the Clapham Sect (Altick, *English*, ch. 3; Feather, *History*, 161–3). What is more important for our purposes is that the growth of the mass reading public from the close of the eighteenth century can in no significant way be seen as indebted to the actions of either government or the established book industry.

Not only was there no provision of public funds for elementary education until after the 1832 Reform Bill, but also, in a series of steps from 1776 to 1815, Tory administrations raised to punitive levels the taxes affecting publications, especially those issued periodically. Though there were still those prepared to echo Soame Jenyns's view, voiced in 1757, that, to those born to poverty and drudgery, ignorance was 'a cordial, administered by the gracious hand of providence, of which they ought never to be deprived by an ill-judged and improper education' (cited in Altick, *English*, 31–2), the evangelical view tended to prevail. This was that the spread of literacy was necessary to extend the appreciation of true Christian principles, including the divine sanction underlying social rank, and thus to bolster the existing social arrangements. The aim of what came later to be known as the 'taxes on knowledge' was above all to throttle radical dissent, without providing too much hindrance to evangelical campaigns. There were, of course, also more directly repressive measures such as the prosecution of authors, printers, or hawkers for blasphemy, seditious libel, or obstructing the thoroughfare. But the process of arrest, trial and punishment tended to produce martyrs whose blood, symbolic or real, increased the circulation of their works tenfold.

As Table 1.1 shows, the cost of the newspaper stamp was increased progressively, rising to a maximum of 4d in 1815, while the tax on printed advertisements was raised by increments of 6d, to peak at 3s 6d the same year. Throughout this period there was also in force an excise duty on paper for printing which obviously affected stationers and booksellers as much as the newspaper publishers. These duties, levied at prohibitive rates, remained in force until after the 1832 Reform Bill, and during those years the London dailies were priced at 7d, beyond the purchasing power of all but the wealthy. Yet the political onus of the taxes can be seen most clearly in two of the notorious 'Six Acts' of 1819. These aimed explicitly at wiping out the radical press which had reappeared vigorously after Waterloo, most famously in the form of Cobbett's *Political Register*. One act introduced a strict 'security system' to prevent sedition and blasphemy, whereby publishers were required to deposit substantial bonds as surety against future conviction. Another, without affecting the existing rates of taxation, sought to redefine the term 'newspaper.' The stamp duty was thereby levied on all periodicals containing news or comments on news,[7] published more frequently than once in 26 days, printed on not more than two sheets (eight larger or sixteen smaller pages), and priced at less than 6d before the imposition of the tax. Specifically exempt were papers 'containing only matters of devotion, piety, or charity' and part-issues of books in reprint, but considerable discretion concerning what actually counted as 'news' was left to the Board of Inland Revenue, which alone had the power to initiate a prosecution (*RSC51*). Like their precursors, the 1819 acts succeeded in their primary intention only in the short term. The storm of radical dissent revived once more in the 'War of the Unstamped Press' of the early 1830s,

Table 1.1 'Taxes on Knowledge' imposed in Great Britain, 1712–1861

Year	Advertisement tax	Newspaper stamp	Excise duty on printing paper
1712	1s per advertisement in newspapers	$\frac{1}{2}$d on a half-sheet 1d on a sheet	*
1725	–	$\frac{1}{2}$d per half-sheet	*
1757	2s per advertisement in all periodicals	1d per sheet 1d per half-sheet 1$\frac{1}{2}$d per sheet	*
1776	–	1$\frac{1}{2}$d per half-sheet 2d per sheet	*
1789	2s 6d per advertisement	2d per half-sheet 2$\frac{1}{2}$d per sheet	*
1794	–	–	2$\frac{1}{2}$d per lb
1797	3s per advertisement	3$\frac{1}{2}$d per half-sheet 4d per sheet	–
1802	–	–	3d per lb
1815	3s 6d per advertisement	4d per copy	–
1833	1s 6d per advertisement	–	–
1836	–	1d per copy	1$\frac{1}{2}$d per lb
1853	Abolished	–	–
1855	–	Abolished	–
1861	–	–	Abolished

* Between 1712 and 1794 paper excise duty was imposed at varying price levels per ream (c. 500 sheets) according to vastly complex schedules distinguishing different types of paper. New schedules were created in 1712 (12 types) and 1781 (77 types), followed by periodic increases expressed in percentage terms. During this period duties paid on paper for printing thus rose steadily, but probably averaged below 15% before 1781 and over 20% afterwards. There were, of course, much higher customs duties on imported paper. See Coleman, chs 5 and 12.
Sources: Dowell, 4:323–49; or as noted.

but this time directed largely against the Newspaper Tax itself (Wiener, *War*). However, the side-effects on the periodical market in general, and on that for instalment fiction in particular, were of far longer duration. Among the most significant were the relatively slow growth of provincial journalism, and the encouragement given to monthly rather than weekly serialization, over the first half of the nineteenth century (Read, ch. 3; Cranfield, *Press*, ch. 7).

However, it would obviously be unwise not to recognize that the regime of punitive taxation on periodicals outlined above also had the significant secondary intention of bolstering government revenue during a period of major overseas military commitments and severe domestic inflation, followed by postwar unemployment. This general climate of economic uncertainty and insecurity was also one of the major factors underlying the conservatism of the established metropolitan book publishers, who were in no rush to learn the lessons of mechanization and mass production. Paper was in short supply and, at 36s a week by 1811, London printing-house compositors were among the best-paid skilled workers in Britain (Plant, ch. 18). Even major publishing firms went bankrupt in the financial crisis of 1825–26, notably Constable and Ballantyne in Edinburgh, or Hurst and Robinson in London. Thus respectable publishing houses were generally content to serve the growing market for luxury books as conspicuous signs of wealth, precisely for the class of *nouveaux riches* who had made their fortunes speculatively through manufacture of, or trading in, wartime supplies. The price of the duodecimo volumes then standard for original novels was doubled and redoubled from the half-a-crown (2s 6d) typical of Smollett's time to the gentlemanly sum of half-a-guinea (10s 6d) by the 1830s. The unprecedented commercial success of Scott's Waverley novels, the series of lengthy historical romances issued in sumptuous formats from 1814 at increasingly exorbitant prices by Constable, was a major cause not only of the second doubling but also of the emergence of the three-volume set at a guinea-and-a-half as the standard format for original Victorian fiction (Gettman, ch. 8). The first example at this price was probably Scott's *Kenilworth* of 1821, which, like its predecessors in the Waverley series, sold more than 10 000 copies as a triple-decker within a few years of publication.

Nevertheless, it would be unreasonable to hold Scott responsible for the fact that the three-volume format retained its dominance almost to the end of the nineteenth century, with its inflated 1820s price still intact.[8] The standard Victorian triple-decker was, of course, unlikely to sell more than a thousand copies, never mind 10 000, and was aimed less at wartime speculators than at the patrons of the circulating libraries, who showed a very limited interest in taking risks. The vogue of circulating libraries had begun as early as the mid-eighteenth century, but the custom of borrowing and sharing reading matter, rather than purchasing it for private use, was greatly encouraged by the inflated prices for literature in the first quarter of the nineteenth century.[9] The custom can be seen also in the practice of communal subscriptions to newspapers, and their rental by the hour in coffee and public houses during the same period.

But it was not until the mid-century, when prevailing economic conditions in many ways encouraged a shift to the mass production of copyright works, that the library market came to be dominated by Charles Edward Mudie. Mudie's set up its headquarters in New Oxford Street in 1852, and offered a speedy and efficient service not only to metropolitan readers but to those in the provinces and the colonies also. As the adjective suggested, Mudie's Select Library was particular both about the social standing of its clientele and the 'moral' status of the works it approved for rental. The basic annual subscription was a guinea, which allowed only a single volume to be borrowed at a time, but the most popular was the two-guinea subscription which permitted the taking out of four volumes simultaneously, and was thus geared to the form of the multi-volume novel (Griest, 39). Despite protests in the later Victorian decades from many progressive publishers – as well as voices as disparate as the patrician critic Matthew Arnold, who described the library system as 'eccentric, artificial, and unatisfactory in the highest degree' ('Copyright', 327) and the bohemian novelist George Moore, who compared its function to that of the nursemaid – the triple-decker did not meet its fate until the Mudies themselves decided that it was no longer in their economic interests to promote it. This was after the death of Charles Edward in 1890 (Griest, ch. 7).

The hegemony of Mudie's over the triple-decker is by now something of a cliché, but what often receives less emphasis is that the corollary of the conservatism of the book trade in original Victorian fiction is the enterprise and versatility of both the prior serial and the subsequent reprint markets. In contrast to the immobility of the price of the triple-decker, the cost of reprinted works declined steadily during the century, as Altick has shown (*English*, chs 12–13). Three categories are significant for our purposes: fiction out of copyright; copyright fiction reprinted by the original publisher; and copyright fiction reprinted by subsequent publishers. In all three cases such reprints tended to be packaged and marketed as a series of works by an individual author or in a branded 'library'. Unlike the original triple-decker, they tended to conclude with a number of pages of 'announcements' advertising the publisher's wares in the same or similar series, sometimes amounting to a complete catalogue.[10] Many valuable copyrights were sold on cheaply following the publishing crash of 1826, and Thomas Cadell then issued an edition of the Waverley novels at only 5s the volume. Colburn and Bentley was probably the first established house to begin re-issuing its own triple-decker novels in single volumes at 6s in the Standard Novels series from 1831 (Turner, *Index*), but it was not until around the mid-century that this practice became the norm. The house of Routledge was the most successful in buying up residual copyrights, including those of Bulwer-Lytton, Harrison Ainsworth, and G.P.R. James, and exploiting them in cheap editions. Notable long-running series were its shilling Railway Library starting in 1848, or the sixpenny Caxton Novels issued from the late 1870s (Mumby, *House*). From the late 1860s there were numerous series of 'yellow-back' novels conspicuously on sale up and down the country at W.H. Smith's chain of railway bookstalls (Topp; Wilson, *First*, ch. 5). The popularity of the yellow-backs forced many mainstream publishers to drop the prices of their reissues to 3s 6d – the enterprising new house of Chatto and Windus was among the first to exploit the trend in its Piccadilly Library from the 1870s.[11] By the later Victorian decades fiction expired from copyright was available for pennies, though usually set in minuscule type in double columns. After Scott's copyrights finally gave out, the Waverley novels appeared at 6d the volume in the 1860s (from Hotten, later incorporated into Chatto and Windus), and even at 3d the volume in the 1870s (from John Dicks). Finally, we should note that cheap reprint specialists like Routledge sometimes published original fiction by lesser writers at low prices and in compact formats among their reprint series, thus demonstrating that the hegemony of the triple-decker was short of absolute.

1.3 The Victorian serial market

The prior publication of original fiction in serial form presents an even more varied picture in terms of both medium and mode of transmission. It now seems likely that, for almost the whole of the Victorian period, a significant majority of 'original' novels published as books had appeared previously in monthly or weekly instalments, as independent numbers, in magazines, or in the pages of the newspapers that are our particular interest here (Pollard, 'Serial', 271–7; Altick, *Presence*, 59). In addition, and particularly in the earlier Victorian decades, there was undoubtedly a vast and still largely uncharted sea of stories, published serially in cheap popular periodicals but never reprinted as books, or at least never deposited in the copyright libraries. By the later Victorian decades, editors were turning increasingly to serial fiction to attract readers not only to general miscellanies but also to journals targeted at groups inclined to particular religious and political parties, or affiliated to specific trades, professions, and disciplines (Keating, 36–8). The general trend during the Victorian period was from the predominance of monthly serialization in relatively expensive, low-circulation formats, pro-duced as petty commodities for the bourgeois market by the book publishers, to that of weekly serialization in relatively cheap, high-circulation formats, produced as commodities for the mass market by newspaper proprietors. In order to chart this shift and begin to explain its causation, it is useful to divide the Victorian period into three overlapping stages, early (1830s–1850s), middle, (1850s–1870s), and late (1870s–1890s).

A Early stage

In the early stage the dominant modes of serial transmission of bourgeois fiction are publication in monthly literary magazines and miscellanies, or in independent monthly parts. As we have seen, some of the common miscellanies flourishing in the second half of the eighteenth century, like the *Lady's Magazine*, survived into the following century and continued to feature translated, reprinted and amateur fiction, including some longer serials (Mayo, App. II). However, it was not until after 1819, when the Newspaper Stamp Act finally removed the threat of the imposition of the stamp duty on monthly periodicals, that there began to appear a generation of magazines prominently featuring full-length original serials by es-tablished writers. These new monthlies were of two types. First, there were the salty Tory review magazines led by *Blackwood's*, which from 1820 featured John Galt's anecdotal studies of local life, *The Ayrshire Legatees* and *Annals of the Parish*. Also noteworthy in this category were *Fraser's*, which carried Thackeray's early fiction, and William Curry's *The Dublin University Magazine*, which was edited by Charles Lever from 1842 and serialized a number of his own novels. All three were long-lived and retained their literary import-ance: Sheridan Le Fanu and Rhoda Broughton were major serialists in the *The Dublin University Magazine* from the 1860s, as was Charles Kingsley in *Fraser's* around the mid-century, while *Blackwood's* later carried 'chronicle' sequences of novels by Bulwer-Lytton and Mar-garet Oliphant. Although *Blackwood's* and *Frasers'*, in particular, initially cultivated a liveliness and irreverence in contrast to the ponderous tone of the quarterly reviews, whether the Whig *Edinburgh*

Review (1802–1929) or the Tory *Quarterly* (1809–1967), the new Tory monthlies nevertheless remained relatively sober and solid periodicals.

The second group comprised the lighter, frothier miscellaneous magazines which tended to be Liberal in sentiment and to have a much shorter effective life. Frederick Marryat's *Metropolitan Magazine*, published by Saunders and Otley, was probably the first to carry serial fiction, beginning with his own *Peter Simple* from June 1832. The most successful was *Bentley's Miscellany*, an illustrated magazine initially edited by Dickens and featuring *Oliver Twist* from its second issue, though he was succeeded as editor as early as 1839 by Ainsworth, whose *Jack Sheppard* proved equally successful in its pages. Colburn's *New Monthly* was a well-established journal which quickly shifted to the miscellany format in imitation of *Bentley's* in 1837 and carried serials by Marryat, Ainsworth, and Thomas Hook. *Ainsworth's Magazine*, leading off with the proprietor's *The Miser's Daughter* in 1842, was started after he quit *Bentley's*. Thus by the 1840s original serial fiction by best-selling writers was a firmly established feature of a number of monthly magazines. In general these were owned by established book publishers (*Fraser's* was an exception), priced at half-a-crown or more (the *Metropolitan* and *The New Monthly* sold at 3s 6d), and with subscriptions under 10 000 at best (Altick *English*, 393–4).

By this time there was also a boom in the publication of new novels in independent monthly parts, generally comprising 32 octavo pages with two illustrations inside a coloured paper wrapper, and sold at a shilling. As is well known, this fashion was started, 'virtually by accident' in Robert L. Patten's phrase (46), by the unanticipated runaway success of Dickens's *Posthumous Papers of the Pickwick Club* from Chapman and Hall. As Patten has shown in most detail (ch. 3), *Pickwick* started out in early 1836 as a series of humorous sporting plates to which the young writer was asked to attach a loose narrative, along the lines of Pierce Egan's 'Tom and Jerry' series *Life in London* (1820–21), perhaps the most popular of early nineteenth-century number books.[12] A healthy 1000 copies of the first number of *Pickwick Papers* were issued in April 1836 but sales at first were disappointing. However, they began to pick up from the fourth number with the appearance of Sam Weller and had reached close to 40 000 before the final double instalment appeared in November 1837. Dickens had quickly established personal command of the project, and the 20 monthly numbers in

Table 1.2 Main Victorian metropolitan monthlies carrying serial fiction

Title	Issues	Price*	Character	Notes†
Blackwood's Edinburgh Magazine	(1817–1980)	2s 6d	Review miscellany	Serials from 1820
Fraser's Magazine	(1830–82)	2s 6d	Review miscellany	Prop. Longmans from 1863
Metropolitan Magazine	(1831–50)	3s 6d	Literary miscellany	
The Dublin University Magazine	(1833–77)	2s 6d	Review miscellany	
Bentley's Miscellany	(1837–68)	2s 6d	Literary miscellany	Prop. W.H. Ainsworth, 1854–68
The New Monthly Magazine	(1814–84)	3s 6d	Literary miscellany	Prop. Colburn; serials after 1837
Ainsworth's Magazine	(1842–54)	1s 6d	Literary miscellany	
Douglas Jerrold's Shilling Magazine	(1845–48)	1s	Radical miscellany	
Sharpe's London Magazine	(1845–70)	1s	Literary miscellany	1½d weekly until 1848
The Train	(1856–58)	1s	Literary miscellany	
Macmillan's Magazine	(1859–1907)	1s	Review miscellany	
The Cornhill Magazine	(1860–1975)	1s	Literary miscellany	Prop. Smith, Elder
Good Words	(1860–1906)	6d	Religious miscellany	Weekly until 1861
Temple Bar	(1860–1906)	1s	Literary miscellany	Prop. Bentley from 1866
The Sixpenny Magazine	(1861–68)	6d	Popular literary miscellany	Prop. John Maxwell
The St. James's Magazine	(1861–82)	1s	Literary miscellany	Founded by John Maxwell
London Society	(1862–98)	1s	Literary miscellany	Prop. Kelly's from 1883
The Fortnightly Review	(1865–1954)	2s 6d	Intellectual review	Fortnightly until Oct. 1866
The Argosy	(1865–1901)	1s	Literary miscellany	Prop. Ellen Wood from 1867
Belgravia	(1866–99)	1s	Literary miscellany	Prop. John Maxwell until 1876
Tinsley's Magazine	(1867–72)	1s	Literary miscellany	
Broadway	(1867–74)	1s	Literary miscellany	Prop. Routledge
The St. Paul's	(1867–74)	1s	Literary miscellany	
The Gentleman's Magazine	(1731–1907)	1s	Literary miscellany	Serials from 1868
Cassell's Family Magazine	(1874–1932)	6d	Literary miscellany	Formerly weekly *Family Paper*
Time	(1879–91)	1s	Current affairs magazine	Prop. Kelly's from 1881
Longman's Magazine	(1882–1905)	6d	Popular literary miscellany	Succeeded *Fraser's*

The English Illustrated Magazine	(1883–1913)	1s	Illustrated Literary miscellany	Prop. Macmillan until 1893
Woman's World	(1886–90)	1s	Women's magazine	Until 1887 as *Lady's World*
Woman at Home	(1890–1920)	6d	Popular women's magazine	
The Idler Magazine	(1892–1911)	6d	Illustrated literary miscellany	
The Pall Mall Magazine	(1893–1914)	1s	Illustrated literary miscellany	
The Lady's Realm	(1896–1914)	6d	Illustrated women's magazine	

* Price = Price when serials began to appear regularly.

† For further details concerning editors, proprietors, and changes of title or price, see *Sources*.

Sources: NPD; NCBEL, 3:1839–54; Houghton *Wellesley*; Sullivan, Vol III; Sutherland, *Stanford, Wolff, Waterloo*; and original journals.

their distinctive duck-green wrappers remained his preferred mode of initial serial publication throughout his career, his last complete novel *Our Mutual Friend* (1864–65) appearing in identical format.

However, this fact in itself has tended to encourage exaggeration of the prevalence of the practice in the Victorian period. In reality, new novels in monthly numbers flourished only in the 1840s, were thereafter only a safe economic option for writers at the peak of their popularity, and were rarely written by women.[13] Lever, whose *Confessions of Harry Lorrequer* appeared from Curry from March 1839, Frances Trollope, with *Michael Armstrong* from Colburn starting in the same month, and Ainsworth and Marryat, whose *Tower of London* and *Poor Jack* were issued respectively by Bentley and Longmans from January 1840, were among the first to cash in on Dickens's success. All were to use the method of part publication on subsequent occasions. There were even exceptional cases where novels came out simultaneously in numbers and a monthly magazine, such as Lever's *Harry Lorrequer* and *Charles O'Malley* (1840–41), both of which appeared in the *Dublin University Magazine*, the former at irregular intervals from late 1837. Minor writers who experienced success through monthly instalments included Henry Cockton with *Valentine Fox* (1840) and Frank Smedley with *Frank Fairleigh* (1849–50). Among other works by writers associated with their comic magazine *Punch*, Bradbury and Evans issued Thackeray's *Vanity Fair* and *Pendennis* almost back-to-back in numbers from January 1847, in bright yellow covers and generously illustrated by the author. Though it seems that Thackeray's number sales rarely went much above the 10 000 mark, in the following decade *The Newcomes* (1853–55) and *The Virginians* (1857–59) appeared in the same format from the same publisher (Harden, 1–15). Chapman and Hall similarly brought out a number of Trollope's works at the height of his fame in the 1860s, beginning with *Orley Farm* from 1861 (Hamer). But, as Sutherland has shown (*Victorian Fiction*, 102–5), the number of monthly instalment novels issued had virtually dried up by the early 1870s: Trollope's *The Way We Live Now* (1874–75) was one of the last, and William Black's *Sunrise* (1880–81) probably the last of all.[14]

A number of exceptions obviously exist in the early Victorian decades to the norm that fiction with pretensions to respectability was serialized in monthly portions. Although, as in the later decades of the eighteenth-century, there were still many cheaper weekly periodicals carrying reprint fiction only,[15] Chapman and Hall's experiment with *Master Humphrey's Clock* (1840–41), an illustrated 3d weekly miscellany written entirely by Dickens, was probably unique. Although it was originally planned to feature only shorter pieces, both fiction and non-fiction, poor sales soon forced Dickens to turn to the serial novel (Patten, ch. 6). *The Old Curiosity Shop* and *Barnaby Rudge* thus appeared first in this format. However, the device of the crippled old narrator proved cumbersome and Dickens found the constraints of weekly composition not to his liking, so the trial was soon abandoned. Similarly, though the publication of reprinted fiction in twopenny weekly parts continued to be common, the weekly appearance of Ainsworth's *Jack Sheppard* in threepenny numbers, concurrently with its appearance in *Bentley's Miscellany*, was unusual. Other and perhaps more significant exceptions are to be found in the metropolitan weekly press, following the rise of the French *roman-feuilleton* (discussed at the end of the chapter), and of reductions in the taxes imposed on publications.

With the 1832 Reform Bill, the movement to repeal the taxes on knowledge gained strength. However, the result, as Collet Dobson Collet argued (ch. 3), was a series of unsatisfactory Parliamentary compromises, unwanted by the established daily papers, and offering little encouragement to proprietors who wished to commence cheap journals aimed at a mass audience. The advertisement tax was reduced to 1s 6d in 1833 and the paper duty halved to $1\frac{1}{2}$d in 1836, while the newspaper stamp itself fell from 4d to 1d. At the same time, however, the 1836 Newspaper Stamp Act not only greatly increased the severity of the requirements concerning the security bonds to be posted against the issuing of criminal libel, but also reintroduced the threat of stamp duty being levied on monthly publications if they were deemed to carry news. It thus did little to reduce the heavy fiscal burdens on the resources of the small-scale publisher (Collet, ch. 21; *RSC51*; Lee, 42–3). Though a number of major new provincial weeklies, such as the *Midland Counties Herald* (1836–), started up then, and while some older one, like the *Manchester Guardian* (1821–), switched to bi-weekly issue, the main stimulus from the reduction in the stamp was to the metropolitan Sunday newspaper market. Soon after there were attempts to serialize original fiction in a number of weekly papers experimenting with illustration, most notably the well-established *The Sunday Times* (1822) and the new *The Illustrated London News* (1842–). *The Sunday Times* began to publish novels regularly in 52 weekly parts in January 1840, beginning with Leman Rede's unsigned *The Royal Rake*, with large illustrations. Its circulation jumped immediately from 13 000 to over 20 000 an issue (*RN37–50*, 16–7).[16] *The Illustrated London News* published rather shorter serials less regularly, beginning with Cockton's *England and France; or, The Sisters* (18 March–23 December 1843).[17] A number of other scattered examples of novels in news-papers have also been located in this period.[18] However, priced at sevenpence and sixpence respectively, *The Sunday Times* and *The Illustrated London News* were still well beyond the reach of the masses, and the experiments ceased by the early 1850s as these journals sought to establish a more sober reputation.[19]

This can be explained by the fact that the weekly melodramatic serial had become increasingly associated with the lower depths of the proletarian market during the 1840s. In one sense, Disraeli's lament on the division of England into:

> Two nations; between whom there is no intercourse and no sym-pathy; who are as ignorant of each other's habits, thoughts, and feelings, as if they were dwellers in different zones, or inhabit-ants of different planets.
>
> (*Sybil*, bk. I ch. 5)

applies forcefully to the world of early Victorian publishing. Litera-ture aimed at proletarian readers was then written by a separate set of hack writers, published by a separate group of dubious 'Salisbury Square' publishers, and distributed at weekly intervals through chan-nels anathema to the established booksellers, whether street hawkers or tobacconist's shops. And yet the urban 'penny blood', which from the later 1830s rapidly superseded the traditional rural popular forms of the ballad, broadside, and chapbook (James, *Fiction*, ch. 1), is best understood as a miniaturized, plagiarized, parodic version of the bourgeois monthly serial. The dominant sub-genres of the novel of the 1830s – the Gothic romance, Silver Fork novel, Newgate novel, and domestic melodrama (described by Engel and King, ch. 4) – all soon had their reduced counterparts in the slum market. In-deed, the prefix 'penny' itself in this period not only denotes the price but also connotes this process of diminution. From the second half of the 1830s, serial novels in penny weekly parts, in penny Sunday papers, and in penny weekly miscellanies began to appear in turn, often from the same writers and publishing houses.

Melodrama in penny weekly instalments, generally a leaflet of eight double-column large octavo pages with a fierce woodcut at the head, perhaps began as early as 1835 with Gothic or criminal tales like *The*

Calendar of Horrors (1835–36) or *History and Lives of the Most Notorious Highwaymen* (1836–37) (Haining, 30–1). Blatant imitations of bourgeois best-sellers by Dickens and G.P.R James, for example, were common – beginning with *Post-Humorous Notes of the Pickwickian Club; or, The Penny Pickwick* from 1838 – as were tales of criminal heroes like Dick Turpin or Jack Sheppard, who had already been celebrated by Ainsworth.[20] *Varney the Vampire; or, the Feast of Blood* (1845–47) and *Ada the Betrayed; or, the Murder at the Old Smithy* (1841–42), both probably by James Malcolm Rymer (1804–82), were among the most popular and typical of titles. *The Mysteries of London* (1845–50) and *Mysteries of the Court of London* (1849–56), principally by the Chartist leader G.W.M. Reynolds (1814–79), which aped Eugène Sue's triumphs in the Paris newspapers, must have been among the longest running. Many of the above examples were published by the young Edward Lloyd (1815–90), who moved his offices from Shoreditch to Salisbury Square, off Fleet Street, in 1842, thus producing the sobriquet which was often used for the publishers of penny bloods (*DLB*, 106: 173–7).[21] As Margaret Dalziel has observed (ch. 4), among the Salisbury Square hacks, George Reynolds was probably at the same time the most sophisticated in stylistic terms as well as the most challenging to conventional morality. However, in the bourgeois world, these crude penny bloods had a blanket reputation for scurrility and indecency that they hardly deserved.[22]

From the beginning of the 1840s there is evidence of the Salisbury Square publishers mimicking not only the bourgeois novel in parts but also the periodical. This can be seen initially in a number of unstamped penny Sunday papers which openly imitated the names and formats of established stamped Sundays – like *The Weekly Dispatch, Bell's Life in London and Sporting Chronicle* (1822–86), and *The Sunday Times*, with their varying combinations of radical politics, crime reporting, lively woodcuts, and sports coverage. The penny imitations were generally four-page folios with a prominent woodcut beneath the heading banner. They seem to have narrowly escaped breaching the Stamp Act, since their main appeal was lurid crime reporting that was at least semi-fictional, but they also tended to follow *The Sunday Times* in offering melodramatic serial fiction, usually on the front page. Typically short-lived examples were *Clark's Weekly Dispatch* (1841) and *Bell's Penny Dispatch, Sporting and Police Gazette, and Newspaper of Romance, and Penny Sunday Chronicle* (1842) (Morison, 255–62). The most persistent and significant was Edward Lloyd's *The Penny Sunday Times and Peoples' Police Gazette*, which started in April 1840 and seems to have survived until around the end of the decade (*NCBEL*, 3:1811). Typically in 1843 it ran a serial 'The Waltz of Death', as by 'C.G. Ainsworth', in imitation of the famous scene in *Old Saint Paul's*.

However, the nature of the stamp legislation still made this a hazardous method of cheap fiction serialization, and by the mid-1840s it was apparent that the safer course for the popular publishers was to divide news and fiction into separate periodicals. Thus were started a series of penny weekly miscellanies, miniature versions of *Bentley's Miscellany*, which, in addition to a generous helping of serial and complete fiction, featured a variety of instructive and entertainment material, including verse, recipes, scientific and statistical information, and answers to correspondents.[23] The most common format quickly emerged as 16 quarto pages in two or three columns, once more with a dramatic woodcut on the front page. From the start these journals attempted to appeal to a family audience by maintaining a rather more respectable image than the penny instalment novels (Mitchell, ch. 1). The first and most austere was John Biggs's *The Family Herald* which initially appeared in the form of a four-page newspaper, with no illustrations, and only small doses of fiction. More daring were *The London Journal* (owned by George Stiff, published by George Vickers, and edited in turn by George Reynolds, J.F. Smith, and Pierce Egan the younger), or *Reynolds's Miscellany*, founded by the writer on leaving *The London Journal* and published by John Dicks. At the same time Edward Lloyd began to experiment with a separate 'Companion' to *The Penny Sunday Times* which contained melodramatic fiction only (Altick *English*, 345–6), in addition to a number of shorter-lived miscellanies. Encouraged by the striking success of John Browne Bell's new threepenny radical Sunday paper *The News of the World* (1843–),[24] at least three of the Salisbury Square publishers began also to issue their own legitimate Sunday newspapers, still strong on crime and violence and fiercely radical in opinion, but with no serial fiction and duly and legally stamped. The first was *Lloyd's Weekly Newspaper*, which began in 1842 as a cheap imitation of the *The Illustrated London News* but was soon modelling itself on Bell's successful formula, to be followed in 1847 by George Stiff's *The Weekly Times* and in 1850 by *Reynolds's Weekly Newspaper* (Berridge 'Popular').

The Salisbury Square publishers obviously at first learned something from the mass production methods used on bourgeois best-sellers like *The Pickwick Papers*. There Chapman and Hall had been forced to employ stereotyping (that is, printing with a solid plate cast from a mould taken from the surface of a forme of type), once the copies called for had exceeded 10 000 per month and back numbers were in demand (Patten, 68). But Edward Lloyd and his like were producing many different serials on a weekly basis, and Peter Haining (14) has estimated that a minimum run of 20 000 copies of each issue of the penny bloods would be necessary to clear costs. Indeed, Reynolds's *Mysteries of London* was rumoured to have approached sales of half a million an issue (Sutherland, *Stanford*, 680). Whatever the validity of that rumour, there seems little doubt that, by the mid-1850s, the most popular penny miscellanies were selling well over a quarter of a million copies, while at least one of the threepenny radical Sunday newspapers easily cleared over 100 000.[25] It is thus not surprising that in 1843 *The Family Herald* claimed to be the first journal ever to be produced entirely by machine, including its typesetting (James, *Print*, 46), while in 1855 Edward Lloyd was the first English publisher to install an American Hoe rotary printing press, and among the first to experiment with esparto grass for paper-making and to open up his own paper-mill in Kent (Altick, *English*, 345n; Haining, 31–2; Plant, chs 13–15).

B Middle stage

Moving on to what we have designated the middle stage of Victorian fiction serialization, centred on the decade from 1860, the first trend we should note is the simultaneous erosion of the autonomy of the proletarian market and of bourgeois prejudice against the weekly serial. By the end of that decade, the typical penny instalment novel had shifted noticeably from the 'penny blood' sold in the slums to the 'penny dreadful' aimed at the emerging juvenile market. Edward Lloyd had 'turned respectable' during the course of the 1850s and no longer published serial fiction, and the leading publishers were increasingly of the type represented by Edwin J. Brett of *Boys of England* (1866–99). At the same time the penny miscellanies were increasingly reorienting themselves towards the expanding female market (Mitchell, ch. 7).[26] *Reynolds's Miscellany*, with the lowest circulation among the three major journals, was closed down in 1869 when its position had already been overtaken by John Dicks's *Bow Bells*. By supplementing its serial fiction – notably by the ageing Harrison Ainsworth – with music, needlework and dress patterns, *Bow Bells* seems to have appealed especially to young female servants (James, 'Trouble', 358–9).[27]

An even more interesting sign of this crossing of borders is the nature of the alarm caused by the fashion in the early 1860s for what were soon being called 'Sensation Novels' – serials like, most famously, Collins's *The Woman in White* (1859–60) or Braddon's *Lady Audley's Secret* (1862), which set improper and mysterious events within respectable domestic environments. The outrage was due at least in part to the fact that sensation fiction transgressed accepted social boundaries. It did this not only by inserting what had hitherto been seen as the proletarian themes of violence, infidelity and insanity into bourgeois settings, but also by encouraging the middle classes to participate in the proletarian mode of weekly serialization. Braddon had succeeded in 'making the literature of the kitchen the favourite reading of the Drawing-room', as Fraser Rae (98) put it in 1865, while a review of Collins's *Armadale* the following year saw 'Sensational Mania' as a 'virus . . . spreading in all directions, from the penny journal to the shilling magazine, and from the shilling magazine to the thirty shillings volume' ('Belles Lettres', 270).[28]

The general point is that during this middle stage, the dominant position of the monthly serial underwent a serious and finally successful challenge from the weekly serial, both in the form of cheap family miscellanies issued in the metropolis, and led by Dickens's own journals, and in the many news miscellanies that sprang up like mushrooms in the provincial cites in the wake of the removal of the taxes on knowledge. However, this development has often been obscured in conventional accounts of the Victorian periodical, which have tended to place an undue emphasis on the brief boom in new shilling monthly literary magazines in the 1860s.[29] These new journals were generally illustrated, ran to 120 pages or more, and carried at least one original serial novel, as well as a wealth of miscellaneous entertainment material. They clearly offered value for money to circulating library subscribers, and quickly dented the market both for the older generation of miscellanies like *Blackwood's*, and for the novel in shilling monthly parts. Smith, Elder's *The Cornhill Magazine*, begun with a fanfare at the beginning of 1860, attracted the most attention. With Thackeray as its first editor, and with serials by both him and Trollope and also illustrations by Millais, the magazine went all out for quality (Huxley, 100). Nearly 110 000 copies of the first issue were sold, and the circulation remained above 70 000 for the first two years, allowing George Smith to offer extravagant sums for serials, like the £10 000 initially offered for Eliot's *Romola* (1862–63) or the £5000 accepted by Collins for *Armadale* (1864–66).[30] But within three years sales had fallen to below 50 000 and to little more than half of that by the end of 1868. This was partly because of the explosion of similar journals, but also because of competition from the growing market for weekly magazines, thus supporting Charles E. Pascoe's contention in the *Atlantic Monthly* of 1884, that the shilling monthlies represented the end rather than the beginning of a publishing tradition.

The most distinguished of the other house magazines was *Macmillan's*, where serial fiction was intended, at least at first, to be only a minor attraction. In this it shared common ground with Chapman and Hall's new review, *The Fortnightly* which, despite its title, became a monthly from 1866, and frequently carried superior serials.[31] Lesser publishers soon followed suit, including Bentley with *Temple Bar*,[32] *Tinsley's Magazine*, and Routledge with *Broadway*. These house magazines predominantly featured fiction by their own regular authors, and, even if not entirely self-financing, served to provide valuable advertising for the novels when published in volume (Schmidt, 143). Other shilling monthlies of second rank were mainly vehicles for the work of their popular editors: Mary Braddon's *Belgravia, Argosy* which was sold to Mrs Henry (Ellen) Wood by Alexander Strahan, and James Virtue's *The St. Paul's*, planned as a Trollope vehicle.[33] Like *Cornhill*, one or two of these shilling monthlies started spectacularly with circulations in six figures, though many soon had to be satisfied with an audience below ten thousand (Altick *English*, 359–60). *Belgravia* was typical with an average circulation of around 15 000 in its first decade, with a peak of over 18 000 in 1868 falling to around 13 000 in 1876, when it was sold to Chatto and Windus (Sullivan, 3:31). By the early 1870s the boom in the shilling monthlies was clearly over, and a couple of the weakest journals expired at this point, although many others continued publication with declining circulations until well after the demise of the triple-decker in the mid-1890s. By the 1880s, however, the menu of fiction offered by, say, *Belgravia, Temple Bar*, or even *Cornhill*, often appeared second-rate when compared with that in the liveliest provincial and metropolitan weekly journals.

For, by the mid-1860s, there was also a wide variety of cheap weekly magazines combining instalment fiction with other instructive and entertainment features, aimed at a broad family audience ranging from the solid middle classes down to the servants and skilled artisans of the 'respectable' working class. The origins of these journals can be traced back to the penny papers started up in the early 1830s by bourgeois philanthropic bodies, whether utilitarian or evangelical, aiming to bring the gospel of political economy or of Christ, or often a combination of the two, to the benighted poor. As has often been shown, though in many ways admirable in the quality of both content and form, these publications seem only initially to have circulated below the reaches of the lower middle classes.[34] The most important were the *Penny Magazine* (1832–46), sponsored by Henry Brougham's Society for the Diffusion of Useful Knowledge and published by Charles Knight, and the *Saturday Magazine* (1832–45) from the Society for the Promotion of Christian Knowledge. Both were illustrated and sold for only a penny. Early on the *Penny Magazine* claimed a circulation in six figures, but, despite the pictures, there was no leaven of imaginative fiction and its diet of instructional material was often experienced as indigestible, so that sales had fallen below a break-even point of 50 000 by the mid-1840s and the venture was terminated. Though the *Saturday Magazine* suffered a similar fate (James, *Fiction*, ch. 2), *Chambers's Edinburgh Journal*, produced commercially by the brothers William and Robert Chambers but with a very similar programme, had an opposite trajectory. It was unillustrated and sold for a $1\frac{1}{2}$d but included 'wholesome' complete tales from its early issues. It started in 1832 with a circulation of little over 20 000 limited to Scotland, but by the mid-century was selling all over the country in quantities approaching six figures. In 1854 the title was changed to *Chambers's Journal of Popular Literature, Science and Arts*, and instalment novels began to appear with the new editor Leitch Ritchie's 'Wearyfoot Common'. In 1858 the Scot Ritchie was joined (and soon replaced) by the glittering London writer James Payn, and in 1861 production was largely shifted to London. By then serial fiction from established names had become a major attraction, including those by Captain Mayne Reid and Payn himself, whose mystery novel *Lost Sir Massingberd* achieved a major success in 1864 and singlehandedly raised the circulation by 20 000 (*VFRG*, 17: 3).

By then *Chambers's Journal* had a host of weekly competitors prominently featuring serial fiction. Notable evangelically inclined weeklies included the Religious Tract Society's *The Leisure Hour*, while *Cassell's Family Paper* was the best-known among the magazines in the 'useful knowledge' tradition. By the mid-1860s, however, there was little difference in form or content between *Cassell's* and the original proletarian miscellanies like *The Family Herald*. Even *The London Journal*, whose editor and star writer J.F. Smith had been lured away by *Cassell's* in 1855, was sold in 1858 to the Ingram family of *The Illustrated London News*, and began to feature reprints of Scott's Waverley novels, alongside the work of Reade, Braddon, and Pierce Egan, Jr. There were also many more short-lived entrants into the same market. The Irish publisher John Maxwell, for example, attempted a variety of formats, including the penny *The Welcome Guest* (purchased from Henry Vizetelly in 1859), the twopenny *Robin Goodfellow* (July–September 1861 only), and *The Halfpenny Journal*.

Nevertheless, it is difficult to underestimate the importance of Dickens's family journals in establishing the acceptability of the weekly miscellany in the bosom of the middle class. Both *Household Words*, published by Bradbury and Evans, and its successor *All the Year Round*, published as well as conducted by Dickens following his falling out with his publishers over his marital difficulties, were unillustrated 16-page double-column octavo miscellanies, selling at 2d a week.[35] *Household Words* was more instructive and reformist, sold a healthy average of perhaps 40 000 copies a week, but only carried shorter serial fiction latterly and occasionally.[36] *All the Year Round* seems regularly to have sold over 100 000 copies while Dickens was alive, was noticeably less agitative in tone, and led off each issue with an instalment of a full-length serial, beginning with *A Tale of Two Cities*, but including many of the best-selling sensation novels of the 1860s.[37] On hearing the news that Bulwer-Lytton was to write a serial for *All the Year Round* in 1861, the *Publishers' Circular* declared, with only a touch of exaggeration, that 'the eminent author may now descend from the six shilling Quarterly even to the penny weekly without the slightest fear of losing caste' (cited in Sutherland, *Victorian Novelists*, 187).

In sum, by around 1870 the weekly miscellanies offered a serious challenge in the serial fiction market to the dominance of the monthly magazines which had already passed their peak of popularity. The weeklies were published not only by established novel publishers like Bradbury and Evans but also by a wide range of periodical specialists, philanthropic bodies, and newspaper companies, with the capital and technology to produce *en masse*. They had penetrated the circles of circulating-library readers, but also extended much further down the social scale.[38] Alvar Ellegard's comparison of the estimated circulations of the principle monthly and weekly miscellanies (13–22) makes the point clearly.

The marked success of the weekly miscellanies seems to have militated against the reintroduction of serial fiction into metropolitan

Table 1.3 Major Victorian metropolitan weeklies carrying serial fiction

Title	Issues	Price*	Character	Notes†
The Sunday Times	(1822–)	7d	Sunday newspaper	Serials in 1840s only
The Penny Sunday Times	(1840–50?)	1d	Popular Sunday newspaper	Prop. Edward Lloyd
The Illustrated London News	(1842–)	6d	Illustrated newspaper	No serials 1854–1882
The Family Herald	(1843–1940)	1d	Popular literary miscellany	No serials initially
The London Journal	(1845–1912)	1d	Popular literary miscellany	
Reynolds's Miscellany	(1846–69)	1d	Popular literary miscellany	Pub. John Dicks
Household Words	(1850–59)	2d	Literary miscellany	
The Leisure Hour	(1852–1905)	1d	Religious miscellany	Monthly from 1881
Cassell's Family Paper	(1853–74)	1d	Popular literary miscellany	As *Cassell's Magazine* 1861–74
Chambers's Journal	(1832–1956)	1½d	Literary miscellany	Serials from 1854
The Welcome Guest	(1858–61)	1d	Popular literary miscellany	Prop. John Maxwell from 1859
All the Year Round	(1859–95)	2d	Literary miscellany	
Once a Week	(1859–80)	3d	Illustrated literary miscellany	Prop. initially Bradbury and Evans
The Weekly Budget	(1861–1913)	1d	Popular news miscellany	Pub. jointly in Manchester during 1860s
The Queen	(1861–1970)	6d	Illustrated women's newspaper	
The Halfpenny Journal	(1861–5)	½d	Popular literary miscellany	Prop. John Maxwell
The Quiver	(1861–1926)	1d	Religious miscellany	Prop. Cassell
Bow Bells	(1862–97)	1d	Popular literary miscellany	Prop. John Dicks
The Graphic	(1869–1932)	6d	Illustrated newspaper	Serials from 1873
The World	(1874–1922)	6d	Society newspaper	Prop. Edmund Yates
The Pictorial World	(1874–92)	6d	Illustrated newspaper	
The Whitehall Review	(1876–1912)	6d	Society newspaper	
Life	(1879–1906)	6d	Society newspaper	
The Lady's Pictorial	(1880–1921)	6d	Illustrated women's newspaper	
England	(1880–98)	1d	Popular newspaper	
The People	(1881–)	1d	Popular Sunday newspaper	

Cassell's Saturday Journal	(1883–1921)	1d	Popular literary miscellany	Serials from mid-1880s
The Weekly Times	(1847–1912)	1d	Popular Sunday newspaper	Serials from mid-1880s
The Weekly Dispatch	(1801–1928)	1d	Popular Sunday newspaper	Serials from early 1890s
Reynolds's Weekly Newspaper	(1850–1967)	1d	Popular Sunday newspaper	Serials from early 1890s
Lloyd's Weekly Newspaper	(1842–1931)	1d	Popular Sunday newspaper	Serials from late 1880s
Tit-Bits	(1881–1994)	1d	Popular miscellany	
Answers to Correspondents	(1888–1956)	1d	Popular miscellany	Answers from 1890
Pearson's Weekly	(1890–1939)	1d	Popular miscellany	
To-day	(1893–1905)	2d	Illustrated miscellany	

* Price = Price when serials began to appear regularly.

† For further details concerning editors, proprietors, and changes of title or price, see Sources.

Sources: NPD; NCBEL, 3:1839–54; Houghton, Wellesley; Sullivan, vol. III; Sutherland, Stanford; Wolff, Waterloo; and original journals.

weekly newspapers for a considerable period after the removal of the taxes on publishing. The campaign of the Association for the Promotion of the Repeal of the Taxes on Knowledge, led by the radical MP Thomas Milner-Gibson with Collet as secretary, and finally backed, against its own economic interests, even by *The Times* (1785–), eventually achieved adequate Parliamentary support. Again as shown in Table 1.1, the advertisement tax, the newspaper stamp (except as an optional postal charge), and the paper duty, were all finally removed, in 1853, 1855, and 1861 respectively, though the security system was not abolished until 1869 (Collet, chs 6–20; Altick, *English*, chs 14–15; Lee, 43–9). Thus the organization of the press was freed of fiscal distortion for the first time since the reign of Queen Anne.

The immediate results for existing papers were rapid decreases in prices, and increases in both circulation and advertising revenue, with the last by no means the least important. Magazines were designed from the first to be bound up into volumes for preservation, and thus the monthly miscellanies, like novels issued in monthly parts, tended to carry ephemeral advertising material only on their disposable coloured paper wrappers. The weekly miscellanies continued this custom, although many also followed the practice of the reprint volumes in inserting in their final pages internal notices by the publishers, as can be seen in the 1850s in weeklies as different as *Household Words* and *Reynolds's Miscellany*. However, from their beginnings the newspapers were thought of as disposable and thus were not designed for binding into volumes, so that they were free to include advertising material within the body of the publication (Andrews, 1:88–92). Already by the later decades of the eighteenth century, in the case of both metropolitan as provincial papers, revenue from advertising was significant, though probably on average less than a third of that derived from sales (Raven; Cranfield, *Press*, 84–5, 184–6). However, according to Terry Nevett's calculations ('Advertising', 15–22), national expenditure on newspaper advertising more than tripled during the first half of the nineteenth century to reach a total of more than half a million pounds even before the repeal of the tax. So, by the 1860s and 1870s, for even the smaller provincial papers 'the proportion of total revenue made up by advertising was between one-half and three-fifths' (Lee, 87),[39] and similar figures were recorded by major dailies like *The Times* or the *Manchester Guardian* around the same period (Brown, 15–16).

These financial changes obviously had important long-term effects on the London daily press, including the appearance of the penny morning paper (when the *Daily Telegraph* halved its price in 1856), the ending of the hegemony of *The Times*, and the gradual rise of what, in 1887, Matthew Arnold labelled the 'new journalism' ('Up to Easter', 638–9). The principle markers of New Journalism in the metropolitan press of the 1880s were innovations both in visual style (the use of banner headlines, cross-headings, illustrations, and display advertisements) and in verbal content (less political and more miscellaneous material, including interviews, 'human interest' stories, feature pages, and sports news). While Arnold recognized the vitality of this new mode, he derided it as essentially 'feather-brained', like the new generations of voters enfranchised by the Reform Bills of 1867 and 1884. However, as Joel Wiener has suggested ('How'), to understand the cultural determinants of these changes requires a more systematic and balanced analysis than Arnold offers. Along with both Alan Lee (ch. 4) and Laurel Brake (*Subjugated*, ch. 5), Wiener argues that the phenomenon of New Journalism should be seen not simply as an abrupt consequence of commercialization, but also as the slower filtering into the mainstream press of developments visible rather earlier in the century in popular and provincial weekly newspapers. Indeed, the more immediate, and, from our point of view, more immediately significant, effects of the repeal of the taxes on knowledge occurred in the provincial press, where there was an explosion of new newspapers, predominantly Liberal in affiliation.

As Collet shows (2:32–3) with reference to the relevant volumes of Mitchell's annual *Newspaper Press Directory*, while only a dozen new journals appeared in London itself between 1854 and 1856, the number of English provincial newspapers jumped suddenly from 264 to 379 during the same period. Regular and stable local daily newspapers were established for the first time in the major cities, whether entirely new organs like the *Sheffield Daily Telegraph* and *Liverpool Daily Post* (both 1855), or by conversion from established weekly papers, as in the case of the *Glasgow Herald* (1859) and *Leeds Mercury* (1861). All of these sold at only 1d an issue, and there were at least 50 such dailies outside London by 1865. From the late 1860s there was a new wave of halfpenny daily evening papers in the provinces, with the *Bolton Evening News* (1867) in industrial Lancashire among the first. Most urban areas of any importance quickly had at least two competing newspaper proprietors of different political persuasions (Lee, ch. 5). As shown in detail in Chapter 2, even the smallest market town soon had its own weekly journal with the assistance of 'partly printed sheets' produced in London – around 100 towns that had never had a newspaper before gained one in the five years following the abolition of the newspaper stamp (cf. Jones, *Powers*, 23–4). Among this profusion of new provincial newspapers, perhaps the most prevalent and distinctive was the weekly news miscellany. This normally appeared on a Saturday, contained not only a summary of the week's local and national news but also a variety of instructive and entertainment matter, as well as increasing amounts of advertising material, was priced at most at twopence, and often reached a wide geographical and social readership. These weekly newspapers gradually began to feature fiction material: at first in Scotland and then in northern and western England and Wales; initially complete tales but increasingly serials; at first local or reprinted material, but gradually original work by established writers. Steady sources of supply soon required the development of various modes of syndication, initially informal and small-scale like those developed for the work of David Pae. This process did not reach its full potential until around 1880 in the late stage of Victorian fiction serialization, but it was already a growing force in the 1860s.

C   Late stage

The late stage of Victorian fiction serialization can be sketched with relative brevity since it forms the substantive content of this volume. Typical circulations for the older generations of monthlies in the last decades of the nineteenth century were the 12 000 claimed by *Cornhill* in 1882 (Altick *English*, 395), the 8000 to which *Temple Bar* had fallen after 1895 (Gettman, 148), *Belgravia's* 3500 in 1887 (*VFRG*, 14: 2), or even the 500 recorded by *Fraser's* in 1879 shortly before its closure (Nelson, 213). By the 1890s there was an entirely new generation of illustrated monthly miscellanies, the first and most successful of which was George Newnes's *Strand Magazine* (1891–1950), followed by *Pearson's Magazine* (1896–1939), both of which were populist and imperialist, sold at only sixpence, and had circulations of over a quarter of a million by the end of the century (Altick *English*, 396). Rather more select and with correspondingly lower circulations and shorter lives were *The Pall Mall Magazine* and *The Idler Magazine*. But, with the exception of *Pall Mall*, these new magazines tended to avoid lengthy serial novels (*VFRG*, 9, 23). In fact the new monthlies, especially that of Newnes, avoided longer items and articles altogether, and complete short stories were the dominant narrative form, though continuity was often provided by the concept of the series of anecdotes.[40] By then the average length of the novel had shrunk dramatically following the rapid demise of the triple-decker, and the new mass-market novels of adventure, mystery and romance relied heavily on the mechanisms of enigma and suspense encouraged by the weekly serial.

For, from around the mid-1870s, the dominant mode of initial British periodical publication (whether measured in terms of the number of works issued, the size of the audience reached, or the remuneration offered to authors) had shifted gradually but unmistakably from serialization in single metropolitan magazines, whether monthlies like *Cornhill* or weeklies like *All the Year Round*, to syndication in groups of provincial weekly papers with complementary circulations. The firm of Tillotson and Son of Bolton, Lancashire, proprietors of the *Bolton Weekly Journal* (1871–) as well as the *Bolton Evening News*, were undoubtedly the pioneers in this development. Their 'Fiction Bureau', a newspaper syndication agency founded in 1873 and specialising in novels in serial, had a nationwide clientele from the beginning and an international one within a decade. Almost immediately, though, there were a number of similar organizations selling serial fiction to provincial newspapers nationwide. But these direct competitors were in the end less of a threat to the Bolton firm than a variety of indirect rivals who began to appear from around 1880. In combination, these new entities succeeding in undermining the brief dominance of the provincial newspaper as a vehicle for serial fiction and returning the initiative to the London press. Some were the new literary agents, most notably A.P. Watt, who by the early 1890s wielded enormous influence in the periodical market. Others were a new generation of metropolitan weekly newspapers targeting a nationwide audience, which began to carry novels in instalments. These included both 'class' and 'mass' journals, that is, papers aimed at either the distinct professional classes or the undifferentiated masses, an antithesis in vogue from the mid-1880s.[41] Among the more expensive and prestigious class weeklies were Society journals like *The World* or pictorial papers like *The Graphic*, both of which began to carry serial fiction as early as the mid-1870s. The new mass penny weeklies of the 1880s included both Conservative Sunday papers like *The People*, and fragmentary news miscellanies led by George Newnes's *Tit-Bits*. This second shift contributed to a much more rapid and unambiguous process of commodification of fictional content and form than had taken place under the provincial syndicators.

Above all this book is concerned with the nature and role of the provincial fiction syndicates, and the reasons for their rise and demise. The central argument is that the syndication of serial fiction in newspapers represents an important but overlooked transitional phase between the 'Gentlemanly Publishing' of the mid-century, with its cloth-covered volumes and literary monthlies, and the mass-market magazines and paperbacks of the turn of the century (Saunders, *Profession*, ch. 10). During this period the size and social range of the novel-reading public expanded considerably, but the divide between 'quality' and 'popular' modes of production and reception had not yet hardened. This volume rejects as prejudiced the conventional, uniformly negative view of the syndicator (the name itself is likely to mislead) as a philistine and exploiter, who was to the author as the factory owner was to his hands. Instead it demonstrates that such agencies were under-capitalized, economically unstable, and thus unable to wield hegemonic power. By 1870 stereotype machines, the essential tool of the provincial proprietor-syndicator, were available for as little as seven guineas,[42] and fees could be collected piecemeal from the subscribing journals before the substantial payments had to be made to established authors like Braddon or Collins, Besant or Hardy. It argues that the decentralized mode of production of fiction syndication had a dual potential. For a brief period, it created a variety of local sites of interaction with, as well as a marked expansion of readership; it increased the social and geographical range of outlets as well as the remuneration available to authors; and it offered a venue for provincial themes and genres as much as the metropolitan and imperial emphases of the adventure, mystery and romance. With the emergence of the new metropolitan papers, however, the weekly serial began unambiguously to embrace a nationwide atomized mass consumer audience for formula fiction.

In arguing in this way this volume must take issue with N.N. Feltes's *Modes of Production of Victorian Novels*, which pinpoints the major shifts in fiction production, from *Pickwick* in monthly parts around the accession of Queen Victoria, to *Howard's End* in a single volume under the Net Book Agreement not long before the outbreak of the First World War. In particular, in discussing Hardy's attempts to have *Tess of the D'Urbervilles* serialized at the end of the 1880s, Feltes is in error, I believe, in fusing the distinct moments of the provincial syndicate and the metropolitan weekly, and subsuming both within the undifferentiated category of the capitalist 'journal':

> The writer's work was produced in a journal within relations of production analogous to those prevailing in a textile mill. When the *Bolton Weekly Journal*, for example, announced itself as 'Liberal,' and as 'probably the English newspaper distinctively wedded to the publication of fiction, as a feature of the family newspaper,' and then went on to extol its 'Ladies Column, Children's Hour, London Letter, and other special articles,' or when the *Graphic*, to take another instance, advertised itself as "Independent. An admirably illustrated journal, combining 'Literary excellence with artistic beauty,'" fiction writers entered their pages as hand-loom weavers entered a factory...
>
> (Feltes, *Modes*, 63–4)

The misrepresentations involved here will be demonstrated in detail in the following chapters. Here, perhaps we can generalize by suggesting that, compared to the book, which seems to sit squarely in the technological middle ground, there is a fundamental economic doubleness about the periodical form. Serial production can represent the most stable, complex, organized form of commodity production, requiring high levels of capital investment in advanced technology and a complex distribution system to reach a mass market, dependent on revenue from advertising mirroring the most general form of economic production; but it can also represent the most unstable, simple, piecemeal form of petty commodity production, requiring minimal levels of capital and technology, a traditional mode of distribution in a limited local area, at its simplest taking place entirely outside the market economy. This doubleness can be seen in the early days of newspapers and serial novels in the first half of the eighteenth century, and it is equally apparent in the rise of fiction syndication in the mid-Victorian period.

1.4   International comparisons

It must finally be acknowledged that the boom in the newspaper novel in later Victorian Britain diminishes to some extent in scale when seen from an international perspective. It occurs considerably later, is briefer, and remains less significant culturally than that of the French *roman-feuilleton*, which was a major mode of fiction transmission from the early 1840s until after the turn of the twentieth century. Original French serial fiction had begun to appear in the late 1820s in prestigious bimonthly reviews like *La Revue des Deux Mondes*, and continued to do so. But, while there were self-conscious artists like Flaubert who were serialized only in the reviews, throughout this period works by the most popular novelists appeared in instalments in the metropolitan daily newspapers of widest circulation, and were often reprinted in major provincial organs. The taxes on newspapers in the earlier decades of the nineteenth century were considerably lighter in France than in Britain (Bellanger, 2:3–10), and in the early 1830s the circulation of daily newspapers in Paris seems already to have been almost three times that of London.[43] The French Société des Gens de Lettres, founded in 1837, was quick to set up an agency to protect the rights of authors from unauthorized reproduction of serials in newspapers (Sprigge, 1889). In the early decades of the nineteenth century, the French market for fiction in book form developed along similar lines to the British, with lavish and expensive multi-volume first editions aimed at the rich and at circulating libraries, followed at some distance by cheaper single-volume reprints. Thus the capitalist mode of mass production began to enter the fiction industry in connection with the newspaper serial, which can thus be seen as the first of the mass narrative media. Although by 1860 the French circulating libraries were in decline, cheap railway editions of fiction were on sale, and there were alternative popular modes of serialization – notably the illustrated fiction-weeklies (*journaux-romans*) and novels in parts (*livraisons*) – the *roman-feuilleton* retained its dominance for another half-century.[44]

As Lise Queffélec has shown, the *roman-feuilleton* first appeared in 1836 in *La Presse*, a Parisian daily which had reduced its price by half and needed urgently to double its circulation in order to remain in profit, and the success of this venture made it a model for all progressive dailies. Queffélec distinguishes two major periods of the *roman-feuilleton* separated by a brief interim stage occupying the years 1866–75. The early period is dominated by Romantic chroniclers of the stature of Balzac, Sue, and Dumas who appeal to a very wide social cross-section. However, critical opinion was generally dismissive of the *roman-feuilleton*, while the government was often suspicious, even imposing a special five-centimes stamp (the 'Riancey' tax) on journals carrying serials during the political repression of the press under the Second Empire. In the transition period a clear partition occurs within the daily journals, as lighter papers devoted to *'faits divers'*, like *Le Petit Journal* (1863–), begin to challenge the dominance of the heavier organs of political opinion. At the same time, a division emerges among the contributing novelists, as social and literary theorists like Zola and the Goncourt brothers begin to attack the simple assumptions of melodramatic story-tellers such as Ponson de Terrail or Emile Gaboriau. In terms of quantity, the later period represents the peak of the popularity of the newspaper novel, as both the number of participating journals and their readership expand rapidly, with two or three *roman-feuilletons* appearing simultaneously in most national and provincial dailies. In terms of quality, however, the later period marks the beginning of decline, as the narrative contents become uniform as they conform increasingly to a dominant nationalist ideology. This is the period of popular genre fiction in the newspapers, whether the romances of Emile Richebourg or the detective stories of Gaston Leroux. The *roman-feuilleton* retains a certain following until around the Second World War, but after the end of the Great War it is merely one among many mass media purveying serial narrative (radio, cinema, cartoons), and that increasingly old-fashioned and marginal.[45]

For an example of an industrialized nation where original newspaper novels first appeared in any quantity not in the national press as in France, but in syndicates of regional journals as in Britain, we need turn no further than the United States. This is hardly surprising given that, even today, the constraints of social-geography effectively preclude the emergence of the national newspaper in North America. Building on the pre-war research of Elmo Scott Watson, Charles Johanningsmeier has shown in his recent book that, while a certain amount of reprinted shorter fiction did appear earlier in American newspapers on the 'exchange' system – that is, the reproduction of material from other periodicals (in the first instance, British or American magazines) with acknowledgement though without formal permission – there was little original or serial fiction until after the emergence of the syndicates. Johanningsmeier (chs 2–3) offers a detailed descriptive history of the rise of the fiction syndicators, which occurred in three stages. Firstly, from the 1860s, there appeared the 'ready print' services, most notably that of A.N. Kellogg, offering 'patent insides', which provided fiction material – still generally 'exchanged' from other journals – alongside general news, mainly to smaller rural journals appearing weekly. Secondly, in the 1870s came 'plate service', that is, the provision of fiction along with news and other entertainment material in the form of stereotype columns by companies such as the American Press Association. Here the fiction tended to be a combination of reprinted material and original work by minor authors, and the receiving journals to include both larger rural newspapers, and medium-sized urban journals, both weekly and daily. And thirdly, in the 1880s, there emerged the 'galley-proof' syndicates, dedicated to the provision of original short or serialized stories, increasingly by mainstream authors like Rudyard Kipling or Mark Twain, in the form of sheets of flimsy, sold predominantly to daily metropolitan newspapers with mass circulations. Here, among the principle operators were S.S. McClure and Irving Bacheller, though the latter's firm had already folded by the time fiction syndication began to decline around the turn of the new century. Again unsurprisingly, it is clear that, at its peak in the early 1890s, the American fiction syndication industry operated on a considerably larger scale than that in Britain. Novels by well-known writers might be placed in almost a hundred journals simultaneously rather than the ten or so common in Britain, while a federal structure composed of central and branch offices became necessary to effect economies of scale.

What is remarkable, however, is that, as Johanningsmeier acknowledges in each case, these three methods of syndication had been previously developed by the British newspaper industry, where they tended to be referred to respectively as 'partly printed sheets', 'stereo' and 'proof' or 'reprint'. Further, Johanningsmeier notes that Tillotsons of Bolton was the first agency to sell original serial fiction by well-known authors to American newspapers, and thus largely determined the structure of the market at least in its first decade. Pioneering scholars of fiction serialization in Britain, like Graham Pollard ('Novels', 73), had assumed automatically that British fiction syndication techniques had been learned from the United States.[46] The overturning of this assumption thus helps to confirm not only the unusual enterprise of the British provincial newspaper proprietors in the decades immediately following the repeal of the 'taxes on knowledge', but also the global as well as the local significance of the topic to which this volume is dedicated.

Part II
Narrative

2
Before Tillotsons

Sometime in the first half of 1873 an innovative deal was struck between William Frederic Tillotson (1844–89; Plate 3), proprietor of the *Bolton Weekly Journal*, and John Maxwell (1820–95; Plate 4), then companion, publisher, and literary representative of the popular novelist Mary Elizabeth Braddon. For the sum of £450 Maxwell sold to Tillotson's the serial rights for a limited period to Braddon's new novel *Taken at the Flood*. The novel appeared in a dozen provincial newspapers in lock-step in 34 parts from Saturday 30 August 1873 to 18 April 1874, with the minor variations noted in Table 2.1.[1] On the whole, the papers tended to be cheap weekly journals with a Liberal outlook, containing not only a synopsis of the week's news, local, national and international, but also a miscellany of feature material. The marked exceptions were the *Portsmouth Times and Naval Gazette*, a staid journal which commenced publication before the repeal of the 'taxes on knowledge', and which had no history of publishing fiction or features, plus the Dublin *Penny Despatch*, which was struggling to establish its new identity as a popular literary miscellany with no news content at all. For Willie Tillotson the transaction represented a major advance in the growth of his business. Serial fiction had been acquired for the *Bolton Weekly Journal* from its opening issues, but he advertised his new deal with Maxwell widely and seized the opportunity to expand his original weekly into a chain of local journals. But, since simultaneous serial rights were sold on to seven other provincial proprietors whose territories covered almost the length and breadth of the United Kingdom (the notable exception being the Home Counties), in the process he succeeding in more than recouping his initial outlay. This was to be merely the first of many successful syndicates or 'coteries' that 'Tillotsons's Fiction Bureau', as it later became known, would put together over the next half-century and more. But that,

Table 2.1 The first Tillotsons's syndicate

Journal Established	Politics Proprietor	Frequency Price	Claimed Circulation	Notes
Bolton Weekly Journal 1871	Lib. W.F. Tillotson	Weekly (Sat.) 1½d	?	Also in four new Tillotson papers – (All parts): *Farnworth Journal & Observer, Tyldesley Weekly Journal*; (Summary + pts 23-34, 31 Jan.–18 Apr. 1874); *Leigh Weekly Journal, Eccles & Patricroft Journal*
People's Journal (Dundee) 1858	Lib. John Leng	Weekly (Sat.) 1d	125 000	Later Tillotsons's novels tended to appear in sister publication, the *People's Friend*, a literary miscellany
Sheffield Daily Telegraph 1855	Neut./Con. W.C. Leng	Daily (Mon.-Sat.) Mon.–Fri. 1d/Sat. 2d	20 000	In Sat. Supp.; circulation in 1876 (March, 121-2)
Newcastle Weekly Chronicle 1864	Lib. Joseph Cowen	Weekly (Sat.) 2d	31 000	–
Weekly Mail (Cardiff) 1870	Con. Lascelles Carr	Weekly (Sat.) 2d	13 000	–
Western Daily Mercury (Plymouth) 1860	Lib. Isaac Latimer	Daily (Mon.–Sat.) 1d	35 000	In Sat. edn; (33 pts) 30 Aug. 1873–11 Apr. 1874
Penny Despatch (Dublin) 1861	Neut. R. Williamson/ E. Dwyer Gray	Weekly (Sat.) 1d	?	(35 pts) 30 Aug. 1873–25 Apr. 1874; on 30 Aug. 1873 began New Series as literary miscellany, discontinued Dec. 1875
Portsmouth Times 1850	Con. R. Holbrook	Bi-weekly (Tue. & Sat.) Tue. 1d/Sat. 2d.	?	In Sat. edn; no fiction preceding or following *Taken at the Flood*

Sources: NPD; original journals; or as noted.

as they say, is another story, one that will be told in detail in Chapter 3.

Here, I want not so much to look forward to the repercussions of W.F. Tillotson's enterprise, as to go back to what happened before. There is no doubt that the deal between Maxwell and Tillotson was original in the sense that it created the first syndicate of British provincial newspapers systematically covering most of the country for new work by an author with a reputation already established in the metropolitan book market. It thus set a trend which would lead to an entirely new phase in the periodical publication of Victorian fiction. This is attested to by a series of informed contemporary observers.[2] But it was by no means original in the sense of introducing serial fiction into provincial papers for the first time or of inventing the practice of fiction syndication itself. This point requires emphasis, as there seems some danger of the opposite passing for truth in mainstream newspaper history of the period, where political coverage in the provincial daily is generally given priority, and the more miscellaneous contents of the provincial weekly are often overlooked.

Alan Lee seems a particular culprit in his seminal 1976 study, *Origins of the Popular Press in England 1855–1914*, which, in a brief paragraph on the emergence of the news miscellany as an early manifestation of the New Journalism, states:

> News, sensational or otherwise, was not the only ingredient of the 'new journalism'. The newspaper was coming to resemble more closely the magazine, in response to the demand for papers to be entertaining as well as informative. One aspect of this was the emergence of the serialised novel in the ordinary press. It began in 1871 in the Tillotsons' weekly *Bolton Journal and Guardian*, extending afterwards to their chain of Lancashire papers.
>
> (128–9)

The error has resurfaced more recently in slightly garbled form in Dennis Griffiths's *Encyclopaedia of the British Press* (the inclusion of Scotland is significant) under the entry for 'W.F. Tillotson':

> The serialised novel first appeared in 1871 in Tillotson's *Bolton Journal* and *Guardian* series, and was extended through the other newspapers in its Lancashire chain.
>
> (562)

Yet, even a cursory survey of the new cheap urban provincial newspapers springing up after the repeal of the taxes on knowledge, particularly in weekly journals or weekly editions, reveals that serial fiction was by no means uncommon at a significantly earlier date.[3]

In Scottish newspapers, examples of full-length serial novels can be found without difficulty as early as the mid-1850s; in English provincial journals, although many examples of complete tales or short serials have been located around this period, examples of longer serials are difficult to find before the mid-1860s. To demonstrate this clearly, and in order to provide a small database for discussion of the functions and characteristics of novels in newspapers before the 1870s, I have carried out a survey of the fiction content of the eight principle journals which composed the first Tillotsons's syndicate from their opening issues up to at least 1873. The results are summarized in Table A.1. Both as a control, and in order to highlight the importance of local newspaper rivalry in encouraging the growth of newspaper novels, I have also included detailed information on the serials located in five other competing journals in relevant years. In addition to the 13 journals listed in this way in Table A.1, briefer references will be made in what follows to a large number of other weekly newspapers where fiction appeared during this period.

Before proceeding to a discussion of the survey results, however, it should be pointed out that this is not entirely uncharted territory. In particular, William Donaldson's *Popular Literature in Victorian Scotland* offers a concise account of serial fiction in the Scottish press from the mid-century, based on an extensive informal survey of weekly newspapers, while Michael Turner's dissertation on the Tillotsons' operation offers invaluable pointers towards earlier attempts at fiction syndication in England. What both lack, however, and what, in the first place, this chapter will attempt to provide, is a recognition of the impact of Scottish developments on the English provincial newspaper market.

2.1   North of the Border

The factors, at once economic and ideological, discouraging the early development of newspaper novels in England and described briefly in Chapter 1, did not apply with anything like the same force in Scotland. On the contrary, and with justification, William Donaldson is able to propose as a working definition of popular literature in Victorian Scotland, the phrase 'material which has been written specifically for publication in newspapers' (154n). According to Donaldson (14), a major reason for the earlier rise of the newspaper serial novel there is to be found in the increasing orientation, during the first half of the nineteenth century, of the Scottish bourgeoisie towards English metropolitan culture, and the concomitant slump in the indigenous book and serial markets. One consequence was a marked decline in locally produced fiction, whether in volume or in periodicals (Craig, chs 7, 9). The drift of Scottish publishers towards the English market can be illustrated by the case of the house of Blackwood and Son, which first set up a London office in 1840 (Tredrey), and by that of *Chambers's Journal* which, as we saw in the previous chapter, took on an English editor and shifted its production to London early in the second half of the century. On moving to Edinburgh in 1858, the new editor James Payn discovered that 'it had for years ceased to be "the Modern Athens"; the exodus to London had set in; and men of letters no longer made it their residence by choice' (*Gleams*, 137–8). With the final removal of the taxes on knowledge in the mid-century, the newspaper press in Scotland moved quickly to fill this gap with new 'miscellaneous' weekly journals costing only a penny and combining news summaries, political discussion, and literary material. They were distinctively Scottish in tone and content, and aimed mainly at the upper-working and lower-middle classes, who, due in large part to the popular education system developed by the Presbyterian Church of Scotland, and despite considerable erosion of its effectiveness in the urban areas during the process of industrialization, remained both more literate and less tolerant of scurrility than their English counterparts (Anderson, *Education*, ch. 1; Saunders, *Scottish*, pt IV).

The Dundee *People's Journal* (1858–1992) was by no means the first of these new popular Scottish weekly news miscellanies, but it was quickly to become the most distinctive and successful. It began with a limited local subscription of around 7000, but by the 1870s was covering most of Scotland with a number of regional editions, and claiming the largest circulation for a British weekly published outside London. It was created by John Leng (1828–1906; Plate 1), an enterprising young Englishman from Hull, who after a period as sub-editor on the *Hull Advertiser* (1794–1867), had been invited in 1851 to take over the bi-weekly *Dundee Advertiser* (1839–). But the *People's Journal*'s editor and guiding spirit from December 1860 (shortly before the *Advertiser* moved to daily publication, thus claiming more of Leng's energies) until near the end of the century was William Latto (1823–99), an autodidact from Fife with links to the Chartist, Free Church, and Free Trade movements, who had previously worked as a handloom weaver and a schoolmaster. To him was due in large part the *Journal's* distinctiveness, which lay in its combination of radicalism in politics, celebration of Scottish popular culture, and active encouragement of contributions from readers.[4] As Plate 10 illustrates, these included: 'The People's Opinion' – a generous section devoted to readers' correspondence; literary submissions which were rigorously criticized in a weekly column entitled 'To Correspondents'; plus regular prize competitions for poetry, tales, and songs, held mainly at the winter and summer holiday seasons.

The readers' competitions were strikingly successful. They had begun in the earliest issues of the *Journal*, and were soon offering small cash prizes. On 4 June 1859, for example, a total of £5 was offered for the best three 'Competition Tales' submitted, as judged principally by readers themselves. Over 30 tales were received, 14 being published by September, each of just over three columns in length. In requesting readers' votes, the editor suggested that a minimum of a 1000 votes would be necessary for a prize to be awarded. Not surprisingly this proved over-optimistic, given that the circulation of the journal was then less than 15 000 (see Chapter 5), and in the event the first prize was given to a tale receiving no more than 201 votes. As time went on the value of the prizes increased, attracting a response that eventually came to overwhelm the paper's human resources. The result was the creation of a separate literary miscellany, the *People's Friend*, which started up as a monthly supplement in mid-1869, but soon began a new series as an independent weekly with its own editorial staff. Other Scottish popular weeklies, like the Edinburgh *North Briton* (1855–79) and the *Glasgow Times* (1855–69), had already taken up the idea in the early 1860s, and by the 1870s such competitions, particularly for short fiction, were a regular feature of many provincial newspapers all over Britain. We should note here that the tales appearing in other early weeklies were by no means always Scottish ones – the *Glasgow Times*, for example, ran a number of serials with American settings around 1860. However, until John Leng and Co. joined the syndicate for Braddon's *Taken at the Flood* in 1873, all the stories in the *People's Journal* were local in content and/or origin.

The encouragement of readers' contributions first by the *Journal* and later also by the *Friend* succeeded not only in generating a steady supply of Scottish tales to help fill the papers' expanding columns, but also in launching the professional literary careers of a number of local talents. Though his work had previously been published in a number of other local papers like the *Fife Herald* (1839–), William Latto himself first came to John Leng's attention as a contributing reader. He began to submit correspondence in vernacular Scots under the pseudonym of Jock Clodpole in February 1858, and was the winner of the *Journal's* 1859 New Year's Prize Tale with 'Clouds and Sunshine', this time in standard literary English. As editor, he continued to contribute the 'Tammas Bodkin' column, which ran regularly for more than thirty years. Again in Scots, it mixed comic pseudo-autobiography with trenchant social and political comment (see Donaldson, 39–53). Further, a number of the serial novelists later to appear regularly in the pages of the *People's Friend*, including Annie S. Swan and Adeline Sergeant, achieved their first literary success in the fiction competitions of the Dundee weeklies (*How a Newspaper*, 15).

But in the early days of the *Journal*, fiction contributions from readers were limited to short tales published complete in a single issue or at most in three to four parts. When, to meet the demands of the growing size and circulation of the *Journal*, in 1863 John Leng sought to introduce regular serial novels, he turned not to his own subscribers but to a professional writer, who had become founding editor of the Dunfermline *Saturday Press* in 1859 and whose serials had already appeared in a wide range of other papers – David Pae. Pae (rhymed with 'hay') was raised and educated in Berwickshire, before being apprenticed to Thomas Grant, an Edinburgh bookseller who was later to publish several of Pae's novels in weekly numbers or in volume. In Edinburgh, Pae fell in love with the theatre and began to write both theatrical reviews and original plays. At the same time he became influenced by the liberal trends in contemporary evangelicalism, both anti-Calvinist (believing in the unlimited nature of the Atonement) and millenarian (arguing for the imminence of the Second Coming of Christ), and issued a number of controversial pamphlets on these subjects. His earliest novels unmistakably reveal these preoccupations, and, particularly in their endings, partake of the quality of the religious tract. *George Sandford; or, the Draper's Assistant*, probably his first novel, was published in 1853 by Thomas Grant. His subsequent novels, perhaps 50 or more, seem all to have been published first in serial in newspapers, and less than a quarter of them seem to have appeared in volume form.[5] The bibliographical details are inevitably tentative: the titles of Pae's serial tales seem to have been changed at will by many newspaper proprietors, possibly with the intention of passing off old work as new, and nearly all his written work was published anonymously.[6] Although he was quite probably the novelist most widely read in Scotland and the North of England in the mid-Victorian years, his name was virtually unknown in his own day and had been generally overlooked by literary historians until Donaldson drew attention to it in 1986.

As Table A.1 suggests, anonymity was the rule rather than the exception in newspaper fiction in the 1850s and 1860s, but the degree of Pae's reticence about his own acts of authorship seems to have been exceptional. Strangely, in 'Lucy, the Factory Girl', which, along with 'Jessie Melville', was his most perennially popular serial, he leaves an obscure pointer to his identity. There Mr Hay, a novelist from Edinburgh, visits Glasgow to inspect the Tontine area – notorious as a sink of poverty and crime – with a view to gathering copy for a tale which sounds suspiciously like 'Lucy', and asks an unsympathetic police captain to accompany him for the sake of safety. The following dialogue then occurs:

> 'Have you ever written any books before?'
> 'Yes, I have written several tales.'
> 'I don't know you. I never heard your name.'
> 'Possibly not, sir. I am not in the habit of publishing my name. I publish the tales, not myself.'
>
> (Pae, 165)

Pae's first novel to appear in the newspapers was probably 'Jessie Melville' in the *North Briton* in 1855 (Norrie, 23–4), and, even before he began to write for John Leng in 1863, at least 15 of his serials had appeared in various journals covering much of Scotland. A rapid search at the British Library Newspaper Library turned up examples between 1856 and 1863 in the following papers: the *Airdrie Advertiser* (1858–), *Berwick Journal* (1855–), *Falkirk Herald* (1845–), *Galloway Post* (1859–78), *Hamilton Advertiser* (1856–), (Glasgow) *Penny Post*, *Glasgow Times*, and Pae's own (Dunfermline) *Saturday Press*, and there must have been many others. In most cases Pae's early novels appeared successively rather than simultaneously in a number of papers, hence the remarkable fluidity of the titles. However, the data in

Table A.1, despite its incompleteness, does indicate that between 1858 and 1864 at least, the *North Briton* in Edinburgh and the *Glasgow Times* cooperated in the serial publication of at least four works by Pae, plus four others by unknown authors: in each case the dates of publication were virtually simultaneous, allowing for the fact that the Edinburgh paper appeared twice a week and the Glasgow one only once.[7]

The existence of such an agreement is confirmed by a surviving letter from Robert Buchanan of the *Glasgow Times* (father of the later Victorian poet–novelist) to Pae:

> I have arranged with Mr Cunningham for your story of "Lucy the Factory Girl" to appear in the "Glasgow Times" (Wednesday) paper, commencing next Wednesday. We shall keep up as close to the "Briton" as possible, and the rate at which I propose to pay for it to you is one pound a week. Trusting this arrangement will be satisfactory . . .
>
> (ALS, 25 November 1858, Pae)

The arrangement was presumably informal, since a hand-written agreement between Pae and the *North Briton* for 'The Heiress of Wellwood', one of the works in question, makes no mention of the *Glasgow Times*:

> It is agreed between Mr Bertram (on behalf of the conductors of the North Briton Newspaper) and Mr Pae, that the latter shall write a Scottish Story for the North Briton to be entitled "The Heiress of Wellwood; or Swindlers and their Victims" to consist of sixty chapters or upwards. One chapter to be supplied for each publication, or as much matter as shall fill $1\frac{3}{4}$ or 2 columns. . . . And shall receive for the same One Pound One shilling per week – payment weekly – the Copyright of the tale belonging to the Author.
>
> (5 November 1859, Pae)

Cases such as this, where two or three newspapers with complementary circulations came to a gentlemanly agreement to carry the work of one or more local authors at the same time, I propose to call a proto-fiction-syndicate.

John Leng's initial contact with Pae by letter has also fortunately been preserved. Again it concerned the story 'Lucy, the Factory Girl':

Having read over the Chapters of "Lucy" you forwarded the other day I shall be obliged by your informing me whether this story has appeared in the Family Herald, London Journal, Budget or any of the English publications of similar character.

If it has not please send on the remaining Chapters and I will remit you ten guineas on the understanding

I That the Story shall not appear in any other paper in Scotland while we are publishing it

and

II That we shall be at liberty to curtail it and alter the title or the headings of the chapters as we may think expedient.

(ALS, 13 July 1863, PAE)

The details are interesting. They suggest the following possibilities:

1 that Pae was in the habit of forwarding manuscript chapters of his work to likely editors to obtain new outlets for his work;
2 that Leng was aware of previous appearances of 'Lucy' and wished to change the title to disguise its provenance; and
3 that Leng may already have been thinking about his journal as a national rather than a local publication, and as such a potential competitor of the London penny miscellanies.

The novel was in fact published in the *People's Journal* under the title 'The Factory Girl; or, the Dark Places of Glasgow', from 5 September 1863 to 23 April 1864. Although 'Lucy' was old stock, having already appeared in book form as well as in the newspapers,[8] following its success Leng obviously agreed to buy the first serial rights of Pae's latest fiction exclusively for the *People's Journal*. Beginning in July 1864 with 'Mary Paterson', over a dozen of Pae's new serials appeared in the *Journal* before John Leng and Co. joined Tillotsons's first syndicate (cf. Plate 10). Others appeared after that date, though with considerably less frequency. When the *People's Friend* commenced independent weekly publication, David Pae was invited to become its founding editor. He remained in this new post until his death 15 years later, and during the period of his editorship a mixture of his old and new material was published in its pages. In addition to their publication in the Dundee weeklies, Pae's new stories once again appeared in serial form at a later date in a variety of newspapers throughout Scotland.

2.2 South of the Border

Let us now return to the situation south of the Tweed. Though new provincial weeklies beginning in the early 1870s, such as the Cardiff *Weekly Mail* or indeed W.F. Tillotson's own *Bolton Weekly Journal*, carried serial fiction from their opening issues, major journals starting up a decade or so earlier, like the Plymouth *Western Morning News* or the *Newcastle Weekly Chronicle*, tended initially to carry half a column or so of verse but no fiction at all. Clearly English proprietors were more nervous than their Scottish counterparts that fiction would lower the tone of their publications. They then normally began to feature complete tales only, before moving gradually and intermittently through the intermediate stages of tales in three or four parts, and stories running for a couple of months, towards full-length serials, that is, novels equivalent in length to a triple-decker and running for at least half a year.

The sources for these early tales and serials in provincial papers in England and Wales were varied. Initially the most common was again local authors. Although they seem likely to exist, I have not been able to locate any examples of fiction competitions in weekly newspapers outside Scotland before Christmas 1870, when they have been traced in both the radical *Newcastle Weekly Chronicle* and the conservative Cardiff *Weekly Mail*. The Newcastle competition attracted around 600 authors, and the winning entry was by Northumbrian Dora Russell with *The Miner's Oath*, which appeared in book form from Routledge the following year. The Cardiff *Weekly Mail* printed four prize tales in its Christmas Supplement. Francis Vacher, one of the winners with 'The Property Man's Story', went on to write a number of tales exclusively for the *Mail*, including the 1872 serial 'Disappearances Extraordinary', though none of them were local in setting. However, the *Mail* obviously did find other sources for local tales, such as the two serials which ran simultaneously for a period in 1871: the unsigned 'Mystery of Paul Wakenden' set among the Rhondda Valley coal fields, and Carl Morganwg's 'Gwendoline Margrave' set during the 'Rebecca Riots' of 1843, when turnpike gates in South Wales were destroyed by gangs dressed in women's clothes. In a similar way, and rather earlier, other provincial editors found a way to tap local sources without using the device of prize competitions. Examples include the short Devonshire tales which appeared in the Plymouth weeklies from 1862, or the serial stories by 'Reuben Hallam' concerning the Sheffield cutlery trade, or by 'John Thomas'

set among the South Yorkshire coal fields, which appeared in different
Sheffield journals from 1866. In some cases the writers were already
on the editorial staff of the papers concerned, just as Latto and Pae
were in the case of the *People's Journal* and *Friend*.[9]

Yet there was also clearly a demand for stories from further afield,
whether for the positive reason that such material proved attractive to subscribers or for the negative one that the supply of local
material was insufficient. The imported stories included both those
translated from other languages, and those originally in English
but reprinted from metropolitan or overseas journals. Typically, from
the early 1860s both the *Western Daily Mercury* in the southwest
and the *Newcastle Weekly Chronicle* in the northeast, mixed local
tales with those 'adapted' from French and German sources, and
those reproduced from London family weeklies like *The Leisure Hour*
or *Once a Week*, metropolitan literary monthlies like *Belgravia* or
The St. James's Magazine, plus American or colonial magazines like
Harper's or the *Anglo-Colonial Monthly*. Both the above newspapers
were scrupulous in acknowledging the provenance of their stories,
and presumably paid for the privilege of reprinting the British ones
at least. Others, like the Dublin *Penny Despatch*, rarely declared the
sources of their tales, and some proprietors obviously flouted copyright legislation. As early as 1859, for example, the *Liverpool Daily
Post* provoked Dickens's wrath by lifting the opening chapters of *A
Tale of Two Cities* from *All the Year Round* without permission (to
W.H. Wills, 30 April, Dickens, *Letters*, 9:57–8). The problem was
still apparent over a decade later, as revealed by cases involving
both serials and complete stories recorded in the first issue of the
Newsvendor (a trade journal for newsagents and booksellers), which
appeared in August 1873:

> 'Clytie', a new novel [by Joseph Hatton] in one of our leading
> magazines [*The Gentleman's Magazine*], was recently announced
> for publication in a north country paper. The author had to apply
> for legal power to stop the reprint. It is strange that there should
> be a general ignorance in the trade with regard to copyright law.
> (Leading Article, 4)

or

> Mr John Maxwell, the proprietor of *Belgravia*, and husband of
> Miss Braddon, has lately commenced actions against several

proprietors of cheap newspapers for reprinting tales from *Belgravia*.
('Trade Chit-Chat', 5)[10]

What we have seen so far suggests that one of the main constraints on the growth of serial fiction in provincial newspapers outside Scotland after the repeal of the taxes on knowledge was the shortage of suitable material. So it is then perhaps not surprising that there is scattered evidence of attempts to syndicate fiction in English newspapers well before 1873. As Michael Turner has shown ('Syndication', 8–20), although the practice of producing different provincial journals by adding local material to a common set of news sheets printed in London can be traced back to the 1830s at least, this mode of news syndication was given an enormous boost by the repeal of the taxes on knowledge. With the sudden reduction in the costs of advertising, publication and newsprint, if a page or two of general intelligence could be received regularly, ready-printed and cheap from London, it was relatively simple for a printing concern in even a small provincial town to set up a journal by employing a couple of editorial staff to attract a handful of advertisements from local traders and to add a leader and a few columns of local news. Of the more than a hundred new English provincial newspapers founded between 1854 and 1856, well over half, and the overwhelming majority of those serving smaller communities, seem to have been published initially in this way.[11] Unsurprisingly there were very quickly a number of London companies willing to provide such material, whether as inserts, supplements, or partly printed sheets, from lavishly illustrated miscellanies to more austere epitomes of national and international news, and on a monthly or weekly basis.

At least two companies offering illustrated miscellanies included fiction material. More than a dozen monthly journals, based in market towns as widely separated as Crediton in Devon and Alnwick in Northumberland, incorporated identical partly printed sheets with engravings of good quality, issued from early 1854 by an unknown source, and regularly featuring short serials and complete tales (see Plate 9).[12] And from June 1855, London engraver George Dorrington supplied more garish material with crude woodcuts to at least eight new 'Illustrated' weeklies, including the *Illustrated Derbyshire Chronicle*, *Illustrated St. Neot's Chronicle*, and *Illustrated Hull Mercury*, material which included a single six-part serial.[13] But many of the new local papers based on illustrated sheets, like the *Crediton Advertiser*, folded quickly, while those that became established were often keen to drop their use – on abandoning Dorrington's sheets, the editor of the *Hull Mercury* confessed that 'we have long sighed silently over the illustrations' (Editorial, 20 December 1855, 1). Thus neither of the London suppliers continued in this line of business for long.[14] Some local papers, like the *Alnwick Mercury*, continued to include short fiction, often from local sources, even after the supply of illustrated sheets dried up.[15] More commonly, however, such papers shifted to the use of unillustrated sheets with more news content, less miscellaneous matter, and no fiction, the *St. Neot's Chronicle* and *Hull Mercury* being typical examples.

By the 1860s there were a number of companies, both in London and the provinces, offering unillustrated news sheets and supplements for the use of provincial proprietors, but the largest and most successful were undoubtedly those run by William Eglington, of Aldergate Street, London, and by the popular periodical publishers, Cassell, Petter, and Galpin, both of which remained in the business for several decades.[16] A brief article in the *Newsvendor* of November 1873 (157–8) on 'Provincial Newspapers', noting a decline in the use of partly-printed sheets, stated: 'At the present time there are only two firms which supply these news sheets, viz. Mr. William Eglington, who claims to be the originator of the plan, and Messrs. Cassell, Petter, and Galpin . . .'. Little is known about the news syndication business run by Eglington, although he placed a prominent advertisement in the *Newspaper Press Directory* for 1865 claiming that he 'had supplied partly-printed Newspapers for the last Ten Years' (174). It is perhaps safe to assume, then, that it was Eglington who gained the business of many papers at the end of 1855 when Dorrington ceased to produce his illustrated sheets, since at least one of those journals, the *St. Neot's Chronicle*, continued to use what are recognizably sheets of the same provenance from then until at least the mid-1870s. Among the many papers employing the same sheets in the mid-1860s were the *Yorkshire Advertiser* (1859–69) and *Wigton Advertiser* (1859–).

Cassell began to produce partly-printed newspapers for smaller provincial proprietors in 1862 under the banner of 'Cassell's General Press' (Nowell-Smith, *House*, 78; Advertisement, *NPD*, 1864, 170).[17] A significant number of the new local weeklies starting up in the 1860s seem to have turned to them for material, at least in the early stages: the *Pontefract Advertiser* and *Yarmouth Chronicle* (both from 1863) were typical early examples. Other papers of longer standing, like the *Shepton Mallet Journal* (1854–) and *St. Alban's Times* (from 1855) changed their allegiance to Cassell around 1864. Some remained faithful for decades, like the *Alcester Chronicle* (from 1864) which was still relying on Cassell for half of its copy in the mid-1880s.[18] In 1864, all of these papers consisted of a single sheet of four pages, with the inner side featuring a common summary of general news courtesy of Cassell.[19]

However, from the admittedly incomplete evidence available, it seems likely that Eglington's sheets contained little in the way of fiction material apart from a few short seasonal tales at the end of the year,[20] and that Cassell's sheets only began to include serial fiction with any regularity after Tillotsons had started up. From the beginning of August 1865, there was a short-lived experiment with three consecutive, anonymous serial tales ('The Missing Coin', 'Paul Radcliffe's Adventures', and 'Leaves from the Diary of a Working Man'), which ran for three, five, and seven weeks respectively, in Cassell's country papers. Though no explanation was offered when the series came to an end in mid-November, there were perhaps objections from subscribing proprietors, for it was not until 10 years later, in October 1875, that the unsigned 'The Wrecker' began, launching a virtually unbroken sequence of lengthy serial tales in Cassell's partly printed sheets.[21]

We should also note in passing here another London newspaper publisher who provided serial fiction in quantity for provincial readers, though not in the form of pre-printed sheets. In 1861, immediately following the repeal of the last of the taxes on knowledge, there appeared a single partial exception to the English trend to keep serial fiction out of the popular metropolitan weekly newspapers. This was the *Weekly Budget: a Family Newspaper and Magazine* (1861–1913), one of the metropolitan journals referred to in John Leng's letter to David Pae. Unlike the cheap miscellanies, this penny Saturday publication had the form of a newspaper and carried social and political news with a Liberal slant, but also gave around three of its eight pages over to popular serial fiction, with three or four stories generally running at one time. However, although it was principally published in London it appears to have had relatively few metropolitan readers, but regularly claimed to have 'the largest Provincial Circulation of any Newspaper in the United Kingdom' (*Weekly Budget*, 7 January 1865, 1, for example), a circulation which seems to have reached half a million by the early 1880s (Altick *English*, 395). The first issue bore the title *The Lancashire Yorkshire and Northern Weekly Budget: A Family Newspaper and Magazine* and during the 1860s it was published jointly in Manchester by John Heywood of Deansgate, and in London by James Henderson.[22] By the 1870s the Manchester edition had stopped and Henderson was the sole proprietor, though judging from the lists of prize winners announced regularly in the *Budget*, its readership remained strongest in the northwest of England. It was thus a direct competitor of W.F. Tillotson's own Lancashire Journals and may have helped to encourage their use of serial fiction. To begin with the serials were virtually all anonymous, but by the 1870s many were signed by writers who also served the northern syndicates like Mrs G. Linnaeus (Isabella) Banks, Compton Reade, George Manville Fenn, and Eric St C.K. Ross. Adventure stories seem early to have become popular in the *Budget* and from the same period there were also a significant number of stories by American writers like Leon Lewis and W.F. Cody (Buffalo Bill).[23]

Following pre-printed sheets, a further technique for news syndication was soon available. The practice of stereotyping goes back to the eighteenth century, but by around 1860 the technology had advanced sufficiently so that it could be used for the syndication of newspaper columns, as a more flexible and individuated alternative to pre-printed sheets (Dooley, ch. 3; Wilson, *Stereotyping*, 1–24). Samuel Harrison, proprietor of the *Sheffield Times* (1846–74), was probably first to set up a news agency dedicated to providing 'type-high stereo news columns' to other journals (*NPD*, 1863, 175). By 1862 Harrison had a foundry and office in London as well as Sheffield, and was offering around 24 columns of news per week to all-comers. He was soon followed by new organizations such as the Central Press, set up in 1863 in London by William Saunders of the Plymouth *Western Morning News* (Hunt, ch. 7), plus some of the existing suppliers of partly printed sheets like Joseph Bruton, C.W. Allen, and Cassell.[24] In 1865 Harrison's annual advertisement in the *Newspaper Press Directory* offered to other proprietors, in addition to the usual supply of stereotype news, 'Casts or Copy of Original Copyright Tales of thrilling interest' (171). Both the nature of the fiction offered and the clients who purchased it, remain something of a mystery – no records of Harrison's business survive, and the *Sheffield Times* itself appears only to have carried fiction only occasionally during the 1860s.[25]

Actively involved in both the literary and production sides of the enterprise, Harrison himself was obviously overworked. He gave up the editorship of *Sheffield Times* in 1869, but, according to an obituary in the same paper of 25 February 1871 (8), died suddenly at the age of only 44. It seems that his newspaper and syndication businesses were continued briefly by his wife Mary, before both were sold in early 1873 to Leader and Sons, proprietors of the long-running moderate Liberal organ the *Sheffield Independent*, which had itself carried fiction on Saturdays from 1866.[26] Leaders ran the re-named *Sheffield Times and Iris* for only just over a year before merging it with the *Independent*'s weekly edition. An early announcement in the *Sheffield Times and Iris* again suggests that as a fiction syndica-tor Harrison might have concentrated on complete rather than serial tales: it promised 'High Class Original Tales by Distinguished Au-thors. The Tales will be short, and in that respect they may be more acceptable than serial stories' (27 September 1873, 1). One regular among the 'Distinguished Authors' seems to have been James Skipp Borlase, who had recently returned from Australia and some-times wrote under the signature J.J.G. Bradley. As we shall see in Chapter 3, there is circumstantial evidence that the syndication agencies belonging to Leaders and Tillotsons cooperated with each other regularly in the mid-1870s, when neither was in a position to offer a complete fiction syndication service, and documentary evidence that they did so occasionally in the mid-1880s.

To take the story thus far is obviously to trespass into the Tillotsons era itself, but, given the paucity of documentary evidence concern-ing the operation of the agency under Samuel Harrison, such an excursion seems necessary to establish the case for the existence of an agency systematically syndicating fiction in stereotype before Tillotsons's Fiction Bureau started up, though obviously on a much smaller scale, and with less well-established authors. I propose to call such early operations as the distribution of stories within the partly printed news sheets offered by Dorrington, Cassell, and others, or among the stereotype news columns of Samuel Harrison, minor fiction syndicates, as opposed to the type of major syndicate initi-ated by Tillotsons.

Nevertheless, the data in Table A.1 suggests that the earliest regular pattern of publication of full-length serial fiction in English pro-vincial newspapers derived not from English sources at all, whether local, metropolitan, or syndicated, but from Scotland and once again from the prolific pen of David Pae. Though no business records from the period survive today in Dundee or Sheffield, there is still sufficient circumstantial evidence to suggest that one of the first presentations of Pae's work to an English audience was by means of an arrangement between the two Leng brothers, John and William, which we can again term a proto-fiction-syndicate. W.C. Leng (1825–1902; Plate 2), was the elder of the two sons from Hull, and had served as an apprentice chemist and operated a successful business there. He began to write material for the *Dundee Advertiser* on his brother's taking up the editorship in 1851, and was persuaded to move to Dundee in 1859 and take up the post of Assistant Editor, marrying his brother's sister-in-law the following year. He remained in Dundee until December 1863, when he left to become the editor and joint-proprietor with Frederick Clifford of the *Sheffield Daily Telegraph*. The relationship between the two brothers appears to have remained warm despite growing ideological differences. John Leng was throughout a political radical, went on to represent Dundee as a progressive Liberal MP from 1889 to 1905, and was knighted in 1893 for his prominent support of Gladstone's second Home Rule bill. William Leng was first disillusioned by Liberal opposition to municipal renewal back in Hull, and went on to become a staunch supporter of the Conservative Party, responsible for producing the influential Tory Reform Broad Sheet (March; *How We Publish*, 19).

William Leng was coming towards the end of his time in Dundee when his brother struck the deal with David Pae to write his new serials exclusively for John Leng and Co., and presumably recognized Pae's talent and potential to raise circulations single-handed. 'The Heir of Douglas', Pae's first serial to appear in the *Telegraph*, was announced the previous week as being by 'one of the most popular tale writers in the kingdom' (25 March 1865, 1). The information given in Table A.1 for the *Telegraph* is incomplete,[27] but still demonstrates that, in the decade from 1865, at least eight new Pae novels began to appear in the pages of the *Telegraph* before or on their completion in the *People's Journal* (beginning with 'Mary Paterson' under the title 'The Fatal Error'), and that over the same period there were issued at least four other older Pae serials which had appeared in the *North Briton* between 1857 and 1863, including 'The Heir of Douglas' and 'Lucy, the Factory Girl', the work which had initially attracted John Leng's attention. The fact that the proto-syndicate for Pae's fiction carried on by the Leng brothers involved sequential publication rather than the simultaneous publication apparent in the earlier deal between the *North Briton* and the *Glasgow Times*, reinforces the idea that John Leng came early to the conception of his weekly journals as national organs, reaching Scottish subscribers not only all over their homeland but in England as well.[28]

Just as the precise nature of the business arrangements between Pae and the two Leng brothers remains obscure, so it is uncertain whether either of the brothers acted as agents for Pae's work with other newspaper proprietors, or whether Pae himself continued to market his own second serial rights. But whatever the detail of the arrangements, soon Pae's stock of old stories was turning up in newspapers not only throughout Scotland, but also all over the north of England.[29] Table A.1 shows this in W.F. Tillotson's own *Bolton Weekly Journal* plus its main Bolton rival the *Guardian* in the early 1870s. Eddie Cass (*Cotton*, ch. 4) has traced what may be Pae's earliest appearance in English newspapers: a sequence of 23 stories in the *Ashton Reporter* (1855–) of Ashton-under-Lyne, east Lancashire, between 1863 and 1886, most following their serialization in the *People's Journal* or *People's Friend*. But the first was Pae's tale of the recent Lancashire Cotton Famine, 'Very Hard Times: or, The Trials and Sorrows of the Linwood Family', which ran from June to December 1863, simultaneously with its appearance in the Edinburgh *North Briton* and thus predating not only the first Pae story in William Leng's *Sheffield Telegraph*, but also the agreement with John Leng in Dundee. Appearances almost as extensive have been traced in the *Middlesbrough and Stockton Gazette* and *Gorton, Openshaw and Bradford Reporter* soon after their respective beginnings in 1869 and 1874, and in daily rather than weekly portions in the halfpenny evening paper the (Blackburn) *Northern Daily Telegraph* from its first issue in late 1886. But this must represent only the tip of the iceberg, if William Westall's contemporary witness is to be credited (81). Westall cites Jesse Quail, editor of the *Northern Daily Telegraph*, as stating that the most popular newspaper novelists of the Tillotsons era, 'William Black, James Payn, Walter Besant, and even Miss Braddon . . . cannot hold up a candle to David Pae.'[30] If the data presented in Table A.1 gives the impression that David Pae was personally responsible for almost half the full-length serial novels appearing in British provincial newspapers before Tillotsons, the exaggeration may not be too great.

2.3 Local rivalry

Clearly the major forces encouraging the exponential growth in the British provincial press from the mid-1850s, whether political like the removal of the taxes on knowledge, social like the growth of popular literacy, or technological like refinements in stereotyping or the invention of rotary printing, were national in scope. These are perhaps sufficient in themselves to explain in general terms the increasing presence of fiction in local newspapers and the gradual shift from the prevalence of complete tales to serial novels. But to understand the changing patterns of fiction publication in more detail we must take into account the complex local rivalries between competing newspapers in the same city or district, which could in time themselves give rise to national trends. These were occasionally between political opposites – radicals versus conservatives. However, they tended rather to begin in fine shades of difference around the terms liberal, independent, neutral, and reformist, and often to end in naked clashes of personality or economic interest. John Leng's acquisition of exclusive first serial rights to the new work of David Pae in 1863 was almost certainly designed to steal a march over the rival *North Briton*. However, the two papers advocated not dissimilar progressive politics and cultural policies. In the long-term, the arrangements with Pae, whose later novels seem to have been rather less radical in their political and religious implications, at the same time contributed to the emergence of the *People's Journal* and *People's Friend* as national organs, and tended to drive a wedge between the political and literary aspects of Leng's enterprise and perhaps to diminish its power as a vehicle of radical thought.

Similar clashes can be seen in England and Wales, in both minor and major keys. In Plymouth, for example, the radical Isaac Latimer started the *Western Daily Mercury* in 1860 in immediate response to the foundation by William Saunders and Edward Spender of the *Western Daily News*, which was declaredly 'independent' though decidedly Whiggish in tone. The gradual introduction of fiction – both complete tales and serials, and including works of local, metropolitan and foreign origin – into their respective weekly editions proceeded almost in lock-step over the next decade, down to the parallel publication of serials by Selwyn Eyre in 1873. The *Mercury*'s decision to introduce original work from writers with national reputations by joining most of Tillotsons's early syndicates was obviously intended to break the deadlock. In Cardiff, as Aled Jones has suggested ('New', 167–72), the Tory press, in the form of the *Western Mail* and its companion the *Weekly Mail* owned by the coal magnate, the Marquess of Bute, was perhaps more adventurous than its

Liberal rival. The decision of Lascelles Carr, moderate Tory editor of the *Weekly Mail*, to join the Tillotsons's syndicate for Braddon's *Taken at the Flood* provoked the Liberal *Weekly Times* also to introduce serial fiction, beginning with John Saunders's *Israel Mort, Overman* the following year. In volume this novel, 'A Story of the South Wales Coal and Iron Districts', was dedicated to Lord Aberdare, former Home Secretary under Gladstone, who had sponsored legislation protecting the coal miner.

However, the most bitter and prolonged rivalry between local journals in this period was probably to be found in Sheffield. The *Sheffield Independent* had started up in 1819 and was bought by the Leader family in 1829, but, as we have seen, it did not move to daily publication until relatively late in 1861, having been pre-empted by the *Sheffield Daily Telegraph* which started up in 1855. When W.C. Leng took over the *Telegraph* in 1864 and began to shake things up, a fierce rivalry began between the Leng and Leader families which was to last until the Leaders sold up in the 1890s. This was only in part political. In principle the *Independent* was a Liberal journal, but the Leaders were rather Whiggish and politically inactive; although W.C. Leng was formally a Tory, he seems to have had rather more in the way of reformist zeal than his rivals. In his stand against the Sheffield Trade Union outrages of the late 1860s, Leng became an ally of John Arthur Roebuck, the maverick Liberal MP who had played a major role in the early days of the fight for the repeal of the taxes on knowledge (Collet, ch. 3), and who had represented Sheffield from 1849. Leng used the *Telegraph* to support Roebuck vociferously against the radical Liberal candidate John Mundella, who defeated him in the election of 1868, and who the Leaders were forced reluctantly to defend in the *Independent* (March, pt II, ch. 3). The powerful forces of Nonconformist radicalism in Sheffield found little more sympathy with the outlook of the *Independent* than that of the *Telegraph*: 'too much Leng and Leader' was how Hyslop Bell described the situation in 1874 (cited in Lee, 138).

In fact, the bitterness of the rivalry was more often due to economic and personal conflicts. After the Great Flood in Sheffield of 1864, the two papers clashed over where the responsibility lay (March, pt II, ch. 1). In 1876 there was a notorious incident when the two dailies traded accusations of plagiarism of exclusive news (Guthrie, ch. 6). More generally, J.D. Leader (1835–99) and R.E. Leader (1839–1922), the two sons who had taken over the editorship of the family papers in the 1860s, had strong literary and antiquarian interests, and this was reflected in the content of their daily, while the rival journal tended to excel in reporting crime, punishment and disaster in bloodthirsty detail. This contrast of tone and style was exaggerated when the two papers began to include fiction in their weekly editions in the mid-1860s. Leaders responded to the publication in 1865 in the *Telegraph* of two of Pae's Scottish melodramas and a series of rollicking local tales entitled *Wadsley Jack: or, Travels and Humour of a Flatback Cutler*, with a sober local historical serial, which, though unsigned, was in fact written by R.E. Leader himself.[31] It was prefaced by the following careful defence:

> The most enthusiastic politician sometimes wearies of politics, and the most indefatigable "Common Reader" occasionally, especially in uneventful times, finds his newspaper a tax instead of a delight. By way of varying the contents of the *Independent*, and affording a change from our constant record of past events, we propose for a short time to carry our readers backward in the history of our town, and to place before them a narrative which we hope may enable them to realise to some extent the kind of place Sheffield was in the days of our forefathers. We do not aspire to be mere tale-tellers, but if possible to be chroniclers of the state of the town some hundred or two years ago. This purpose will be best achieved under the guise of fiction, and we now therefore give the First Part of "Judith Lee: A Tale of Old Sheffield".
>
> (6 January 1866, 1)

Leaders's persevered with such earnest local material for two or three years, but by the end of the decade, presumably due to the success of Pae's stories at the *Telegraph*, they were commissioning George Manville Fenn to produce more sensational material, including a stirring story based on the 1864 flood. The Leaders's decision to take over Harrison's fiction syndication operation, then, may well have been prompted also by a pressure to compete which was rendered even more acute by the decision of W.C. Leng and Co. to switch from Pae to Braddon as their star writer in 1873.

Specific local newspaper rivalries, then, often had more general repercussions, frequently exercising an influence on the long-term development of the newspaper novel. Indeed, as we shall see in the following chapter, W.F. Tillotson's own enterprise in setting up the first major fiction syndication agency can be seen at least in part to have a similar local determination. Finally, we can say not only that novels in newspapers were much more prevalent in the British provinces in the decades before the deal between Tillotson and John Maxwell than has generally been recognized, but also that the operations of the minor and proto-syndicates during those years raised a number of the crucial issues for both novels and newspapers that were to be worked out later in the century. One of these was the role of the miscellaneous news weeklies in shaping cultural and social discourse in provincial communities, which we shall return to in Chapter 5. Another was the opening of new means of access to publication for aspirant authors, especially those without contacts in metropolitan literary circles, one of a number of topics relating to authorship addressed in Chapter 6. A third was the tension between local and metropolitan settings, styles and themes in newspaper fiction in the period, which will be taken up in Chapter 7.

3
Tillotsons

When, in 1866, shortly after he had completed his apprenticeship, the young Willie Tillotson was taken into partnership with his father John Tillotson (1821–1906), the family firm operated a small though thriving printing, bookselling and stationery business in the cotton town of Bolton, whose population then totalled less than 80 000 people. John was the son of a Primitive Methodist clergyman, and the firm's specializations included the publications of the Religious Tract Society and the Sunday School Union. When W.F. Tillotson died in 1889, the firm was running a series of successful newspaper concerns with Nonconformist Liberal leanings. The first was the *Bolton Evening News*, which began to appear in March 1867, one of the first halfpenny evening papers in England, and unique in being started from scratch without the benefit of building on the reputation of an established morning or weekly journal. Next, and thus reversing the order typical of provincial development, came a chain of six weeklies known as the 'Lancashire Journals', each based in a different Lancashire township and each with distinct local characteristics, but all deriving from the original *Bolton Weekly Journal* which began in 1871.[1] Finally there was the 'Fiction Bureau', a newspaper syndication agency specializing in novels in serial with an international reputation, which had its beginnings in 1873.[2] There seems little doubt that the enterprise and energy underlying all these risky but finally successful business ventures derived largely from W.F. Tillotson himself.

Fortunately, the nineteenth-century business records of the firm, and particularly those relating to the fiction syndication operation, were thorough and have survived in large part, most now being housed at either the Bodleian Library, Oxford or the Central Library,

Bolton. However, by no means all of these documents were available to the writers of the fullest existing accounts of the early days of the firm of Tillotson and Son – Frank Singleton's centennial history of the firm of 1950, and Michael Turner's 1968 dissertation on the 'Fiction Bureau', both of which inform the paragraph above. In consequence, the process of the foundation and early expansion of the Tillotsons's syndication operation, and the importance to it of W.F. Tillotson's business relations with M.E. Braddon's partner John Maxwell, as well as a number of newspaper proprietors across the Pennine hills in Sheffield, have yet to be satisfactorily described. It is the aim of the present chapter to carry out that task. The narrative will be conducted under three headings: 'Growth and Cooperation', 'Outreach and Competition', and 'Retrenchment and Decline', corresponding in turn to the last three decades of the century. Detailed illustration of many of the points made can be found in Table A.2.

3.1 Growth and cooperation

When the *Bolton Weekly Journal* first appeared on Saturday, 11 April 1871, it became the third local Liberal weekly on sale in the Bolton area. The rather staid *Bolton Chronicle* dated back to 1824, but had been taken over in the 1860s by George Toulmin, the owner of a growing Lancashire newspaper empire based in Preston. The cheaper *Bolton Guardian*, founded in 1859 and owned locally by Thomas Cunliffe, was a more immediate rival. W.F. Tillotson was obviously aware of many of the developments discussed in the previous chapter, and, in order to give his new journal a distinctive popular appeal, decided to include from the opening issue a serial novel of proven worth. 'Jessie Melville', one of David Pae's earliest and liveliest evangelical melodramas, ran, as usual anonymously, for over a year. It is unclear what payments were made or whether the right to reprint was purchased directly from the author, from John Leng and Co. in Dundee, or even from W.C. Leng and Co. in Sheffield. It was presumably successful in helping to get the new paper off the ground, since *Jessie* was followed by three further full-length second-hand Pae serials, each unsigned and published with a short overlap, so that Pae's work was running continuously in the *Bolton Weekly Journal* until mid-December 1873. Thomas Cunliffe responded by including fiction in the *Guardian* towards the end of 1873 – starting off with Pae's 'Lucy'.

By that time also, W.F. Tillotson had reached his seminal agreement with John Maxwell, Miss Braddon's first newspaper novel *Taken at the Flood* was almost half way through its run, and four new Lancashire Journals were being set up on the back of the publicity created. Although much of the later correspondence between Tillotson and Maxwell has survived, there is no record of the initial contacts between the two men, whose appearance and character seem to have been in stark contrast. Tillotson was precise and meticulous, rather short in stature, almost dapper, and normally gentle and reticent in manner, though he could come close to the stereotype of the blunt and stubborn Northerner when roused (Singleton, 11–15). Maxwell was, according to Robert Buchanan, who had worked for him in the early 1860s, 'a big, burly, florid-faced loud-spoken Irishman' (cited in Jay, 93–5), notorious for bullying the female authors he published, rather emotional, nervous, and erratic in his business dealings.[3] Given this contrast in style, and the fact that Maxwell had worked in London during the 1850s as a newspaper and advertising agent, had already succeeded in placing Braddon's work in Colonial newspapers (Morrison, 'Serial', 311), and had taken legal action against British provincial proprietors who had stolen work from *Belgravia*, it is possible that it was the London publisher who made the first move. It is even conceivable that it was Maxwell who first approached the other provincial proprietors to set up the syndicate for *Taken at the Flood*, and only at some later stage passed on the administration to Tillotson, its youngest and most enthusiastic member.[4]

But whatever the nature of the initial encounter, it is apparent that the deal that was eventually clinched gave full satisfaction to both parties. Before the end of the serial run of *Taken at the Flood*, Braddon, in revising the novel for publication in three volumes from the house of Maxwell, had dedicated it warmly to W.F. Tillotson, while the Bolton man had made the following announcement to his weekly readers:

> The proprietor of the Journal begs to announce that, in continuance of his plan of providing his readers of the Paper Stories by one of the most brilliant Novelists of the day, he has again arranged with Miss Braddon for the publication of a New Story from her facile pen, entitled 'A Strange World'. The portions of the Manuscript which have been received from the Author, embracing the earlier part of the Story, open a plot of striking interest, and display the marvellous realistic power which gives life to

all the characters she portrays, a vividness to every scene she describes . . .

(Bolton Weekly Journal, 21 March 1874, 3)

During the 1870s alone Tillotsons purchased the serial rights to a total of seven new works by Braddon. There was some variation in price, but the average was around £500 for a three-volume novel. The first two ran back to back in the *Bolton Weekly Journal*, and until late in the decade Tillotsons's regular subscribers were seldom without a weekly portion of Braddon's fiction for more than a few months. But the provincial newspaper-reading public could not live by Braddon alone, any more than they could from every word proceeding from the pen of Pae, and from the beginning Tillotsons had been on the look-out for other sources of fictional supply. Though there is again no surviving documentary evidence in either case, circumstantial evidence suggests strongly that, early on, Tillotsons turned for assistance in acquiring new sources of fiction both to John Maxwell and to Leader and Sons of the *Sheffield Independent*, who, as shown in the previous chapter, in 1873 took over the syndication business founded in Sheffield by Samuel Harrison.

W.F. Tillotson seems to have gone to the Sheffield syndication agency in order to provide a cheap supply of shorter fiction by lesser writers simply to fill out the literary pages of his own Lancashire Journals. In 1874, two 10-part serials (the unsigned 'The Peasants' War' plus 'Sixty per Cent: An Experience' by the broad church clergyman Dr Maurice Davies) were published in the columns of the *Bolton Weekly Journal*. Both had appeared slightly earlier in the *Sheffield Independent* and, according to the records, neither was syndicated by Tillotsons. Similarly, a number of the complete tales published early on in the *Bolton Weekly Journal* had appeared previously in the Leaders's newspapers, including 'What Dick Blaize Found at Church' by James Skipp Borlase (as J.J.G. Bradley). In fact, the records indicate that Tillotsons did not begin to supply short stories to other journals until near the end of the decade.[5] It should be noted here that Leaders in turn were purchasing serial fiction for their own papers from Tillotsons, including Florence Marryat's *Fighting the Air* in 1874–75 and Blanchard Jerrold's *Black-Eyed Susan's Boys* the following year, while in the same period a number of provincial journals seem to have bought stories simultaneously from both agencies, including the Cardiff *Weekly Mail* and Dublin *Penny Despatch*.[6] This suggests that from their earliest days, when neither agency was in a position to offer a complete fiction syndication service but both had complementary strengths in serial and short fiction, Tillotsons in Bolton and Leaders in Sheffield actively cooperated with each other. As shown below, this inference is supported by the existence of documentary evidence of occasional acts of cooperation during the 1880s. In addition to the material taken from Leaders, anonymous local authors provided Tillotsons with a number of short stories and a single serial, 'Grace Barton, Heiress of Smithills Hall', which ran for 22 weeks in the second half of 1875, and cost Tillotsons £10.[7] In 1878, a Prize Competition in the *Bolton Weekly Journal* produced three winning serials which occupied the fiction columns of the paper for nearly nine months, at a total cost of only £50 in prizes. The third prize went to 'The Lasses of Leverhulme', a short novel set in industrial Lancashire, by local author Jessie Fothergill, who had already attracted a lot of attention in the London literary world with *The First Violin* (1878), her third published novel.

Singleton (41) states that established London writers at first 'did not like the idea of treating with a provincial publisher for the production of their novels in cheap newspapers week by week.' But, as an experienced metropolitan publisher both of miscellanies prominently featuring serial fiction and of novels in volume, John Maxwell had wide contacts among journeymen novelists and obviously pushed some of them in W.F. Tillotson's direction. Besides Braddon, of the writers with metropolitan reputations who began to sell serials to Tillotsons in the mid-1870s, most were protégés of Maxwell. Dora Russell, B.L. Farjeon, Frederick Talbot, Florence Marryat, and Mary Cecil Hay were all sensation novelists published by the house of Maxwell, while the last three were also regular contributors to *Belgravia* until it was sold to the new and adventurous house of Chatto and Windus in 1876 (*VFRG*, 14). The payments to these writers for syndication rights were still substantial, though significantly less than those paid to Braddon, and varied, in the case of full-length serials, from 50 guineas to Hay up to £360 to Marryat.

In the mid-1870s it seems likely that the combined weekly circulation of the penny Lancashire Journals was still below 50 000 copies,[8] and thus entirely inadequate to justify regular payments such as these. Thus, apart from those by Pae and those probably purchased from Leaders, virtually all the serials appearing in the *Bolton Weekly Journal* were sold on to a number of other provincial newspapers. In addition, from as early as 1875, Tillotson was purchasing serial rights to novels which would not appear in his own flagship weekly, nor sometimes indeed in any of the Lancashire Journals. To begin with these tended to be cheaper works by less eminent writers, coming on to the market when the fiction pages of Tillotson's own papers were occupied with Braddon's latest. Among the earliest examples were R.G. Haliburton's 'Waif in the Wilderness' and Selwyn Eyre's 'A Woman's Shadow'. But by the end of the decade, there were cases where the subscribers to Tillotson's own newspapers were denied the chance to read the agency's star writers. Braddon's *Cloven Foot*, for example, began to appear in the newspapers in autumn 1878, when the winning entries in the Prize Competition were running in the Lancashire Journals, which thus passed up the opportunity, and the syndicate was led by the *Newcastle Weekly Chronicle*. This suggests that towards the end of the decade, the fiction syndication operation had gained considerable independence and was no longer simply an off-shoot of the newspaper publication business.

The technical and economic aspects of syndication were not unduly complex but the process depended on efficient communications systems and required vigilant attention to detail if varying agreements were to be kept and constant deadlines met. The system used by Tillotsons generally involved two distinct stages, concerning the sale of first and subsequent serialization rights. In the first instance, as with Braddon's *Taken at the Flood*, for each serial purchased they worked to create a 'coterie' of up to a dozen major British provincial weeklies with complementary circulations, which would pay substantial sums (by the early 1880s, up to £100 for the biggest names in the largest journals) to serialize new novels simultaneously, or virtually so, in advance of volume publication, which typically occurred shortly before the appearance of the final serial instalment.[9] Copy was normally provided by established authors in a previously agreed number of weekly parts (often over 30 in the mid-1870s, but declining to around 26 by the mid-1880s, in the case of a 'triple-decker') which were set up and forwarded part by part in advance to the members of the coteries. In addition, Tillotsons began to maintain backlists of fiction already published in volume, but for which the firm retained serial rights. These works were sold to lesser journals for as little as a shilling per column, in the case of little-known writers. Text was available from Tillotsons in the form of proofs to be reset by the local publisher or, from perhaps around 1876, as thin column-length stereotype plates made from papier-mâché molds, which could be simply cut to the required length (if necessary), mounted, and locked into the forme.[10] The major city journals joining the coteries were often content to receive material in proof, while the country papers generally preferred it in stereo form. From the late 1880s, however, the stereo plates often included illustrations, of the width of a single or double column, and thereafter tended to appeal even to the major papers.[11]

To begin with, W.F. Tillotson probably sold his wares by writing round individually to offer specific works to likely proprietors, but he quickly developed more efficient methods of advertising. By at least 1875, he was inserting announcements in trade journals offering a number of named serials to all-comers.[12] Soon also Tillotson was producing fliers for individual works, programmes announcing fiction available over the coming months, and catalogues giving details of the growing backlist, all of which were sent around liberally to prospective customers.[13] Of the seven proprietors who joined the original syndicate for *Taken at the Flood* (see Table 2.1), all but two remained coterie members for many years. They were soon joined regularly by other major proprietors like those of the *Nottinghamshire Guardian, Leicester Chronicle, Liverpool Weekly Post, Aberdeen Weekly Journal*, and *Bath Herald*. Typical of the smaller local papers buying second-hand serials at knock-down prices were the *Wiltshire Times, Lymington Chronicle*, and *Todmorden Weekly Advertiser*.

Although the record for individual serials is not always complete, as Tables A.2 and 3.2 both indicate, the 'Story Account' section of the surviving Trade Ledger at Bolton for the years 1874–79 suggests that, in general, income from subscribing journals within twelve months of the appearance of the first instalment of a serial comfortably outran the payment arranged beforehand with the author. Braddon's *Dead Men's Shoes* and Collins's *Jezebel's Daughter*, for example, were respectively £320 and £400 in the black, and even the First Prize tale in the 1878 fiction competition cleared the cost of the prize money by at least £12. Though these figures obviously overlook the cost of wages, communications and other overheads, they also do not take into account income accruing from sales from Tillotsons's backlists after, often long after, the first year had passed. Florence Marryat's *Fighting the Air*, for example, found more than one taker and earned almost £12 in 1882, eight years after first publication, while Frederick Talbot's *Sophie Crewe* (1877) was still in demand in 1898.

Moreover, there were soon auxiliary sources of profit from sidelines to the fiction syndication business. Towards the end of the 1870s,

Tillotsons began to provide a limited but regular syndication service of non-fiction material. A weekly 'London Letter' and 'Ladies Column' were offered from 1879, and the 'Children's Column' and 'Chess Column' were added in 1881. The last proved to be short-lived but the other three lasted well into the twentieth century. The subscribers to these services seem generally to have been the country papers who purchased second-hand fiction, and many small proprietors were doubtless content to fill their feature pages from a single source of supply. More interesting for our purposes was W.F. Tillotson's small venture into book publishing. In July 1876 Tillotson signed an agreement with Dora Russell, who had won the *Newcastle Weekly Chronicle* Fiction Competition in 1870, whereby he purchased for £250 absolute copyright to her latest triple-decker *Footprints in the Snow*, that is, the right to issue the work not only in serial form but in volume also (ZBEN, 4/4). Similar deals were struck with the same author for half a dozen further novels over the next decade, and in 1879 Tillotson was even buying up copyrights to her previously issued work.[14] The purpose was not to sell on the volume rights to another publisher at a profit, as Tillotsons's syndication agency was sometimes to do later,[15] but to engage in a cooperative publishing venture – once again with John Maxwell. It seems that the sheets of Russell's novels were printed in Bolton and then sent to London to be bound into volumes and issued under the Maxwell imprint, while costs of advertising and profits made were both to be shared. Frederick Talbot's *Sophie Crewe* seems to have been dealt with in the same fashion. The surviving ledgers at Bolton suggest that, at least in the early days, there was steady income also from these sources (Publication Account, ZBEN, 1/2–3). Overall, then, there is little doubt that W.F. Tillotson's enterprise in building up his fiction syndication business in the 1870s was rapidly and amply rewarded, and yet it is equally apparent that this task was not accomplished single-handedly. Clearly he looked to and learned much from the early experiments in fiction serialization and syndication by the Sheffield newspapers. But the assistance in the early stages from John Maxwell was even more valuable. As a progressive newspaper proprietor himself, Tillotson had access to a network of contacts with other provincial owners through organizations such as the Press Association and the Liberal Association (Singleton, 11). What he lacked was any standing in metropolitan literary circles, and this was precisely what Maxwell helped him to achieve.

3.2   Outreach and competition

From the early 1880s, however, there occurs something of a sea-change in the workings of Tillotsons's syndication agency. At first sight this appears to be simply a natural process of expansion, leading to ventures into new markets overseas, in America, the Colonies, and Continental Europe, and accompanied by contracts with a wider range of metropolitan authors of higher standing. However, on closer investigation, this new phase of growth seems to be not so much an aggressive move into vacant space as a defensive response to increasing competition in the Fiction Bureau's own home territory, as new agencies entered the market for newspaper fiction more rapidly than the market itself expanded. In this, of course, it reflects the motivation of Britain's wider political and economic imperialism in the same period. As there, evidence is apparent in the emergence of rivalry and conflict in a number of forms. A direct economic result is a marked inflation of sums paid to authors for newspaper serialization rights, without a corresponding increase in sums paid by subscribing newspapers, and thus a squeeze on profit margins. An uncomfortable edge seems suddenly to enter the striking of every bargain at this stage. A more indirect legal consequence is an increase in squabbles between authors and syndicators over questions of copyright, in the context of the complexities and inadequacies of copyright law, both international and domestic. This leads to increasingly formal contracts and the intervention of third parties, either solicitors or literary agents. On the personal level, the effect can be seen in Willie Tillotson's changing relationship with those who had cooperated with him in the previous decade, again most notably John Maxwell. Fortunately, a large part of one side of the correspondence between Maxwell and Tillotson in the 1880s has survived at Bolton, so that it is possible at last to see a little human flesh on the bare bones of the business records.

After the Chace Act of 1891, foreign authors who were citizens of states (like Great Britain) judged to satisfy the condition of reciprocity, could acquire copyright protection in the USA – if their publications were physically produced there. Before that time, there was no such protection and all that writers not citizens of or residents in the country could sell to American publishers, whether of periodicals or books, was advance copy of their work which would give the publishers in question a start over unauthorized rivals and thus a chance to recoup their outlay (Briggs, pt 5; Nowell-Smith, *International*, ch. 4). Although there were occasional instances of Tillotsons explicitly buying the right to sell 'advance sheets' in America in earlier years, and indeed as early as 1874,[16] it seems likely that such rights were sold on to individual periodicals or to agents on the East Coast. It was probably not until the early 1880s that the Fiction Bureau began to establish direct links with regional American newspapers and to form coteries outside the United Kingdom. Early in 1882, after an unusually lengthy break, Tillotsons had accepted a further Braddon novel from Maxwell, and agreed to an increase in payment to £750 if rights outside Britain were included (6, 17 March, 19 April, ZBEN, 4/3). From the 1860s Maxwell had been selling advance sheets to Harpers through a London agent, and many of Braddon's earlier novels had thus appeared in the pages of *Harper's Weekly* (11 October 1882, ZBEN, 4/3). W.F. Tillotson seems originally to have planned to make a similar arrangement, but a hitch in the negotiations led him to an experiment which was encouraged by Maxwell (26 October 1882, ZBEN, 4/3). In December Tillotson prepared a detailed circular advertising for a coterie of state-wide papers to take up advance sheets of Braddon's latest work at £25 pounds per journal. After having it checked by Maxwell, he mailed it to many newspaper proprietors in the United States.[17] The novel was only offered to major city journals with wide circulations, and copy was available in proof rather than stereo. Perhaps only four such journals took up the offer and serialized *Phantom Fortune* on this occasion (telegram, 3 February 1883, ZBEN, 4/3), but the technique was soon repeated for novels by B.L. Farjeon and John Saunders, and for full yearly programmes of fiction from 1885. The first such offering included serials by Dora Russell, Justin McCarthy and Wilkie Collins, as well as others by Braddon and Farjeon. The Bolton agency seems to have established regular business relations with eight American newspapers by late 1885 (TLS to A.P. Watt, 23 November 1886, Collins Acc., BERG). According to Johanningsmeier (53), these included the *Cincinnati News*, Louisville *Commercial*, *Fort Worth Gazette*, Springfield *Republican*, Philadelphia *Press*, and St Louis *Republican*, though the *Chicago Daily News* was among the first and remained one of the longest-standing of the Fiction Bureau's American customers.

As Johanningsmeier has shown (50–61), in spring 1884 W.F.

Tillotson made his first trip to the States to meet his existing clients and find new ones. It is unlikely that on that occasion he came into contact with S.S. McClure, then working for the New York *Century* magazine, but who was shortly to start his own syndication agency (Lyon, pt II). Sam McClure acted as American representative for Tillotsons for around two years from mid-1886, and for the second of those years, after McClure met Willie Tillotson on his first trip to England in March 1887, there was also a reverse agreement for Tillotsons to market McClure's American serials in Britain. According to Lyon (92–3), the understanding came abruptly to an end in the summer of 1888, when McClure attempted to sell Robert Louis Stevenson's 'Outlaws of Tunstall Forest' (a shortened version of *The Black Arrow*) independently to British journals, including the *Nottinghamshire Guardian* and *Cardiff Times*, both regular Tillotsons's clients.[18] Certainly that autumn Willie Tillotson once again made the journey across the Atlantic, this time to set up his own New York Office, which opened at the beginning of 1889 and continued in business into the new century. Fortunately it is still possible to view correspondence between Victor Lawson at the *Chicago Daily News* and Tillotsons, both in Bolton before 1889 and in New York afterwards.[19] Although their business relationship was of long standing, these letters suggest that it was by no means always cordial. In addition to perennial troubles over late arrival of copy or high and inflexible prices, regular and often angry complaints from Lawson concerned: the agency's inability or reluctance to allow the editor to read stories in their entirety before purchase; the fact that the fiction material was geared to weekly rather than daily serialization; and, most significantly, the perception that American audiences seemed to prefer more incident and less immorality than British ones. Domestic novels by Margaret Oliphant, and David Christie Murray were rejected as tedious, while sensational works from Dora Russell and Miss Braddon were often judged unacceptable for an American family audience. In rejecting a novel by 'Ouida', Victor Lawson pointed out primly to W.F. Tillotson that:

> there seems to be a latitude about the publication of a certain sort of fiction in England which does not obtain in this country, we are happy to say, among readers of first-class publications. We must therefore ask you to always bear in mind, in offering us fiction, that stories which are in any sense coarse or 'sugges-

tive' we cannot accept, no matter how distinguished the author.
(TLS, 26 March 1888, Outgoing, VFL)

In the long run, adventure stories from the likes of W. Clark Russell,
Hall Caine, and, especially, H. Rider Haggard seemed the most likely
to find favour and guarantee good prices in the American newspapers (see Table 3.3). That the problems outlined above were not
unique to the Chicago paper, but were typical of those Tillotsons
faced in syndicating their wares in the unfamiliar American market, is suggested by the case of Wilkie Collins's *The Evil Genius*.
The novel was the leading product in the Fiction Bureau's 1885
programme, and as such proved attractive to many editors – the
Chicago Daily News alone was prepared to pay $550 for serializa-
tion rights, spent even more on advertising its appearance, and
thus increased its circulation by many thousands. But not long after publication began, complaints poured in from all sides, not only
that the story was both tedious and immoral, but also that the
instalments were far shorter than stipulated. W.F. Tillotson protested to Collins and his agent, and claimed that *The Evil Genius*
lost him several of his principal American clients (see Chapter 6).

The Colonial and Continental markets seem to have presented
less in the way of risks but also offered more modest returns, though
reliable documentation remains thin.[20] As Toni Johnson-Woods shows,
novels by established English authors probably began to appear in
weekly newspapers in major Australian cities as early as 1856, when
Dickens's *Little Dorrit* started its run in the Melbourne *Leader*. In
the same journal appeared many of the serials from Dickens's family
weekly *All the Year Round* from its start in 1859. Other early examples
include Trollope's *Phineas Finn* in the Melbourne *Australasian* from
November 1867, and Wilkie Collins's *Moonstone* in the Brisbane
Queenslander from July 1869. John Maxwell was also quick to begin
placing Braddon's work in a number of Australian city journals
through the agency of George Street, beginning with *To the Bitter
End* in 1872 and continuing up until *Just as I Am* in 1880 (Morrison,
'Serial', 311–12). But from *Phantom Fortune* onwards, this task also
was left to Tillotsons, who arranged for that novel to be serialized
in the *Illustrated Sydney News* from April 1883. Somewhat earlier,
Tillotsons had explicitly purchased Colonial serial rights from a
small number of writers, the first case probably being B.L. Farjeon's
No. 119 Great Porter Square in 1879, where the payment of £300

included serial rights in America and the British Colonies (ZBEN, 4/4). The novel appeared in the monthly Melbourne *Australian Journal* from January to August 1881. Dora Russell's *Beneath the Wave*, for which Tillotson held absolute copyright, appeared in the same journal rather earlier, from November 1878 to June 1879. Further, two works handled by Tillotsons in Britain at least, Eliza Lynn Linton's *My Love!* and John Saunders's *Victor or Victim?*, have been located consecutively in the Melbourne Age in 1881, immediately following the serialization of Braddon's *Just as I Am* (Table A.3). It thus seems possible that Willie Tillotson may have received advice from John Maxwell on Australian publication at earlier stages also.

In any case, the process itself was relatively simple, and the passage of the International Copyright Act of 1886 must have made the task slightly easier as regards the timing of Colonial publication, in that it extended Imperial copyright protection to works first issued in any part of the Empire rather than merely in Britain itself (Briggs, pt 4, ch. 2). In the early years, a London agent was almost certainly employed, possibly again George Street, and approaches were only made to major city journals. A standard arrangement for works by well-known writers like Braddon seems to have been to offer serial rights in a single colony for £75, or entire Australian and New Zealand rights for £100, thus leaving a Colonial editor or agent to sell on copy to other journals. On many occasions serialization seems to have occurred in only a single newspaper, although Braddon's *Ishmael* (1884), for example, has been traced in three major Australian journals (Johnson-Woods), while Hall Caine's *The Bondman* (1889–90) has been found appearing simultaneously in twelve local journals in Victoria alone, in addition to slightly earlier appearances in the *Adelaide Observer* and Melbourne *Daily Telegraph* (Elizabeth Morrison, personal communication).

In Canada, where the ease of entry from America of cheap unauthorized books and periodicals made the enforcement of Imperial copyright legislation problematic (Briggs, 618–32), serial rights seem to have been marketed along with those in the USA. They were generally sold to a single major city newspaper, often the *Toronto Globe*, which took Justin McCarthy's *Camiola* and Wilkie Collins's *Evil Genius* in 1885, for example. Arrangements with journals in India, in the Cape, and in other parts of the Empire seem to have been less frequent, commanded relatively small payments, and again tended to involve only a single major journal – such as the *Calcutta Englishman* or *Overland Mail* in India. But the market in Australia and New Zealand remained the centre of the Bolton agency's Colonial ventures and represented a steady if unspectacular additional source of income. As Table A.3 shows, the Melbourne *Age*, for example, received almost half of the serial novels appearing in its columns in the last 20 years of the century from Tillotsons's Fiction Bureau, including works by William Black, Walter Besant and Margaret Oliphant.

Documentation concerning Bureau's venture into the European market is even sparser. Braddon's *Phantom Fortune* appears again to be one of the first cases where Tillotsons explicitly purchased European serial rights – France, Germany, Italy, and Spain being specified in this case (17 March 1882, ZBEN, 4/3), while the 1885 agreement for Besant's *Herr Paulus* simply ceded European rights (Notebook A, 1, TURNER). John Maxwell offered Willie Tillotson advice on the implications for his business of the 1886 Berne Convention on International Copyright (6 September 1886, ZBEN, 4/3), which was signed by Britain and most major European countries, though not, of course, by the United States.[21] Slightly later there is evidence of a concentration on the German market, though the sale of rights to Baron Tauchnitz, the publisher of European editions of English-language novels in Leipzig, is reserved on many contracts. Agreements with Wilkie Collins and William Black from around 1887 allow extra payments for rights of German translation and newspaper publication. According to a note in the *Publishers' Circular* (1 March 1889, 224), around this period Tillotsons also appear to have begun to pay an agent in Berlin and employ German translators and compositors in Bolton in order to provide serial stories. Translation and Continental serial rights were still specified on a number of contracts after the turn of the century.

As this survey of the entry into markets outside Britain suggests, by the end of the 1870s the Bolton firm had established something of a reputation in London literary circles and had begun regularly to purchase fiction from a new group of established metropolitan authors who had no formal connection with John Maxwell, and who were a cut above the general run of his protégés. These included F.W. Robinson, George MacDonald, Robert Buchanan, Eliza Lynn Linton, Henry Lucy, James Payn, Justin McCarthy, Charles Reade, and Walter Besant, though the biggest catch of all, and one of the earliest, was Wilkie Collins, with whom a contract was signed for *Jezebel's Daughter* in July 1878 (ZBEN, 4/4). All of these commanded from Tillotsons at least £200 for serial rights to a full-length novel, though only Payn, Besant, Reade and Collins achieved sums matching those then being offered to Braddon. Though there is ample evidence of W.F. Tillotson simply writing round to distinguished authors to solicit stories by this time (ZBEN, 4/6),[22] it is noticeable that many of the established writers then signing up with Tillotsons, including all of those listed above, belonged to the Chatto and Windus 'stable', as regular contributors to *Belgravia* (*VFRG*, 14), and/or as prominent members of the house's popular list of 'Piccadilly' novelists. Andrew Chatto's new publishing house, which had quickly established a reputation for its approachability and progressive publishing policies, seems positively to have encouraged its writers to explore the provincial newspaper market (see Chapter 4). Indeed, a number of the writers listed above had already seen their work published in the provincial press before their first contracts with Tillotsons. Leader and Sons, for example, syndicated Payn's *Less Black than We're Painted* in 1877, and reprinted Collins's tale 'Percy and the Prophet' from *All the Year Round* in five parts in the *Sheffield Independent* early in 1879.

These are important early indications that Tillotsons were encountering growing competition in the fiction serialization market. Here a brief outline will suffice as this topic will be dealt with at length in the following chapter. As we have seen, from the mid-1870s London publishers like Cassell and Co. started to offer regular serial fiction among their news material. From the early 1880s the pioneering literary agent A.P. Watt set up his own *ad hoc* newspaper syndicates and quickly attracted well-known authors like Collins, Payn and Besant, while expensive metropolitan weeklies like *The Graphic* began to pay top prices for serial fiction by name authors. At the same time there were American-based syndicates being created who wanted popular British authors on their books. And closest to home, there were the proprietors of rival northern newspapers who needed a steady supply of fiction material and saw the chance to turn a profit by themselves selling copy in proof or stereotype to other journals. W.C. Leng and Co. in Sheffield, as we shall see, were to set up their own syndication agency from around 1885 and become one of the Bolton firm's fiercest rivals.

Table 3.1 Costs of serials in the *Bolton Weekly Journal* over five-year periods

Period*	Total Cost (A)[†‡] (£)	Annual average (A/5)[‡] (£)
1875–79	4 085	817
1880–84	4 782	956
1885–89	10 870	2 174
1890–94	3 178	636
1895–99	3 392	678

* Based on the year when the serial runs commenced.
[†] Includes the proportional and estimated sums shown in Table A.2.
[‡] To the nearest pound sterling.
Sources: Notebook A, TURNER; and Table A.2

Table 3.2 Crude profit margins on certain Tillotsons's serials

Year serials began in *Bolton Weekly Journal*	No. of serials where data available	Payments to authors (A)[‡] (£)	Receipts from syndicates within one year (B)[‡] (£)	Crude margin (B-A)/A (%)
1875	4	800	1275	59.4
1879	4	958	1605	67.6
1882	3	575	751	30.6
1884	3	780	1128	44.6
1885	2	1800	2051	13.9
1886	2	1825	1622	−11.1

[‡] To the nearest pound sterling.
Sources: Table A.2,: Notebook A, TURNER; and ZBEN, 1/2–3.

While the gradual increase in payments to authors in the early 1880s might be explained by the additional remuneration offered for overseas serials rights, the abrupt leap in prices offered by Tillotsons to major authors from around 1885 must have been largely due to the intensity of competition experienced in this period. Certainly this was the explanation W.F. Tillotson offered to Victor Lawson when the latter protested the inflation of fees charged to subscribing papers (TLSs, 22 August, 24 November, 31 December 1885, Outgoing & ALS, 12 January 1886, Incoming, VFL). Suddenly Collins and Braddon were able to command sums well in excess of £1000 for a single novel, and similar amounts were offered to eminent new acquisitions like Walter Besant, William Black, and Thomas Hardy.[23] As Table 3.1 shows, the total amount Tillotsons paid for the serials which appeared in the *Bolton Weekly Journal* from 1885–89 was £10 870, more than double the £4782 paid in the preceding five-year period. But, with alternative sources of supply, the provincial coteries were reluctant to match such increases in the subscriptions they paid to Tillotsons. The Fiction Bureau's profit margins were thus noticeably squeezed and in some case even vanished. Though the data available (summarized in Table 3.2) is patchy, we can see that the combined receipts from syndicate members within twelve months for two novels appearing in the *Bolton Weekly Journal* in 1885 (by Collins and McCarthy) were little above 110 per cent of the payments to authors, while those for novels by Oliphant and Black in 1886 came to below 90 per cent. The general trend is indicated in Table 3.2. It seems likely that this form of financial pressure in their home market encouraged Tillotsons to search more energetically for returns elsewhere. In other words, the ventures into America, the Colonies, and Europe were as much a consequence as a cause of the inflation of payments to authors.

The specific agreements framed between the Fiction Bureau and its authors in the nineteenth century are again summarized schematically in Table A.2, and will be discussed in detail in Chapter 6. The general pattern is clear enough: in most of the earliest agreements authors ceded unspecified 'Serial' or 'Newspaper' copyright to Tillotsons, whereas by the early 1880s the majority cited time limits and/or place restrictions. Although the increasing complexity of the agreements may seem at first simply a further consequence of the expansion into overseas markets, the acrimonious nature of some of the contract negotiations suggests that growing rivalry in the syndication market was once more a determining factor.

To varying extents all the public determinants described above underlie the tensions growing between Willie Tillotson and John Maxwell throughout the mid-1880s and leading to a final break between them in 1887, though the situation was exacerbated by personal factors. As I have shown elsewhere (Law 'Engaged'), the letters from Maxwell to Tillotson reveal a fluid mixture of commercial and social intercourse. Detailed negotiations concerning rights conceded, rates or methods of payment, and publication dates stand side by side with social invitations, family news or inquiries, and personal banter. Tillotson and his wife Mary (an avid reader of Braddon and other Tillotsons's authors, who took advantage of her husband's business to collect the autographs of eminent writers) were both fully a generation younger than Maxwell, but so nearly was Braddon herself; despite the distance between Bolton and the Home Counties, there were occasional social engagements involving the two families, particularly at holiday times, while Tillotson himself was a frequent visitor to London. Despite Maxwell's overbearing manner, the relationship which emerges with 'gentle Willie' seems generally warm and personal, and after conflicts in the business negotiations, Maxwell is always quick to protest eternal trust and friendship. But as Maxwell became older and frailer (he turned 60 in 1884), he became more irritable, and, although he was much less actively involved in running the publishing business, seems to have spent much of the time on his hands in worrying. During the 1880s, the Maxwells bought land in the New Forest and built a substantial second home, and John seems to have been unnecessarily anxious about the financial outlay involved (for example, 19 July 1884, ZBEN, 4/3). The sheaves of letters and telegrams that he fired off to Bolton at times of tension bear witness to his anxieties, and there are obvious signs of Tillotson's impatience.[24] The general pattern in the negotiations was for Maxwell to claim greater remuneration, which Tillotson would only agree to if wider publication rights were granted. As no formal contracts were produced, there were a number of misunderstandings and disputes over what payments had been agreed and what rights conceded. A regular irritation to Maxwell at this time was the risk of copyright loss in the American newspaper market, although he had himself encouraged Tillotson to begin syndication there. Maxwell's fear was that Tillotson's tendency to send advance sheets too early to clients in the United States risked allowing American newspaper publication to conclude before the first complete appearance in a British journal, thus perhaps imperilling the entire British copyright (see for example, 27 December 1882, 5 September 1883, 5 March 1885, ZBEN, 4/3).[25]

Perhaps the biggest row of all erupted in early 1886 and concerned the cooperative book-publishing venture between Maxwell and Tillotson. In 1879 Maxwell had transferred ownership of his publishing house to his two sons by his first marriage, John and Robert, who carried on business as 'J. and R. Maxwell', and continued to publish and distribute the Dora Russell novels printed at Bolton (Wolff, *Sensational*, 332–3). Early in 1885 Maxwell and Tillotson had come up with a new publishing scheme to take advantage of the growing fame of the Bolton firm, the 'Tillotson's [sic] Shilling

Fiction' series, whereby Tillotson would purchase the volume rights to short novels by popular authors and have them published by Maxwells as before, with the aim of selling cheap volumes in tens of thousands to the readers who normally only encountered fiction in newspapers (Turner, 'Syndication', 97–9; Law, 'Engaged', 27–8, 34–5). Only the first two books in the series had been produced (Ouida's *A Rainy June* and Joseph Hatton's *John Needham's Double*) when a rude and incoherent letter from the London publishing house caused Willie Tillotson, who was already suspicious that Maxwell's sons were making little effort in marketing his books, to lose his temper. The result was that, at considerable expense, he abruptly switched all his volume publishing to the firm of George Routledge.[26] Both sides in the dispute were obviously hit badly by this outcome. The house of Maxwell was sold up to Spencer Blackett not long afterwards, and 'Tillotson's Shilling Fiction' series fizzled out in 1887 after only seven volumes had appeared (Turner, 'Reading', 70–2).

Both men were aware that, though the Bolton firm were pioneers in the syndication of fiction in Britain, competition was growing. Maxwell habitually forwarded to Tillotson not only requests from individual journals wishing to serialize Braddon's work but also details of offers from rival syndicators, with ambiguous motives. He claimed that he was acting out of openness and friendship, but he obviously used the rival offers to influence negotiations and Tillotson was sensitive to any hint of treachery. When Maxwell wrote to Tillotson pointing, with justification, to other syndicators offering 'greater sequence of employment and at higher prices than you have ever given' (26 March 1887, ZBEN, 4/3), it was the first of the two complaints that was more crucial. On more than one occasion Maxwell had happily agreed to accept lower payments from the Bolton firm in order to preserve the relationship. To begin with Tillotsons had been pleased to publish Braddon's works back to back, but by the late 1870s, with other well-known sensationalists like Wilkie Collins and Joseph Hatton also on their books, the Bolton firm was obviously finding this too much of a good thing. But since *Belgravia* had been sold, serial publication of Braddon's work in the literary monthlies was becoming more intermittent, and Maxwell kept pushing for W.F. Tillotson to take a Braddon every year, as his wife was still producing two novels annually. In autumn 1885 when Maxwell was trying to place Braddon's 1886 novel *Mohawks*, he was shocked when Tillotsons replied that he would not have an opening until 1887. Maxwell then forced a reluctant

Tillotson to accept the shorter novel *One Thing Needful* for the interim, by threatening to sell to A.P. Watt who had already offered
a considerably higher sum for the work on behalf of a client (Law,
'Engaged', 26–33).

The client in question was almost certainly W.C. Leng and Co.
in Sheffield, who also approached Maxwell directly earlier the same
year (9 June, ZBEN, 4/3). The Sheffield firm renewed the attack in
the spring of 1887, when Maxwell was asked to name his price for
an annual Braddon novel for the following three years.[27] Maxwell
once again tried to force Tillotson's hand. Tillotson wrote for advice to R.E. Leader of the *Sheffield Independent* and received the
following reply:

> I am much obliged to you for asking my opinion on the latest
> Sheffield effort to trump your best card. My feeling is that it
> would be most unfortunate to let Miss Braddon get 'out of your
> hands for ever' – and yet I think Mr Maxwell far too shrewd to
> let anything of the kind take place. But I quite agree with you
> that an annual tale from her pen would be quite too much.
>
> (ALS, 25 March 1887, ZBEN, 4/3)

Neither Maxwell or Tillotson would concede and a separation became inevitable. Maxwell accepted the Sheffield offer of £1250 for
each of Braddon's next three novels, to be published annually from
January 1888, with an option on succeeding works. On the day
that the serialization of *The Fatal Three* was to begin in the Sheffield paper, Maxwell wrote what sounds almost like a lover's farewell:

> So let it be! again and again so let it be! . . . I was not to blame
> in our correspondence last year. Your language was firm: mine
> only informing: the result unavoidable. I warned but in vain!
> New arrangements merely succeeded. Our dearest 'Willie' pro-
> nounced the decree of severance after long years of peaceful and
> pleasant servitude.
>
> (14 January 1888, ZBEN, 4/3)

Just over a year later, shortly after returning from his second trip
to New York, and when plans were well under way for his firm to
move into new and enlarged premises, W.F. Tillotson contracted
pneumonia and died suddenly at home on 19 February 1889,
according to obituary notices in *The Journalist* (22 February, 6; 1

March 1889, 2). Like Samuel Harrison on his death in 1871, he was only 44. Perhaps also like Harrison he finally found the dual role of running newspapers and a syndication agency too much for his strength. Together, the loss of its first novelist and the death of its founder effectively mark the end of the second stage of development of the Fiction Bureau.

3.3   Retrenchment and decline

After the heady literary successes and the commercial turbulence of the 1880s, the following decade was a period of retrenchment and consolidation for the Fiction Bureau, leading gradually into a slow retreat and decline in the new century. This process also had both private and public determinants.

The untimely death of W.F. Tillotson undoubtedly left the family firm in a difficult position. In 1889, his father John Tillotson was nearly seventy and had long retired from active duty, but his three sons were still in their teens. The eldest, John Lever Tillotson, had just entered the firm as an apprentice, while James Lever and Fred Lever were still at school. William Brimelow, a lay minister in the local Independent Methodist Church as well as a professional journalist, had joined Tillotsons in 1871 as editor of the *Bolton Evening News*. He become a partner in 1874 and was also involved in the day-to-day running of the syndication business. Brimelow took control of the firm on Willie Tillotson's death, though the widow Mary (whose brother William Lever was in the family soap-manufacturing business and was to become the first Lord Leverhulme) became a partner and assisted in the business for an interim period. Both seem to have concentrated their energies on the core newspaper publication activities. John Nayler, who had entered the firm in 1879 as a reporter and later become W.F. Tillotson's literary secretary, temporarily took over the running of the fiction agency until he was replaced by the 18-year-old James Lever Tillotson in 1893. When John Lever Tillotson left the family firm to join the board of Lever Bros at the end of the decade, James took over his responsibilities, and a series of managers were recruited to run the Fiction Bureau, the first being the young Philip Gibbs who interrupted his glittering Fleet Street career for a spell of two years at Bolton (Turner, 'Syndication', 51–3; Johanningsmeier, 58–9). For none of these later chiefs did the management of the Fiction Bureau offer the intensely personal satisfaction that it had given to its founder.

For Willie Tillotson, the Bureau was not only a vindication of his own ingenuity and enterprise, but also a passport to new worlds, the literary circles of London as well as the journalistic spheres of New York. It is easy to imagine the smile on the Bolton man's face as, say, he made his way to his appointment with Ouida at her London hotel (Singleton, 49), or presented his wife with the auto-graphed letter of Charles Dickens that Wilkie Collins had just sent him for her collection (ALS, 15 February 1880, ZBEN, 4/6/16).

But in the early 1890s there were also pressing commercial reasons to cut back the expenditure on payments to authors. As we have already seen, Tillotsons were facing increasing competition and diminishing profit margins from the middle of the previous decade, which were not adequately compensated by the ventures into overseas markets. In the following chapter, we shall see that the Bolton firm's fiercest rivals followed them quickly into the field of international syndication, and often had greater technical and financial resources behind them. In addition, the early 1890s experienced a major readjustment in the market for new fiction in book form, as it became apparent that the circulating libraries would no longer support the expensive three-volume format that they had so long dictated, and publishers and authors alike prepared themselves for a new era of shorter original novels which could be sold in single volumes, more cheaply, and in much larger quantities in the book shops. One almost immediate economic result was a significant increase in the payments for novels in volume by the most popular writers, accompanied by the exclusion of many marginal authors from the book market altogether (Griest, chs 7–8). It is from this period that the phrase 'best-seller' begins to have a currency. Most importantly, as we shall see in Chapter 4, by the end of the decade it was clear that the provincial weekly newspaper was no longer in the vanguard as a periodical vehicle for the latest metropolitan fiction, but had been superseded by the mass-circulation periodicals produced in London.

Indeed the first indications of the impact of these changes can be seen even before W.F. Tillotson's death. From autumn 1888 the Fiction Bureau began to contract with a number of reliable but undistinguished authors to produce a given amount of fiction per year at a pre-determined salary, with Tillotsons retaining absolute copyright of the stories thus produced (Notebook A, 18, 20, 31, 110, TURNER). The authors in question were: Adeline Sergeant, a Scottish writer specializing in love stories who had first been published in John Leng's *People's Friend*, and who had first been syndicated by Tillotsons in 1883; J. Monk Foster, a former miner from Lancashire writing local tales of agricultural and industrial life, who was new to the Bureau but who had already published a number of stories in James Henderson's periodicals;[28] and Dora Russell, the sensationalist who had been linked continuously with Tillotsons since 1876. The periods lasted from 5 years in a single contract for Sergeant, at least ten in two stages for Russell, and at least 13 years in five shorter periods for Foster. Sergeant and Foster were each to produce a full-length serial and a short story totalling around 160 000 words annually, while Russell generally had to come up with over 200 000 words a year in the form of a full-length serial and a novella. Annual salaries varied from £78 for Foster at the end of the 1880s to £600 for Russell at the end of the 1890s, while Sergeant earned £162 per annum throughout her single five-year contract. As though to emphasize his inferior status, in Foster's contract the quantity of fiction was calculated in quarterly amounts, while the remuneration was expressed as a weekly or monthly wage. This rose slowly but steadily from 30s a week in 1889 to 10 guineas a month in 1902, that is, from £78 to £126 a year. In contrast, Russell earned £5500 from the Bureau between 1889 and 1899. However, we should remember that, the book-publishing ventures now having come to an end, Tillotsons could sell on volume rights of Russell's work to London houses like Hurst and Blackett, whereas none of Foster's novels appear to have been published in London.

The overall purpose of the exercise was presumably to have a steady supply of saleable fiction, at a range of levels from low to middle ranking. This must have been part of a new policy to reduce significantly the agency's dependence on big name writers demanding inflated sums. Table A.2 demonstrates the suddenness of the decline in the appearance of top-priced serials by top-ranking authors in the pages of the *Bolton Weekly Journal* in the 1890s. If we exclude William Black's *Stand Fast, Craig Royston!* of 1890, which, since the contract was almost certainly signed before W.F. Tillotson's death, should be regarded as a residue of the boom years of the 1880s, no work there cost anything approaching a £1000 and only two broke the £500 barrier – Oliphant's *Sorceress* in 1892 and Black's *Wild Eelin* in 1898. Although a small part of the data for the late years is the result of estimation, Table 3.1 indicates that spending on serials published in the Bolton paper over the decade not only fell dramatically from the heights scaled in the later 1880s, but even failed to reach the levels of the 1870s. The five serials appearing in 1899, for example, together cost less than the £450 that Braddon had received for *Taken at the Flood* back in 1873. This was despite the fact that, after 1893, when Tillotsons took over the rival *Bolton Guardian*, the re-titled *Bolton Journal and Guardian* added a new four-page supplement which significantly increased the space devoted to fiction and other entertainment material. Other little known and even lower paid authors, who also found it difficult to get their work published in volume form, like William Henry Moyes or Mary H. Tennyson, began to enter the ranks of Tillotsons's authors in number during the decade. New authors with metropolitan reputations beginning to appear were generally writers specializing in distinct sub-genres and commanding prices around the £200 mark. These included 'John Strange Winter', pseudonym of Mrs Arthur (Henrietta) Stannard, the prolific writer of love stories, and William Le Queux, the equally prolific producer of thrillers, both of whom were to become regular clients at and after the turn of the century. In literary terms, comparing the *Journal* in the 1890s and in the 1880s shows two marked trends: a decline in the prestige of the authors featured, together with a return to the earlier provincial newspaper tradition of reliance on local fiction, thanks to J. Monk Foster. It should be noted that only a single serial by each of Russell and Sergeant appeared in the pages of the *Journal* during the decade, though there were nine from Foster.

Another impact of the changes in the 1890s fiction market visible in Table A.2 is the sudden reduction in the average length of the serial stories in Tillotsons's lists which occurs from around 1893. This was well before Mudie's Library announced their refusal to accept any further original novels in the expensive triple-decker format from the beginning of 1895 (see Chapter 1). It suggests that, by the beginning of the decade, novelists and publishers were aware that this outcome was inevitable, in general welcomed it, and were thus keen and able to anticipate.[29] The Bolton firm had bought quite a few shorter serials from the earliest days, and their newspapers continued to publish occasional serials of triple-decker length until the late 1890s, especially by aging sensationalists like Braddon and Russell who seemed to cling to the ampler format,[30] or by J Monk Foster who had a quota to fulfil and no interest in the book market. But there is no doubt that before the middle of the decade the dominant serial form in Tillotsons's lists shifted rapidly from the longer novel of around 150 000 words/24 parts to the shorter novel of around 80 000 words/15 parts. What Table A.2 does not reveal clearly is the equally marked surge in importance of the short story in Tillotsons's fiction programmes and backlists from around the same time. The only indication there is the thinness of the serial offering at the beginning of the decade. The *Journal* had normally run two serials concurrently from the middle of the 1870s, yet for most of the period from 1890 to 1892 there was only a single serial running, while for six months in the middle of 1891 there was no serial at all, apart from a few longer tales in two to four parts. The rest of the fiction columns, which were not noticeably reduced, were devoted to complete tales. This emphasis continued after 1893 when the added pages of the new supplement allowed the regular inclusion of a number of complete tales as well as the customary instalments of two serials. The Story Account pages in the Trade Ledgers for the 1890s at Bolton (ZBEN,1/5–6) reveal a similar surge in the sale of short stories to other papers from around the same period. Five complete tales by Braddon in the later 1890s were among the more popular.

Two caveats are in order here concerning what Table A.2 does *not* show, and the way in which it thus tends to exaggerate the rapidity of the movement away from best-selling authors in Tillotsons's lists. First, some of the higher sums paid by the Bureau during the 1890s were for works by W. Clark Russell, Hall Caine, and H. Rider Haggard, purchased particularly or exclusively for the American market, as noted above. Secondly, compared to the previous two decades, a noticeably higher percentage of works by established metropolitan authors purchased by Tillotsons for publication in provincial newspapers failed to appear in their own journals during the 1890s. Table 3.3 shows all such serial stories, in cases where £500 or more was paid and data is available. Clearly the dropping of top-rank authors was not quite as rapid or absolute as Table A.2 suggests. Nevertheless, it is noticeable that the works in Table 3.3 tend to congregate in the first half of the decade and around the £500–600 level. Only in exceptional cases involving absolute copyright (and thus book rights) or the American market (potentially more lucrative after the Chace Act) does the payment reach four figures, and even then £1000 is an absolute ceiling. These prices are restrained when compared with the amounts that some of the Fiction Bureau's rivals were prepared to pay during the decade. In this context, Dora Russell, under contract for 10 years, almost certainly emerges as Tillotsons's highest paid author of the 1890s.

Table 3.3 Expensive Tillotsons's serials not appearing in the *Bolton Weekly Journal* in the 1890s

Author	Work	Year	Payment (£)	Length	Rights Purchased
Hall Caine	'The Prophet'	1890	1000	150 th.	S-US
Margaret Oliphant	'The Heir Presumptive and the Heir Apparent'	1890	600	156 th.	S
Robert Buchanan	'The Wedding Ring'	1891	500	100 th.	A
James Payn	'A Modern Dick Whittington'	1891	1000	100 th.	A
H. Rider Haggard	'Nada the Lily'	1892	800	110 th.	US
Thomas Hardy	'The Pursuit of the Well-Beloved'	1892	525	60 th.	S–US
David Christie Murray	'Bob Martin's Little Girl'	1892	650	125 th.	S–Con
W. Clark Russell	'Alone on a Wide, Wide Sea'	1892	600	120 th.	S–Con–US
William Black	'Highland Cousins'	1893	850	140 th.	S
M.E. Braddon	'All Along the River'	1893	500	110 th.	S
H. Rider Haggard	'Montezuma's Daughter'	1893	(500P)	150 th.	US
H. Rider Haggard	'The People of the Mist'	1894	(500P)	150 th.	US
M.E. Braddon	'When the World was Younger'	1895	850	150 th.	S–Con–US
Mrs Hungerford	'The Professor's Experiment'	1895	750	156 th.	A
Walter Besant	'The Master Craftsman'	1896	500	65 th.	S
Justin McCarthy	'The Ring'	1896	500	100 th.	A

(nP) = Proportionate sum calculated on length of story, in case of payment for more than one work.
th. = Thousand words
S = Simple serial/newspaper copyright.
A = Absolute copyright.
US = Advance sheets/serial copyright in USA.
Con = Serial copyright in Continental Europe.
Source: Notebook A, TURNER.

Where Tillotsons's 1890s fiction was not second-rate, it was increasingly often second-hand. This is true in more than one sense. The letters of condolence from the Bureau's authors received at Bolton on the death of W.F. Tillotson show that his relationship with many established novelists had become quite intimate through correspondence or interviews (WFT). But now the Bureau was increasingly to

have little in the way of personal contact with its major clients as
more and more acted through intermediaries. Of the 13 authors
listed in Table 3.3, seven (Besant, Black, Buchanan, Haggard, Oliphant,
Murray Payn) were already clients of A.P. Watt by 1885. Four more,
Hardy, Hungerford, McCarthy, and even (after Maxwell's incapacitation in 1891) Mary Braddon, were soon to follow them. Many of
the new generation of popular Tillotsons's authors (Guy Boothby,
Anthony Hope, Arthur Morrison and William Le Queux, for example) quickly joined the Watt stable. In addition some lesser names
would soon sign up with Watt's rivals, J.B. Pinker (often American
writers like Ulysses Rogers) or William Colles (usually unknowns
like Frances Gribble). Others dealt with Tillotsons through forgotten minor agents or their publishers (Notebook A, TURNER). Although
these agents valued the Bolton firm's experience in creating newspaper syndicates, whether in the British provinces, America, or
Australia, they could themselves handle the arrangements with the
metropolitan newspapers or magazines, thus depriving the
Bolton firm of the lucrative auxiliary market that W.F. Tillotson
was beginning to add to his repertoire in the mid-1880s. As we
shall see in Chapter 6, there were occasions when conflicts arose as
a result of too many middlemen scrambling in the space between
author and publisher.

The more literal meaning of 'second-hand' here refers to the practice
of buying residual serial rights to the works of name authors on
the cheap from rival syndicators, which begins in this period. Ironically enough, the most consistent example of such purchases was
from Lengs of Sheffield. From the turn of the century, E. Phillips
Oppenheim's work was frequently acquired in this way, but during
the 1890s the author in question was generally Braddon herself. As
Table A.4 indicates, between 1889 and 1901, W.C. Leng and Co.
sold on to Tillotsons various rights – first serial, second serial, and
colonial – to a total of nine Braddon novels.

All these changes are symptoms of a probably inevitable period of
retrenchment immediately following the death of W.F. Tillotson.
When precisely that process becomes one of retreat is difficult to
pinpoint, though Michael Turner's detailed description of the 1909
programme, for which unusually full records survive, offers a useful landmark. In the appendices to his thesis, in addition to

transcribing the programme itself in its entirety, Turner provides a comprehensive listing of where the short stories appeared, and a summary of the serials ('Syndication', 170–225). A number of points emerge which show the consequences of the developments in the 1890s which have been discussed. The programme itself has become rigid to facilitate the regularity of supply to subscribing papers, producing a marked commodification of the fiction: the 15 serials available are virtually all of 13 episodes to fit into a quarterly programme, the 104 complete tales are either 'Short Stories' of 4000 to 4500 words or 'Storyettes' of 2000 to 2500, and compiled into series running 26 weeks. The names of the authors feature rather less prominently than titles, dates and lengths, and are in any case virtually all unmemorable, apart from Arnold Bennett who contributes both a 'Short Story' and 'Storyette'. Otherwise, William Le Queux and Arthur Marchmont are the top names among the serialists, while John Strange Winter, and L.T. Meade stand out among the writers of complete tales. Payments to authors are correspondingly low: the entire cost to Tillotsons of the complete tales is just over £500, while the serials probably cost around not much over £1000 in total (Turner, 'Syndication', 94–6). According to the corresponding trade ledger (Ledger A, TURNER), overseas sales no longer figure very prominently and the American market may have dried up altogether.[31] The coterie of newspapers for first serialization seems to have narrowed to six or seven larger journals, only two (the *Bristol Observer* and the *Cardiff Times*) outside the North of England, and later sales from the backlists to small local papers are vital to balance the books. Although Tillotsons's fiction syndication business continued until 1935 under family control and along the lines established by its founder, there is little doubt that, in both literary and commercial terms, from the first decade of the new century at least the story is one of long and slow decline.

4
Rivals of Tillotsons

As was suggested in the previous chapter, although W.F. Tillotson could claim to be the creator of the first major fiction syndicate in Britain, others were planning to enter the field almost before the ink was dry on the agreement with John Maxwell. By the mid-1870s there were at least three other organizations selling serial fiction to provincial newspapers nationwide. From the middle of the following decade the Bolton firm was forced to modify its business strategies significantly in response to the activities of its rivals. It is important to distinguish here between narrower and broader definitions of the competition Tillotsons faced. Like all agents, Willie Tillotson was a middleman, first buying the serial rights to fiction from authors and then selling them on to a number of other newspaper proprietors. From Leader and Sons in 1873 to the Northern Newspaper Syndicate 20 years later, throughout the last quarter of the nineteenth century there were agencies being created which tried to do more or less the same thing. But these direct competitors proved less of a threat to the Fiction Bureau than the indirect rivals who began to emerge after 1880. Some were the new professional London literary agents who normally did not buy and sell at all, but took a commission from the price paid by a wide range of publishers or further middlemen to the author. Others were a new generation of large-circulation metropolitan weeklies, which began to purchase serials by popular novelists at top prices. In this chapter, we will look at the different bodies competing with Tillotsons under three headings: 'Direct competitors'; 'A.P. Watt and the literary agency'; and 'W.C. Leng and Co. and the metropolitan weekly'. The activities of A.P. Watt and W.C. Leng and Co. will receive rather more detailed attention, and not only for the reason that more detailed evidence has survived in these cases. The two are of particular interest because both began in direct and predatory competition with Tillotsons, but soon evolved into even more theatening indirect competitors.

4.1 Direct competitors

Of course throughout the Golden Age of the major fiction syndicates it was still possible to by-pass the middlemen altogether. As they had been in the 1850s and 1860s, authors were free to make direct approaches to individual provincial newspaper publishers. This still seems to have happened commonly in the case of local writers, like the Revd W.M. Philip who in 1878 was offered £20 for the publication of a short serial novel in the *Aberdeen Weekly Journal* (Finance Committee Minutes, 4 October, AJR). There were also cogent ideological or economic motives on the part of certain editors and novelists for avoiding the syndicators. Some of the most successful provincial city newspapers with large circulations, like the *Glasgow Weekly Herald*, *Glasgow Weekly Mail* or *Manchester Weekly Times*, obviously considered that they were above the necessity of joining 'coteries' and were sometimes prepared to pay for exclusive rights to the work of established writers. Alexander Sinclair, editor of the *Herald*, suggested that the use of syndicated fiction by an established newspaper was 'apt to give readers the impression that they are being asked to pay for matter which is cheap common property' (184).

As already noted, the *Weekly Herald* began to feature serials by members of its own editorial staff at the end of the 1860s, but appears not to have accepted material through the syndicators until 1880, Wilkie Collins's *The Black Robe* from Leaders perhaps being the first (Law, 'Wilkie', 257–9). But during the 1870s, alongside anonymous works by local writers or members of the editorial staff, readers had the exclusive privilege of reading the latest works by authors with established metropolitan reputations. These included the Scotsmen William Black (*A Daughter of Heth* in 1870) and George MacDonald (*Malcolm* in 1874), as well as George Meredith with *The Egoist* in 1879–80 (under the title *Sir Willoughby Patterne, the Egoist*). Similarly, the Manchester weekly seems to have accepted material from the syndicators only occasionally until the 1890s, but exclusive arrangements were nevertheless made with a number of well-known authors: most notably Jessie Fothergill (*Kith and Kin* in 1881), David Christie Murray (*Joseph's Coat* in 1882 and *Val Strange* in 1883), or Francis Hodgson Burnett (*Howarth's* in 1883). Fothergill, Murray, and Burnett all had some claim to be local authors, though it should be noted that in each case publication took place *after* the appearance of the novel in London, both in serial and in volume form. Clearly there were limits to what even the largest provincial journals were prepared to pay for their serials. This is also implied by circumstantial evidence of an informal arrangement to share serial fiction between the *Glasgow Weekly Mail* and the *Manchester Weekly Times* from the late 1870s, along the lines of the proto-syndicate between the Edinburgh *North Briton* and *Glasgow Times* described in Chapter 2. The works in question this time included George MacDonald's *Sir Gibbie* in 1878, Anthony Trollope's novella *Cousin Henry* in the spring of 1879, and William Westall's *The Old Factory* in 1880. Although Trollope at least seems to have made the arrangements himself (Sadleir, *Trollope*, 175–6), we should also note that in some cases such provincial newspaper appearances were set up by agents like Watt, or by the London volume publisher who had bought the novel outright. The latter was the case with Meredith's *Egoist*, where serial rights were sold on to the Glasgow paper by Kegan Paul for £100, without the author's knowledge and much to his annoyance (Collie, 43–4).

At the same time there were well-known authors who felt that they were underpaid by the syndicates, or resented the loss of control over their work, and attempted themselves to arrange for their fiction to be published at the same time by a number of newspapers. This practice can be distinguished from that of David Pae in earlier decades both in the number of journals involved and in the fact of simultaneous publication. In 1882, for example, Walter Besant's *All Sorts and Conditions of Men*, was serialized in around half a dozen provincial newspapers including the *Sheffield Telegraph*, simultaneously with its appearance in *Belgravia* (see Tables 4.1 and A.6). It seems that these appearances were arranged by James Rice, Besant's co-author from 1872, who took no part in writing the book due to ill health.[1] However, the best-documented case remains that of Captain Mayne Reid, whose letters to the *Newcastle Weekly Chronicle* were edited by Graham Pollard in 1942. As Table A.2 shows, following his return from the United States in 1870, Reid had sold the serial rights to 'A Brother's Revenge', a full-length novel, for one year only to Tillotsons for £200 in 1875. While that novel was still appearing in the *Bolton Weekly Journal*, Reid began to write around to a series of local proprietors to syndicate his next novel himself, and continued the practice until at least 1880, close to the end of his writing career. He succeeded with at least two new works (*Gwen Wynn* in 1876 and *No Quarter!* in 1880), and two other novels which had already appeared elsewhere (*The Flag of Distress* in 1877 and *The Free Lances* in 1879). All have been located in at least two provincial papers. Reid's widow (Reid, 220) later wrote that her husband negotiated for *Gwen Wynn* to appear in 10 country newspapers – including the local *Hereford Times* (1832?–) which thus featured fiction for the first time – though less than half have been traced.[2] Judging from his comments in the letters reprinted by Pollard, Reid's motives seem to have been chiefly financial. If the £50 that Reid seems to have received from the *Newcastle Chronicle* for *No Quarter!* is representative, he would have only to have contracted with four such journals on each occasion to have matched the remuneration obtained from the Fiction Bureau.[3]

There is also some evidence of lesser-known authors taking a more systematic approach to syndicating their own work, at a rather later date. Towards the end of 1888 a number of full-column advertisements began to appear in the pages of the new weekly trade paper *The Journalist* (1886–1909), advertising serial and short stories at cheap rates for publication in provincial journals. James Skipp Borlase (5 October, 4) and one Hawmon Queznal (28 December, 8) were the writers principally involved and they presumably placed the advertisements themselves. Queznal is an unknown quantity. His advertisement claimed previous appearances in a number of minor local papers including the *Lichfield Mercury*, and, judging from the titles, he may have been Australian. During the 1860s Borlase had undoubtedly been on the staff of the *Australian Journal*, a Colonial equivalent of *The London Journal* (Sussex & Burrows). From the early 1870s, he had not only contributed stories regularly to Edwin Brett's juvenile magazines, but also often written romances with local themes to order for a wide range of local newspapers (see note to Chapter 7). In addition, he had also sold work to Tillotsons, Leaders, and Cassell on more than one occasion, as his advertisements point out prominently. Presumably for him at least self-syndication was not merely a sign that his work was unwanted by the big market players.

Nevertheless, there were plenty of other writers of the status of Reid or Borlase willing to take their place in Tillotsons's lists, as there were other big city weeklies quite content to be served almost exclusively by the Fiction Bureau, like the *Liverpool Weekly Post* or

Birmingham Weekly Mercury. Ironically, immediately on the success of *Gwen Wynn*, Reid's local *Hereford Times* became a regular customer of Tillotsons and did not take any of the other novels Reid syndicated himself. Obviously these scattered attempts to by-pass the syndicating agent were in no way a significant threat to Tillotsons's business. But then, there is also little suggestion that the Fiction Bureau was seriously troubled by the three competing agencies which had already emerged by the mid-1870s. To put it another way, if Tillotsons had remained the sole major fiction syndication agent, it would have been difficult to attract a sufficiently wide range of established authors and major provincial journals into the market. Without the spur of such competition newspaper syndication would have been unlikely to form the dominant mode of 'respectable' fiction serialization as it clearly had by at least the early 1880s.

The three rival agencies which had entered the serial syndication market by 1875 were of course Cassell, Leaders and the National Press Agency. Concerning Cassell and Leaders there is little to add to the information presented in previous chapters.[4] The National Press Agency was established in early 1873 in Shoe Lane, Fleet Street (alongside John Maxwell's publishing house) with E. Dawson Rogers as General Manager. It began as the Liberal Press Agency but had changed its name by around June of the same year, though it retained explicit links to the Liberal Association (Brown, 118), and aimed to supply journals of Liberal persuasion with appropriate news and feature material in the form of proofs, stereo plates, or partly printed sheets. It appears to have had ample financial resources and expanded rapidly, judging by its annual advertisements in the *Newspaper Press Directory*, which began in 1874 and continued well into the twentieth century.[5] In addition to news services, the first such announcement already promised 'Serial Tales in proof or stereotype' (NPD, 1874, 142), while the Agency's partly printed sheets soon included 'Good Serial Stories... when desired' (*NPD*, 1882, 231). Even at the end of the century the Agency, now based on the other side of Fleet Street in Whitefriars House, Carmelite Street, was still offering both 'Partly printed Newspapers supplied in all sizes' and 'Original Serial and Short Stories in Proof or Stereo by the Most Popular Authors' (*NPD*, 1899, 83).

Unfortunately the Victorian business records of the National Press Agency have not survived, and details concerning the authors recruited and newspapers supplied must be largely conjectural. There is little in the way of documentary evidence, apart from the case of another late work by Anthony Trollope, the serial rights of whose full-length novel *Ayala's Angel* were sold to the Agency in November 1880 for the sum of £200 (Sadleir, *Trollope*, 182–3). However, the novel has only been located in a single journal, the (Plymouth) *Western Weekly News* from 5 February 1881 to 15 April 1882.[6] The Plymouth weekly's featured fiction shifted suddenly in mid-1877 from short serials by local writers to those of triple-decker length by metropolitan authors, presumably indicating a new source of supply. Elizabeth Owens Blackburne's *The Love that Loves Always* (1877) and *Shadows in the Sunlight* (1879), plus Emily Spender's *Secret Chains* (1878), were among the first of the new longer serials, and these have been located in a similar sequence in local papers as widespread as the *Moray Weekly News* (1877–80), and *Wakefield Herald* (1872–1913). Since the works in question appear not to have been provided by known competing agencies, it is possible that they might have been supplied by the National Press Agency.

It is significant that all four major agencies syndicating fiction in the 1870s were Liberal in leaning. However, under Petter and Galpin, Cassell's was noticeably less radical following the death of the founder John Cassell in 1865, and at some point their General Press seems to have started to offer news sheets with different ideological perspectives to cater to the varying needs of Tory, Whig and Radical journals (Nowell-Smith, *House*, 78). Moreover, from the beginning a minority of Tillotsons's regular client newspaper proprietors were known Tories. Nevertheless, it was not until the 1880s that fiction syndicators with explicit Conservative affiliations began to emerge. One was run by W.C. Leng and Co. in Sheffield, to whom we shall return. The other was the Central Press, which had changed its character since it was set up by William Saunders in 1863 (see Chapter 2). Saunders was one of the prime movers in the formation of the Press Association in 1868, when the nationalization of the telegraph allowed major provincial proprietors to combine to control their own supplies of urgent national and international news. But, as the owner of an existing private news agency, Saunders was placed in an anomalous position, and decided to sell off part of his business. It was bought by an organization wishing to set up a news agency serving the Conservative interest. After a law suit, it emerged that Saunders had lost control of the name 'Central Press' as well, and thereafter ran his own reduced agency under the name of 'Central News' (Hunt, ch. 10; Brown, 116–19). Under its new management, as under Saunders, the Central Press at first limited itself to the syndication of news material, but from 1885 at least began to offer 'Original Tales, by well-known authors, in manuscript, at moderate prices' (*NPD*, 1885, 245).[7] Though this service continued at least until the early 1890s, again almost nothing is known of its client newspapers or authors, and thus of whether or how the Conservative interest was reflected in the fiction it offered.[8]

Religious as well as political affiliation was also possible. Around the same time, the Catholic Press Company of Great Britain and Ireland, for example, was offering 'fiction in proof or stereo' suitable for publication in Catholic journals (*NPD*, 1890, 148). Then there were more minor and short-lived direct competitors about which even less is known, including their ideological leanings. Judging from the advertisements in the *Newspaper Press Directory*, it seems possible that the Central Press dealt only in short stories. This is probably also true of the Reporter Press Agency, discussed as a new provincial supplier of partly printed sheets in *The Paper and Printing Trades Journal* (June 1881, 24), which states that the agency was managed by R.N. Christie, editor of the *Luton Reporter*, and offered sheets 'well edited and filled with a careful selection of general news and other interesting matter, some of them containing short tales, which are inserted by arrangement'; and also of NOPS' Illustrated Press, which listed stories among its illustrated material offered to country newspapers in advertisements in *The Journalist* in 1891 (18 April, 10). On the other hand, the Literary and Newspaper Press Bureau of Ramsgate, which also advertised regularly in *The Journalist* in 1889, offered serials prominently, as well as 'Leaders, Leaderettes, Gossip Notes, Tales, etc' (22 February 1889, 1). The Scottish writer James Simson seems to have been one of the main suppliers of fiction material to the Bureau at that time.

By the late 1880s the major new American fiction syndicates were also opening offices in London, offering not only fiction by American writers to British newspapers but also serialization in the States to British authors (Johanningsmeier, 81–2).[9] A few months after Tillotsons cancelled their mutual arrangements with S.S. McClure in summer 1888, Sam McClure's younger brother was placed in charge of the London office of the 'Associated Literary Press', as it was by then known. Robert McClure remained in this position until after the turn of the century, though in 1899 Joseph Conrad was to describe him as a 'perfectly harmless man who knows nothing of literature' (to Edward Garnett, n.d., Conrad *Letters*, 2:121). Yet

Sam McClure himself made frequent trips to London, and secured novels from up-and-coming stars like Stevenson, Doyle, and Kipling, as well as *One of Our Conquerors* from the ageing Meredith (Lyon, 94–100). McClure's biggest rival, Irving Bacheller, also organized representation in London on his first visit there in 1887 (Johanningsmeier, 81). Arthur Waugh was his London agent, obtaining stories from James Payn and George Gissing among others, and the office remained in business until the syndicate folded in 1898. By then, as we shall see, Victor Lawson of the *Chicago Daily News* was becoming a major syndicator and operating a mutual agreement with W.C Leng and Co.

The last major British fiction syndication agency to open for business in the Victorian period was the Northern Newspaper Syndicate based in Kendal, Lancashire, which started up in 1891. The principal owner was one John Watson of Kendal, though he seems to have had little involvement in the day-to-day running of the business. Watson's partner and the first manager of the Syndicate was the young Ernest E. Taylor, a devout Yorkshire Quaker who went on to write a number of pamphlets for, and lives of distinguished members of, the Society of Friends (Whiting, especially ch. 2). At first the Syndicate offered only news articles and was barely profitable, but things looked up when stories were added to the lists. The first advertisement in the *Newspaper Press Directory* offered 'high-class articles on the foremost subjects of the day' and claimed a specialization in agricultural matters, but also mentioned that '[f]iction is represented by popular novelists' (*NPD* 1893, 51). In the equivalent notice in 1900, Grant Allen, Justin McCarthy, Mrs (Mary Louisa) Molesworth, Dean Farrar and Helen Mathers were mentioned as recent client authors (57), while that for 1905 (60) listed 'J.M. Barrie, H.G. Wells, Andrew Lang, Count Tolstoi, Hall Caine, Miss Braddon', and claimed to serve 'the London, Provincial, Colonial and Foreign Press'. A number of these authors had earlier been clients of Tillotsons and then used A.P. Watt as their literary agent. There is also evidence among the A.P. Watt papers held at the University of North Carolina that Watt used the Kendal Syndicate for the periodical placement of his client's work from the mid-1890s.[10] According to his biographer, Ernest Taylor was increasingly uncomfortable with the sensational material the Northern Newspaper Syndicate came to rely on. He resigned his partnership in 1905, returned to Yorkshire and began to work for newspapers linked to Arthur Rowntree, though he was later to renew his connection with newspaper syndication as a director of the National Press Agency (Whiting ch. 2). James E. Lyons, C.W. Shepherd, and William Wilkinson acted in turn as the Syndicate's manager until it folded around 1929 (annual advertisements in *NPD*).

But whatever his distaste for the material he was handling, by the time that Taylor left, the Northern Newspaper Syndicate was a major force in fiction syndication. In 1903 Joseph Conrad was even considering submitting *Nostromo* (then still thought of as a novella) to the Syndicate (to J.B. Pinker, 19 January, Conrad, *Letters*, 3:10–11). By the beginning of the new century, the Kendal firm may already have been challenging Tillotsons as the leading fiction agency serving the British provincial press. Given the fact that Leaders sold up in 1896, and Cassells continued to concentrate on lesser writers and smaller local newspapers, at the turn of the century, the strongest direct competition the Fiction Bureau faced probably came from the Syndicate in Kendal and the National Press Agency in London.[11] But by then the market for serial novels had shifted once again, and provincial newspaper syndication could no longer lay claim to be the dominant mode of serial publication. This was in part as a result of the intervention of agents like Watt for whom syndication was only a temporary or auxiliary means.

4.2   A.P. Watt and the literary agency

In his brief, pioneering study of the rise of the literary agent, James Hepburn notes as forerunners of dedicated professionals such as Watt, not only author's solicitors or personal acquaintances (John Forster for Dickens, or G.H. Lewes for George Eliot, most notably) but also a variety of newspaper agencies (chs 3–4). The correspondence between John Maxwell and W.F. Tillotson discussed in the previous chapter indeed suggests that both men were involved on Braddon's behalf in performing the role that would, after their deaths, be sustained by A.P. Watt. More generally the surviving letters addressed personally to W.F. Tillotson by other author–clients of the Fiction Bureau (ZBEN, 4/6) suggest that the Bolton man's role was by no means always limited narrowly to that of syndicator, but sometimes entailed the disposing of other copyrights, and the offering of literary advice and encouragement. Johanningsmeier similarly notes that the early syndicators 'often thought of themselves as agents and were described as such by others' (66). To illustrate this he notes two interesting cases where the terms syndicator and agent

were conflated: by the British author Ouida in an angry letter to
The Times (22 May 1891, 3, headed 'New Literary Factors'), in which
she saw the activities of these upstart middlemen as 'new methods
of treating for and dealing with books . . . fraught with considerable menace to the small modicum of artistic excellence which
remains still extant in English fiction'; and by the American syndicator
S.S. McClure a year earlier in a letter to Robert Louis Stevenson,
where he boasted that there would be 'no more A.P. Watt nor
Tillotson & Son. There is just room for one person in this business
of mine.' (cited in Johanningsmeier, 66).

What neither Hepburn nor Johanningsmeier picks up on, however, is the reciprocity of the relationship – that is, around the
1880s not only did syndicators behave like literary agents, but literary agents also behaved like syndicators. This is true both of Watt
and, to a lesser extent, of W.M. Colles, the agent affiliated to the
Society of Authors from the end of the decade. Johanningsmeier
argues that this conflation of terms was finally a matter of subjec-
tive perception only, and that there was an objective, economic
distinction between the two roles, in that syndicators risked their
own capital to purchase serial rights whereas agents merely received
payment for arranging the sale of the property of others. However,
given that both syndicators and agents acted as middlemen between novelists and periodical publishers, that fiction syndication
was normally carried on as an enterprise ancillary to the production of newspapers, and that organizations like Tillotsons and Leaders
generally collected subscriptions from their client-newspapers before making payments to their client-authors, the distinction does
not seem to have been of fundamental importance in the early
1880s. Certainly there is ample evidence that Watt was prepared to
compete head to head with the provincial syndicators, by writing
round to large numbers of newspaper proprietors in order to set up
simultaneous serialization of his authors' latest novels.

There is unfortunately still no authoritative, detailed account of
Watt's early years as an agent, and it is necessary to supplement
the brief sketches by Hepburn and others with information gleaned
from scattered business correspondence, mostly unpublished.[12] A.P.
Watt (1834–1914) was born in Glasgow, brought up in Edinburgh,
and began to work in London at some point during the later 1860s
for his brother-in-law, the evangelical literary publisher Alexander
Strahan who had himself moved down from Edinburgh in 1862.
Strahan's most distinguished regular author was the Revd George

MacDonald, but the house was perhaps better known for its periodicals, most notably *Good Words*, the *Sunday Magazine* (1864–1910), and the *Contemporary Review* (1866–). Watt became a partner in 1876, but by then the firm was in major decline with its periodicals being taken over by the firm of Isbister, and he seems to have struck out on his own not long afterwards (Srebrnik, chs 6–8). At first he sold advertising space in periodicals and gradually shifted into the negotiation of fiction serial rights.[13]

MacDonald was already a friend, and Watt seems to have acted first on his behalf, taking over the arrangements for the serialization of his novels, probably from around 1878.[14] Surviving correspondence in the Berg Collection suggests that other early clients-authors also generally had Scottish connections – William Black, Robert Buchanan, his sister-in-law Harriet Jay, Edward Jenkins (with a Colonial background, but radical MP for Dundee from 1874), and Bret Harte (then American consul in Glasgow) – all of these novelists were on Watt's books by at least the end of 1880. Still at this stage Watt's role was largely limited to arranging periodical publication, in provincial and overseas journals as well as in the London magazines. For example, around 1880, in addition to selling stories by Black to *Cassell's Family Magazine* and Strahan's *Day of Rest* (1872–82), Watt established a link with the Boston publisher Lothrop for MacDonald, arranged serialization of Jenkins's *Lisa Lena* in the *Glasgow Weekly Mail*, offered stories by Buchanan and Jay to John Leng and Co. in Dundee, tried to organize the simultaneous serialization of a Harte novel in two or three English provincial papers, and eventually sold both MacDonald's *Mary Marston* (after its rejection by *The Family Herald* and *The Graphic*) and Buchanan's *Martyrdom of Madeleine* (not required by John Leng and Co.) to Tillotsons (Letterbooks, 2–3, BERG).

But the earliest Berg correspondence also suggests that many of Watt's first paying clients were publishers who wished to dispose of or acquire serial rights. In particular, Andrew Chatto seems to have used Watt's services extensively to sell the serial rights to triple-decker novels for which he held absolute copyright. For example, towards the end of August 1880, Watt offered Tillotsons serial rights to a wide selection of already-published Chatto novels, notably works by either John Saunders or his daughter Katherine Saunders.[15] Among the clients' letters of recommendation which Watt later reprinted for advertising purposes, were those from Bentley, Longmans, and Murray, as well as Chatto and Windus (*Collection*), the dates suggesting that this practice continued well into the 1880s.[16] However, towards the end of 1881 at least Watt had also started sending round prospectuses to leading authors in England. By 1885 David Christie Murray, Walter Besant, James Payn, James Grant, Margaret Oliphant, Eliza Lynn Linton, Joseph Hatton and H. Rider Haggard, among others, had all accepted Watt's services. However, Wilkie Collins was perhaps the first to respond in early December 1881 (Peters, 393–4) and this engagement led Watt to attempt his first full-scale exercise in fiction syndication.

Collins wrote to ask whether Watt would take on the task of arranging the simultaneous serialization in a number of country newspapers of the novel on which he was then working, *Heart and Science*. His two previous novels had already been syndicated in the provincial weeklies, respectively by Tillotsons and Leaders, and, although Collins did not wish either of these agencies to act for him on this occasion, he wanted Watt to operate in very much the same way that they had done. He set out the conditions in great detail in a two-page memorandum entitled 'Notes for Consideration' (Enclosure, 5 December 1881, PEMBROKE). But *Heart and Science* was a work on which Collins placed great hopes for the revival of his fast-fading literary reputation (Peters, 399–404), and the appearances in the provincial weeklies were to be in addition to publication in monthly parts in *Belgravia*, now the Chatto and Windus house magazine. It thus seems likely that Collins consulted Andrew Chatto before responding to Watt's approach. Around this period, in addition to selling on serial rights to novels already published in volume to country journals, Chatto and Windus seem to have allowed or even encouraged their authors to serialize their new works simultaneously in *Belgravia* and with the syndicates. As already noted, from January 1882 Besant's *All Sorts and Conditions of Men* was placed by James Rice in a series of provincial weeklies as well as in Chatto's monthly, and there is evidence of earlier arrangements of a similar nature (see Table 4.1).[17] The reason for Chatto's policy must have been largely financial. By 1880, the print-run of *Belgravia* was below 10 000 and falling rapidly (*VFRG*, 14: 2), thus severely limiting the remuneration that could be offered to authors for serial rights. Granting freedom to syndicate simultaneously in newspapers must have enhanced considerably the attractiveness of Chatto's offers to distinguished writers.

Watt obviously jumped at the chance to act for such a well-known author as Collins. He thus pulled out all the stops by writing batches of letters to over 40 different journals throughout the United Kingdom between December 1881 and June 1882. The initial approaches all took virtually the same form, among other things assuring editors (rather dishonestly, given the work's preoccupation with the issue of vivisection) that the new novel would not concern 'anomalies in the marriage laws' or other 'painful social subjects' (for example, ALS to the *Liverpool Daily Post*, 2 March 1882, Letterbook, 2:420, BERG). Some editors did not even take the trouble to reply, while there were many objections and rejections – because the date of commencement was too near and other arrangements had been made, because the asking price was too high, because of the simultaneous publication in *Belgravia*, because the same offer had been made to rival newspapers, or simply because the journals in questions did not take fiction. But as soon as an objection or rejection came in, Watt was willing to renegotiate or to fire off a proposal to another journal in the same catchment area, and by the spring had firm acceptances from ten weeklies. As Tables 4.1 and A.5 show, in addition to journals all over Scotland, Ireland, Wales, and the English North, West and Midlands, Watt arranged serial appearances in *Frank Leslie's Illustrated Newspaper* in New York, as well as in the new London journal *England: the Only National and Conservative Weekly Paper for All Classes*, through its owner, populist Tory MP Ellis Bartlett. The *Liverpool Weekly Post* agreed to set up the novel in type first and provide proofs for the other journals, probably in return for a reduction in price (ALS to Watt, 13 May 1882, Collins Acc., BERG). In addition to £100 received from the New York journal and around £300 from *Belgravia*, payments by British newspapers totalled £565, as compared to the £500 Collins had received from Tillotsons for *Jezebel's Daughter*.[18]

Both Watt and Collins were presumably satisfied with the outcome, as the experiment was repeated for the author's next novel '*I Say No*', ready at the end of 1883. Watt prepared another circular letter, including a puff from the highly favourable review of *Heart and Science* in *The World*, and began to send it out at the end of May of that year. Of the journals taking *Heart and Science*, only the *Cardiff Times* was interested, in part because the earlier serialization had only concluded in January or February, but also in some cases because of annoyance that they had not been informed of the simultaneous serialization in the two London journals, which circulated well beyond the metropolitan area. Nevertheless, as Tables 4.1 and A.5 again show, Watt managed to place the novel in six provincial weeklies for a total of £400, in *Harper's Weekly* in the States for £200, and for an unknown sum in the new metropolitan Conservative Sunday paper *The People*, the first of many instalment novels it was to carry.[19] The likely slight drop in receipts for weekly serialization was more than compensated for by the fact that Watt also managed to sell the novel as a monthly serial for as much as £900 to Kelly's, the directory publishers, who issued the novel in *London Society*.[20]

The correspondence surviving at the Berg also shows that, while Watt never again put as much effort into the arrangements as he did with Collins's two novels, he had constructed a significant number of provincial syndicates for novels by other writers by the mid-1880s. These generally seem to have comprised three or four journals and usually included a major Glasgow or Manchester paper. Early examples of novels dealt with in this way included George MacDonald's *Donal Grant* (1883) and *What's Mine's Mine* (1885), or Robert Buchanan's *Foxglove Manor* and Sarah Tytler's *St. Mungo's City* (both 1884). Perhaps more characteristically, however, he continued to set up a number of 'belt-and-braces' syndicates, that is, ones combining both London journals and provincial papers, as in the case of Collins's novels. If, as suggested in Chapter 1, the rise of the provincial syndicates is itself best understood as a transitional phase between two distinct stages in the periodical publication of new fiction, in both of which the market is dominated by metropolitan publishers, the belt-and-braces approach can then be seen as reflecting fine adjustments in the balance of power between the provincial and metropolitan press within that phase of transition. As Table 4.1 suggests, nearly all the examples of belt-and-braces serialization noted before 1885 involve monthly metropolitan appearances of limited circulation paired with wide-ranging provincial syndicates, where the aim of the London publishers can properly be described as defensive. Most of the examples of belt-and-braces arrangements traced after 1885 feature weekly metropolitan serialization in newspapers with large and growing national circulations, like *The Illustrated London News*, *The People*, and *The Graphic*, coupled with limited provincial appearances, where the role of the London proprietors is more aggressive. Novels thus serialized included those by Robert Buchanan, James Payn, Walter Besant, and William Black, though the serialization of Hardy's *Tess* exhibits the same pattern and seems to have been arranged at least in part by Watt.[21]

By this stage Watt's reach obviously extended also to the Colonial

Table 4.1 Some 'belt-and-braces' syndicates

Work in volume	Metropolitan serialization(s)	Provincial serialization(s) traced	Agent(s)
James Payn, *A Confidential Agent* (Chatto & Windus, 1880)	*Belgravia* (Jan.–Dec. 1880)	*Sheffield Weekly Independent* (from Jan. 1880)	?
William Black, *Sunrise* (Sampson Low, 1881)	Monthly parts, Sampson Low (Apr. 1880–June 1881)	*Sheffield Weekly Independent* (from Mar. 1880)	A.P. Watt (?)
Walter Besant, *All Sorts and Conditions of Men* (Chatto & Windus, 1882)	*Belgravia* (Jan.–Dec. 1882)	*Birmingham Weekly Post, Leicester Chronicle, Sheffield Weekly Telegraph, Liverpool Weekly Post,* & (as 'All Sorts of Men') *Glasgow Weekly Mail* (Jan.–Aug. 1882)	James Rice
Wilkie Collins, *Heart and Science* (Chatto & Windus, 1883)	*Belgravia* (Aug. 1882–June 1883) *England* (July 1882–Feb. 1883)	*Aberdeen Weekly Journal, Bristol Observer, Cardiff Weekly Times, Liverpool Weekly Post, Manchester Weekly Times, Nottinghamshire Guardian, Scottish Reformer,* & *Weekly Irish Times* (July 1882–Feb. 1883)	A.P. Watt
Wilkie Collins, *'I Say No'* (Chatto & Windus, 1884)	*London Society* (Jan.–Dec. 1884) *The People* (Dec. 1883–July 1884)	*Cardiff Weekly Times, Glasgow Weekly Herald, Leicester Chronicle, Newcastle Weekly Chronicle,* & *Belfast Weekly News* (Dec. 1883–July 1884)	A.P. Watt
Robert Buchanan, *Master of the Mine* (Bentley, 1885)	*The Illustrated London News* (July–Dec. 1885)	(Aberdeen) *Weekly Free Press, Leeds Express,* & *Scottish Reformer* (late 1885)	A.P. Watt
James Payn, *The Heir of the Ages* (Smith, Elder, 1886)	*The Illustrated London News* (Jan.–June 1886)	*Birmingham Weekly Post,* & *Glasgow Weekly Herald* (early 1886) [*Sheffield Weekly Independent, Leeds Mercury, Liverpool Weekly Post, Newcastle Weekly Chronicle, Bristol Observer,* U]	A.P. Watt
Walter Besant, *The World Went Very Well Then* (Chatto & Windus, 1887)	*The Illustrated London News* (July–Dec. 1886)	*Sheffield Weekly Telegraph,* & *Glasgow Weekly Herald,* (July–Dec. 1886)	A.P. Watt
Emile Zola, *Germinal* (tr. Vandam) (Vizetelly, 1885)	*The People* (Nov. 1884–Apr. 1885)	*Sheffield Weekly Telegraph* (Nov. 1884–May 1885)	A.P. Watt (?)

R.E. Francillon, *King or Knave?* (Chatto & Windus, 1888)	*The People* (Mar.–Sept. 1886)	*Sheffield Weekly Telegraph* (mid-1886)	A.P. Watt
Robert Buchanan, *The Moment After* (Heinemann, 1890)	*The People* (early 1887)	*Sheffield Weekly Telegraph* (early 1887)	A.P. Watt
Margaret Oliphant, *The Heir Presumptive and the Heir Apparent* (Macmillan, 1892)	*London Society* (Jan.–Dec. 1891)*	*Birmingham Weekly Post, Hereford Times, Newcastle Weekly Chronicle, Newport Advertiser, & Yorkshire Weekly Post* (Oct. 1890–Apr. 1891)*	A.P. Watt/ Tillotsons
Thomas Hardy, *Tess of the D'Urbervilles* (Osgood, McIlvaine, 1891)	*The Graphic* (July–Dec. 1891)	As 'A Daughter of the D'Urbervilles' *Nottinghamshire Guardian, & Birmingham Weekly Post* (July–Dec. 1891)	A.P. Watt
William Black, *Wolfenburg* (Sampson Low, 1892)	*The Graphic* (July–Dec. 1892)	*Nottinghamshire Guardian* (late 1892)	A.P. Watt/ Tillotsons
S.R. Crockett, *The Grey Man* (T. Fisher Unwin, 1896)	*The Graphic* (Jan.–June 1896)	*Newcastle Weekly Chronicle, & Glasgow Weekly Mail* (early 1896)	A.P. Watt
Walter Besant, *No Other Way* (Chatto & Windus, 1902)	*The Lady's Realm* (Nov. 1901–Oct. 1902)	*Sheffield Weekly Telegraph* (Dec. 1901–May 1902)	A.P. Watt

* Based on *VFRG*, 11.   U = Unconfirmed.

Source: Farmer and Law; or as noted.

market. In 1888 Thomas S. Townend, London manager of the Melbourne *Argus* group of papers, wrote a letter of recommendation for Watt in which he declared that 'For some years I have made purchases through your agency of the serial stories of many English authors, for publication in the *Australasian*' (25 May, *Collection*, 58). Judging by the indexes compiled by Toni Johnson-Woods, however, the *Sydney Mail* seems to have relied even more heavily on Watt's services, and the majority of the English serials it ran during the 1880s and 1890s came from Watt's client-authors, having initially appeared in London in either *The Graphic* or *The Illustrated London News*. To begin with Watt seems often to have contacted the Colonial journals directly. In early 1884, for example, after arranging for James Payn's *Luck of the Darrells* to appear in *Good Words*, Watt sent a circular letter to seven major city journals in Australia and New Zealand offering serial rights, either for £75 in a single colony, or for £100 in the case of syndication in the whole of Australasia (ALSs, 28 March 1884, Letterbook, 7:688–701, BERG), and the novel appeared in the *Sydney Mail* from January 1885. He also wrote later to offer the same novel to the *Calcutta Englishman*, though the result is uncertain (ALS, 4 July 1884, Letterbook, 8:16–17, BERG). Soon, however, he began to work through other agents to sell serial rights in Australasia, India, and the Cape – there is evidence, for example, in the Watt papers at the Wilson Library of his frequent use from the later 1880s of the London agency Gordon and Gotch, of St Bride Street, Ludgate Circus.

In a similar way, from the middle of the decade Watt increasingly began to leave the work of placing serials in provincial newspapers to other agencies, and initially to Tillotsons's Fiction Bureau itself. Watt's experiences in syndicating Collins's two novels, in particular, must have revealed to him that negotiating with more than a dozen provincial proprietors was time-consuming and that he lacked the intimate knowledge of country newspapers that he could claim of London periodicals.[22] By the middle of the decade he had obviously concluded that there was no longer any necessity to fight the Fiction Bureau head on. On one of W.F. Tillotson's regular trips to the capital, Collins was unable to receive him due to illness (ALS to Watt, PEMBROKE, 30 October 1884), so on the morning of the 6 November 1884 an appointment was made for the Bolton man to call at Watt's office in Paternoster Square. The consequence was that Collins's next two novels were again syndicated by the Bolton firm, not only in the British provinces but also in America and Australia, with Watt simply taking a commission on the terms arranged. Similar negotiations were soon under way for the works of Bret Harte and Rider Haggard, and these were to be merely the first of many deals struck between the two middlemen in the mid- to late 1880s. There were two immediate and unwelcome results for the Fiction Bureau which have already been mentioned in the previous chapter – marked increases in both the prices paid to authors and in the length and complexity of the agreements drawn up – which proved to be the first signs of the decline of their position in the serial market. The ease and rapidity with which Watt was thus able to challenge the market leader, and in the slightly longer term to reduce Tillotsons to a sub-agency for serials by major writers, suggests that he was being given momentum by a wider historical shift in publishing practice then just beginning.

It seems clear then that Watt acted as a direct competitor to Tillotsons and the other provincial syndicators for only a relatively short period before his name became widely known. As suggested by Table A.6 listing the serializations of Walter Besant's fiction (arranged entirely by Watt's Agency from 1883 onwards, although three of the later novels were sold to the Fiction Bureau), by the end of the 1880s at least Watt was tending to overlook the provincial press and sell British serial rights to a single major metropolitan journal. He had understood that, as the London weeklies began to reach a mass nationwide audience, the 'belt-and-braces' approach was not feasible in the long term, and that a timely placement in a single aggressive metropolitan journal could match the remuneration from all but the most meticulously-constructed provincial syndicate. However, there is little doubt that the selling of serial rights remained at the centre of his business for at least another decade. This is in part because there was little flexibility in the British book-publishing market until the collapse of the triple-decker novel in the mid-1890s, and in part because his clientele was concentrated heavily on well-established authors for whom striking a deal with London houses was unproblematic.

Watt's first collection of recommendatory letters, published in 1893, began by emphasizing the wide range of professional services offered by the firm of A.P. Watt and Son, known modestly at that time when there was little competition as 'The Literary Agency'. The Agency's business was:

to place Mss. to the best advantage; to watch for openings; to sell COPYRIGHTS, either absolutely or for a limited period; to collect ROYALTIES, and to receive other moneys due; to conduct Arbitrations; to transfer Literary Property; to value Literary Property; to obtain opinions on Mss., etc etc.

(Collection, ix)

But in the letters of recommendation themselves the focus is still predominantly on Watt's role in placing short stories and novels in periodicals at home and abroad. The interview with Watt recorded in the *Bookman* of October 1892 begins by describing the agent's office in Paternoster Square as the place where 'some of the most important periodicals in this country, America, Australia, and elsewhere are supplied with the greater part of the novels and stories so necessary to their existence' (reprinted in *Collection,* 65). And in the course of the interview, Watt proudly checks off an impressive list of periodicals currently handling serials from his clients:

The *Illustrated London News,* the *Graphic,* the *Lady's Pictorial, Longman's Magazine, Macmillan's Magazine,* the *English Illustrated Magazine, Tit-Bits,* the [*Christian*] *Million,* the *Leisure Hour,* the *People,* the *Atlantic Monthly, Harper's,* the *Cosmopolitan, Chambers's Journal, Pearson's Weekly, Temple Bar,* and a number of other periodicals (all sorts and conditions, as you can see), not to mention the Provincial Press, are all either running, or have just concluded, or are about to run stories which I have sold them.

(Collection, 73–4)

It is symptomatic that the provincial papers now appear as little more than an afterthought, following the list of representatives of all major kinds of metropolitan periodical – in London, the illustrated weekly, the literary monthly, the weekly miscellany, the religious paper, and the new mass-market entertainment magazine, or in America, both the traditional heavyweight literary monthly and the fashionable lightweight literary weekly. The long-term success of Watt's intervention in the market for serial fiction must be seen as in part cause and in part consequence of a shifting back of the balance of power in periodical publishing from the provincial to the metropolitan press. We will return to this development shortly.

The only other dedicated literary agent of any note to emerge before the circulating libraries decided to bring the curtain down on the three-volume novel was W.M. Colles. (J.B. Pinker and Curtis Brown, who were to emerge in the new century as the keenest rivals to A.P. Watt and Son, did not set up shop as literary agents until 1896 and 1899 respectively, and thus need not concern us greatly here.) The son of a clergyman, William Morris Colles (1855–1926) graduated from Cambridge in 1877, was called to the Bar in 1880, and started a career as a journalist in London. The biographer of publisher William Heinemann, a personal friend, described him as 'a big, burly, bearded lawyer, with a wheezy infectious laugh – a sort of well-spoken, decent-minded, entirely reputable, nineteenth-century Falstaff' (Whyte, 123), though Colles was destined to cut something of a smaller figure as a literary agent. Sometime in the mid-1880s Colles had joined the recently founded Incorporated Society of Authors, serving early on the Executive Council and Committee of Management, offering legal advice, and even acting as stand-in Secretary at one point (Bonham-Carter, 167–8). In June 1887 the Society moved into new premises at 4 Portugal Street, Lincoln's Inn Fields, where Colles already had his office on the same floor, and where he was soon drawn even more closely into the activities of the Society. He became the author of one of the first three publications issued by the Society in 1889, *Literature and the Pension List*, a painstakingly detailed investigation into the functioning of the Civil List over the past half century, and the arbitrariness of its treatment of authors. When, in the same year, the Society announced the formation of a non-profit-making agency to sell to periodicals the serial rights of work produced by its members, it was Colles who was appointed as Honorary Secretary.

Although the Incorporated Society of Authors was by no means the first attempt by authors to act collectively to protect their own interests, it was the first to achieve any degree of success and survive for more than a brief period.[23] It was conceived at a meeting of 12 author–members of the Savile Club in autumn 1883, one of whom was the novelist Walter Besant. Besant was to be the driving force behind the organization in its first two decades and personally 'conducted' its periodical *The Author* from its commencement in 1890 to his death in 1901. The Society in many ways took as its model the French equivalent, which reached its fiftieth anniversary in 1887 and which was celebrated in another of the Society's 1889 publications, *The History of the Société des Gens de Lettres*, by S. Squire

Sprigge who was later to become the Secretary. But the French society had arisen out of a specific grievance against the unauthorized reprinting of novels as *feuilletons* in newspapers, and had quickly formed its own literary agency to handle such rights, whereas the British organization had spent its early years and energies in attempting to define and defend the underlying concept of literary property, and its initial campaigns had concerned international copyright or abuses by book publishers.

When the Society finally got around to setting up its own agency at the beginning of the 1890s, it was a case of too little and too late. There is no doubt that Colles lacked the personal drive as well as the necessary contacts and experience in the publishing world to make a success of the venture. He had in any case been placed in an invidious position by his mentor Besant: the status of the Authors' Syndicate, as it was known, was radically ambiguous. It was not formally an organ of the Society, but merely an affiliated association which happened to share the same postal address.[24] Its services were not at first available to those who had not paid dues to the Society, but neither were they open to members who had not 'already attained a certain amount of popularity' as writers (advertisement, *Author*, 1 February 1892, 292, seriatim). It claimed to cut out the middlemen between authors and periodical publishers, but was forced to farm out much of its day-to-day work to other agencies and had to charge similar rates of commission.[25] In theory the Society was against the private syndicators and agents, and in favour of authors acting collectively to market their own property, but in practice Besant, and with him many of the established authors joining the Society, like Wilkie Collins and H. Rider Haggard, had been among the first to sell their wares to Tillotsons and to sign up with A.P. Watt.[26] Watt himself had close links with the Society and seems to have been recommended to its members as a reliable agent during the 1880s (Bonham-Carter, 133). Later he acted as advertising agent and publisher of *The Author* during the first year of its publication, so that prominent advertisements for The Literary Agency often appeared in its pages (for example, 16 March 1891, 307). Early on Besant warned Colles not to 'worry too much about the small fry whom you really cannot help' (cited in Colby, 'Tale', 7), but most of the big fish seemed already to be in Watt's net.

What is most interesting for our purposes, however, is how quickly the Society moved to extend Colles's role from fiction syndicator to literary agent. The first conception of the Executive Committee, in its annual Report issued in January 1890, was of 'a Syndicate for supplying the papers with works of fiction' (13). By the time the first advertisement appeared in *The Author* in February 1892, the purpose had broadened to 'syndicating or selling the serial rights of authors in magazines, journals, and newspapers' (292). Finally, in a signed article in *The Author* of April 1892, Colles announced that 'the work is being put on an extended basis, so that it may now undertake the management of all forms of literary property' (349). Thus Besant could announce to the authors assembled at the Society's AGM that year that the Authors' Syndicate now undertook 'to take all the trouble of your business affairs off your hands' (Besant, *Society*, 32). The speed of this transition is indicative not only of the confused nature of Besant's thinking when he asked Colles to act for the Society (Colby, 'Tale', 9; Colby, 'What', 77–80), but also of change and uncertainty in the fiction market itself in the early 1890s. The fact that it did not seem necessary to change the name from the Author's Syndicate when Colles began to take on the wider role of literary agent is yet another example of the original intimacy of the connection between the two functions.

The first piece of business transacted by the Authors' Syndicate was to assemble two quarterly batches of short tales by established authors in order to sell them to the provincial newspapers. However, those newspapers turned out to be booked up with fiction material from agencies like Tillotsons for at least a year ahead, and Colles ended up asking Watt to negotiate sale of the package to individual periodical publishers in Britain, America, Australasia and India, and seems to have made little more than £3 out of the arrangement ('On Syndicating', *The Author*, 15 May 1890, 10–11; Colby 'Tale', 10; WILSON, 5.17). In fact it seems likely that, despite its initial aims, the Authors' Syndicate rarely managed to sell anything directly to the newspaper proprietors. Although *The Author* put a brave face on things, a sense of failure continued to dog Colles's efforts when he took up the wider role of literary agent. George Gissing, H.G. Wells, and Arnold Bennett all used his services briefly during the 1890s but had defected to J.B. Pinker by the turn of the century.[27] George Meredith, who became the President of the Society of Authors in 1892 on the death of Tennyson, its inaugural head, signed up with Colles in 1893. He used him both to negotiate with Chapman and Hall to recover the copyrights of his earlier works, and to place the serial versions of his latest novels in magazines in

London and New York. However, when he changed publishers in 1895 to the firm of Constable, now revived in Edinburgh, and began to arrange a collected edition, he also dropped Colles and allowed his son to take over all his literary negotiations (Collie, 67–70, 248–9, 256–8). Thomas Hardy, who took over the Presidency of the Society on Meredith's death in 1909, had been wooed assiduously by Colles from 1891 until then, but only seems to have placed a single short story through the Author's Syndicate, though he seems to have used A.P. Watt's services regularly enough (to W.M. Colles 1891 to 1908, Hardy, *Letters*, vols I–III). Eden Phillpotts and Flora Annie Steel were probably Colles's most faithful clients of any note, but even the small fry were not always appreciative of Colles's efforts (Colby 'What'). Colles's agency somehow soldiered on virtually until his death in 1926, still under the name the Author's Syndicate, but the link with the Society of Authors was broken, amicably but decisively, as early as 1898 (Colby, 'Tale', 11).

In themselves, then, the activities of W.M. Colles and his Authors' Syndicate represented little serious competition, direct or indirect, to the established newspaper syndicators. Nevertheless, they do serve to point out by contrast the power of the threat posed by Watt. In the process, they provide further illustration of the long-term shift taking place in the fiction market away from the provincial newspapers and towards the metropolitan journals, and thus from the dominance in the serial market of the role of the syndicator to that of the literary agent.

4.3   W.C. Leng and Co. and the metropolitan weekly

As was suggested in Chapter 1, by the early 1870s the boom in the shilling literary monthlies was over, although many of the magazines continued publication with declining circulations until after the demise of the triple-decker in the mid-1890s. Already by the later 1870s there were signs of another major shift in the London periodical market as a new generation of 'class' weekly journals began to emerge, many of which, sooner or later, introduced serial fiction into their pages (Fox Bourne, ch. 23). One group was the sixpenny Society weeklies, where the news material was principally gossip and rumour about those in high places, led by Edmund Yates's highly successful *World*. Yates's paper notably carried Collins's *Fallen Leaves* from the beginning of 1879, though the first serial was the editor's own 'A Decree Nisi' (*Two, by Tricks* in volume) which began in the opening issue of 8 July 1874. Imitators of some standing and longevity were *The Whitehall Review* and *Life*, both of which were carrying serials by around 1880 – Anthony Trollope's novella *An Eye for an Eye* appearing in the former in 1878–79, and his unfinished *The Landleaguers* in the latter in 1882–83, for example. Considerably larger in circulation and more important in their impact on the fiction market were the sixpenny illustrated newspapers. The grandfather of these was, of course, *The Illustrated London News* which had dominated the market from its beginnings in 1842. But as we saw in Chapter 1, it had ceased to feature serials in the early 1850s and did not return to them until the beginning of 1883, when William Black's *Yolande* appeared in its columns. The most immediate reason for the revival was the intense rivalry growing up with *The Graphic*, which had been started in late 1869 by William Luson Thomas, a disgruntled engraver from the *Illustrated* (Fox Bourne, 297–8). *The Graphic* began to include serial fiction at the beginning of 1873, with Margaret Oliphant's *Innocent*. Both the major illustrated weeklies ran a full programme of instalment fiction virtually throughout the 1880s and 1890s: the *Illustrated* insisted from the beginning on 26 part serials (Besant, *Autobiography*, 192), shifted smartly to 13 parts in 1894 when the triple-decker was about to crash, and opted for a programme of short stories from early 1897. *The Graphic* was more flexible as regards length, though it too shifted to shorter serials in the mid-1890s, and continued to feature serial fiction well into the new century. *The Graphic* perhaps paid higher prices for serials by popular authors (see Chapter 6), while, as Table 4.1 suggests, *The Illustrated London News* was perhaps readier to permit simultaneous provincial appearances. Wilkie Collins, Thomas Hardy, William Black, James Payn, H. Rider Haggard, W.E. Norris, Bret Harte, and Robert Buchanan were among the writers who had novels appear at least once in each paper during this period, though Walter Besant was far and away the most frequent contributor with four full-length novels in *The Graphic* and five in the *London News* (see Table A.6)

As has already been suggested, and as this list of authors confirms, A.P. Watt obviously played a major hand in supplying stories for both journals from the early 1880s. William Ingram, editor of the *London News*, wrote a letter of recommendation for Watt in 1887, in which he declared: 'I have now for some years past through your agency arranged for the publication of nearly all our Serial Novels and Special Number Stories' (20 March, *Collection*, 30), while there is ample evidence among the correspondence in the Berg

Collection and at Chapel Hill of Watt supplying *The Graphic* (see Table 4.1). The success of both *The Graphic* and *Illustrated London News* seems to have stimulated rather than swamped the market for sixpenny illustrated papers, and there were soon other competitors appearing, most notably *The Pictorial World* and *The Lady's Pictorial*. Both of these started off as cheaper threepenny papers but soon switched to the price and format of the major players, and both included serial fiction by the early 1880s. On the other hand, there were also soon much cheaper popularizing versions of the class weeklies, both Society journals and illustrated newspapers, like *Modern Society* (1882–1917) or James Henderson's *Penny Pictorial News* (1877–92), and they too sometimes included fiction.

But a more important development at the cheap end of the metropolitan newspaper market was that, from the early 1880s, a number of the mass-circulation penny weeklies began to feature serials and take on the appearance of miscellanies, as the Scottish or English provincial city journals had done decades earlier. This trend seems to have begun with the new popularizing Conservative weeklies which used fiction to attract a working-class audience. *England* and *The People* were the main examples, and we have already seen how they were successfully approached by A.P. Watt for the two Collins novels which he syndicated personally in the early 1880s; *The People*, indeed, seems to have been regularly supplied with serials by Watt throughout the 1880s (see Table 4.1). The older radical Sunday papers soon followed suit, beginning with the *The Weekly Times* and *The Weekly Dispatch*, which began with complete tales but were carrying serials by the middle of the decade. *The Weekly Times* took material regularly from Tillotsons for at least a decade, and at the end of the century carried H.G. Wells's *Love and Mrs. Lewisham*. *Reynolds's Weekly*, which, as Berridge has shown ('Content', 207–17), remained closest to its original working-class readership and old-style radical politics, began to carry a series of 'Stories for the People' in 1888, while *Lloyd's Weekly*, increasingly targeted at the lower-middle class, resisted the trend until the early 1890s. James Henderson's local weekly the *South London Press*, which, as noted in Chapter 2, carried serial fiction from its opening issue in 1865, switched from mainly local sources to material from the provincial syndicates around this time.[28] Leaders sold Collins's *Black Robe* to this journal in 1880, and it became a regular client of Tillotsons in the mid-1880s, featuring a fine range of stories by Charles Reade, Margaret Oliphant, William Black, M.E. Braddon and again Wilkie Collins.

By the early 1890s even the cheaper metropolitan daily newspapers were occasionally publishing fiction in weekly supplements: William Black's *Donald Ross of Heimra* and *The Blue Pavilions* by Arthur Quiller-Couch appeared in the Wednesday supplement of the *Daily Chronicle*, for example, both being provided by Watt (*Collection*, 73). But, before the turn of the century, no metropolitan daily seems to have dared to go as far as the large American dailies, like Victor Lawson's *Chicago Daily News*, or even some of the English provincial evening papers, like the *Staffordshire Sentinel* or Jesse Quail's *Northern Daily Telegraph* in Lancashire, and publish instalments of serial fiction every day, though both Watt and Besant enthusiastically supported the idea in the early 1890s (*Collection*, 72–3; Besant, 'Place', 18–19). However, William Le Queux's anti-German fantasy *The Invasion of 1910* (1906) was later to prove an immense success when first serialized in the columns of Alfred Harmsworth's *Daily Mail*.

However, with the exception of *Lloyd's*, none of the existing cheap London weekly papers was to reach anything like the readership of the new generation of mass-circulation penny news magazines which were inaugurated with George Newnes's *Tit-Bits* in October 1881 (Jackson, 203–5). *Tit-Bits*, as its title suggests, was manufactured almost entirely from bits and pieces extracted from other journals, and according to its founder, had the aim of providing 'wholesome and harmless entertainment to crowds of hardworking people, craving for a little fun and amusement' (cited in Friedrichs, 116–17). By the early 1890s, there were a number of competing journals, most notably Harmsworth's *Answers to Correspondents* and *Pearson's Weekly*. All three were soon reaching a mass nationwide readership and beginning to include light serial fiction. James Payn's *The World and the Will* was the first serial to appear in *Tit-Bits* (from 21 December 1889 to 16 August 1890), but was soon followed by shorter tales, mostly of mystery and adventure, by the likes of John Strange Winter, Fergus Hume, and E.W. Hornung. Grant Allen won £1000 at the end of 1890 with *What's Bred in the Bone*, in the first *Tit-Bits* prize story competition.

There is thus no doubt that novelists had a far wider range of choice for the publication of their new work in London periodicals in the early 1890s than they had twenty years earlier. Though by then there were a number of new amply illustrated monthly miscellanies beginning to enter the market, most notably Newnes's *Strand Magazine* (1891), the new fiction-carrying organs which had emerged in the 1880s were overwhelmingly weekly journals. This huge expansion of demand for weekly supplies of serial fiction in the metropolitan press, which could be met more efficiently by agents in London, was obviously a major setback for the provincial syndicators. But one of the most surprising twists in the tale of the rise and fall of novels in Victorian newspapers, is that the Sheffield firm of W.C. Leng and Co. were among the first proprietors to launch a mass-circulation metropolitan weekly entertainment magazine featuring instalment fiction.

W.C. Leng and Co. began to introduce serial fiction in the Saturday edition almost immediately after taking over the *Sheffield Daily Telegraph* in 1864. For almost a decade the stories featured were mainly a combination of local material and tales by David Pae, passed on by John Leng and Co. in Dundee. In 1873 the *Telegraph* joined the first Braddon syndicate and continued to receive most of its fiction from Tillotsons until around 1880, although there were still a good number of Scottish and South Yorkshire stories. From that point on, though material was still occasionally received from the *People's Friend* or from local authors like Eric St C.K. Ross, the Sheffield firm appears to have turned more frequently to London sources for its serials. Some, by the methods described earlier, were obviously offered by the authors themselves, including Besant's *All Sorts and Conditions of Men* in 1882, or James Skipp Borlase's 'Nina the Nihilist' and J.E. Muddock's 'Only a Woman's Heart', both in 1883. In the middle of the decade, however, many seem to have been supplied by A.P. Watt and to have run simultaneously in the London weeklies (see Table 4.1). But from around 1885, there is also evidence that W.C. Leng and Co. were beginning to purchase fiction on their own account and looking to sell it on to other journals. Major commissions undoubtedly by the Sheffield firm themselves were *Living or Dead* (early 1886), the last novel of the then hugely popular 'Hugh Conway' (Frederick John Fargus), for which he received £1000 for serial rights, and *The Deemster* (1886–87), Hall Caine's third novel, based on the Biblical parable of the prodigal son (*Sheffield Daily Telegraph 1855–1925*, 25–6).[29] In doing this, they also were going into direct competition with Tillotsons, and, as described in Chapter 3, they took the process literally by persistently attempting to poach the Fiction Bureau's star writer, Mary Braddon, until they finally succeeded in 1887.

By this time, W.C. Leng was well into his sixties and much of the day-to-day running of the papers had been passed on to his sons and those of his partner, Frederick Clifford. In the mid-1890s W.C. Leng retired completely from active duty. The *Telegraph's* Saturday Supplement became the *Sheffield Weekly Telegraph* in January 1884, and C.D. Leng (1861–1921), the elder son, who was based mainly in London and had already been handling the fiction negotiations for some time, took over the editorship and soon had ambitious plans to turn the journal into an illustrated metropolitan weekly with a nationwide circulation (*Sheffield Daily Telegraph 1855–1925*, 25–33). In this he was perhaps following the lead of his uncle John Leng's *People's Friend*, 'A Miscellany of Popular and Instructive Literature', which was already circulating throughout Scotland and beyond. However, the Scottish weekly remained rather strait-laced (see Plate 13), whereas C.D. Leng had something altogether brasher in mind, almost certainly under the influence of Newnes's *Tit-Bits*. In October 1887 the *Sheffield Weekly Telegraph* was reborn as the *Weekly Telegraph*, declaring itself 'A Non-Political, Amusing, and Instructive Weekly Household Journal'. It moved to a tabloid format, with bold headlines, plentiful graphics, and a largely anecdotal and fragmentary content, including regular prize competitions. In the process, all serious news material was dropped, although the weekly supply of fiction, both serials and complete stories, continued to occupy a prominent place in the opening pages of the sixteen-page penny paper (see Plate 14). It should be noted here that the first issues of the new *Weekly Telegraph*, now printed in London, thus preceded not only the opening of Newnes's biggest rivals *Answers to Correspondents* and *Pearson's Weekly*, but also the first appearance of serial fiction in *Tit-Bits* itself.

Taking Braddon from Tillotsons was a vital move in C.D. Leng's overall strategy. She indeed remained the chief literary attraction of the modernized *Weekly Telegraph* for some time, and 10 of her novels were serialized between 1888 and 1901. During the 1890s, however, C.D. Leng must often have found there was an over-supply of Braddon's fiction and sold on to Tillotsons either first or second serial rights to stories, while the remuneration she received had dropped noticeably by the end of the century (see Table A.4). During the same period, a number of other regular clients of Tillotsons sold their work to W.C. Leng and Co., including Adeline Sergeant (initially *A Dead Man's Trust* in 1888), Hawley Smart (*Without Love or Licence*, 1889–90, among others), and B.L. Farjeon (*The Mystery of Mr Felix*, 1890). Newer authors syndicated included, in the later 1880s, James McGovan, Richard Russell, or R.T. Casson and, in the early 1890s, J.H. Yoxall, Frank Barrett, or M.E.O. Malen. Arthur Conan Doyle's second Sherlock Holmes novel, *The Sign of the Four*, was serialized in the *Weekly Telegraph* (from 20 September 1890), after an appearance in *Lippincott's Magazine*, though its provenance is uncertain. However, by the turn of the century, E. Philips Oppenheim had become the *Weekly Telegraph*'s most prominent and consistent contributor, with over 30 thrillers between 1890 and 1925.

Advertisements in the *Newspaper Press Directory* for 1888 (142), 1889 (155) and 1890 (156) show that the new Sheffield agency was then known as 'The Editor's Syndicate', and suggest that at first it handled fiction in serial only, and did not maintain backlists. On each occasion at least five novels were listed with the date of commencement, and from 1889 details of the number of weekly instalments were added. Stereo plates with illustrations seem to have been offered even earlier, probably beginning with Braddon's *The Fatal Three* available in January 1888 (Table A.4). The message was clear by 1889:

> During the year 1888 the circulation of the *Weekly Telegraph* increased from 80,000 to 230,000 per week, owing to the excellent Stories it published. These Stories are carefully selected from a large quantity submitted by experienced readers, and are offered for simultaneous publication in other papers by the Editor's Syndicate.

I have only been able to trace novels thus syndicated by W.C. Leng and Co. in a limited number of British weeklies between 1886 and 1896, including John Leng's *People's Friend*, the metropolitan *Pictorial World*, the *Nottinghamshire Guardian*, the Cardiff *Weekly Mail*, the *Birmingham Weekly Mercury*, the *Glasgow Weekly Herald* and *Glasgow Weekly Mail*, plus Tillotsons's Lancashire Journals. Perhaps C.D. Leng also tended to concentrate less on British provincial than Colonial and American outlets. Braddon's 'newspaper novels' continued to appear regularly in major Australian weeklies such as the Melbourne *Age* or *Leader* and the Sydney *Town and Country Journal* through W.C. and Co. Leng although this was sometimes effected by selling Colonial rights on to Tillotsons (see Table A.4). But Conway's *Living or Dead* and Smart's *Without Love or Licence* have been located in the Melbourne *Australasian* and the Brisbane *Queenslander* respectively, while in the later 1890s six of the Oppenheims purchased by W.C. Leng and Co. been traced in the Melbourne *Age* and *Leader* and the Sydney *Town and Country Journal* (Table A.3; Johnson-Woods). In addition, there is evidence that C.D. Leng had initiated direct contacts with American regional newspapers before 1890, and that his material appeared frequently in the *Chicago Record* and *Boston Globe*, at least. In establishing regular links with the Chicago paper, C.D. Leng was once again encroaching on Tillotsons's territory. The correspondence between C.D. Leng and Victor Lawson has again survived among the Lawson papers at Chicago. The tone is rather more amicable than in the letters between Lawson and Tillotsons, though similar problems surface. Lawson tended to find Hawley Smart tedious and Rayne Butler objectionable. He accepted the first two Braddons offered but found the rest unsuitable or disappointing. B.L. Farjeon's late sensational works seemed to go down well, but there was no doubt that E. Phillips Openheim's thrillers were in greatest demand. His *Postmaster of Market Deignton* was used as a prize mystery story in early 1895 in the *Weekly Telegraph* and the *Chicago Record* (in the latter case under the title *John Martin, Postmaster*) in both cases with overwhelming success. Lawson was disappointed when Oppenheim's next offering was not a mystery and was even more distressed when a further Oppenheim, *The World's Great Snare*, proved to be 'unavailable' because it dealt 'so largely with immoral relations and situations' (TLSs, 12 April & 17 October 1895, Outgoing, VFL).

The result was that in 1896 Lawson decided to offer 12 money prizes totalling $30 000 (£6000) for mystery serials submitted by his readers, and received 816 entries from all over the English-speaking world. Harry Stillwell Edwards won the first prize of $10 000 for *Sons and Fathers*. It and the 11 runners up were not only published in the *Chicago Record*, but also sold on to other journals ('Our New Serial Stories', *Weekly Telegraph*, 6 June 1896). As well as all over the United States, they appeared in the *Weekly Telegraph* and in Australia, where they were handled by W.C. Leng and Co. (Johnson-Woods). So, from early 1896, C.D. Leng and Victor Lawson of the *Chicago Daily News* entered into an agreement for the mutual exchange of popular serial fiction, whereby each would receive 25 per cent commission on sales handled by the other, Lawson covering the USA and Canada, and the Editor's Syndicate Britain and her remaining Colonies (TLSs between Leng and Lawson, February to April 1896, Outgoing & Incoming, VFL). It soon emerged that the American side might be the more powerful in the partnership, which nevertheless allowed the Editor's Syndicate to consider abandoning the British provincial newspaper market altogether. At the beginning of the following year, it was announced that '[n]otwithstanding the great cost, the proprietors of the "Weekly Telegraph", intend to try the effect of publishing Miss Braddon's 1897 story . . . exclusively in this journal' ('The Queen of Novelists and the Weekly Telegraph', 2 January 1897, 2). The precise results of this experiment are unclear, but it seems more than likely, given C.D. Leng's arrangements with Lawson in America and his successful transformation of the *Weekly Telegraph* into an entertainment magazine with a large national circulation, that, from around the turn of the century, the Editor's Syndicate may have simply ceased to be economically necessary. From then on Leng may have purchased serial rights from authors for publication in Britain exclusively in the *Weekly Telegraph*.

In little more than a decade W.C. Leng and Co. of Sheffield had transformed their position in the fiction market from provincial syndicators to the operators of a mass-market entertainment weekly identical in style and function with the latest popular metropolitan journals. In 1897 the Sheffield firm purchased a colour printing machine, mainly to produce the new wrapper of the *Weekly Telegraph*, which then took on the appearance of a magazine, with 32 quarto pages (see Plate 15). Two years later, a *Weekly Telegraph* library of fiction was started, providing, at the bargain price of threepence, a complete novel every month by a popular author, usually a writer familiar from the pages of the journal. The series was still going strong in 1925, when over 300 volumes had been issued, and obviously proved considerably more successful than Tillotsons's earlier venture into the book publishing business. The *Weekly Telegraph* itself only began to decline in popularity sometime after the Great War, though it continued publication until December 1951.

Once again the phase of direct rivalry in the end represented a less severe threat to Tillotsons's business than the later indirect competition. We shall return to the cultural implications of the different courses pursued by the Bolton and Sheffield firms in the following chapter.

Part III
Analysis

5
Readership

Between the Newspaper Stamp Acts of 1836 and 1855, each registered newspaper in Britain was issued with a distinctive numbered stamp which had to be impressed upon every copy issued. The official stamp returns from this period can therefore be taken as a fairly reliable guide to actual sales.[1] Before that period, newspapers purchased sheets bearing a generic stamp through paper agents, whose often informal records formed the basis of the returns. Given also that such purchases were made irregularly and the practice of selling on stamped sheets to other journals was common, the pre-1836 stamp returns must be taken as fairly arbitrary (Cranfield, *Press*, 199–200). Between the abolition of the compulsory newspaper stamp in 1855 and early in the twentieth century when advertisers began to demand audited evidence of sales, that is, precisely the period of the rapid expansion of the press dealt with in this study, there was what A.P. Wadsworth calls 'the period of secrecy' (1), when circulation figures for specific newspapers are generally hard to find and sometimes questionable.[2] Information of this kind could only come from the proprietors themselves, whether made public in their own journals and in the various trade directories aimed principally at advertisers, or hidden away in files of company records or correspondence which have occasionally survived.[3] However, numerical indications of circulation were often advertised in the far vaguer form of information concerning the population of the area served or the output of the printing machines used.[4] When precise circulation figures were issued, they sometimes conflated figures for morning, evening and weekly papers or editions, and were occasionally challenged by rival journals.[5]

If quantitative evidence of sales alone thus lacks comprehensiveness and reliability, more complex and interesting questions concerning readership, such as the average number of readers of each copy sold, the composition of readership in terms of religious and political affiliation, class, or gender, and the specific sections of the paper favoured by sub-groups of readers, must remain entirely outside the range of statistical analysis. House-to-house surveys of newspaper readers, their practices and preferences, of the kind carried out by Northcliffe's *Daily Mail* in provincial towns shortly after the end of the First World War (cited in Brown, 27), were unthought-of in the nineteenth century.[6] To imagine, then, that it is possible 'to fully understand the experiences of the millions of readers of syndicated fiction in the nineteenth century', in Johanningsmeier's phrase (184), is to enter the realm of fantasy. Fortunately, however, the Victorian newspapers themselves offer a wealth of circumstantial evidence concerning the qualitative nature of their readership which is available to a more informal mode of inquiry. An underlying assumption here is that newspapers, both generically and individually, must be seen to create as much as to discover their readership.

In order to explore the nature of such Victorian communities of readers, it is useful at the outset to establish two sets of journal categories. The first is the simple distinction among local, regional, and national newspapers according to their socio-geographical circulation, which has been commonly used to describe modern newspaper developments by no means restricted to Britain. The second is a more complex distinction, and more specific to later Victorian journals, between 'autonomous' and 'supplementary' weeklies, that is, between those operated as independent journals with an integral news service, regardless of whether the proprietors ran a separate daily paper, and those which functioned as a weekend edition of or companion to a daily paper, which tended to give greater weight to features and entertainment material (see Plates 11–12). In extreme cases, such as that of the *People's Friend* or the Sheffield *Weekly Telegraph*, the 'supplementary' weekly could even evolve into an independent entertainment miscellany, with little or no news content and assuming the format of a magazine (Plates 13–15). Serial fiction was a common component of all three types of weekly, but each tended to construct its readership in different ways.

This chapter then will begin from an analysis of a sample of circulation data concerning Victorian papers regularly carrying serial fiction, before moving on to a more general discussion of what can be learned about communities of newspaper readers from the contents and forms of representative journals, beginning with a consideration of reader's contributions, and touching on the way political and religious affiliations, plus divisions of gender and class, might contribute to the definition of communities of readers. Finally, given the vast amount of such information available and in order to keep the topic in sharper focus in the limited space available, I have chosen to concentrate on the way in which two major fiction syndicators working out of provincial newspapers in northern industrial communities, Tillotsons in the Lancashire cotton town of Bolton, and W.C. Leng and Co. of Sheffield, centre of the cutlery trade, came to conceive of and to construct their reading publics in almost diametrically opposed ways.

5.1 Circulations

In the circumstances described above, it is obviously difficult, even if we limit ourselves to publication in Britain, to calculate with any precision the circulation of a given serial story, particularly so in the case of syndicated fiction, and thus to judge the average size of the readership reached by newspaper novels. In 1890 William Westall (79) attempted to estimate the total possible market for English newspaper fiction, and came up with the highly speculative figure of at least 18 million readers. His starting point, provided by an unnamed 'competent authority', was a circulation of 3 million copies for all penny Saturday and halfpenny evening papers in England. He guessed that similar papers in the rest of the English-speaking world must have at least twice as many subscribers since the countries concerned had twice as many inhabitants, and added for good measure the assumption that each copy was read by two individuals. However, while the sources are varied and scattered, enough figures are available to fit together a coherent general picture of the growth of potential readership for newspaper novels in Britain. A representative sample of circulation figures encountered in the process of researching this book, which seem to be trustworthy, and which have been checked for consistency with the limited relevant data already presented by modern scholars, notably Altick, Ellegard, and Wadsworth, appears in Table 5.1.

In the later 1850s and 1860s, the period of the minor and proto-syndicates discussed in Chapter 2, circulation claims are particularly hard to come by. We should then perhaps recall that the largest

Table 5.1 Claimed circulations of some victorian newspapers carrying serial fiction

Provincial papers Per issue/ thousands	1854	1858	1863	1864	1868	1870	1872	1873	1876	1880	1882	1883	1884	1886	1887	1888	1889	1890	1893
Alnwick Mercury (Monthly)	1[J]	2.5[J]																	
Paisley & Renfrew Gazette			3[J]																
Glasgow Penny Post		27[J]				3.25[J]													
Dundee People's Journal	12[J]		49[J]	80[J]	120[J]			125[J]		140[D]			150[D]	160[J]		200[J]			235[N]
(Sheffield) Weekly Telegraph				3.3[L]		10.5[L]			20[L]			30[S]		25[N]	80[N]	230[N]		215[N]	215[N]
Newcastle Weekly Chronicle						7[M]		31[N]		55[D]			60[D]	65[D]					
Cardiff Weekly Mail								13[N]											
Plymouth Western Weekly Mercury								35[N]											
Hereford Times										24[J]									
Tillotsons's 'Lancashire Journals'												87[S]		100[S]			110[S]		
Cardiff Weekly Times														81[S]					

Per issue/ thousands	1854	1858	1863	1864	1868	1870	1872	1873	1876	1881	1882	1883	1884	1886	1887	1888	1889	1890	1893
Manchester Weekly Times								30[N]											
Liverpool Weekly Post													60[D]	60[S]	91[D]			160[N]	200[N]
Glasgow Weekly Mail							103[J]	130[N]		207[D]			222[D]	270[D]					275[N]
Metropolitan papers																			
The World									20[N]					22[E]					
Lloyd's Weekly Newspaper														612[D]					710[D]
Reynold's Weekly Newspaper														300[D]					300[D]
The Weekly Dispatch														180[D]					180[D]
England											40[D]								40[D]
Weekly Budget										500[A]									
Tit-Bits														300[D]					607[D]

A = Altick *English*, App. C; D = *Deacon's*; E = Edwards, 142–3, on Edmund Yates; J = In the Journal itself; L = March, 121–2, on W.C. Leng; M = *May's*; N = *NPD*; S = *Sell's*

Sources: As noted.

regular provincial circulations recorded in the 1836–54 stamp returns rarely exceeded 10 000 per issue. The (Lincolnshire) *Stamford Mercury* and *Leeds Mercury*, two of the oldest provincial weeklies, dating back to before 1720, plus the *Manchester Guardian* (bi-weekly from 1837), *North British Advertiser* of Edinburgh, *Glasgow Herald*, *Liverpool Mercury* and *Birmingham Journal* were perhaps the most consistently successful, while the sales of the *Sheffield Independent*, belonging to the Leader family, later important syndicators of fiction, achieved just over 5000 at best.[7] English provincial weeklies in the major cities tended to remain suspicious of serial fiction for far longer than their Scottish counterparts. Some older journals with wide regional circulations like the *Leeds Mercury* did not take the risk until the 1870s, while the *Manchester Guardian* avoided them absolutely. The *Independent* in Sheffield was among the first to experiment, along with its new rival the *Telegraph*, but neither seems to have circulated far beyond the city itself or have achieved sales of over 10 000 until the 1870s. On the other hand, the English country papers relying on partly printed sheets containing serial fiction from the mid-1850s often served small communities and began with tiny circulations, often as small as the 500 sales claimed by the *Crediton Advertiser* in 1854 (January 1854, 1). The circulation of 3000 claimed in 1864 by the *Alnwick Mercury*, which persisted with serial stories for at least a decade, and which served an extensive rural area in Northumberland, was probably unusual. Many of the Scottish papers which carried David Pae's stories from the mid-1850s, like the *Falkirk Herald* or the *Galloway Post*, must have had similar limited sales, so that the circulation of 3250 claimed by the *Paisley and Renfrewshire Gazette* as late as 1870 is not surprising. The Liberal journals targeting a working-class audience in the major cities, notably the *Glasgow Times* and (Edinburgh) *North Briton* which formed a proto-syndicate for Pae's fiction around 1860, must have had far larger sales, perhaps in the region of the 27 000 claimed by the short-lived (Glasgow) *Penny Post* as early as 1858. Other more venerable and conservative Scottish city journals proceeded with English caution, like the *Glasgow Weekly Herald*, whose editor later commented:

> When the *Weekly Herald* was started, the Editor aimed at suiting the class of readers most likely to appreciate well-selected news and general literature, but it contained no fiction. . . . After a few years' experience, it became evident that one of the best

means of attracting readers was the publication of serial tales. The idea was comparatively new, and for a time the best papers hesitated to entertain it. But its success elsewhere dissipated the doubt, and it was at length resolved to make an experiment with a serial story in the *Weekly Herald*.

(Sinclair, 181–2)

But in the longer term, none of these city journals could match the sales accumulated by the different regional editions of the *People's Journal*, which amounted to well over 100 000 by the end of the 1860s. Already by that time it was in a position to claim that it had the widest geographical and largest numerical circulation of any British newspaper published outside London. Apart perhaps from the *Weekly Budget* (see Chapter 2), it was then the only newspaper carrying serials which could approach the largest sales achieved by the popular London monthly and weekly magazines.

A decade later the situation was very different. By then, not only did the quality of the fiction syndicated in the provincial newspapers often at least equal that in the London magazines, but the quantity of potential readers far exceeded anything that the respectable metropolitan periodicals could claim. As Table 2.1 suggests, if we take merely a conservative guess at the sales of the three journals where data is lacking, even the first Tillotsons's syndicate for Braddon's *Taken at the Flood* in 1873 must have achieved a circulation of over a quarter of a million copies. Around 10 years later, given the sales of the *Glasgow Weekly Mail* alone, Besant's *All Sorts and Conditions of Men* probably received in excess of 350 000 impressions in different city weeklies outside London (Tables 5.1 and A.6). These figures not only dwarf the 8000 copies issued of the metropolitan monthly *Belgravia* in which *All Sorts* also appeared (*VFRG*, 14: 2), but even comfortably outstrip the total number of copies of the novel produced in book form in all British editions up until the end of the First World War (Eliot, 'His Generation', 54). The (again often incomplete) details of the newspapers composing the syndicates for later works by Braddon and Collins (Tables A.4 and A.5), suggest that by the late 1880s well-constructed syndicates for works by such major writers could easily achieve well over half a million sales in Britain alone, since by then a number of other major city weeklies featuring serial fiction, like the *Liverpool Weekly Post* and *Birmingham Weekly Mercury*, individually commanded circulations comfortably in excess of 100 000 copies. Both of these, plus the *Glasgow Weekly Mail* and the *People's Journal* itself, were then regular clients of Tillotsons.

Obviously the local town and country papers which bought re-print fiction cheaply from Tillotsons's backlists, like the *Todmorden Weekly Advertiser* or *Wiltshire Times*, still probably had circulations below 10 000 copies in the mid-1880s, while regular members of Tillotsons's coteries for original works based in smaller cities or in rural areas, like the Cardiff *Weekly Mail*, Plymouth *Western Weekly Mercury*, or *Hereford Times*, clearly had sales significantly under 100 000. In contrast, the provincial weeklies with the largest circulations listed at the end of the previous paragraph all reached a wide regional audience. This could be demonstrated in detail with reference to a number of different forms of evidence. First, there are the claims to geographical circulation in the trade directories; secondly there is the provenance of the announcements in the classified advertisement sections of these papers; thirdly there is the place of origin, where recorded, of the various readers' contributions to the journals; finally, and for our purposes most economically, there is the composition of the syndicates themselves, which was based on the concept of complementary circulations. The negotiations in the early 1880s between A.P. Watt and the various provincial proprietors/editors in arranging the syndicates for Collins's *Heart and Science* and '*I Say No*', provide the clearest evidence. There papers like the *Manchester Weekly Times* or *Glasgow Weekly Herald* are seen to explicitly demand 'that the Northern Counties be reserved' or 'the right of publishing . . . in Scotland',[8] while the *Cardiff Weekly Times* or *Aberdeen Weekly Journal* are content respectively with Glamorgan and Monmouth or the area to the north of Dundee. It is noticeable from Tables A.4 and A.5, that Tillotsons never combined one of the major regional Scottish weeklies with other Scottish papers, and always included only one of the major northern English regional journals. Similarly W.C. Leng and Co. in Sheffield must have been well satisfied with the core of the syndicate for their third Braddon novel, *One Life, One Love* in 1890, which comprised their own *Weekly Telegraph*, the *Glasgow Weekly Mail*, and the (London) *Pictorial World*.

Such a perspective confirms the impression that the belt-and-braces syndicates Watt finally achieved for Collins's novels tended distinctly to 'milk' the periodical market, not only in combining monthly and weekly serialization, but also in forcing papers with significantly overlapping circulations such as the *Manchester Weekly Times* and *Liverpool Weekly Post*, or the *Bristol Observer* and the *Cardiff Weekly Times*, to feature the same novel at the same time. Again Alexander Sinclair of the *Glasgow Weekly Herald*, writing around 1895, comments appositely:

> a 'syndicate' system had some years before [1880] come into vogue, by which one serial would be run simultaneously in several papers in different parts of the United Kingdom. Of course it was possible for us to arrange, as we always did, that we should combine only with papers outside of Scotland. But despite the advantage of this plan, by which several high-class novels have been brought out, it had sometimes the serious disadvantage of overlapping, when stories appeared across the border where our paper also circulates, and were at the same time published in the *Illustrated London News* or in the *Graphic*, which circulate far and wide.
>
> (Sinclair, 184)

In the long term, the only rational way to command the sorts of circulation that Watt attempted to create in his *Heart and Science* syndicate was to serialize fiction exclusively in those metropolitan journals beginning to achieve mass-circulations nationwide, which, as shown in Chapter 4, is precisely what Watt went on to do.

As Table 5.1 suggests, I have been unable to trace reliable figures indicating average circulations for some of the main 'class' weeklies carrying serial fiction around this period. However, while Edmund Yates was editor of *The World*, one of the most successful of the Society weeklies, it seems rarely to have exceeded a circulation of 25 000 copies, priced as it was at sixpence (Weber, 36; Edwards, 142–3). Though sold at the same price, the top-rank illustrated weeklies obviously reached a much wider audience. Sales of *The Illustrated London News* had topped 100 000 copies before the newspaper stamp was abolished in 1855 (*RN51–3*, 6). Though this was probably down to around 70 000 by the late 1860s, it could still reach double that on special occasions, and by the mid-1880s, when serials had again become a regular feature, special issues occasionally reached half a million readers (*Deacon's* 1886, 84). The same source (114) suggests that *The Graphic* sold even more widely: regular issues occasionally reached the quarter million mark, while the Christmas numbers for 1881 and 1882 both sold well over half a million copies. By the late 1880s some of the 'mass' weeklies, whether the new Tory *England* or the old radical *Weekly Dispatch* and *Reynolds's Weekly*, with circulations ranging from 40 000 to 300 000 copies, could do no more than hold their readership stable, and this was obviously a reason for their recourse to regular serials. Nevertheless, in the mid-1890s, the most popular of the Sundays and the one which held out longest against the newspaper novel, *Lloyd's Weekly*, had a circulation rising towards the three-quarter million mark. Around the same time, *Tit-Bits, Answers to Correspondents*, and *Pearson's Weekly*, the three leading new-style miscellaneous weeklies, which by then were all carrying genre fiction in serial, had circulations already around or above the half-million point and climbing much more rapidly, with *Tit-Bits* the first and biggest (Jackson, 203). Despite its regular quota of serial fiction, in the 20 years after W.C. Leng took over, the *Sheffield Weekly Telegraph* seems not to have succeeded in establishing a wide regional readership. Thus it opted in the mid-1880s to leap-frog its provincial competitors and aim for a national circulation as a popular magazine along the lines of *Tit-Bits*. The rise in circulation claimed by C.D. Leng between 1886 and 1888 is extraordinary but appears to be accurate. Unfortunately, I have not been able to trace any precise indications of the growing circulation of the periodical which had preceded the *Telegraph* in this course, John Leng's *People's Friend*, though it seems likely that its circulation was broader geographically and higher numerically than its companion weekly newspaper the *People's Journal*, and thus might have been well over a quarter of a million copies by the early 1890s.[9]

However, before turning in more detail to the contents of the provincial weeklies and the communities of readers they fostered, we must at least briefly consider the possibility, discussed by Johanningsmeier in the American context (184–8), that the serial fiction in such journals might have been read in its entirety by only a tiny proportion of purchasers, and often served merely as padding to bulk out the contents to the required eight pages or so. This theory is obviously attractive to modern witnesses, who, surfeited with reading material and pressed for time, absorb only a fraction of the jumbo Sunday newspapers that they subscribe to, and who are likely to be daunted by the vast size of the pages of papers like the *Bolton Weekly Journal*, packed tight with tiny and sometimes barely legible print. A couple of accidents in the serialization of Braddon's novels in the pages of the Cardiff *Weekly Mail* might seem to offer the theory some support. In early 1879, the order of chapters 14–15 and 16–17 of *The Cloven Foot* was reversed without any acknowledgment, while in late 1886, two chapters of *The One Thing Needful* were entirely omitted for three weeks, after which they were finally published, out of sequence, and with the briefest of announcements. There were other occasions when a serial was dropped in the middle, as with Richard Dowling's Irish romance 'Tempest-Tossed' (*Tempest-Driven* in volume) appearing in James Henderson's *South London Press* in the second half of 1885, where after reaching chapter 22, readers were abruptly informed that:

> the demands upon our space, owing to the ensuing Elections, make it impossible to give the rest of this story in the *South London Press*. It is appearing in the *Weekly Budget*, particulars concerning which are to be found on Page 15.
>
> (*South London Press*, 24 October 1885, 9)

But amusing incidents such as these are unrepresentative, and the theory itself untenable on economic grounds alone. For why then should Tillotsons or W.C. Leng and Co. have troubled to recruit writers of the stature of Collins and Braddon and pay them more than a thousand pounds for first serial rights to a novel, when they could easily pick up absolute rights to an anonymous local work for little more than ten? We should note that in the same column of the *South London Press* apologizing for the premature termination of Dowling's Irish tale, there was an announcement of the commencement of Wilkie Collins's *The Evil Genius* the following week. For both W.F. Tillotson in 1873, and C.D. Leng nearly 15 years later, the winning of the exclusive rights to the first serial publication of Braddon's latest work was heavily advertised and a crucial factor in the marketing of their new ventures. In the case of serials by well-known authors for which substantial sums had been paid, from the second instalment onwards a synopsis of the preceding chapters was normally included to encourage readers who had missed the beginning to pick up at a later stage. Such summaries often ran for as long as the first third of the entire serialization.[10] Announcements of the serialization of a new Braddon novel were often accompanied by explicit appeals to existing readers to spread the news and boost the circulation. Braddon's first two serial novels for Tillotsons were published back to back, and the final instalments of *Taken at the Flood*, were accompanied in all the Lancashire Journals by a notice from the proprietors to the effect that 'The Opening Chapters of "A Strange World" will appear in our columns on Saturday April, 18, 1874; and we avail ourselves of this opportunity to request our readers to recommend the Journal to all their friends and neighbours as the best Local Paper . . .' (for example, *Bolton Weekly Journal*, 21 March 1874, 3). Similarly the announcement of the 1897 decision by C.D. Leng to publish Braddon's latest work exclusively in the *Weekly Telegraph*, cited in Chapter 4, concluded with the following appeal:

> Miss Braddon possesses a larger army of readers than any other writer, and we feel assured that when we have advertised our new enterprise all over the Kingdom, and the public know that, for some time to come, they can only read Miss Braddon's latest story in the 'Weekly Telegraph', we shall secure many more thousands of readers.
>
> If you value the efforts made to supply you with the best and most popular reading, you can show your appreciation, and help us considerably, by telling your friends what we are about to do.
>
> ('The Queen of Novelists and the Weekly Telegraph',
> *Weekly Telegraph*, 2 January 1897, 2)

So it is unsurprising that the advertisements announcing the tripling of the circulation of the *Weekly Telegraph* in 1888, were convinced that it was due to the excellence of the stories it published (*NPD*, 1889, 155). Similarly the noticeable surges in the circulation of the *People's Journal* in the mid-1860s and mid-1870s must be due in part to the introduction of sensational stories by first Pae then Braddon. Certainly R.M.W. Cowan was convinced that the *North Briton*, the *Journal's* fiercest rival at the mid-century, 'quickly reached a circulation of 10,000 not so much by "independence" in politics as by popular features like serial fiction' (286). When the directors of the limited company owning the *Aberdeen Journal* decided in 1884 that 'the Weekly Journal should be more pushed', their main suggestion was that the manager should be 'authorised to allow the agents to distribute the returns among farm servants on some occasions when a new story was commenced' (Minutes of Directors' Meeting, 14 November, AJR). It would then be rash for us not to assume that the large circulation figures for the weeklies run by Tillotsons and W.C. Leng and Co. themselves, and for those of many of their clients, indicated a large and enthusiastic following for much of the fiction they were offering (see Turner, 'Syndication', 85–90).

5.2 Contents and communities

If enthusiasm for newspaper fiction is expressed most generally in surges in sales, it can also be seen more occasionally but also more explicitly among readers' own contributions to journals, whether in the form of letters to the editor or, more characteristically, of submissions to story competitions. Autonomous weeklies tended to have correspondence columns of letters from readers who wished to contribute to debates of both local and national import, usually initiated by editorial stories and comments. These were sometimes lengthy and frequently political, as in the case of James Henderson's *South London Press*, where the future of Liberalism was often enthusiastically discussed throughout the 1870s and 1880s. Supplementary weeklies often contained no correspondence columns at all, leaving it to the companion daily, or, like the *Sheffield Weekly Independent*, carried 'Questions & Answers' features focusing on factual information, household hints, and romantic problems in the tradition of *The Family Herald*. 'Answers to Correspondents' was, of course, also a staple feature of the magazine-format weeklies. Indeed this was the central idea underlying Alfred Harmsworth's *Answers* when it began in 1888, though the weekly soon shifted to the more miscellaneous model of *Tit-Bits*. As Jackson has shown (203–6), *Tit-Bits* itself offered a guinea a column for all original contributions to the paper, including letters sent to the 'Correspondence' page. In the issue of 1 June 1895, for example, it was taken up by four lengthy essay-style missives on 'How Best to Learn a Foreign Language', 'Who are Most Polite – Men or Women?', 'Should Infant Life Insurance be Permitted?', and 'Is Early Rising a Mistake?', each of which presumably earned its author something approaching 17s.

However, even in the autonomous weeklies, published comments by readers on the serial stories carried seem to have been relatively rare. David Christie Murray relates how, during the period of his employment at the *Birmingham Morning News* in the early 1870s, an abrupt and unexpected conclusion to Edmund Yates's serial 'A Bad Lot' forced Murray to attempt to fill the breach by setting about his own first novel.[11] This proved to be 'the most formless and incoherent work of fiction which was ever put in type' so that '[s]cores of letters were sent week by week to the editor protesting against its continuance' (Murray, *Recollections*, 189–90). But in the extensive, though inevitably cursory, scans of runs of a wide range of later Victorian weekly papers carried out in the preparation of this volume, I have come across few examples of published letters to the editor concerning serials, nearly all concerning stories with a strong local or political theme. In 1879, for example, when the *Sheffield Daily Telegraph* announced the appearance of Isabella Banks's Yorkshire serial 'Under the Scars' (syndicated by Tillotsons and published in volume as *Wooers and Winners*), a reader wrote from Rotherham in favour of the choice. The letter praised the historical and local verisimilitude of the same author's *Manchester Man*, claiming that the character Madam Broadbent was 'true to the very life. Hers was the first school I ever attended' (30 March 1879). Or in 1874–75, when Henderson's *Weekly Budget* carried Compton Reade's 'Hard Lines', championing the cause of the agricultural labourers, there was a wave of sympathetic responses from the North of England. Complaints seem to have been rare, though 'One who Reads' wrote to the *South London Press* to suggest that Dr Carden's 'Mabel Mortimer' 'should be continued . . . the heroine being brought to repentance and happiness' (21 May 1870, 10). I have not, however, found any published readers' comments on syndicated novels by novelists with an established metropolitan reputation of the stature of Collins or Braddon.[12]

Altogether, then, the stories submitted by readers, normally for specific prize fiction competitions and often in large numbers, provide a more consistent indication of their engagement with newspaper fiction. From the *People's Journal* and other popular Scottish news-miscellanies in the late 1850s (see Chapter 2) to *Tit-Bits* at the turn of the century (Chapter 4), such competitions remained perennially popular in the Victorian weekly paper. Competitions for serial stories were irregular and exceptional. During this period there was a marked inflation of the first prizes offered, from the £25 in the *Bolton Weekly Journal* in 1878, through the £150 in the *Glasgow Weekly Herald* in 1880, to the £1000 put up by *Tit-Bits* in 1890, and professional writers were often attracted. Grant Allen who won the *Tit-Bits* competition had already published at least half a dozen volumes of popular fiction. Indeed, even the first and third prizes in the Bolton competition had been won by writers who had already published in London – Frederick Talbot and Jessie Fothergill. Competitions for short complete tales were much more regular and

1 John Leng.

2 W. C. Leng.

3 W. F. Tillotson.

4 John Maxwell.

5 David Pae.

6 M. E. Braddon.

7 Wilkie Collins.

8 Walter Besant.

LOVE OR MONEY.

A TALE OF THE TIMES.

CHAPTER I.

IN THE SUNSHINE AND—THE SHADE.

It was the height of the season. The aristocracy of England, (by which term is to be understood, not all those nobly born, but those also whose enormous wealth sets them so far above their fellow-creatures,) had hastened from their country seats to their town mansions, and London was "full."

It is always full enough, Heaven knows! It can always boast of its two millions and a half of human beings crowded together in a little space; but that is not what is meant by the term. Whitechapel may be filled to suffocation, and in the courts and alleys of Drury Lane and Somers Town, sixteen grown-up persons may and do lie in one small room; but that is not being full, in the polite sense of the term: to be full in that sense, the east, the City, and the lower suburbs may be deserts, so that Belgravia has its complement of fashionable people, and Regent Street and Bond Street be made impassable by the equipages of these persons—so impassable, indeed, that every now and then the streets are blocked up, and the footmen, who in harlequin liveries hang on to my lady's carriage, are in constant fear of the pole of some one else's vehicle being run into their calves, or knocking them off their "perch." The word last employed is, we believe, vulgar and low, applied to those excellent gentlemen in livery—but let it pass.

As London was full, of course all the fashion was to be found there, and, of course, also the Honourable Mrs. Bezant—and the Misses Bezant had, to quote the *Morning Post*, arrived at their family mansion in Hill Street. Everybody knows where Hill Street, Berkeley Square, is, or at least everbody ought to know. It is short but pleasant, and is to its extent full of great people. It is in the immediate neighbourhood of the parks, and boasts of large houses. A bishop lives at one corner, and an ambassador from an Emperor at the other; and the street consequently claims the appellation of aristocratic.

The Honourable Lady Bezant had a vast house, of which she and her daughters might occupy about four rooms. The rest were set aside for state, show, reception—for the servants, and for domestic purposes. The lady, who was a widow, "with two accomplished and lovely daughters"—again to quote the *Morning Post*—had been left with a very fine jointure, and had determined to spend it in a way most conducive to the advancement of her family in the *beau monde*. She was a proud and haughty woman, well versed in the petty affairs of the world, and ready to use every effort to get and secure the best places in it to herself and children.

At the period our story commences, she was to be seen seated upon a sofa in a luxuriously fashioned chamber—a boudoir common to the mother and daughters—between her two children—giving them lessons in that domestic economy which all worldly mothers, at one time or another, are sure to offer to their children.

"You have not a particle of manner about you, Sophy," she said to the youngest, "and although, to be sure, your face and figure are superior to your sister's, still you seldom make an impression, and more seldom preserve it when made. At the flower-show the other day, when Sir John Malcolm was so attentive and complimentary, I was obliged to answer all those compliments myself. You were mute, dumb, confounded."

"Because, mamma," said Sophia—a very pretty and innocent-looking girl of about nineteen years of age, but looking as those invariably do who are of the *ton*, much older—"because, mamma, I do not understand compliments. I sometimes think an overstrained compliment is meant more to show the speaker's wit, than his sincerity."

"Precisely so," returned the mother, "your understanding is not bad—"

"And then," interrupted Agnes, a bold and dashing-looking girl, a year and a half older than her sister, bending over a work-box which was on the table, and which was made rather for show than for anything else—"there is this to say for Sophy, Sir John, a north country baronet, is no great catch after all."

"The observation, Agnes, is vulgar, but is true," said Lady Bezant; "but that is no reason why your sister should not show her *esprit*, and should omit to make an impression. Let the men talk about her, let them once get *epris* with her charms, and she will become the *mode*. Her wit and beauty, or whatsoever the people choose to assign to her, will strike at a distance. Young fellows with weak heads will fall in love with ere they see her. She may then hope," continued the mother, warming with her subject, "to marry an earl, a marquis, nay, a duke. The career of that woman may be indeed splendid."

Agnes smiled at her mother's enthusiasm, and Sophia looked on the ground, muttering to herself a certain line from Tennyson's poems. Neither of them spoke: the mother was meditating some sage and worldly maxim whereon again to enlarge, when a thundering rap was heard at the hall door, and the visitor's bell was pulled with a vigour and ability which so peculiarly distinguish the fashionable footmen of England.

"My dears," said the Lady Bezant, gracefully rising, "our *séance* is concluded. "We shall now no doubt have morning calls till the carriage is ordered, everything is prepared. Agnes, go with your sister, you will receive in the crimson drawing-room."

As she said this, she opened a door to the left, and departed swiftly, waving her hand to her daughters. Agnes, at once arose, and opening a door to the right, entered the room indicated. Her sister followed, and both took their places, Agnes at a piece of tambour work prepared by her maid, (and it must be confessed stationary at the same rose-bud for at least three weeks,) and Sophia at some velvet tinting, which she was doing with great taste.

So quickly and cleverly was this little passage accomplished, that when the footman threw open the door to announce Lord Claude Graham and Sir John Malcolm, one might have supposed that the young ladies had sat there for the whole morning. Of course, the tambour work and the tinting were thrown by, and the ladies rose slightly to welcome their guests, who made the usual polite inquiries.

There were three gentlemen, but one was unannounced. He was a pale, intellectual looking man, the tutor of Lord Claude, a fair sickly boy of nineteen. Sir John Malcolm might have been thirty-five, and was bluff, bold, and handsome. He was well-made, and of redundant health, and not very polished in his actions.

After a short time in which Agnes led the conversation, Lady Bezant entered the room and uttered quite a little scream of surprise when she saw her guests. She was an admirable actress, and the manner in which she welcomed her guests was a study in itself. The bow to Mr. Taunton, Lord Claude's tutor, was frigidly polite; the welcome to Sir John warm, but still distant; but that to Lord Claude Graham, the third son of a duke, and with the benefit of having two sickly elder brothers, was kindly, matronly, and lady-like, and so warm that the poor young fellow stammered out a modest expression of surprise, and then stopped short.

"We called to know, Lady Bezant," said Sir John, "whether you are going, with these charming young ladies to the archery fete in the Park. You must go; we shall be quite dull without you," and Sir John bowed to Sophia—"shall we not, Lord Claude?"

"Yes, we shall, indeed" stammered his Lordship, blushing up to the roots of his light hair.

"And it's a beautiful sight, is it not, my lord?" continued Sir John.

"Yes, it is indeed," answered the young man, stealing a glance at Agnes, who met it in so bold a way, that his eyes fell confusedly.

"Well, your lordship, we are very much obliged and delighted," returned Lady Bezant, "but to tell the truth, this week is a busy week. To-morrow is the Fancy-fair till four. Myself and daughters have prepared for and keep stalls."

"I'm sure I'll be a customer" lisped Claude.

"Next day," continued the Lady with a graceful bow, "but I forgot—in the evening we go to the opera. The day afterwards Lady Finionbrum gives her *thé dansante*. That is on Tuesday. On Wednesday there is a drawing-room and of course we must be there, and to the opera in the evening; on Thursday the Honourable Mrs. Thogot gives her *matinée*; then the—"

"Toxopholites," interrupted Sir John, "you must come."

"Well," since you will insist my lord," answered the lady, looking at his lordship, who was perfectly mute—"we will be with you. In the evening, the opera. On Friday a lecture at the Royal Institution, and Lady Drumclog's fète champetre—in the evening Madame Alto's concert. And on Saturday a quiet dinner party at home and Alboni at the Opera. I really think, my lord, that you must own that our time is filled up."

LADY BEZANT AND HER DAUGHTERS.

"Oh yes it is, indeed," lisped Lord Claude.

"'Egad, your Ladyship works harder than a horse" cried Sir John.

Mr. Taunton did not speak, but he looked earnestly at Sophia, and then at Agnes, and lastly at her Ladyship, and muttered to himself—"What a vortex of folly and amusement: There is enough in a week spent, as these women spend it, for a whole life time."

As he said this to himself, a footman entered bearing a card upon a silver salver. It was for Sophia, and had merely a name and two lines in pencil written on it. The young lady took it, and rose instantly and with a graceful inclination to the company rose and withdrew hastily to the housekeeper's room, where we will follow her.

As she entered this room a very pretty but pale girl of her own age, in a common bonnet and shawl rose to greet her. She was pale and sickly—her dark hair hung dankly over her forehead. Her eyes were cast down, her lips parted, and as she spoke, modesty so flushed her pale clear cheek, that Sophia thought she had never seen any one so beautiful.

"I have brought home all the work for my lady, Miss," said the young workwoman; "the slippers, the braces, and the tambour work;" and she pointed to a little heap of things which she had unpacked, and placed on the table. "I hope they are in time; I have worked night and day to finish them. Here also are some drawings by my brother."

"Thank you," said Sophia, with a blush; "they are quite in time. They are for to-morrow." And she blushed still more deeply, for she knew that the articles would be sold as the work of, to quote again the *Morning Post*, 'The Honourable Lady Bezant, and her accomplished and beautiful daughters, the Misses Agnes and Sophia Bezant.' The list of articles, and that stereotyped phrase, had been sent that very morning to the paper to be in time for its insertion for the next day.

"Thank you, again and again, Miss Sinclair; they are very beautiful indeed, very beautiful. Mamma will pay you to-morrow."

"Will you pay me *now*, miss?" said the girl firmly, with a heightened colour. "I am very poor, and my brother is very ill. We are in need of the money."

The pain which this avowal caused the workwoman had a great effect on her. She had been sitting up all night to finish the work, and was overwrought in body and mind. She pressed her hand on her side, and sat down in a chair.

"You are very ill," cried Sophia, alarmed.

"I am, indeed, miss," gasped the girl, as she suddenly lay back her head and fainted.

"Mamma! mamma!" shrieked Sophia, frightened out of her wits, and running suddenly into the crimsom drawing-room, which, with its satin hangings and gilt furniture, contrasted strangely with the bare plainness of the apartment she had just quitted. "Mamma, mamma, she is dead!"

All arose suddenly.

"Who is dead?" cried Lady Bezant, in a voice which would have suited Lady Macbeth.

"Oh, come here, come here," answered her daughter, in a tone of anguish, running to the housekeeper's room. The guests and ladies frightened beyond their propriety followed her, and found the poor workwoman still fainting. Mr. Taunton at once saw what it was, and hurriedly untied the course bonnet, and sprinkled the pale face. "Don't be alarmed, ladies," he cried, "she is only fainting!"

"Only fainting!" ejaculated Lady Bezant; "how could you, Sophia, be so foolish as to disturb us for a person of that condition!" and she swept back with a regal air, leading Lord Claude, Sir John, and Agnes with her.

Mr. Taunton stayed behind. He had studied medicine at Edinburgh, and soon brought Miss Sinclair to her senses. Sophia, too frightened to conceal anything, told him all.

"Poor girl!" she said, "whilst we have been enjoying ourselves, she has been working and starving. She wants air and rest and exercise."

"True, Miss, true—too true," said Taunton, sadly. "How pale she is. You have had hitherto all sunshine in your lifetime; she has had too much of the shade—too much of the shade."

CHAPTER II.

"A LITTLE LOW LIFE."

Fox Court, Gray's Inn Lane, has of late years gained an unenviable notoriety, but it is by no means the worst of that cluster of courts and alleys which form the little veins which carry off the circulation from the main arteries—Gray's Inn Lane and Holborn. Two hundred years ago it used to be a very pretty place, no doubt. The high blank wall forming the back of one side of the quadrangle of Gray's Inn Square did not then exist to shut out the pure air, and students at law who could not reside in the Inn, lived there in the modest little houses. Baldwin's Gardens, which approximates to it, might have then boasted of a garden, and a few hundred yards down the Gray's Inn Road brought you into pleasant fields, and refreshed your sight with hedge-rows and wild-flowers.

All this is changed now. The courts have become crowded with poor people, and the houses therein, which might comfortably lodge six or eight people, have sometimes as many inhabitants as forty or sixty. In a court running out of it, the thieves' kitchen was established, which at the time we write flourished in its glory.

It was a wet day, and the rain poured down incessantly. Now it has been a question with those who observe such things whether the poverty of the poor is more apparent on a fine or a wet day. In the sunshine their rags and dirt stands out in strong contrast to the bright sunshine and the sky; in the rain they hang and cling about them, and get sodden and darker, and more dirty. The rain pours off from their miserable caps or hats and channels their faces with dirt.

The people of these courts are of a peculiar class; that some of the worst characters in London do live there, there is little doubt; but the great majority are of a kindly class, feeling for their fellow-creatures, who they fancy are in a lower condition than themselves, and constantly imposed upon by professional beggars. Newspapers, cheap as they have become, are a luxury there, or are, when old used, for trading purposes, that is, to cover the bottoms of the large trucks upon which some of the more adventurous inhabitants of the courts have placed their speculations in nuts, oranges, and, in the summer, of pine-apples. The consequence of this is, that in this network of courts, the itinerant newsvendor has full play. He does not generally meddle with politics, but is extremely forcible upon anything which relates to the horrible. The most successful of these travelling editors was, at the time we write, a gentleman who went by the name of Bullmouth, who was roaring out—

"H'yar yer have the full and perticklar account of the bloody and brutal murder of ——— only a ha'penny, my dears."

Bullmouth stopped to detach one of his broadsides, and his his commentators, youthful beings who listened attentively, exclaimed joyously,—

"Oh, crikey, don't he give it out, don't he just now."

—— "A perleeceman in 'Ighbury Lane, with the captur of the murderer, with the dreadful oaths he swore, and his committal afore—only a ha'penny, my dears," and Bullmouth sold another.

"A magistrate this mornin' with the whole account of his hexamination, when there was found on him—only a ha'penny." Another purchaser was found, Bullmouth being as before hinted popular in the district he worked, and celebrated for the depth of his horrors.

It was a wet day in the middle of June, and in addition to the actual misery of wet, the contrast to the late fine weather seemed to bring out the dirt and degradation of the little crowd of audience round Bullmouth. Draggled children, with hair which had never seen the comb or felt the brush, were listening with looks of intense interest, tall thin unwashed girls, just bursting into womanhood at that period when they should be clothed with every grace, listened also with a look which seemed to sharpen their already sharp faces.

There was one respectably dressed person among the crowd, from whose wet garments an atmosphere steamed up by no means pleasant nor wholesome. He was Mr. Taunton, protected by an umbrella, and listening or rather watching the crowd with as much interest as any one of the youthful admirers of the itinerant bookseller.

"H'yar you have," cried he, beginning the story over again.

"Oh, it's jest the same," related a big girl. "Can't yer tell us some more, Tommy Bullmouth."

"Only a halfpenny,—now, miss, why don't yer buy one and read it yerself. It wouldn't do for me to tell the whole court about it, 'cos I should sell none. H'yar you have a full, true and peetickler account'—and Bullmouth shouted again in his worn-out voice, loud enough to split the ears of the listeners.

(To be Continued.)

9 *Alnwick Mercury*, 1 July 1856, tenth page.

10 Dundee *People's Journal*, 21 April 1866, second page.

will be made to surviving personal correspondence with their literary and syndication agents, and issues of class and gender will be discussed. At its most general level, the argument is that, while the newspaper novel initially served to broaden the range of writers who could make a living by their pens and to undermine prevailing assumptions concerning class and culture, it did so eventually at the cost of imposing inflexible commercial constraints on writing and creating significant barriers to the entrance of women to the emerging profession of authorship.

6.1 Making a living

The boom in periodical publishing in the latter part of the Victorian era entailed large relative increases not only in the number of subscribers but also in the number of persons employed as writers in the broad sense (Cross, 225–30). And, without seriously challenging the dominance of the London publishing industry, the particularly vigorous growth of the provincial press seems to some extent to have increased the chances of making a living by the pen without taking up residence in the metropolis. As Lucy Brown has shown with reference to the occupational tables of the decennial Census (37–9), the number of people in England and Wales classifying themselves as authors, editors, journalists, reporters, or shorthand writers increased from 2403 to 8145 between 1871 and 1891, that is, a factor of 3.4, while the total population increased by a factor of 1.3 only. In addition, the tables distinguishing different occupations by region over the same period show that the number of such writers based in London increased by a factor of only 2.5, as against the 5.8 recorded in Lancashire, for example, with its vigorous regional press. (Even so, it should be noted that in 1891 the proportion of writers resident in London and Lancashire respectively represented 39.4 per cent and 9.5 per cent of the total, as compared to 14.5 per cent and 13.6 per cent in the case of the general population.) While somewhat similar trends can be seen among those working in other occupations directly related to the publishing industry, notably printers and bookbinders, there both the rate of increase and the extent of the shift in the weighting towards the regions were rather less marked. In addition, in those occupations the increase in the number of workers was rather more prominent in the 1880s, while in the case of writers the 1870s showed significantly stronger growth.

11 *Leigh Journal and Times*, 31 October 1890, second page.

The Leeds Mercury

No. 18,163. Price 1d.

ISSUED EVERY SATURDAY.

JANUA...

LIFE IN LONDON.

By J. MEIKLEJOHN.

LATE INSPECTOR OF DETECTIVE POLICE, SCOTLAND YARD,

Author of "Leaves from a Detective's Note Book," "Meiklejohn's Detective Experiences," &c.

A TRAGEDY OF ERRORS.

A Tale of Revolution Times.

(By the Author of "In Troublous Land," "The Mystery of Roath's Farm," "Thrall of Fate," &c. &c.)

Book III.—Sixes: 1793.

CHAPTER IV (Continued).

THE QUAKER.

THE KEEPER OF THE...

By F. W. ROBINSON

Author of "Grandmother's Money," "Lazarus in London," "The Courting of Mary Smith," "Mr Chinck," &c. &c.

For plots she was pretty, chastity, the Keeper of the Keys of whatsoever...

Book I.—Rumous.

THE PROFESSOR AND HIS SON.

THE PEOPLE'S FRIEND

A Miscellany of Popular and Instructive Literature.

No. 994   MONDAY, JANUARY 14, 1889.   PRICE ONE PENNY.

M. E. BRADDON.

Mary Elizabeth Braddon is the daughter of Mr Henry Braddon, solicitor, and was born in Soho Square, London, in 1837. Her mother was a woman of much refinement and working taste, qualities which have descended in large measure to her daughter. At an early age Miss Braddon began to contribute to magazines in prose and verse, but it was not till 1862, when she published "Lady Audley's Secret," that she became famous. By this, and a host of novels that have succeeded it, she has established the right to be placed in the front rank of English novelists. Nor has she confined herself to fiction alone, but has written for the stage, and some of her works —"Henry Dunbar," for instance—show that if she had turned her attention to the writing of sensational plays, she would have achieved as great a success on the stage as she has done with the reading public.

Miss Braddon lives a quiet and comparatively retired life at Lichfield House, Richmond. Here she devotes two hours a day to putting her story in form for the press, but spends a good many more quietly thinking out the development of her plots. Miss Braddon's method of working is peculiar. She keeps in a carefully-locked drawer of her workroom the skeletons of many stories, which from time to time she draws from their seclusion, and slowly and laboriously clothes them with flesh. In the centre of her workroom is a large square table, covered with books of reference, and a litter of books and pamphlets; but Miss Braddon usually writes her novels in a low chair near the fireplace, with a large piece of stiff cardboard on her knee, and in the course of two hours will produce three or four pages of printed matter, written in a neat legible hand, not a trace of feminine character being about it. Her great difficulty, she confesses, is to adhere to the plot, which she has carefully thought out and decided on as final. Her characters have the troublesome knack of displaying new developments and wandering into fresh and untrodden tracks, but when once she has decided on the fate of her several characters, she compels them to pursue their destined path to the end.

Miss Braddon has dealt with the troublous side of human life—with its crimes, its deceptions, and its vices—and while she has produced pictures startling from a vividness of colour, she has never once allowed her pen to depict a scene at which the most innocent might blush. She has set herself to deal with hard naked realities, and to strip the cover off some of the cancers and malformations of modern society. Of late years her stories have decidedly improved in their tone. A refinement of sentiment, and an elevation of thought and feeling, pervade them now to a greater extent than formerly, making their perusal a source of keen and pure enjoyment. She is a literary artist in the highest and truest sense. Her style is unexcelled among British novelists, and she paints her scenes and characters with an almost photographic fidelity to truth and nature. She is a most omnivorous reader—fiction, of course, occupying much of her time—and a most ardent devotee of literature, and this is why her latest novels still display the freshness and originality of her earlier works, while they are mellowed by that wider reading and deeper study of human nature which have so fully occupied her leisure time. Her popularity is as great to-day as it ever was, and she is bound to take one of the highest places among the writers of fiction in the Victorian era.

THE DAY WILL COME.

By M. E. BRADDON,

Author of "Lady Audley's Secret," "Vixen," "Ishmael," "Like and Unlike," "The Fatal Three," &c., &c.

CHAPTER I.

"Farewell, too—now at last—
Farewell, fair lily."

The joy bells clashed out upon the clear, bright air, startling the rooks in the great elm trees that showed their leafy tops above the gray gables of the old church. The bells broke out with sudden jubilation; sudden, albeit the village had been on the alert for that very sound all the summer afternoon, uncertain as to when the signal for that joy peal might be given.

The signal had come now, given by the telegraph wires to the old postmistress, and sent on to the expectant ringers in the dusky church-tower. The young couple had arrived at Wareham Station, five miles off, and four eager horses were bringing them to their honeymoon home yonder amidst the old woods of Cheriton Chase.

Cheriton village had been on tiptoe with expectancy ever since four o'clock, although common sense ought to have informed the villagers that a bride and bridegroom who were to be married at two o'clock in Westminster Abbey were not very likely to appear at Cheriton early in the afternoon. But the village having made up its mind to a half-holiday, was glad to begin early. A little knot of gipsies from the last race meeting in the neighbourhood had improved the occasion and set up the friendly and familiar image of Aunt Sally on the green in front of the Eagle Inn; while a rival establishment had started a pictorial shooting gallery, with a rubicund giant's face and gaping gargantuan mouth, grinning at the populace across a barrow of Barcelona nuts. There are some people who might think Cheriton village and Cheriton Chase too remote from the busy world and its traffic to be subject to strong emotions of any kind. Yet even in this region of Purbeck, cut off from the rest of England by a winding river, ostentatiously calling itself an island, there were eager interests and warm feelings, and many a link with the great world of men and women on the other side of the stream.

Cheriton Chase was one of the finest places in the County of Dorset. It lay South of Wareham, between Corfe Castle and Branksea Island, and in the midst of scenery which has a peculiar charm of its own, a curious blending of level pasture and steep hillside, barren heath and fertile water-meadow.

Cheriton House was almost as old as Corfe in the estimation of some of the country people. Its history went back into the night of ages. But while the Castle had suffered siege and battery by Cromwell's ruthless cannon, Cheriton House had been cared for and added to century after century, so that it presented now a picturesque blending of old and new, in which almost every corridor and every room was a surprise to the stranger.

The present master of Cheriton was a lawlord, created about fifteen years before this day of clashing joy bells and village rejoicings. He had been owner of the Cheriton estate for more than twenty years, having bought the property on the death of the last squire, and at a time of unusual depression. He was popularly supposed to have got the estate for an old song; but the old song meant something between seventy and eighty thousand pounds, and represented the bulk of his wife's fortune. He had not been afraid to swamp his rich wife's dowry, for he was at this time one of the most popular silk gowns at the equity bar. He was making four or five thousand a year, and he was strong in the belief in his power to rise higher.

Under Mr Dalbrook's improving hand the Cheriton estate, which had been gradually sinking to decay in the occupation of an exhausted race, became as perfect as human ingenuity, combined with judicious outlay, can make an estate. The famous advocate's only idea of a holiday was to work his hardest in the supervision of his

The Weekly Telegraph.

No. 1410. | Established April, 1862. | REGISTERED FOR TRANSMISSION ABROAD. | **SATURDAY, APRIL 27, 1889.** | REGISTERED FOR TRANSMISSION ABROAD. | PRICE ONE PENNY.

A CONCEIT.

S WINGS at each ear a pendant pearl
That whispers softly to the girl—
... such a lovely, perfect shell!
And if I did, then, posy pen tell
What dires shock'd me not, that I
To his small worth may bode'ry
Else in this shell once let me lie,
Then I shall prove the choicer thine
From ocean far might me unto you,
And, happy there, shall know he knew
How much a sea-born pearl would prize
A place in a shell-paradise.

— *F. D. Barnum.*

Instead of quietly stepping aside he struck out from the shoulder right and left, and quickly found himself confronted by three or four men, each one, apparently, having some knowledge of the art of boxing.

NEW STORY, MR. LEAGRAVE, OF LONDON.—SEE PAGE 262.

THE PRIME OF LIFE

JUST as I thought I was growing old,
To watch the world with a heart grown cold,
And smile at a folly I would not share,
Some came by with a smile for me,
And I am watching that forty year
Isn't the age that it seems to be,
W'h is the pretty lower eyes are near.
Blow me if life it is just the prime,
A fact t at I hope she n'd and t stand;
And forty year is a perfect p time
To thit harves eyes and a pre tty hand.
These grey hairs are by chance, you see;
Pow are sometimes over, I am told;
Br w cares to w e a smile for me,
Just so I thought I was getting old.

— *Walter Learned, in the "Century."*

A CONGO MASHER.

ABOVE the shoulder both of the A...

HE WOULDN'T SUBSCRIBE.

THE SMALL BOY WAS FOND OF MUSIC AND HE GOT THE TICKETS.

WHY SHE MARRIED HIM.

DELINDA : "How can I excite misery that old fool Clondil ?"...

WELL REPRESENTED.

YOUNG Man (up p ng for situation) : "I h had considerable experience as a commerc...

THE Weekly Telegraph.

APRIL 27, 1889.

A NON-POLITICAL, AMUSING, AND INSTRUCTIVE WEEKLY HOUSEHOLD JOURNAL.

BRAZILIAN authorities know what they are about...

✂ CUT THE PAPER AT THE TOP AND PLACE THE SECOND INSIDE THE FIRST HALF ✂

15 London *Weekly Telegraph*, 23 June 1900, front paper cover.

2. *Paternoster Square*,

LONDON, E.C.

Memorandum of Agreement made this eleventh day of February 1889 between the Proprietor of "The New York World" of New York of the one part, and Alexander Pollock Watt of 2 Paternoster Square in the city of London of the other part.

1. The "New York World" agrees to buy the exclusive serial use for *North America* in a new story to be written by Wilkie Collins , on the following terms.

    1. The said story to commence publication in England in the first Satur--day in July of this year.

    2. That the said story shall run for 26 weeks - consecutively- publishing each week an instalment of not less than 4000 words .

    3. That the "New York World" shall have the privilige of publishing the first 12 instalments of the story one week in advance of its publica--tion in "The Illustrated London News" , in this country, and three weeks in advance of the reprint of the story in the American edition of the "Il--lustrated London News" published in America. After the publication of the 12th instalment "The New York World " to divide the next five weekly instalments as published in "The Illustrated London d News" into six parts , and thereafter to continue publishing simultaneously with the "News"

    4. Duplicate proofs to be delivered to "The New York World" at their New York office 6 days in advance of the date of publication as arranged.

    5. If the publication of any instalment in "The New York World" be for --stalled/without fault on the part of the purchaser of this story)by publication in any other paper in the United States , then the agreement regarding this story to be at an end ; and if at such time part payment shall have been made , then that payment shall be returned .

    6. Subject to the above "The New york World" agrees to pay to the said A.P. Watt the sum of £150 on the receipt by them of the thirteenth instalment of the said story ;and a further £150 on the receipt of the final instal--ment of the said story .

    7. A.P.Watt guarantees that no new story by Wilkie Collins shall be pub--lished in newspapers before June 30th of this year ; also that the said

or Canada apr

story shall not appear in authorized book form in the United States before its publication shall have been completed in the " New York World ".

16 New York World agreement with A. P. Watt, 11 February 1889.

frequent, could reflect local readers' interests more closely, and were less subject to inflation. The four prizes for Christmas tales in the Cardiff *Weekly Mail* in 1870 included one for a story in Welsh; in 1887 the '*Weekly Mercury* Prize Tale Competition' was won by local readers in Plymouth and Bristol; and for the 1904 Christmas number the *Nottinghamshire Guardian* offered three prizes for original stories 'of which the scene is laid within and by writers resident within Nottinghamshire, Derbyshire, Lincolnshire, or Leicestershire' (10 September). The first prizes of two guineas put up by the *Mercury* and the three pounds by the *Guardian* were on a par with the 50s offered by the *People's Journal* back in June 1858. The first prize in a competition held in early 1881 in the Saturday evening edition of the *Staffordshire Sentinel*, edited by local socialist William Moody, was given to 'Won by Peril', 'A North Staffs Story of the Working Class' by 'Ouvrier' (from 9 February), indicating that prize-winning entries could sometimes reflect the ideology of the paper itself.

The political affiliation or orientation of British newspapers, whether national or provincial, was then public knowledge, and the annual press directories provided such information on the listed journals for the information of potential advertisers. As has been shown by Alan J. Lee (ch. 5) and Lucy Brown (ch. 3), the large majority of the new newspapers founded on or soon after the repeal of the taxes on knowledge were Liberal in outlook, whereas there was something of a resurgence of the popular Tory press in the last two decades of the century. Lee has summarized succinctly the general political trends:

> It seems clear that in numerical terms the decline of Liberal press representation between the 1860s and the 1900s was slight. The clear Liberal domination of the 1860s and 1870s had been due largely to the lack of a Conservative press, and the development of this in the 1880s and after served to obscure somewhat the fact that the Liberal press shared about equally in the general expansion of those years.
>
> (Lee, 133)

As was suggested in Chapter 2 in relation to the situation in Sheffield, as the nineteenth century progressed, competition between newspapers often tended to become as much a matter of economic as of political interest, but in the 1870s and 1880s there were still a number of lively battles between, especially, rival Tory and radical organs, which sometimes spilled over into the fiction pages. In the metropolitan Sunday press, soon after the new Tory weekly *The People* began to attract a growing working-class readership through its publication of original popular fiction, the older radical Sundays responded by including serials of their own, this time overtly political. From 1885, *The Weekly Dispatch* began a sequence of 'radical serials', beginning with John T. Day's *Under the Hoof*, followed by *Something Wrong* from 'Fabian Bland' (Edith Nesbit), while the following year *Reynolds's Weekly* began its 'Stories for the People' including the unsigned stories *The Book of Erin* (actually by John Morrison Davidson) and 'Orange and Green' (decidedly not the work of the same title by G.A. Henty), though both had moved towards a blander menu of adventure, mystery, and romance by the following decade. An interesting example in the provinces emerged from the long-standing battle in Newcastle-on-Tyne between the Tory *Courant* and the *Chronicle*, owned by the radical M.P. Joseph Cowen, and one of the members of Tillotsons's first syndicate. This was reflected in the correspondence between Mayne Reid and W.E. Adams, the Republican editor of the *Newcastle Weekly Chronicle*, when, as noted in Chapter 4, Reid was attempting to syndicate his own fiction in provincial papers in the 1870s. In 1879 Reid attracted Adams's interest with a story of the English Civil War entitled *No Quarter!*, which would be 'very *radical* in tone, taking the Cromwellian side, and bitterly hostile to Toryism' (29 September Pollard, 'Novels', 80). He had, however, to explain carefully why he had also sold two of his novels to the rival *Courant*: 'but for the *res angustae domi* [sic] – the sheer gaining of bread – [I] would not write for a Tory paper at all.' (7 October, Pollard, 'Novels', 82). When *No Quarter!* began to appear in the *Weekly Chronicle*, it duly featured a savage diatribe against Disraeli and his Government as its Prologue.

Some provincial weeklies also had declared religious affiliations. In 1864 two devotional serials 'written expressly for the *Glasgow Free Press*' by one Shandy McSherry appeared in that staunchly Catholic journal, while, as previously noted, from at least 1890 the Catholic Press Company of Great Britain and Ireland provided appropriate syndicated fiction for papers serving Catholic communities. These included the *Wigan Catholic Herald* which carried two serial stories simultaneously in 1895; at the same time the paper offered a salary of 30s a week to any reader capable of writing circulation-boosting stories with a Romanist slant. There were obviously more and larger city journals whose proprietors had strong Nonconformist sympathies. These included P.S. Macliver, the radical Scots Congregationalist owner of the *Western Daily Press* and its weekly counterpart the *Bristol Observer*, or T. Wemyss Reid, Gladstonian editor of the *Leeds Mercury* and *Weekly Mercury* from 1870–87. In both cases these autonomous weekly journals carried serial fiction, but the two dailies carried the stamp of their owners' religious and political convictions much more explicitly, and the sequences of stories they ran give only indirect hints of this ideology. Tory proprietors staunchly supporting the Established Church, like Thomas Forman in his *Nottinghamshire Guardian* or Robert Redpath of the *Newcastle Courant*, were even less inclined to insist on doctrinal purity in their serials and seemed to have no objection to carrying works by such anti-establishment figures as Mayne Reid, Thomas Hardy or Wilkie Collins.

As the cases of Hardy and Collins might remind us, issues of religion and sexuality were often complexly intertwined in later Victorian literature. The question of dominant later Victorian assumptions concerning gender will be discussed at greater length in the following chapters in relation to the themes of authorship and genre. Here we may simply note the gradual solidification of the concept of the female newspaper reader in the second half of the nineteenth century. Just after the mid-century Victorian newspapers seem still to be largely addressed to a male audience, both in their advertising and editorial material. In the weekly news-miscellanies becoming common by the 1870s, there is a growing recognition of female readers, but often as belonging a separate sphere, meriting specific women's pages and features. As had occurred 30 years earlier with the proletarian weekly miscellanies like *The Family Herald*, during the 1890s the new mass-market magazine weeklies, notably the *People's Friend*, *Weekly Telegraph*, and *Tit-Bits*, gradually come to see the woman reader as their dominant target.

From the advertising agent's viewpoint, in the absence of reliable circulation figures, the information concerning political affiliation in the press directories must often have functioned as coded information about the social class, and thus the economic potential, of the readership of a given journal. Until at least the 1860s, and especially in English newspaper circles, the attitude was prevalent that weekly serials were intrinsically base, melodramatic, and thus suitable only for the lower classes; Alexander Sinclair's comments cited above refer to this perception. It is interesting then to see the same assumption emerge in a more complex form, after novels in newspapers had become commonplace by the late 1870s, in the discrimination between different qualities of serial fiction aimed at different classes of readers. The following letter from the editor of the *Western Daily Mercury* (owned by the Plymouth Liberal Isaac Latimer, another member of Tillotsons's first syndicate), in reply to the offer of a serial in 1883, encapsulates this mode of thought:

> I am much obliged for your offer of a story by Wilkie Collins. It may seem a little strange to say so but for our purposes his stories are too high class. When our Saturday was a combination of daily & weekly we had, of course, before all else to satisfy our educated readers as their patronage brought advertisements, but since we have divided the old Saturday paper into two distinct papers, a daily and a weekly, the latter now appeals almost solely to the working classes. For those we find a different, & from an artistic point of view, <u>far inferior tale the more telling,</u> & as furthermore the inferior tale is much the cheaper it would be folly to waste the extra money.
>
> (ALS to A.P. Watt, 12 Oct. 1883, Collins Acc., BERG)

Thus it is clear that the conversion of the supplement to the Saturday edition of the *Daily Mercury* into the supplementary weekly, the *Weekly Mercury*, which took place in 1879, entailed a redefinition of its readership, of its value as an advertising medium, and finally of the novels it published.[13] The question of assumptions concerning class will once again be discussed at greater length later in relation to themes of authorship and genre.

The comments above do little more than suggest possibilities for areas of analysis. We must acknowledge that much detailed work yet remains to be done, of the type that Donaldson has carried out in the case of Scotland, to chart the role of the miscellaneous news weeklies south of the border in shaping popular culture and democracy in specific communities in Wales and the English provinces in the second half of the nineteenth century.[14] Let us then turn our attention in a more sustained way to the nature of the journals published by Tillotsons and W.C. Leng and Co. themselves, to the types of syndicate that they tended to set up, and by extension, to the ways they came to conceive of and to construct their reading publics.

5.3   Atomization: Tillotsons and W.C. Leng and Co.

The main contrasts which emerge between the concepts of the reading public fostered respectively by the Tillotson and Leng operations can be summed up in the terms integration and segregation. These apply equally to the content and style of their publications, their ideological orientation, and their chosen markets. (Many of the points which I wish to make are illustrated both in Tables 5.2 and 5.3, analysing general contents – using the model established by Raymond Williams and admirably deployed in the study of Victorian newspapers by Virginia Berridge ('Popular' and 'Content') – and also by Plates 11–15, showing pages from the different types of fiction-carrying weeklies.)

Firstly, Tillotsons's own Lancashire Journals, and probably also the bulk of the papers which belonged regularly to their coteries, were local autonomous weeklies.[15] The proportion of their columns devoted to the coverage of local and national news was significantly larger than that given to entertainment, as Table 5.2 shows, and there was generally little stylistic distinction between the presentation of fiction and news material, which tended also to be in continuous prose. Although a portion of the local and general news offered concerned crime and scandal and was fragmentary and anecdotal, there was usually in-depth coverage of major European political events, the week in Parliament, and national developments with local implications, most doubtless taken from one of the London press agencies, as well as internally produced copy offering an extensive discussion of local issues. In their leaders, editors addressed their readers with gravity. In 1888 for example, the Tory *Nottinghamshire Guardian* of 30 June devoted a column to a measured discussion of the treatment of denominational schools in the report of the Education Commission, which had just been leaked, while the Liberal *Leigh Journal and Times* of 27 April came out strongly in support of Gladstone's Irish Home Rule Bill at similar length, in addition to pithier comments on local disputes, such as the politicization of a local Parish Board election, or the lack of action to create a municipal recreation ground. Correspondence from readers generally maintained a similar tone. In the *Leigh Journal* of 17 February of that year there were three letters, together occupying a column and a half, on Sabbath Observance, Irish Home Rule, and the problems of London Traffic, while the *Bolton Weekly Journal* of 27 July 1889, had six letters occupying two and a half columns, three on

Table 5.2 Contents analysis of provincial weeklies in newspaper format

	Autonomous weeklies				Supplementary weeklies			
	Leigh Journal & Times 27 Apr. + 26 Oct. 1888*		Nottinghamshire Guardian 23 Jun. + 1 Dec. 1888*		Sheffield Weekly Telegraph 3 Apr. + 12 Oct. 1886*		Sheffield Weekly Independent 7 Jan. + 7 Jul. 1888*	
	Cols.†	% of total	Cols.†	% of total	Cols.†	% of total	Cols.†	% of total
Fiction	7+6	10.2	8+3	8.6	10+8.5	14.5	9+14	20.5
Features	4+4	6.3	13.5+17	23.8	20+23.5	34.0	27.5+21	43.3
Entertainment	**11+10**	**16.4**	**21.5+20**	**32.4**	**30+32**	**48.4**	**36.5+35**	**63.8**
Crime/Gossip	5+5	7.8	1.5+3	3.5	3+4	5.5	2+3	4.5
Leaders/Letters to Editor	3+1.5	3.5	1+1	1.6	0+0	0	0+0	0
Local News	14+19	25.8	7+8	11.7	12+11	18.0	11+10	18.8
National/International News	13+10.5	18.4	15+15	23.4	7+6.5	10.5	3+4	6.3
News	**35+36**	**55.5**	**24.5+27**	**40.2**	**22+21.5**	**34.0**	**16+17**	**29.5**
Advertisements	**18+18**	**28.1**	**18+17**	**27.3**	**12+10.5**	**17.6**	**3.5+4**	**6.7**
Total‡	64+64	100	64+64	100	64+64	100	56+56	100

* Two issues of each journal were analysed, both from the same year and separated by around six months, but avoiding abnormal patterns of editorial/advertising material around the summer/winter holidays.
† Column sizes vary from journal to journal
‡ Percentage figures may not add up to 100 due to rounding.
Source: Original journals.

Table 5.3 Contents analysis of provincial weeklies in magazine format

| | (Dundee) *People's Friend* 22 Apr. + 21 Oct. 1889* | | (Sheffield) *Weekly Telegraph** 11 Jan. + 12 Jul. 1890* | |
	Cols.†	% of total	Cols.†	% of total
Serials	19+15	28.3	17+15.5	20.3
Complete Stories	8+10	15.0	3+4	4.4
Fiction	27+25	43.3	20+19.5	24.7
Verse	1+2	2.5	1+2	1.9
Special features	10+10	16.7	22+25.5	29.7
Regular features	10+11	17.5	27+24	31.8
Advertisements	12+12	20.0	10+9	11.9
Total‡	60**+60**	100	80+80	100

* Two issues of each journal were analysed, both from the same year and separated by around six months, but avoiding abnormal patterns of editorial/advertising material around the summer/winter holidays.
† Column sizes vary from journal to journal.
‡ Percentage figures may not add up to 100 due to rounding.
** Includes four-page coloured-paper cover devoted entirely to advertisements.
Source: Original journals.

'Butter and the Irish Question', one on a local lecture series, and two involving a heated exchange concerning an incident at the Bolton Cricket Club. Typically, until around the turn of the century, these autonomous local weeklies were austere in appearance, with the front page devoted entirely to advertising. Much of this was classified announcements, while the display adverts still tended to rely for their visual impact on the imaginative use of typography, rather than illustration. Even when the then *Bolton Journal and Guardian* added a four-page Supplement in the late 1890s, which was mainly given over to entertainment, including a good deal of illustration and anecdote, at least one of the serial stories continued to appear in the main part of the paper.

W.C. Leng and Co. took over the *Sheffield Daily Telegraph* in 1864, and the paper almost immediately began to carry fiction in a supplement to its Saturday edition. This Saturday supplement, in which the space devoted to news was considerably less than that given to features and entertainment, later evolved into a weekly illustrated magazine with no news at all and which showed a marked tendency to follow the fragmentary content and presentation of George Newnes's *Tit-Bits* (Table 5.3; Plate 14). Although there was an occasional article of historical or practical interest in the *Weekly Telegraph*, the content was largely a miscellany of sentimental, comic, or scandalous anecdotes, often in the form of scraps from other journals, and prize quizzes and competitions for both younger and older readers. Those in the 'Children's Corner', conducted by 'Captain Trim of the Kind-Hearted Brigade', which youthful readers were encouraged to join, included picture puzzles and prize essays ('On Cricket' or 'How I Spent the Christmas Holidays'). In addition to a column of word puzzles, adult readers were offered prize competitions giving opportunities to write both verse ('Our Parody', 'Our Valentine') and prose (short Christmas tales, or anecdotes on 'How I Spend my Wages' or 'Deeds of Pluck and Heroism'). There was also the 'Mutual Aid Column' where readers requested and offered factual information and household tips, though in addition there was a short section of general correspondence addressed to the editor. In the issue of 11 January 1890, for example, this consisted of four letters occupying less than a column, respectively concerning a reader's parody of Browning, the format of the *Weekly Telegraph* itself, a problem of prominent ears, and the value of sulphur, of all things, as a hair tonic. Together these features produced large quantities of copy from readers themselves: again in the 11 January issue, for example, this amounted to fully 20 per cent of the total content. Already by 1890, apart from the serial fiction, very few artices entered a second column: typical in the same issue were the 'Ladies Corner', with 14 discrete items in two-and-a-half columns, or the single column devoted to 'Science, Art, and Literature', and comprising seven 'tit-bits'. In short, W.C. Leng and Co. tended to segregate news from entertainment material and atomize both, whereas Tillotsons usually encouraged integration and continuity.

Secondly, the Tillotsons were Nonconformist Liberals, and this ideological orientation can be seen immediately in their newspapers' coverage of political and religious issues, at both the local and national level. As Johanningsmeier has suggested (134), they were not averse to the use of fiction as a vehicle of social criticism and reform. In the early days of the Lancashire Journals there were a number of works by local authors touching on social conditions experienced by agricultural or mill workers in the north of England, such as J. Bradbury's 'Grace Barton', Jessie Fothergill's prize-winning *The Lasses of Leverhouse*, or Isabella Banks's 'Under the Scars'. In the 1880s there were advertisements promoting novels 'with a purpose': one praised the political novel because of its 'vitality and strength which lift it above the merely sensational competitors' (*Bolton Weekly Journal*, 27 May 1882, 2). In the 1890s, of course, J. Monk Foster's mining stories appeared regularly in the Tillotsons's papers (see Plate 11). Like the majority of provincial journals at the time, most of the members of Tillotsons's early coteries seem to have been Liberal in leaning, although the *Sheffield Telegraph, Cardiff Weekly Times*, and *Nottinghamshire Guardian* were notable exceptions. When Leaders in Sheffield took over the syndicate for Braddon's *One Thing Needful* in 1886, W.F. Tillotson asked John Maxwell to assure the author that the 'chief subscribing paper, and most others, are liberal nay radical.'[16] At the beginning of 1890, when the *Sheffield Weekly Independent* itself began to serialize Rosa Mulholland's stirring tale 'Giannetta: A Story of the Irish Eviction' (published the previous year by Blackies as *Giannetta: a Girl's Story of Herself*), blazoned prominently on the front page was the invitation 'Be sure to read "Giannetta" the book the Tories fear' (11 January). Although N.N. Feltes (*Modes*, ch. 4) has implied that Tillotsons were motivated by Grundyism in refusing to publish *Tess of the D'Urbervilles* as submitted, the evidence suggests that the Fiction Bureau acted with some candour in the case (see Chapter 7). The Bolton firm's willingness to deal regularly with the likes of Thomas Hardy, Wilkie Collins, and Ouida rather argues that, by the standards of the time, W.F. Tillotson and his successors were relatively unpuritanical and flexible concerning social and sexual *mores*.

The Lengs in Sheffield, on the other hand, were supporters of the Tory establishment, and though their daily was eminently political, they moved quickly to create a declaredly apolitical entertainment weekly, which appealed to the pocket rather than to the civic-mindedness of the reader.[17] Around the turn of the century there was a series of prize coupon schemes designed to boost readership, such as the 'Charity Coupon Competition' of 1896–97, or the 'New Readers' Competition' of 1902.[18] Beside the 'Weekly Telegraph Fiction Library', there were other long-running spin-offs from the journal, including the 'W.T. Dolls' (cardboard cutouts), 'W.T. Portrait Enlargements', and the annual 'W.T. Guide to Holiday Resorts', all of which were promoted as offering value for money and helped to place the magazine as an organ of entertainment rather than of information. It is thus not surprising that the *Weekly Telegraph* encouraged a view of fiction as fantasy and escape, typified by the role of E. Phillips Oppenheim as leading story writer. C.D. Leng's 'Editor's Syndicate' selections for 1888 and 1889 seem to rely especially heavily on detective stories, spy thrillers and military romances, and there were no novelists of local colour comparable to J. Monk Foster at Tillotsons. Although, in the mid-1880s, the *Sheffield Weekly Telegraph* had taken the risk of publishing Zola and Ouida, from 1887, under its new guise as a 'Household' magazine, it carefully avoided accusations of impropriety in its fiction. An advertisement for the Editor's Syndicate proclaimed in large bold capitals that 'None but suitable stories are selected' (*NPD*, 1890, 156). On the occasion of the journal's Diamond Jubilee in 1922, two long-standing contributors specifically commended its dedication to 'clean amusement' (*Sheffield Daily Telegraph 1855–1925*, 31–2). Braddon herself, of course, was a far less dangerous presence in 1888 than she had been in 1873, when she was still 'living in sin' with John Maxwell, and still best known as the creator of those socially and sexually transgressive heroines, Lady Audley and Aurora Floyd. In short, W.C. Leng and Co. increasingly treated fiction as an imaginary sphere divorced from social issues, whereas Tillotsons consistently attempted to unite the two.

Finally, Tillotsons's aimed with their Lancashire Journal Series to meet the interests of a number of discrete and specific local audiences, and, through the flexible way the Fiction Bureau operated, encouraged other provincial proprietors to do the same. Members of the Tillotsons's coteries could encourage the illusion among local readers that they alone had access to the new work of such household names as Braddon and Collins.[19] Profits were made by the Fiction Bureau from the multiplication of such coherent local markets. Civic pride and local identity remained important values, as the columns of readers' correspondence indicate. Interestingly, after the creation of the *Bolton Journal and Guardian Supplement*, the stories which still appeared in the main part of the paper were often by a local writer with a local setting, most notably those by J. Monk Foster, such as 'The Watchman of Orsden Moss' (1897). The range of both editorial and advertising material in newspapers such as the *Leigh Journal and Times* or the *Nottinghamshire Guardian*, also makes it apparent that they were aimed at a wide social audience, centring on the solid middle classes as much as more skilled and literate working-class readers, and appealing fairly equally to women and men. There is coverage of local rugby and cricket fixtures as well as the activities of local political and religious groups. Alongside the serial fiction are chess and draughts problems as well as 'The Children's Hour', 'Our Ladies' Column', and 'Fashions for this Month'. Similarly many of the extensive columns of classified advertisements in these journals are listed under such commercial headings as 'Sales by Auction', 'Business Announcements', and 'Saleshops To Be Let', while the displays are as likely to be for local banks, tailors, or merchants as for foodstuffs, household goods, and medicines. Noticeably sparse are slots devoted to mass-produced and nationally-available consumer goods such as Pear's Soap or Beecham's Pills.

In contrast, despite W.C. Leng's active involvement in civic life, the *Weekly Telegraph* moved rapidly to sever its Sheffield roots. From the beginning there were far fewer local stories than in Tillotsons's Lancashire Journals or John Leng's *People's Friend* (where well over half the stories were Scottish in setting and origin), and Eric St C.K. Ross's 'Frankie Farrall's Flute: The Story of a Sheffield Cutler's Boy' and 'Sons of Sheffield; or, Scarlet and Steel' (both 1881) were probably the last local stories carried in the *Telegraph*. By the 1890s Crown and Empire had became more prevalent themes. The limited range of novels offered by the Editor's Syndicate gave little choice to subscribing papers, and the national circulation of the flagship journal spoilt any local claims to exclusivity. By the 1890s, not only do the contributions from readers in the *Weekly Telegraph* show that it was achieving its goal of a nationwide audience, but also the advertising material suggests strongly that that audience was in the main to be found among women of the lower-middle and working classes. Contributors' offerings provide substantial numbers of readers' addresses. Already by 1890 they thickly cover the whole of the Midlands and the North of England, with more scattered occurrences in London and the Home Counties. By 1900, England and Wales are covered more evenly, and there are even occasionally missives from Ireland and India, though Scotland tends not to show – perhaps there was an understanding not to encroach on the territory of John Leng's *People's Friend*. And so, inevitably, there is no need for columns of classified and local advertisements. The most prominent and well-illustrated display advertisements are for nationally available brands of household products such as soap, metal polish, or cocoa, as the reproduction of the front cover of the issue of 23 June 1900 illustrates (Plate 15). Significantly, the cover for the new format employed from 1897 onwards prominently featured a picture of a woman reading a magazine. In thus targeting a market spread nationwide but limited in terms of both class and gender, C.D. Leng was again emulating *Tit-Bits* and its metropolitan rivals. Increased subscriber participation in such journals was inevitably devalued by the absence of any topic worthy of serious debate, and by the loss of the sense of a common local identity among their readership. In short, Tillotsons attempted to broaden the social range of existing communities of readers, whereas Lengs sought to embrace a distinctly modern atomized mass consumer audience.

Obviously the two fiction syndication operations described above did have a number of things in common. Both W.F. Tillotson and W.C. Leng were northern bourgeois heroes, full of civic pride, and ignorant of the decline of the industrial spirit; both relied fundamentally on a similar recipe for their syndicated fiction – strong 'cliff-hanger' narratives, driven by enigma and suspense to meet the demands of weekly serialization; both took full advantage of the rapid changes in taxation, technology, and education in the second half of the nineteenth century which led to such an exponential growth throughout the newspaper industry, and especially in the provincial press; both were aware of the economic implications for the publishing industry of the global spread of English, the language of Empire. And yet, while all this is true, there were also stark differences between the way Tillotsons and W.C. Leng and Co. ran their syndication businesses, which emerged most fully when the family firms were taken over by the next generation in the late 1880s, and which had significant implications for the development of journalistic and literary culture in the twentieth century. Above all these differences are questions of the socio-economic and cultural constitution of the readership they attempted to target and helped to construct. It is important here to emphasize that the contrast between the Tillotsons and W.C. Leng and Co. operations is not in any significant sense one of old against new, of reaction against progress. In technological and commercial terms Tillotsons were at least as innovative and forward-looking as their competitors. Both represent different aspects of the complex interaction (both contribution and response) of the provincial press with the emergence of New Journalism in the metropolis in the 1880s, as discussed in Chapter 1. In other words, Tillotsons's vision of the reading public did indeed represent a possible course for the future, though one that in the event was not followed by most cultural producers. But given the great gulf which by the early twentieth century had become fixed between 'serious' and 'popular' newspapers, between 'literary' and 'pulp' fiction, above all, between an 'elite' and a 'mass' audience, it is difficult not to feel regret that the Sheffield rather than the Bolton projection of the modern reading public proved triumphant. Lucy Brown (102) makes the point powerfully, when she suggests that, though press histories conventionally assume that proprietors such as Newnes and Harmsworth 'brought newspapers to the masses', the evidence is rather that journals such as *Tit-Bits*, *Answers*, or indeed the *Weekly Telegraph*, worked to create 'a cultural division which had not existed before.'

6
Authorship

In the final chapter, among other issues relating to fictional genre, I will consider the forms of composition encouraged by publication in weekly newspapers, and the degree of explicit control of content exercised by syndicators and editors. Here the concern is more with writing as property than as production, with authorship considered as an occupation rather than an act. The increasing professionalization of the role of the later Victorian novelist has recently been discussed both in relation to specific authors – notably, Michael Anesko on Henry James or Simon Eliot on Walter Besant – and in more general terms by scholars such as Peter Keating in *The Haunted Study* (1989) and Norman Feltes in *Literary Capital and the Late Victorian Novel* (1993). Here the intention is to consider specifically the function of the newspaper market, which has thus far received little emphasis, as a catalyst for change in that process. First, in 'Making a Living' I shall outline the way in which two modes of connection with newspapers, regular employment as journalists and the occasional contribution of short or serial stories, help to explain the increase in the number of professional writers suggested by the statistical record. Then, in 'Agreements and Agents' we will look at how the practice of syndication, in particular, encouraged an increasing complexity in the contracts drawn up between authors and publishers, and increasing intervention by new types of 'middlemen'. In both these sections, accumulations of examples and brief case histories will occupy an important place in the argument. In the final section under the heading 'Professionalization', however, we will look in more extended fashion at the impact of newspaper serialization on the careers of two novelists, Collins and Braddon. In both cases, extensive reference

To what extent these trends affected the activity of the novelist in particular is not easy to quantify, though it is known that the number of novels appearing in volume form increased markedly in the last decades of the century. Indeed, this was the principal reason given by the circulating libraries for bringing down the curtain on the triple-decker (Griest, chs 7–8). At the end of each year the *Publishers' Circular* included tables showing publishing trends, and these indicated that the number of new novel titles published annually increased from 516 in 1874 to 1315 in 1894, the growth coming almost entirely in the latter half of the period. However, these figures explicitly excluded fiction aimed at the rapidly expanding juvenile market, and almost certainly underreported publications both in the cheapest sector of the market and outside London (Keating, 32–3). The increasing importance to fiction writers specifically of serial publication and the provincial press, however, is suggested by:

- the growth in the numbers of 'novelist-journalists';
- evidence concerning the remuneration obtained from serial publication, particularly in relation to that from volume publication; and
- the strength of the demand for fiction with local and provincial settings.

The final point has already been touched on in the first part of this volume and will be returned to in the following chapter, while the first two will be illustrated in some detail here.

On the basis that they contributed material of some form at some point to periodicals, probably all Victorian novelists could be classed in the broadest sense as 'journalists.' The numbers of those who were so in the sense intended by Leigh Hunt when he welcomed the 'congratulations of friends and brother-journalists' in *The Examiner* (31 August 1812, 1), that is, those regularly involved in the writing and editing of periodicals, was still substantial as Colby has shown ('Goose'). The number was much smaller of those who were involved in journalism in the sense intended by a reviewer of the French work *Du Journalisme* in the *Westminster Review* (January 1833, 195–6) – '"Journalism" is a good name for the thing meant.... A word was sadly wanted' – that is, the regular work of writing and editing newspapers. However, that number increased significantly in the later Victorian decades, thus probably facilitating both the growth of the newspaper novel and the ability of a wider range of novelists to make a living. By the beginning of the new century,

Arnold Bennett could write, with the third sense in mind, that 'very many, if not most, authors begin by being journalists' (Bennett, *How*, 14).

In the earlier decades of the nineteenth century, as was implied in Chapter 1, it is easy to find examples of major novelists editing literary magazines, whether Bulwer-Lytton and Hook (both *New Monthly*), Marryat (*Metropolitan*), Dickens (*Bentley's Miscellany*), Lever (*The Dublin University Magazine*), or Ainsworth (*Bentley's Miscellany, Ainsworth's*, and *The New Monthly*). More minor novelists editing less literary journals might include R.S. Surtees at the *New Sporting* (1831–36), or Frank Smedley with the short-lived *George Cruikshank's Magazine* (1854), while many of the most popular authors in the 'penny blood' market went on to run penny miscellanies, including G.W.M. Reynolds, J.F. Smith, and Pierce Egan, Jr, who all in turn edited *The London Journal*. Thackeray and Dickens are certainly the most illustrious among the few examples of earlier Victorian novelists who edited newspapers, though both did so for only a brief period. In the 1830s, before acting as Paris correspondent for the *Tory Constitutional* (1836–37) and contributing regularly to the *Morning Chronicle* (1769–1865) and *The Times*, Thackeray had financed and edited a new weekly paper, the *National Standard* (1833), which soon failed. Even more famously, after working as reporter for the *Morning Chronicle* and other papers in the early 1830s, Dickens was prominent in the foundation of the radical *Daily News* in 1846, though he handed over the role of editor to John Forster after only 17 issues. For a more consolidated career, one would have to turn to a distinctly minor novelist like Douglas Jerrold, who, after the failure of his own weekly paper in 1847, edited *Lloyd's Weekly Newspaper* from 1852 until his death in 1857.

In the later decades of the nineteenth century, as the number of weekly and monthly literary miscellanies increases markedly, examples of novelist–editors naturally proliferate. A far from exhaustive list would include: Dickens (*Household Words, All the Year Round*), James Payn (*Chambers's Journal, Cornhill*), Anna Maria Hall (*Sharpe's London Magazine, St. James's*), Thackeray (*Cornhill*), Le Fanu (*Dublin University Magazine*), Trollope (*St. Paul's*), Mary Braddon (*Belgravia*), Ellen Wood (*The Argosy*), Charlotte Riddell (again *St. James's*), Florence Marryat (*London Society*), James Rice (*Once a Week*), L.T. Meade (*Atalanta*) and Jerome K. Jerome (*The Idler*). Other distinguished novelists edited 'class' monthlies aimed at more specific audiences and where serial fiction was less prominent or entirely absent. Notable examples would include: Charlotte M. Yonge and the *Monthly Packet* (For Younger Members of the English Church), 1851–90, Oscar Wilde at the *Woman's World*, 1887–89, and Walter Besant with *The Author*, 1890–1901. Still other major fiction writers, while not formally taking the title of editor, made significant and prolonged contributions to the operation of a range of periodicals. These would include: Wilkie Collins working as staff writer on Dickens's weeklies in the 1850s and early 1860s, George Meredith assisting John Morley at the *The Fortnightly Review* in the later 1860s and 1870s, and Andrew Lang acting as literary adviser to *Longman's* in the 1880s.

Further, the later Victorian years reveal a marked increase in the number of practicing novelists who also played an active role in newspaper production, thus helping to strengthen what Altick calls the 'developing affinity between fiction and journalism' (*Presence*, 78). Interesting examples from the metropolitan newspaper world include Blanchard Jerrold, George Sala, and Edmund Yates, all three among the young bohemians who gathered around Dickens in the 1850s (Edwards, 1–3; Cross 93–117). Jerrold took over his father's job as editor of *Lloyd's Weekly* from 1857 until his own death in 1884, but, among a variety of literary activities, also published a handful of novels from around 1860. These included *Black-Eyed Susan's Boys*, a reworking of his father's famous stage melodrama, which was sold to Tillotsons in 1875 and proved one of their most perennially popular serials. In the 1850s both Sala and Yates wrote extensively for Henry Vizetelly's *Illustrated Times* (1855–72) and for John Maxwell's journals. As Joel Wiener has suggested ('How', 62–5), both played an important role in the early development of what came to be known as the New Journalism. Together they founded the shilling comic monthly *The Train* in 1856 and, after it folded in 1858, moved on to Maxwell's *Temple Bar*. Sala wrote a series of meandering novels from the late 1850s, *The Baddington Peerage* in the *Illustrated Times* (1857) being the first and weakest and *The Seven Sons of Mammon* in *Temple Bar* (1861) the most popular. However, the florid articles that he began to contribute regularly to the *Daily Telegraph* at around the same time seem to have absorbed much more of his energy and concentration. He continued this popular role until the mid-1880s, went on a number of highly publicized overseas jaunts as special correspondent, and claims regularly to have earned around £2000 a year from his work as a journalist (Sala, 2:309). Yates also published a series of fast and fashionable novels from the mid-1860s, of which *Broken to Harness* in *Temple*

Bar (1864) was the first and most popular (Yates, 2:84–8). However, his fame and fortune were more largely due to his early reputation as London's most witty gossip columnist, gained on the *Illustrated Times* and Maxwell's *Town Talk* (1858–59) (Wiener 'Edmund'). He put this to greatest effect from 1874, following his retirement after a 25-year career in the Post Office, in his own Society journal *The World* which still seems to have been making a profit of around £4000 a year when Yates died in 1894 (Edwards, 194). Both Sala and Yates were very much London lights, and neither seems to have published to any great extent in the provincial journals.[1] In fact neither wrote much fiction after the mid-1870s and thus, like Jerrold, both are perhaps better classified as 'journalist–novelists', that is, members of the editorial staff who occasionally turned their hand to novel writing for the benefit of their own journals.[2] (In Chapter 2, we have already noted a number of examples of minor provincial journalist–novelists, such as R.E. Leader at the *Sheffield Independent* in the 1860s, or, a few years later, William Freeland and T.G. Smith, both on the staff of the *Glasgow Weekly Herald*.)

A number of prominent newspaper novelists had also had experience of newspaper work overseas. B.L. Farjeon (1838–1903), who from the 1870s sold half a dozen novels to Tillotsons and at least one to W.C. Leng and Co. had escaped to the Antipodes while still in his teens. In New Zealand he had acted as assistant editor of the *Otago Daily Times*, the first daily journal in the Colony, and made his debut as a novelist in the pages of the weekly *Otago Witness*. Captain Mayne Reid (1818–83), who we have noted as a successful self-syndicator in the 1870s, among many other travels and adventures had worked as a journalist in the USA in both the early 1840s and late 1860s. J.E Muddock (?–1934), another adventurer and self-syndicator, acted as Swiss correspondent of the *Daily News* during the 1870s, in addition to a series of other journalistic appointments including those on James Henderson's *Weekly Budget* and Charles Alexander's *Weekly News* in Dundee. The Lancastrian William Westall (1834–1903), eight of whose novels I have been able to trace in the provincial weeklies beginning with *The Old Factory* in 1880, had previously edited the *Swiss Times* in Geneva, as well as acting as foreign correspondent of *The Times* and *Daily News*.

But for our purposes the most interesting group of novelist–journalists is the significant number who published fiction regularly in the provincial journals and through the provincial syndicates after they had established themselves in the metropolitan literary world, but who gained their first experience as professional writers in the world of provincial journalism. Here William Black, Joseph Hatton, and David Christie Murray represent important cases.[3] William Black (1841–98) was born and brought up in Glasgow and worked for the *Glasgow Citizen* until the mid-1860s, when he came to London and established a journalistic and literary career. He worked in turn on the staff of the *Morning Star* (1856–69), *The Examiner* (1808–81), and the evening *Echo* (1868–1905), and became sub-editor of the *Daily News*, also acting on occasion as foreign corespondent. His first novel *James Merle* appeared in 1864, but it was not until the popular success of *A Daughter of Heth* (1871) and *A Princess of Thule* (1874) that he retired from active journalism and wrote fiction full-time. Like *A Daughter of Heth* many of his novels dramatize the clash between provincial and metropolitan culture and first appeared in newspapers outside London.

The son of a Chesterfield printer/bookseller who had founded the *Derbyshire Times* in 1854, Joseph Hatton (1841–1907) became in turn editor of the *Bristol Mirror* (1774–) and the Birmingham *Illustrated Midland News* (1869–71). Not long afterwards he moved to London and took up the editorship of *The Gentleman's Magazine*, also serving as London correspondent of a number of foreign newspapers. He later edited two major Sunday papers, *The Sunday Times* from 1874 to 1881 and *The People* from 1892 to 1907. He also published a series of melodramatic novels from the mid-1860s to mid-1890s, many of which appeared first in weekly newspapers, including five syndicated by Tillotsons, beginning with *Cruel London* in 1877.

David Christie Murray (1847–1907) was born in the English Midlands, also the son of a printer/bookseller, for whom he worked from the age of twelve to eighteen, latterly also acting as an unpaid writer for the local weekly, the *Wednesbury Advertiser* (?–1872). After enlisting briefly in the army, he joined George Dawson's new *Birmingham Morning News* (1871–76) as a junior reporter, where, as was noted in the previous chapter, his first effort at fiction appeared as a serial. In the early 1870s he moved to London and continued his career as parliamentary reporter for the *Daily News*, while also acting as roving correspondent for *The Times* and *Scotsman* (1817–). His second novel, *A Life's Atonement*, was published in 1879 in *Chamber's Journal*, but many later examples appeared in the provincial weeklies, including, as noted in Chapter 4, his two best-known works, *Joseph's Coat* and *Val Strange*, reprinted in the

Manchester Weekly Times in 1882 and 1883 respectively. In describing his own apprenticeship as a novelist, Murray commented:

> I have always held that there is no training for a novelist like that of a journalist. The man who intends to write books describing life can hardly begin better than by plunging into that boiling, bubbling, seething cauldron called journalism. The working journalist is found everywhere. Is there a man to be hanged? – the working journalist is present. Exhibitions, processions, coronations, wars, whatever may be going on, wherever the interest of life and richest and the pulse beats fastest, there you find the working journalist. There is no experience in the world which really qualifies man to take a broad, a sane, an equable view of life in such a degree as journalism.
>
> (Murray, *Recollections*, 69–70)

The aesthetics of fiction articulated here would have been accepted by a good many later Victorian popular novelists.

Before moving on to the question of remuneration to authors from newspaper serial rights, two general observations should be made concerning the foregoing list of examples of novelist-journalists under various categories. First, we should note that women novelists are under-represented, particularly so in the case of the early Victorian decades, the heavier journals, and the newspaper press. The absence of such names as Frances Trollope, Dinah Craik, Margaret Oliphant, and Mrs Humphry (Mary) Ward, none of whom seem to have undertaken any sustained editorial duties, is suggestive (see Tuchman, 105–19); even George Eliot's work as editorial assistant at the *Westminster Review* in the early 1850s seems to have been of a voluntary nature. That this was by no means always a matter of personal preference is indicated by a letter from Margaret Oliphant to George Craik, a partner at Macmillan and Dinah's husband, appealing for help to find a permanent editorial position:

> But as I am growing old I have more desire for a regular quarter day, a regular occupation, and so much money certainly coming in. . . . This is where men have such a huge advantage over us, that they generally have something besides their writing to fall back upon for mere bread and butter.
>
> (24 December 1880, Oliphant, *Autobiography and Letters*, 291)

It is, of course, possible to locate examples of female proprietors/ editors of general newspapers in the second half of the nineteenth century, but they seem often to have been widows like Mary Harrison of the *Sheffield Times* or Mary Tillotson of the *Bolton Weekly Journal*, who took over the family business briefly on the premature death of their husbands. And the small though increasing number of female reporters seems in large part to have been employed specifically on pages and features directed at female readers. This, at least, was the understanding underlying both an article on the topic in the *Newspaper Press Directory* of 1897 (Smith), and Arnold Bennett's brief guide to the subject published a year later. Harriet Martineau, on the staff of the *Daily News* from around 1845, and Eliza Lynn Linton, who later worked regularly for the *Morning Chronicle* and other metropolitan papers (Linton, 11–40), are among the few noteworthy examples of women novelist–journalists.[4]

Secondly, it is significant that, in the last decades of the century, the novelists most closely associated with realist, aestheticist, and modernist tendencies, such as Thomas Hardy, Henry James, and George Gissing, also do not appear among the novelist–journalists. Here, as will be suggested in the following chapter, the issue seems to be much more one of personal and artistic preference. Nevertheless, both of these points suggest strongly that the process of the professionalization of authorship should not be treated as ideologically neutral.

With the notable exception of Tillotsons's Fiction Bureau, evidence concerning payments to authors for newspaper serial rights is again scattered and thin on the ground, particularly so in the period before the major syndicates. However, the surviving agreements suggest that David Pae received £21 from the *Glasgow Times* for 'Lucy, the Factory Girl' in 1858, 30 guineas from the *North Briton* for 'The Heiress of Wellwood' in 1859, both almost certainly original pieces, though only 10 guineas from the *People's Journal* for the subsequent serialization of 'Lucy' in 1863.[5] These are by no means trivial sums, especially when we consider the number both of the serials Pae was producing and of the Scottish journals in which they were published. Despite the fact that few of his works appeared in volume, this must have allowed Pae to make a comfortable living by his pen even before his long-term contract with John Leng and his appearance in English newspapers. However, they begin to look small in the light of the extravagant amounts paid to the most popular writers by metropolitan publishers during the sensation boom of the early 1860s. At the height of his popularity after the runaway success of *The Woman in White* in Dickens's *All the Year Round*, Wilkie Collins was offered £5000 by the house of Smith, Elder for a long novel (*Armadale*) to be serialized in their *Cornhill Magazine* before publication in volume (see Chapter 1). He immediately wrote to his mother asking her now to consider him 'in the light of a wealthy novelist' (31 July 1861, Collins, *Letters*, 1:197). Here it is difficult to distinguish between payments for serial and volume rights, though around the same time Smith had offered Charles Reade £2000 for volume rights to a novel with an extra £1000 if published in *Cornhill* (Sutherland, *Victorian Novelists*, 174). Collins himself gained a total of only £1600 from the serial appearances of *No Name* in Dickens's journal and *Harper's Weekly* in New York, but £3000 from Sampson Low for volume rights, 'the most liberal price that has ever been given for the reprinting of work already published periodically', as Collins claimed to his mother (12 August 1862, Collins, *Letters*, 1:210).

However, after the death of Dickens there was a noticeable decline in the prices paid by metropolitan publishers for publication rights to fiction in both volume and serial, and, as Sutherland has shown (*Victorian Novelists*, ch. 9), this particularly affected sensationalists like Charles Reade, Ellen Wood, and Collins himself. Thus, by the later 1870s, the remuneration offered by the provincial syndicates had not only overtaken that being offered by metropolitan periodicals but was even beginning to match the rewards of initial volume publication. In 1878 James Payn wrote to Bernhard Tauchnitz in Leipzig:

> Literature has taken a curious phase in England so far as fiction is concerned. The largest prices are now got from country newspapers who form syndicates, and each subscribe their portion towards the novel.
>
> ('Autoren-Briefe', *Der Verlag*, 113)[6]

The details of Tillotsons's payments to authors for all serials published in the *Bolton Weekly Journal*, presented in Table A.2, suggest that this was true for a wide range of authors from the distinguished to the obscure, and from those whose careers were in the ascendant to those in decline. Lack of available data concerning volume publication in a large number of cases, plus a much smaller number of cases where royalty or profit-sharing agreements with book publishers complicate the calculation, make a full comparison impossible.[7] However, the following examples are perhaps sufficient to suggest the general pattern:

- Harrison Ainsworth was paid £130 by Tillotsons for *Stanley Brereton* in 1881, though his payments from volume rights from Tinsleys were already down to £120 by 1875 (Sutherland, *Victorian Novelists*, 153);

- Tillotsons paid £150 for serial rights but only £100 for volume rights for a number of novels by Dora Russell between 1876 and 1882;

- Eliza Lynn Linton sold the serial rights to *My Love!* to Tillotsons for £300 in 1880, but only received £250 for volume rights to *Christopher Kirkland* from Bentleys in 1885 (Gettman, 125–7);

- Charles Reade obtained £500 from Tillotsons for second serial rights only to *A Perilous Secret* in 1884, though his payments for volume rights from Chapman and Hall were already down to £600 by 1871 (Sutherland, *Victorian Novelists*, 189);

- Margaret Oliphant received £600 from Tillotsons for *The Heir Presumptive and Heir Apparent* in 1889, and the same price for volumes rights to the novel from Macmillan (Tuchman, 195);

- Wilkie Collins accepted £1300 and £1000 from Tillotsons for serialization rights respectively to *The Evil Genius* (1885–86) and *The Legacy of Cain* (1888), but received only £500 each for seven-year leases on the volume rights from Chatto and Windus (Weedon, 181).

That such ratios were not limited to deals involving Tillotsons is confirmed by the two further syndicates for Collins's novels constructed by A.P. Watt in the 1880s, where, as noted in Chapter 4, the sums obtained from periodicals far surpassed those paid for volume rights by Andrew Chatto.

It should be noted in passing here that the comprehensive Tillotsons's records do not offer any support for an argument that women authors in general were paid less generously than men for comparable newspaper serial rights (see Tuchman, ch. 7). Braddon was undoubtedly the best rewarded Fiction Bureau author in the 1870s, and her fees matched those of Collins, Black and Besant in the 1880s despite the much greater number of her works on the market, while Dora Russell probably reaped the highest rewards during the deflationary 1890s. Margaret Oliphant had sometimes also complained that she was less well rewarded than male authors of comparable standing – 'I can't for my part understand why [James Payn] should get two or three times as much as I do' (cited in Terry, 33) – but the Fiction Bureau records show both writers receiving around £500 for a triple-decker novel in the early 1880s (Table A.2). If Oliphant's payments were lower, her continuing preference for sedate domestic novels after the market had shifted noticeably towards action and adventure, may have been a more important factor than her gender.[8]

The higher figures for Collins's novels noted above obviously reflect the inflation of prices paid for serials by well-known authors in the mid-1880s, which has been shown to be due in part to the inclusion of American and Colonial serial rights, and in part to a new phase of competition from metropolitan papers. Again, evidence of such payments by London papers is scattered and scarce. The *Graphic* seems to have been known for its generosity: Hardy was paid £620 for British and Colonial serial rights to *Tess* in 1891 (Grindle and Gattrell, 10); Margaret Oliphant records receiving £1300 for *Innocent*, the first serial to appear in the paper back in 1873, perhaps exceptionally as copy was required at short notice (Oliphant, *Autobiography and Letters*, 128); and Tillotsons's Notebook A, 27–8, TURNER, contains jottings on serial prices dating from around 1889, where it is noted that '*The Graphic* have paid £1400 for a story.' A detailed survey of the A.P. Watt Collection at the Wilson Library would probably yield a large number of examples from the late 1880s onwards, of which the following have been located in a more casual manner:

- £1000 offered by *Bow Bells Weekly* for a Wilkie Collins novel in 1887 (WILSON, 6.3);
- an 1889 agreement for £1000 from *Lloyd's Weekly* for a William Black novel (WILSON, 5.9);
- £800 each paid for serial rights to Besant's last two novels, *The Lady of Lynn* in 1901 and *No Other Way* in 1902, both of triple-decker length (WILSON, 37.6, 44.5);
- as Braddon's career faded, £420 from *The People* for *The Conflict* in 1903 and £450 from *Tit-Bits* for *The Rose of Life* in 1904, both single-volume works (WILSON, 59.1, 71.17).

By this period, as Keating has shown (15), royalty contracts were much more common and it becomes extremely difficult to compare remuneration from serial and volume rights.

Two comments from the early 1890s from Besant's *The Author*, however, can serve in summary. First, an unsigned article on 'Serial Rights' of July 1892, which described such rights as 'the most valuable of all' and worth up to five times as much as book rights; and secondly, author Lily Spender's letter of December 1893 confessing that 'we novelists make most of our profits in serial publication'.[9] Both forms of connection with newspapers – regular employment as journalists and the occasional contribution of fiction in serial – thus seem to have contributed significantly to the ability of a wide range of later Victorian novelists to make a comfortable living from writing. At the same time, of course, the pressure of writing to deadlines, whether those of regular journalistic assignments or of weekly serial instalments, tended to introduce a new staccato beat into the rhythm of writing, a topic discussed in detail in the following chapter.

6.2   Agreements and agents

British law pertaining to copyright, including that in newspapers and magazines, during the period with which this book is concerned was complex and confusing even to specialists (Copinger, 1904, pt I, ch. 7; Saunders, *Authorship*, ch. 5). The Copyright Commission, appointed in 1875 and reporting in 1878, stated that:

> The first observation which a study of the existing law suggests, is that its form, as distinguished from its substance, seems to us bad. The law is wholly destitute of any sort of arrangement, incomplete, often obscure, and even when it is intelligible upon long study it is in many parts so ill-expressed that anyone who does not give strict study to it cannot expect to understand it. . . . The common law principles, which lie at the root of the law, have never been settled . . .
>
> (cited in Copinger, 1915, 14)

The governing statute, passed before the massive growth in periodical publishing following the repeal of the taxes on knowledge, was the 1842 Copyright Act, which remained in force in very large part until 1911, when extensive changes were introduced under pressure to bring British law into line with the Revised International Copyright Convention signed at Berlin in 1908. The 1842 Act was above all concerned 'to afford greater Encouragement to the Production of literary Works of lasting benefit to the World' (cited in Briggs, 710). It thus centred on copyright in books (the term 'book' being broadly defined to include items such as a volume, pamphlet, map, sheet of music, published drama, or 'Sheet of Letterpress') which was vested in the author. A separate section dealt with collective works, such as encyclopaedias or magazines, where, with certain exceptions and unless otherwise agreed, copyright was vested in the proprietor. Newspapers were not specifically mentioned, and there remained uncertainty for a considerable period in case law as to whether newspapers were to be understood as periodicals, as books, or were not subject to copyright at all under the act. The Copyright Commission summarized:

> Much doubt appears to exist in consequence of several conflicting legal decisions whether there is any copyright in Newspapers. We think it right to draw your Majesty's attention to the defect, and to suggest that in any future legislation it may be remedied by defining what parts of a Newspaper may be considered Copyright, and by distinguishing between announcements of fact and communications of a literary character.
>
> (cited in Low, 665)

A judgement in 1881 established generally that newspapers were to be classed as books under the 1842 Act, but the question of which specific categories of newspaper content were subject to protection was left to a series of subsequent rulings. The extent of copyright in news material itself was still at issue in the 1890s, when there were important decisions on the protection of press agency information (Copinger, 1904, 249–51). An article on 'Newspaper Copyright' in the *National Review* (1883–1950) in summer 1892 (Low), and the correspondence it generated, revealed that the situation remained uncertain even to experts in the field. It is also necessary to remember here the rapid developments in international copyright at this time, as noted in Chapter 3. In this context, given that the provisions of the 1842 Act regarding periodical publication could be overridden by explicit agreements between authors and publishers, the legal complexity and confusion in the last decades of the century presented authors aware of the implications with a clear set of alternatives – that they must either themselves develop greater legal and business acumen, or employ professional agents on their behalf.

The entry of newspapers into the fiction market in itself obviously provoked a rapid growth in the value and variety of serial rights. In the 1860s the most prestigious and remunerative outlets for serials had been the monthly house magazines of book publishers specializing in fiction, to whom authors often sold both serial and volume rights in a single agreement for a simple sum, as in the case of Collins's *Armadale*. Publishers of monthly and weekly miscellanies without such links generally purchased single serial use for a lump sum, while the author retained the copyright and normally sold it independently to a book publisher, as in the case of Collins's *No Name*. The cheapest fiction weeklies, like *The London Journal* and *The Family Herald*, probably followed a similar pattern, but still sometimes seem to have paid their authors a weekly stipend linked to the production of a fixed quantity of fiction. The few scraps of information we have concerning the early appearances of David Pae's serials suggest that, when the weekly newspapers began to carry fiction, they may have followed the same pattern. In many cases a simple exchange of letters seems to have served instead of a formal agreement. Things obviously tended to become much more complicated with the practice of fiction syndication as developed by Tillotsons. Not only was there an inevitable plurality of initial users, but soon there were also subsequent reprint rights which could continue for decades, and potential overseas newspaper users virtually infinite in number (Turner, 'Tillotson's', 353–7; Saunders, *Authorship*, 141–4).

The dominant pattern is clear from the materials surviving at the Bodleian and at Bolton.[10] Tables 3.3 and A.2 provide a schematic summary of most of the available data concerning nineteenth-century agreements for novels. Before 1885 Tillotsons normally issued authors with a simple receipt acknowledging transfer of otherwise unspecified 'Serial' or 'Newspaper' copyright, whereas after that date they regularly used sets of pre-printed multi-leaf memoranda with optional and alternative leaves, each with space for deletions and insertions. Agreements composed in this way seem to have varied from about five to around twelve leaves. They always began with those labelled 'Parties' and 'Consideration' and ended with 'Attestation', normally contained those headed 'Number and length of instalments' and 'Delivery of copy' plus one of several detailing 'Payment', and might include such options as 'Author not to publish in volume form before fixed day' or 'Agreement as to future stories'. From that time the bulk of completed agreements cited limits of time and/or place.

Until the passage of the Chace Act in 1891, the phrase 'together with the right of supply to America of Advance Sheets' was pre-printed, though it was sometimes erased by authors. Typical phrases inserted, sometimes in combination, were: 'serial right outside America', 'serial, American & Continental rights', 'serial & transla-tion rights', 'newspaper publication right in Great Britain, Ireland, America, and British colonies' and 'limited to 2 years'. Neverthe-less, just as a small number of authors, like Florence Marryat, Joseph Hatton and Isabella Banks, specified limitations in the early years in more complex contracts that seem not to have survived but which are summarized in the 'Abstract of Agreements' held at Bolton (ZBEN, 4/4, covering 1874–80), so a minority were still content with a simple receipt for 'serial rights' throughout the 1880s. The term 'serial rights' occasionally led to conflicts, as some inexperienced authors naively understood the phrase to imply only first serial rights in British newspapers, whereas Tillotsons, with their backlists of stories for small provincial proprietors, growing international clientele, and shrinking profit margins, naturally took the wider view. In late 1883, for example, John Maxwell had complained loudly that Tillotsons were continuing to sell Mary Cecil Hay's story 'Missing' to provin-cial newspapers, although the entire copyright now belonged to him. The original agreement with Tillotsons was a simple receipt signed on 30 September 1880 and ceding 'serial rights' to the 40 000 word story for £100. Hay, who was used to selling single serial rights to her stories for the same price to the *Family Herald*, had assumed a similar limitation in this case, had then sold absolute copyright to Maxwell, and the work had appeared in volume form with other tales in 1881.[11]

The opposite case was represented by Wilkie Collins, who like his master Dickens, had become an early advocate of authorial rights.[12] Already in 1868 he had had his solicitor prepare a draft contract for volume rights to *The Moonstone* which the publisher William Tinsley later described as 'a regular corker; it would pretty well cover the gable of an ordinary-sized house' (Downey, 25). Even the summary of the contract for Collins's first novel for Tillotsons, *Jez-ebel's Daughter*, took up two full spreads in the notebook of Tillotsons's Abstracts, at least four times the average length. It introduced a series of unusual restrictions on the process of syndication by in-sisting, for example, that the subscribing newspapers should be limited to twelve 'named by the publisher and approved by the author', should include only one London paper and only one belonging to each publisher, and should issue the novel virtually simultaneously. In addition, there were five clauses explicitly reserving all other rights save British serial rights, and a final proviso specifying the consequences if any of the other clauses were broken (ZBEN, 4/4).

The contracts negotiated by Watt in the 1880s for the newspaper serial right to Collins's novels are often no less complex, though perhaps rather more clearly and concisely drafted. These would include that with Tillotsons for *The Legacy of Cain*, signed on 19 December 1886, where the agreement did not use Tillotsons's pre-printed memoranda, but consisted of ten brief clauses typed on less than two pages of foolscap (f.395/1, BODLEIAN). By this stage Tillotsons were regularly selling stories to papers in the USA, and the timing of the serialization on both sides of the Atlantic was a key issue.[13] In the agreement for Collins's *Legacy of Cain*, while granting the right 'to supply advance sheets to the USA', Watt had guarded against the risk of the loss of British copyright by a simple clause insisting that 'first newspaper publication be in Great Britain', leaving Tillotsons to take care of the details. In the case of Collins's final novel *Blind Love*, where Tillotsons were not involved and Watt personally arranged single newspaper appearances in the *Illustrated London News* and the Sunday edition of the *New York World*, the details were built in to the American contract. The agreement between Watt and the *New York World*, reproduced in its entirety (Plate 15), shows the precise timing required to protect the American journal's priority against the US edition of the *Illustrated London News*, against the pirates who would jump in the case of a delay of more than a few days, and against premature authorized volume publication, while all the time making sure the British copyright was not threatened by prior publication in the USA.[14]

Clearly, by the 1890s, the role of the literary agent was no longer limited to the arrangement of periodical publication and the disposal of serial rights, but these examples do help to suggest how closely the development of the newspaper market for fiction determined the early definition of that role. A simple glance at the authors who became the earliest of Watt's regular clients reveals that a significant proportion were those who, through Tillotsons or otherwise, had already sold their work to the provincial papers – obvious cases would include MacDonald, Collins, Besant, Harte, Payn, Buchanan, Black, Clark Russell, Christie Murray, Rider Haggard, Linton, Oliphant, and Braddon. However, it is again important to emphasize that the changes in the nature of professional authorship implied by the increasing complexity of contracts for fiction and the growing power of syndication and literary agents are not value neutral. This can be seen most simply in the different ways authors responded to the process, including the case of authors who reacted with extreme distaste to the very thought of literary syndicates and literary agencies. In the following section we will look in some detail at the responses to the intervention of the middlemen in two complex cases, those of Collins and Braddon. Here, it may be useful to sketch briefly the extreme responses, both negative and positive, represented by Ouida and Walter Besant in their angry exchange in the correspondence columns of *The Times* in 1891, under the heading 'New Literary Factors'.

On 22 May Ouida was permitted to occupy nearly two full columns in a rambling and ranting complaint to the effect that, because of radical changes in the mode of publication of novels in the previous decade, the 'closing years of the nineteenth century witness a breathless and useless competition of utterly worthless books'. The main thrust of the attack is against the *parvenu* middlemen who have disrupted the gentlemanly understanding between author and publisher. These 'enemies and parasites' are the newspaper syndicates (who handle the author 'precisely as the Chicago killing and salting establishment treat the pig'), literary agents ('the maggot of the nut'), and authors' guilds ('caricatures of literature'). The references were explicit enough to allow knowledgeable readers to recognize specific attacks on Tillotsons's Fiction Bureau, Watt's Literary Agency, and Besant's Society of Authors. The only pause in the flow comes when Ouida is distracted, though only temporarily, by the thought that the publishers themselves might also be considered as middlemen. The heart of Ouida's opposition was unmistakably Romantic and aristocratic, as befits someone who was born Louise Ramé at Bury St Edmunds, but recreated herself as Marie Louise de la Ramée when writing high-flown fiction in purple ink in Florence:

> To every author of imaginative mind and impersonal feeling, the association of trade with literature must always be disagreeable; the question of pounds, shillings, and pence must always chafe and jar when brought into connexion with the children of thought. The feeling of Byron must be the feeling of every true poet and scholar.

Besant derided Ouida's position as 'this poor, old, worn-out, conventional rag of sentiment' in a reply which appeared on 26 May 1891, and, occupying just less than a single column, was fittingly brisk and business-like. He took the position, first articulated by Thackeray in *Pendennis* (vol. I, ch. 37) and analysed in detail by Shillingsburg, that it would not harm Pegasus to be put in harness. He defended the activities of the commercial agents as well as those of the Society of Authors, as enhancing the concept as well as the value of literary property, and, as usual, reserved his harshest words for those 'plunderers and sharks', the dishonest gentlemen publishers. He concluded confidently:

> In a word, Sir, I would beg your readers not to believe a single word of all this sham indignation and froth. English literature is looking very well indeed. . . . The good books are in demand and are extensively read. The literary agent is a great help to us, and I believe to publishers as well. The competition of writers tends to raise the standard instead of lowering it. . . . We are not, in fact, exactly arrived at the Kingdom of Heaven, but we are going along as well as can be expected . . .

We should perhaps note that Sir Walter passed away at his home in Hampstead in 1902, an honoured and wealthy man, while Ouida died of pneumonia in virtual destitution in Italy six years later, despite a Civil List pension charitably conferred in 1906, and although her early novels were still selling strongly as cheap reprints to the greater comfort of her publishers.[15]

6.3   Professionalization: Collins and Braddon

Mary Braddon and Wilkie Collins were the two Victorian novelists of name who sold their work to syndicates of provincial newspapers earliest and most consistently. Interestingly, before the era of the syndicates, both had belonged to bohemian sets and formed domestic establishments that breached bourgeois social and sexual conventions, and both had come to fame as writers of sensational works which transgressed the social and sexual norms of domestic fiction. There is then considerable value in looking comparatively at their complex relations to the new literary middlemen in the light of their earlier careers. It is perhaps not surprising that engagement in modes of fictional production that challenged the conventions of the dominant mode of 'gentlemanly' publishing of the mid-Victorian period should have explicitly raised questions about authorship in terms of class and gender.

From *The Dead Secret* (1857) onwards, all Wilkie Collins's novels were published initially in periodical form. With the notable exception of *Armadale*, from the mid-1850s to the late 1860s most of his work appeared first in Dickens's family weeklies, including the shorter fictional and journalistic pieces. During the 1870s, after Dickens's death and with his own popularity beginning to fade, Collins's fiction was serialized in a range of metropolitan journals, both lighter monthly miscellanies like *Temple Bar* and *Belgravia*, and 'class' weeklies like *The Graphic* and *The World*. As Table A.5 shows, the novels written during the last decade of his life generally appeared in syndicates of weekly newspapers. Money was almost certainly the chief motive: in rapidly failing health and with an unconventional lifestyle that left him with two morganatic families to support, Collins was almost desperately seeking to maximize the return on his literary capital (Clarke, chs 12–13; Peters, chs 22–3). The £500 offered by Tillotsons for *Jezebel's Daughter* in July 1878 must already have appeared generous compared to the £300 he was getting from Andrew Chatto for *The Haunted Hotel* then running in *Belgravia* (Peters, 384), and the gap was much greater by the mid-1880s. Yet Collins was also attracted by the idea of escaping the Grundyism of the London editors, library proprietors, and reviewers, and directly addressing a new mass reading public measured in hundreds rather than tens of thousands. In particular, as we shall see in *The* following chapter, he had clashed in 1875 with the editor of the *Graphic* over 'impropriety' in *The Law and the Lady*. More generally, throughout much of his career Collins had conducted a running battle in the prefaces to his novels in volume with the reviewers, who he addressed provocatively as 'Readers in Particular', as against 'Readers in General' who he welcomed warmly.[16] In the dedicatory preface to the three-volume edition of *Jezebel's Daughter*, he explained that the novel was not the projected second part of *The Fallen Leaves*, which had entirely failed to please the fashionable readers of *The World*, but which, he predicted, would 'appeal to the great audience of the English people' when 'finally reprinted in its cheapest form'.

As early as 1858 in his well-known *Household Words* piece 'The Unknown Public', in discussing the extensive readership of the 'penny-novel-journals' (that is, *The Family Herald*, *The London Journal*, and their lesser competitors), Collins had predicted that 'the readers who rank by millions will be the readers who give the widest reputations, who return the richest rewards, and who will, therefore, command the service of the best writers of their time' (*Collins 'The Unknown'*, 222). Yet the essay as a whole reveals a curious social embarrassment at the prospect of a wider audience. The tone is chiefly comic, but the laughter is directed not so much at the serial stories in the penny-novel-journals, which are dismissed swiftly for their dullness and sameness, but rather at 'the social position, the habits, the tastes, and the average intelligence of the Unknown Public,' as inferred from the columns devoted to 'Answers to Correspondents' (219). The first person plural asserts a yawning social divide between the readers of the penny journals and the 'known reading public', that is, the subscribers to Dickens's twopenny miscellany – 'We see the books they like on their tables. We meet them out at dinner, and hear them talk of their favourite authors.' (218). Yet, as was suggested in Chapter 1, by this time many of the penny journals were targeting a lower-middle-class family audience that must have overlapped to some extent with that of *Household Words*, which claimed in an advertisement for its opening number to be 'designed for the instruction and entertainment of all classes of readers' (cited in Gasson, 49). In fact, in the year before Collins's piece appeared, the editorship of *The London Journal*, still the best-selling of the penny-fiction-journals but now owned by Herbert Ingram of the *Illustrated London News*, was taken over briefly by Mark Lemon, founder of *Punch* (1841–) and Collins's fellow actor in Dickens's amateur theatricals.

Around this time other sensation writers were prepared to take the risk of appearing in the cheapest weekly miscellanies. Charles Reade's *The Double Marriage*, for example, was first published in serial under the title 'White Lies' in *The London Journal* as early as 1857, while in 1863 Mary Braddon's *Lady Audley's Secret* and *Henry Dunbar* (under the title 'The Outcasts') also appeared there. This was in addition to half a dozen 'penny dreadfuls' written especially by her for John Maxwell's *Halfpenny Journal* between 1861 and 1865. In early 1867, at the first signs of the downturn in his sales, Collins had thoughts of reprinting his most successful sensation works in the penny journals, and even of writing a new novel for them based on melodramatic stage pieces like *The Red Vial* (1858). Though nothing seems to have come of these plans (Peters, 279), two of his serials were to appear in *Cassell's Magazine* in the early

1870s, alongside Reade's *A Terrible Temptation*. But, as was noted in Chapter 4, Collins discussed the idea of syndication in country papers enthusiastically with Mayne Reid and J.E. Muddock around the same time, and the novel he sold to Tillotsons in 1878, *Jezebel's Daughter*, indeed proved to be a recycling of the plot of *The Red Vial*. It is then perhaps not surprising that Collins's dealings with the popular newspaper proprietors and syndicators during the last decade of his life, either directly or through his agent, were often unstable and uncomfortable, being bound up with the complex forms of snobbery revealed in 'The Unknown Public'.

As described in Chapter 4, Watt personally negotiated the appearance of *Heart and Science* in around ten weekly papers in 1882. The correspondence with the various provincial proprietors in general reveals a polite and business-like series of exchanges. Since serialization was due to commence as soon as July, some proprietors requested more precise information about the story for publicity purposes, like Alexander Ireland of the *Manchester Weekly Times*, who wanted to know 'the title and drift of the story' on 27 February (ALS, Collins Acc., BERG). E.A. Bartlett, Tory M.P. and proprietor of the new popular London weekly *England*, was more insistent and intrusive, demanding 'some idea of the character of the story, for the majority of our readers belong to the working classes and like exciting though easily written stories' and emphasizing that 'a good striking title is very important' (ALS, 31 Jan., Collins Acc., BERG). When Collins heard of this through Andrew Chatto, he was incensed, regarding it as both a bureaucratic intrusion into the mysteries of artistic creation and an ungentlemanly questioning of his good faith and standing in the literary world. He wrote immediately to Watt asking him to threaten to break off negotiations with these 'curious savages', and enclosed an indignant remonstrance which he wanted copied and sent to 'Mr. Bartlett and . . . those other people in the north': 'In twenty years' experience, this extraordinary form of distrust approaches me for the first time. The late Mr Charles Dickens neither read, nor wished to read, a line of The Woman in White before we signed our agreement . . .' (8 February 1882, Collins, *Letters*, 2:442–3). He later complained to Watt about the 'vile paper' on which the proofs of the first weekly part had been printed by the *Liverpool Weekly Post* (ALS, 1 June 1882, PEMBROKE), and asked Andrew Chatto, who was serializing the novel slightly later in *Belgravia*, to allow him to escape from the clutches of the Provincial press by taking over the printing (ALS, 5 Jun. 1882 PARRISH).

The intensity of his reaction perhaps reflects his insecurity at his own declining powers and kudos, but there was also an element of class and cultural prejudice, the refined bohemian looking down on boorish tradesmen.

This disdain extended to W.F. Tillotson himself, whose role as syndicator removed the distasteful necessity for direct negotiation with newspaper owners in Britain or overseas, and who never himself made outrageous demands for plot summaries, casts of characters in advance, or the like. Examples of polite letters from Collins to Tillotson survive at Bolton (ZBEN, 4/6), as when, after the end of the run of *Jezebel's Daughter* in the provincial papers, Collins complied with a request to supply Mary Tillotson with an autograph letter from Dickens (ALS, 15 February 1880), or when Tillotson had congratulated Collins on the successful completion of *The Legacy of Cain* in the face of illness (ALS, 30 May 1888). But when Collins wrote privately to Watt, he was almost always scathing about the Bolton man, generally referring to him scornfully as 'T'. His reaction was especially irate when Tillotson complained, quite justly and politely, that Collins had breached their agreement by submitting instalments of *The Evil Genius* considerably shorter than the contracted length, and insisted that the same problem should not occur with *The Legacy of Cain*.[17] The author called Tillotson 'this pest', '[t]hat wretched creature', or 'that impudent little cad', and more than once suggested that he would like to get a train to Bolton and 'kick an unmentionable part of Tillotson's person' (ALSs, 17 July 1883, 13 September 1885, 6 July 1886, 8 July 1886, PEMBROKE). This is in marked contrast both to the affection and respect generally afforded to the Lancashire man by his London authors,[18] and to the warmth and friendship that Collins quickly developed towards his own London literary middlemen, Andrew Chatto and Alexander Watt himself (Peters, 369–70, 395–6). This is attested repeatedly in his letters to them throughout the 1880s.[19] In addition to the class snobbery exposed in 'The Unknown Public', the vehemence of Collins's reaction here must be put down in part to the cultural prejudice of the sophisticated Londoner towards the uncouth Northerner. Much earlier, in 1863 on his trip to the Isle of Man in preparation for the writing of a scene in *Armadale*, Collins had written to Charles Ward: 'All Lancashire goes to the Isle of Man and all Lancashire is capable of improvement in looks and breeding' (29 August, Collins, *Letters*, 1:230). And as late as 1887, on experiencing delays in negotiations with a firm in Glasgow, Watt's birthplace, he wrote obliviously to his agent concerning 'another case of North British superiority to the laws of courtesy' on the part of 'those Glasgow savages' (ALSs, 8, 22 August, PEMBROKE).

There is an added tension in the formal correspondence in that, at least in the early 1880s, Watt and Tillotson themselves were professionally suspicious of each other.[20] Here, two middlemen seems to have been one too many. In his efforts to syndicate Collins's fiction widely during the early 1880s, Watt had undoubtedly been guilty of sharp practice in concealing relevant information about other subscribing journals, and reports of this obviously filtered back to Bolton. Tillotson's negotiations with some of his fellow proprietors for The *Evil Genius* were complicated by the fact that Watt had sold *'I Say No'* to the same journals under very different terms and conditions.[21] Tillotson was undoubtedly conscious that Watt had previously taken Collins, one of his two most eminent client novelists, from him in 1882 and tried to lure the other, Mary Braddon, away in 1885. At that time the normally reserved Bolton business man betrayed his anger in correspondence with John Maxwell by referring to the London literary agent as a 'parasite'.[22]

But in the misunderstandings with Tillotson, in comparison with the direct negotiations with individual proprietors, the ideological positions are reversed. Here Collins, through his representative, is the one insisting on increasingly lengthy contracts formulating the bargain in minute detail, while Tillotson, annoyed that his good faith is being questioned, would prefer an informal gentlemanly understanding. Tillotson finally showed his irritation after Collins began to insist on a lengthy agreement replete with nice restrictions in the case of a single short story ('The Ghost's Touch') for the serial rights of which he was to receive the generous sum of £150. Tillotson's protest to Watt is significant because it illustrates the intimate relation in the syndicator's mind between increasing remuneration, contractual restrictions, and expanding markets:

That Authors command much larger sums than formerly is a matter of satisfaction to me. Few men of my generation have been the means of contributing more to that result than I have; and perhaps I have some claim to be heard in support of the contention that when an author is well paid for his work, the purchaser's channels to recoup himself should not be narrowed within unnecessary limits.

(ALS, 22 April 1885, Collins Acc., BERG)

We should remember that at this time Collins was as active as his declining health permitted in supporting the foundation of Walter Besant's Society of Authors. Collins was one of 68 founding members and one of 14 prominent writers appointed as honorary Vice-Presidents of the Society. The new organization had as one off its three objectives, 'the maintenance of friendly relations between authors and publishers, by means of properly drawn agreements' (cited in Bonham-Carter, 122).

It is apparent that Collins, with his early high-cultural connections, was increasingly uncertain of his status in the rapidly changing late Victorian literary marketplace. The tensions visible in the intercourse between Collins or his representative and the popular newspaper syndicators and proprietors are symptoms not only of the growing divide between romantic and professional views of authorship, and between 'gentlemanly' and 'commercial' modes of fiction production, but also of Collins's confusion as to which side of the divide he was on.

That Braddon produced more than three times the 25 or so novels achieved by Collins, is obviously not entirely accounted for by the fact that her career spanned nearly 60 years compared to his 40. Almost from the beginning Braddon's work as a writer had been under the control of her publisher-companion John Maxwell. That she wrote 20 novels within less than a decade of starting to write professionally at the age of 23, might largely be explained by immediate economic pressures – initially the need to support herself and her mother (Wolff, *Sensational*, chs 1–2; Carnell, ch. 2) and later the losses due to the financial entanglements of Maxwell in the mid-1860s (Sadleir, *Things*, 69–83).[23] The same cannot be said of the novels she turned out at a rate of two per year virtually throughout the 1870s and 1880s, for by then the Maxwells were the owners of substantial literary and immovable property. In 1885 John Maxwell wrote to W.F. Tillotson: 'My wife must be occupied. It is as natural for her to write as it is for a mountain torrent to flow' (14 October, ZBEN, 4/3). But there was also a perception in the London literary world that Maxwell was a hard taskmaster adept at exploiting female writers and appropriating their work. This is captured precisely in a cartoon in the short-lived satirical monthly *The Mask* (1868–?) which represents Maxwell as a circus ring master forcing Braddon, a bare-back rider on a winged horse inscribed *Belgravia*, through a tight series of paper hoops named for her novels (1:5, June 1868, 138).[24] Both images probably contain a large grain of truth. There is also little doubt that, whatever the reasons for Braddon's high productivity, in market terms there was often an over-supply of her fiction, and equal or greater reward might have been achieved with less output.

The many letters Maxwell wrote to Willie Tillotson on Braddon's behalf during the 1880s reveal a personal warmth and a professional equality that is a world away from how Collins reacted to the Bolton man. After a relationship of nearly 15 years, Maxwell was writing to offer the latest Braddon serial in the following fashion:

> Kindly let me hear from you in reply at earliest possible convenience. I want to say "engaged to Messrs. Tillotson & Son" as soon as I can; and to choke off all enquiries as soon as enquiries arise. And thus, and thus, we merrily trip along, year after year, without delays, differences, or disputes, each relying upon the other, and each rendering to the other sympathetic and best service! And so let it be to end of time!
>
> (8 March 1887, ZBEN, 4/3)

However, as suggested in Chapter 3, the correspondence also reveals growing tensions in the relationship which cannot be entirely explained by Maxwell's personal qualities. In his correspondence with Watt, Tillotson had compared Collins's lengthy contracts unfavourably with the total absence of formal agreements in the case of Braddon's newspaper novels. He stated that Braddon's novels were 'limited to time in the manner proposed, and have never called for any Agreement. Letters containing the points have always sufficed' (ALS, 17 November 1884, Collins Acc., BERG). In this he was guilty of disingenuity, for at that time he was increasingly drawn into long and heated disagreements with John Maxwell which suggest repeatedly that letters were not always enough. In 1884 Tillotson had put Braddon's *Just as I Am* and *Phantom Fortune* in prominent positions on his new backlists and was selling them off to all comers by the column at 4s 6d in proof or 6s 6d in stereo. Maxwell discovered this and angrily threatened to sever the relationship if Tillotson refused henceforth to limit his sales to first serial user:

Your license to use the new novel must be strictly defined. It
will not do to hunt it out of our correspondence and by piece
and patch extracted here and there from 4 or 500 letters make
up a substitute for a clear understanding. We began with one. It
got altered. We must have another. If you want more time than
will suffice for one clear usor [sic.] and that simultaneously every-
where, postal distances allowed, I shall not be able to give it.
And further, I never intended to give it. Let us start with a thor-
oughly clear understanding that you buy what I sell to use once
and once only in a coterie of newspapers, the license expiring at
an agreed time.

(25 August 1884, ZBEN, 4/3)

Tillotson quickly capitulated, and there thus seems little doubt that
the Bolton man was capable of the sharp practice that Collins had
accused him of in his letters to Watt.[25] Maxwell often complained,
only half in jest, that Tillotson got his own way on terms by taking
advantage of their friendship ('be happy always getting own way
from us hence pleasantest relations,' telegram, 23 May 1885, ZBEN,
4/3), but he was always irate if payment failed to arrive on time
('No remittance! Why?', 10 March 1883, ZBEN, 4/3), and he more
than once objected strongly to accepting deferred payment because
it lowered Braddon's literary dignity ('Authors do not give credit
any more than do Physicians or Barristers, if at the head of their
professions', 5 January 1883, ZBEN, 4/3).

In addition, Maxwell's discourse in the letters to Tillotson can
also be read as an allegory of gender relations in the late Victorian
literary world. The two wives, Mary Maxwell and Mary Tillotson,
represent the female author and reader: background presences, end-
lessly engaged in the isolated domestic activities of knitting and
unravelling a garment of prose fiction, subject to the will of their
masters, the middlemen. In the foreground, the two husbands, neither
of whom show sign of having read the novels in question, represent the publishers and agents, nicely calculating the value of fiction
in shillings to the yard, playing power games of manipulation and
control. 'Author writes two novels yearly, never more, never less.
Shortest offered. Belgravia have longest. Wire acceptance, negotiate
own property' runs one particularly pithy telegram from Maxwell
(3 November 1885, ZBEN, 4/3). Braddon seems to have been prepared to leave the details of the negotiations almost entirely up to
her agent–husband, in contrast to Collins's rather fussy and anxious

supervision of Watt's endeavours. Braddon also was not allowed to have anything to do with the recently founded Society of Authors. In response to Tillotson's inquiry about his wife's attitude to the new development, Maxwell perfunctorily dismissed the effort as a 'vision conceived by Visionaries. Nothing in it' (21 February 1884, ZBEN, 4/3). We should also note that the Society itself functioned almost like a Gentlemen's Club for the first decades of its existence. The controlling Committee of Management of 12 remained entirely male and dominated by members of the Savile Club until after the turn of the century. Though Margaret Oliphant and Marie Corelli were among the women novelists who joined the Society its early years, it was only in 1896 that the first group of women writers were elected to the consultative Council of 60 members. Among this group were the novelists Charlotte M. Yonge, Eliza Lynn Linton and Mary Ward (Bonham-Carter, chs 6–7).[26]

Wilkie Collins and Willie Tillotson were, of course, both dead and buried at the time of the clash between Ouida and Besant about the role of the middlemen. It is notable, however, that Braddon herself wrote personally to exonerate the syndicators, who Besant had not bothered to defend:

it would not . . . become me to allow Ouida's sweeping condemnation of the literary middleman to go by without a word as to my own experience of the two great literary syndicates created by the late Mr. Tillotson, of Bolton, and by Sir [sic. for 'Mr'] Christopher Leng, of Sheffield. My relations with these two gentlemen, extending over very nearly twenty years, have brought me both profit and pleasure; since their payment for the serial use of my novels has been liberal and prompt, and their courtesy as to all business arrangements and minor details has been unvarying.

(*The World*, 10 June 1891, 22)[27]

In January 1891 John Maxwell himself had suffered a seizure, and thereafter required almost constant attention until his death on 3 March 1895 (Maxwell, 163–4; Wolff *Sensational*, ch. 9). Although Braddon was not moved to join the Society of Authors until 1905 (see ALSs from Anthony Hope Hawkins, then Secretary, of 15 October and 1 November 1905, WOLFF), after handling her own literary affairs for a brief period following her husband's incapacitation, from late 1892 she began to employ A.P. Watt as her literary agent (*Collection*, 7; WILSON, 15.15).

Let us summarize. The rise of the news miscellany in the second half of the reign of Queen Victoria, and the concomitant emergence of the newspaper novel as a major form of fiction publication, contributed significantly to the growth in both the number and the economic security of professional novel writers. In the process, along with other forms of weekly serialization, it served to undermine prevailing 'gentlemanly' assumptions in the publishing industry, though this sometimes proved disconcerting even to bohemian authors like Wilkie Collins who railed against the Grundyism of the London literary editors and library owners. But the practice of syndication, in particular, encouraged an increasing complexity in the contracts drawn up between authors and publishers, and increasing intervention by new types of agents, imposing often inflexible commercial and legal constraints on the process of writing. Women authors especially may have suffered from new processes of production and distribution which were controlled by, precisely, 'middlemen', and from the fact that they were excluded from full membership in the emerging profession of authorship. Cases such as that of Braddon must thus be seen to offer qualified support to the argument pressed by Gaye Tuchman in *Edging Women Out*, that British women authors were increasingly marginalized from the last decades of the nineteenth century.[28] But while Braddon was generally content to conform to the commercial and ideological demands of the market-place, she was also quite capable of using popular fictional paradigms in order to challenge specific social and sexual prejudices, as we shall see in the following chapter, when we look in detail at the generic form of the novels written for the newspapers by both her and Walter Besant.

7
Genre

In the first place we must confirm the sheer quantity and variety of Victorian novels serialized in British newspapers after the abolition of the taxes on knowledge. Given both the number of papers where runs appear to have been partially or completely lost, and the volume of surviving material, it is obviously impossible to come up with a total number of British newspapers carrying serial fiction with some regularity during this period. However, in the course of the research for this volume, I have recorded instances: in over 50 provincial journals in the era of the minor/proto-syndicates; after the rise of the major syndicates in around the same number of larger city and regional journals, plus in almost double that number of smaller town and country papers; and in well over half that figure of metropolitan papers in the last 20-odd years of the century. As the searches conducted have been far from comprehensive, these figures must be presumed considerably to underestimate the total. Indeed it seems likely that virtually every community in Britain would have had been served by some form of newspaper consistently featuring fiction material before the end of the century. This was certainly the opinion of William Westall who claimed in 1890 that 'there is hardly a small town in the kingdom without at least one local sheet, whose chief attraction is a serial romance' (79).

Though the process of syndication itself, as practiced notably by Tillotsons, with their 'coteries' of simultaneous first users and their backlists of novels in proof and stereo, obviously created widespread duplication of material, the number and range of different works published must remain very high. The checking of a sample of unrecognized titles against the British Library catalogue suggests that, in the early part of the period in particular, significant numbers of novels were serialized in the newspapers which never appeared in book form, as instanced by those from the pen of David Pae.[1] And yet, towards the end of the century it is apparent that many original novels of the highest quality reached their first audience in the newspapers. 'At the present time nearly all the best fiction is preempted by the newspaper market, which has lately advanced with enormous strides in this direction,' an editorial in Besant's *Author* stated in July 1892 (cited in Colby, 'Tale', 2). Though this volume concentrates on the appearance of original British fiction, it should also be noted that it is not difficult to find examples, in the provincial weeklies especially, of reprinted English classics like Smollett, Scott, or Dickens, contemporary European authors in translation like Zola, Daudet, or Verne, American imports like Harriet Beecher Stowe, Leon Lewis or Bret Harte, plus established Colonial writers like Ada Cambridge, or Fergus Hume. Further, the newspapers also published a vast range of 'complete tales' which have been only mentioned in passing here.

Nevertheless, despite the volume and range of material involved, since the market for newspaper fiction overlaps significantly with those for 'popular' and 'literary' fiction in both books and magazines, it is possible to trace parallels to developments in those areas already described by scholars such as Keating, Terry, and Cross. In the first section of this chapter, 'Modes and settings', the extent to which patterns of weekly serialization can be seen to determine generic form will be discussed. Here we will note the growing power of the metropolitan journals to encourage the trend from the general narrative modes of melodrama and sensation towards the specific popular genres of adventure, mystery, and romance. At the same time, we will discuss the influence of the provincial papers in preserving a tradition of local and regional settings and themes in the face of the drift towards metropolitan and imperial subjects. In the following section, 'Composition and control', we will discuss not only the degree of control over fictional texts exercised by syndicators and editors, specifically through acts of censorship, or generally through the way in which serial novels were 'packaged,' but also the extent to which writers might resist such pressures by contractual or other legal means, as well as by revising their serials prior to volume publication. Finally, in 'Commodification', we will again look in greater detail at two contrasting cases of regular newspaper novelists of some stature, Braddon and Besant, to discuss how much that mode of publication can be seen to influence the forms of their writing.

7.1   Modes and settings

In the course of a review of *Great Expectations*, which appeared in
three volumes towards the end of its run in Dickens's family weekly
All the Year Round, *The Times* literary editor, E.S. Dallas, comments
on the evolution of the Victorian serial novel:

> The method of publishing an important work of fiction in monthly
> instalments was considered a hazardous experiment, which could
> not fail to set its mark upon the novel as a whole. Mr. Dickens
> led the way in making the experiment, and his enterprise was
> crowned with such success that most of the good novels now
> find their way to the public in the form of a monthly dole. . . .
>   But what are we to say to the new experiment which is now
> being tried of publishing good novels week by week? Hitherto
> the weekly issue of fiction has been connected with publication
> of the lowest class – small penny and halfpenny serials that found
> in the multitude some compensation for the degradation of their
> readers. . . . Mr. Dickens has tried another experiment. The peri-
> odical which he conducts is addressed to a much higher class of
> readers than any which the penny journals would reach, and he
> has spread before them novel after novel specially adapted to
> their tastes.
>
> (*The Times*, 17 October 1861, 6)

Despite a number of asides in a patrician vein on modern decline,
which echo Thomas Arnold's anxieties about the intellectual effects
of serialization, expressed as early as 1839 in a sermon at Rugby
(*Christian*, 39–41), Dallas finally judges the success of Dickens's new
work to be 'so great as to warrant the conclusion . . . that the weekly
form of publication is not incompatible with a very high order of
fiction'. At the same time, Dallas recognizes that the mode of weekly
serialization does indeed 'set its mark' upon the form of the novel.
    Without using the term 'sensation' which was not yet in vogue,
Dallas notes that the two other early successes in *All the Year Round*,
Collins's *The Woman in White* and Bulwer-Lytton's *A Strange Story*,
are also fast-paced and rely heavily on the mechanics of enigma
and suspense. At the same time he suggests that the failure of Scott's
historical romances when reprinted in the penny miscellanies may
have been due as much to the more leisurely pace of his narrative
as to the debased tastes of the audience. The weekly portion was

for practical reasons much shorter as well as more frequent that the monthly number. The typical serial instalment found in a monthly miscellany in the 1860s was around 15 000 words. This would not only have over-run the space available in a weekly journal of 24 pages but also have overwhelmed the capacity of the writer to produce it on a weekly basis. Regardless of the gradual reduction in the word-count of the average triple-decker during the second half of the nineteenth century, the ratio of the length of the monthly periodical instalment relative to that of the weekly one seems generally to have remained at between two and three to one (compare Table 7.1). As well as confirming these calculations, Walter C. Phillips suggests that the weekly number tended to increase significantly the importance of three elements already apparent in the monthly serial: the striking opening to the work as a whole to increase the chances of its 'taking' with readers; the episodic integrity of the individual number; and 'climax and curtain' endings to instalments to encourage readers to come back for more (ch. 5).[2] It was undoubtedly Wilkie Collins, three out of four of whose major sensation novels of the 1860s first appeared in the pages of *All the Year Round*, and to whom the formula 'Make 'em laugh, make 'em cry, make 'em wait' has often been attributed, who learned most rapidly and skilfully to exploit these demands.

John Sutherland, a modern commentator who has examined the moment of *All the Year Round* in considerable detail, shares Dallas's recognition that the form of the weekly number carried powerful psychological implications for both contributor and subscriber:

> The pace, narrowness and need for 'incessant condensation' cut away all fat; the responsiveness of the sales to any slackening tension kept the novelist nervous and alert. Weekly intervals meant that a reader came to every instalment primed, which was not the case with monthly serialisation where the plot had that much longer to fade in the memory.
>
> (Sutherland, *Victorian Novelists*, 172)

Yet, in stressing that such 'furnace-like conditions' made Dickens's weekly 'a superb instrument for fiction' only if 'handled properly', Sutherland considerably underestimates the generic constraints imposed. It is easy to assign the failure in *All the Year Round* of Charles Lever's rambling picaresque *A Day's Ride, a Life's Romance* (1860–1) to advancing age and declining concentration, but there

Table 7.1 Length of weekly and monthly instalments in four Collins serials

Novel (serial publication)	Total word count	Monthly parts		Weekly parts	
		No.	Average word count	No.	Average word count
No Name (1862–63) in *All the Year Round*	c.270 000	–	–	45	c.6000
Armadale (1864–66) in *Cornhill*	c.300 000	20	c.15 000	–	–
Heart and Science (1882–83) in *Belgravia/Liverpool Weekly Post*	c.130 000	11	c.12 000	28	c.4500
'I Say No' (1883–84) in *London Society/Manchester Weekly Post*	c.120 000	12	c.10 000	30	c.4000

Source: Original journals

were other writers at the height of their powers who were troubled by the pressures of the weekly number. George Eliot eventually turned down a commission for Dickens's journal because of the 'terseness and closeness of construction' of the weekly instalment (cited in Dickens *Letters*, 9:213), while in 1863 Elizabeth Gaskell produced for it the novella *A Dark Night's Work*, her most melodramatic and least characteristic later work. Almost a decade earlier in writing for *Household Words*, it should be remembered, Gaskell had felt crushed by the limitations of space with her second industrial novel, *North and South*. Moreover, in the course of his own anti-utilitarian tract *Hard Times*, Dickens himself had railed against 'the compression and close condensation necessary for that disjointed form of publication', in marked contrast to the 'patient fiction-writing with some elbow-room always, and open places in perspective' characteristic of the monthly number (to The Hon. Mrs Richard Watson, 1 November 1854, and John Forster, February 1854, Dickens, *Letters*, 7:453, 282).[3] It is then not surprising that writers like Anthony Trollope or Margaret Oliphant whose forte was unmistakably in the domestic novel with its leisurely build-up were not approached to contribute to Dickens's weekly. Indeed, in her attack on sensation fiction in *Blackwood's* in 1862, Oliphant had deplored the effect on the reader of the 'violent stimulant of serial publication – of *weekly* publication, with its necessity for frequent and rapid recurrence of piquant situation and startling incident' (568).

As we saw in Chapter 1, during the 1860s weekly periodicals began to offer a serious challenge in the serial fiction market to the dominance of monthly magazines. Though Dallas probably slightly exaggerates Dickens's role, there is no doubt that his active involvement remained of major practical as well as symbolic importance in encouraging the acceptance of this trend by middle-class readers and literary reviewers. Since newspaper serialization almost always occurred in weekly parts, it is not surprising it should also be subject to the generic determinants noted above, and be particularly unsuited to narrative progressing at a leisurely pace. Within the wide variety of fiction material appearing in the press, it is possible to determine dominant forms which change gradually over the second half of the century. As the ubiquity of Pae's work would suggest, in the era of the minor and proto-syndicates beginning in the mid-1850s, as in the penny journals of the same period, melodrama was the prevalent narrative mode, though the combination of domestic settings and outrageous events in stories such as Pae's *Jessie Melville* prefigure certain elements of the sensation novel.[4] When the major fiction syndicates began to appear from the early 1870s, the first authors to sign up were the sensationalists who had made their names in the previous decade. That mode remained predominant, though we can often see their later newspaper novels, such as Collins's *Jezebel's Daughter* (1879–80) and '*I Say No*' (1883–84), or Braddon's *Wyllard's Weird* (1884–85) and *The Day Will Come* (1889), exploring the evolving formula of the detective story (Brantlinger; Carnell, ch. 5). In the mid-1880s, when the provincial syndicates and metropolitan weeklies were competing head to head for the services of the top authors, newspaper fiction came closest to reflecting the full range of fiction available in volume, but by the beginning of the following decade the compartmentalization of sensation into the popular genres of adventure, mystery and romance was already becoming apparent. Again William Westall notes this shift in fashion:

> I remember asking him [W.F. Tillotson], some years ago, what sort of stories had just then the best chance of success. 'Stories of English domestic life, with a good deal of incident and a little immorality,' was the somewhat cynical answer. But since that time fashions have changed. The 'good deal of incident' and the 'little immorality' may still be 'good business' but tales of English domestic life have ceased to draw. The rage nowadays is

all for strong sensation, rapid movement, and complicated plots.

(Westall, 78)

Thus the sensation fiction of B.L. Farjeon or Dora Russell gradually gave way to naval, colonial or wild-west adventures by William Clark Russell, George Manville Fenn, or Bret Harte, to detective series like those featuring Grant Allen's Hilda Wade, Arthur Morrison's Martin Hewitt or J.E. Muddock's Dick Donovan, and to exotic romances by John Strange Winter or 'Rita' (Mrs Desmond [Margaret] Humphreys).

Obviously these trends in newspaper novels are often apparent in other sectors of the fiction publishing industry, and can be explained at least in part by wider historical forces at work. For example, the growing importance of the formulae of adventure, mystery and romance in the 1890s can be related not only to the economic and political tensions deriving from Imperialism, but also to the sudden reduction in the average length of the novel precipitated by the circulating libraries' rejection of the triple decker. Yet at the same time there are determinants specific to the newspaper market, which can be isolated by tracing changes in the forms of fictional commodity then being offered to readers. In the 1850s and 1860s the vast majority of serials appearing in provincial journals were published anonymously, that is, they were unsigned like the rest of the material in the newspaper and could thus generally be presumed to be of local origin. What was being sold then was principally the novelty of fiction itself in the local context. In the period of the major syndicates the name value of the author became paramount. The appearances of new serials by established writers were prefaced weeks in advance by notices hawking the reputation, and later the portrait, of the author. Only seven serials were published unsigned in the *Bolton Weekly Journal* during the nineteenth century, all of them appearing by 1875, most being by Pae, and none being syndicated by the Fiction Bureau. William Westall (78) reports W.F. Tillotson as saying: 'I buy the author; I don't buy the story, and I would rather give four thousand dollars for a "Braddon" or a "Wilkie Collins" than forty dollars for an intrinsically better story by an author without a name.' By the end of the century, mass market miscellanies like *Tit-Bits*, popular Sundays like *The Weekly Times* and *The People*, and even the provincial syndicates, were in large part selling formula fiction to their readers, whether military adventures, detective thrillers, or spicy romances. Again Westall reports

Christopher Leng of the *Weekly Telegraph* as preferring 'a story by an unknown writer with a good beginning, than the biggest author living and a long wandering descriptive opening' (80). Publicity is now achieved less through a portrait of the author than a stirring illustration of the action. This process also helps to account for the increasing commodification of the fiction programmes offered in quarterly and half-yearly packages by Tillotsons to subscribing papers from around the turn of the century (see Chapter 3).

The implication in the above account – that, between the 1850s and the turn of the century, the dominant subject of the newspaper novel shifts from the local to the imperial – remains true at the broadest level of generalization, but requires some qualification when we come to cases. In particular, it is important that the emergence of the major syndicates should not be seen to herald a sudden and absolute shift from provincial to metropolitan settings and themes. In the first place, Pae himself, who so dominated the years before Tillotsons, was not a local novelist in any simple sense, and further, the material provided from the mid-1870s by Tillotsons was by no means limited to works by writers with established metro-politan reputations like Braddon. In order to demonstrate this in more detail, it is useful to look more closely at the specific situations in Scotland and in Lancashire and to employ the concept of the 'regional' novel.

David Pae's work was not restricted in setting to a single local community, nor documentary in intent, nor written to any signifi-cant extent in the Scots vernacular. His *mise-en-scène* ranges not only all over Scotland from Edinburgh to Glasgow and from the Highlands to Tweedside, but shifts on occasion to the Lancashire cotton towns for 'Very Hard Times', or to Ireland for 'Biddy Macarthy'. His narrative mode of choice is theatrical, indeed melodramatic. Pae's narratorial voice is unwaveringly in standard literary English, and his villains' speech seems to owe as much to the Newgate school as to authentic Glasgow thieves' slang. Although there are poor-but-honest characters who speak in vernacular Scots, like Hugh the knife-grinder in 'Lucy, the Factory Girl', the effect is often cosmetic, perhaps reminiscent of that produced by Dickens in *Hard Times* with Stephen Blackpool's broad Lancashire dialect. This is all in marked contrast to the case of William Alexander, another major and largely forgotten Scottish mid-Victorian novelist–journalist, who was editor of the Aberdeen *Free Press* and published much of his fiction in its pages. As Donaldson has shown in detail (ch. 4), Alexander took great pains to reproduce as accurately and consistently as possible Scots dialect forms specific to Aberdeenshire and over a wide social range, and, in consequence, is now largely inaccessible to readers without specialist knowledge or an extensive glossary and apparatus of notes. Pae, on the other hand, was able immediately to reach and touch audiences across a wide range of Scottish and northern English communities.[5]

In the era of the major syndicates, the big Scottish weeklies circulating throughout the country and beyond, most notably the *Glasgow Weekly Mail*, *Glasgow Weekly Herald*, (Edinburgh) *North Briton*, and the *People's Journal* and *People's Friend* out of Dundee, continued this tradition by retaining a significant balance in favour of regional as against metropolitan stories. The former included works not only by writers who remained based in Scotland, like Pae himself and his son, David Pae, Jr, Andrew Stewart, or William McQueen, but also novelists who developed their careers in London, but continued to work Scottish themes. These would include George MacDonald (notably in *Malcolm* or *Sir Gibbie*), William Black (notably in *A Daughter of Heth* or *A Princess of Thule*), Charles Gibbon, or even Robert Buchanan.[6] Some of these stories were sold direct to the Scottish journals, but others were syndicated by agents like Tillotsons, Leaders, or A.P. Watt. Whether produced north or south of the border, these works obviously varied considerably in the aspects of Scottish life they selected and the way they presented them, but all can be classed as realistic by comparison with the sentimental 'kailyard' school of J.M. Barrie, Ian Maclaren, and S.R. Crockett which emerged at the end of the century.

Let us turn to the situation in the northwest of England. As we saw in Chapter 5, in contrast to rival agencies like the Editor's Syndicate, Tillotsons's Fiction Bureau was never content merely to present a uniform programme of metropolitan fiction which proprietors could take or leave, but rather preferred to advertise a wide range of material to suit the varied needs of journals in specific communities. As well as offering the occasional Scots story by Black or Buchanan, Tillotsons handled a considerable quantity of Lancashire material. The local tale *Grace Barton* was syndicated in 1875, while the *Bolton Weekly Journal* fiction competition of 1878 established a contact with Jessie Fothergill, daughter of a Burnley mill owner and author of *The Lasses of Leverhouse*. William Westall, with long experience in the Lancashire cotton trade before he turned to journalism, was an important client author in the 1880s, with *The Old Factory* and other tales, while J. Monk Foster was, of course, one of the Bureau's most regular contributors after W.F. Tillotson's death, with around 15 Lancashire novels between 1890 and 1906. Rather than the coterie of major regional journals covering most of the kingdom created for, say, Braddon's work, Foster's serials tended to appear in minor local papers concentrated in the English North and Midlands. In addition to Tillotsons's Lancashire Journals, there were many other weekly papers which contributed to the sense of a thriving regional tradition in fiction, as various as George Toulmin's rival chain of Lancashire weeklies, major city journals like the *Manchester Weekly Times* and *Liverpool Weekly Post*, James Henderson's *Weekly Budget* printed in London, or workers' papers like the *Cotton Factory Times*, which has been discussed in detail by Eddie Cass. In addition to the names mentioned above, writers who contributed to the tradition of the Lancashire novel in the later Victorian decades included Harrison Ainsworth – notably in the autobiographical works *Mervyn Clitheroe* (1858, reprinted in the *Manchester Weekly Times* in 1881) and *Stanley Brereton* (also 1881, syndicated by Tillotsons), Francis Hodgson Burnett with *That Lass O' Lowries* (1877) and *Haworth's* (1879), Isabella Banks, Ben Brierley, and Edwin Waugh. The Manchester publishing house of Abel Heywood, the bookseller and wholesale newsagent who had been imprisoned for his activities during the War of the Unstamped Press back in the early 1830s (Wiener, *War*, 206–7), and who had given telling evidence to the Parliamentary Newspaper Stamp Committee in 1851 (see Chapter 1 and Altick, *English*, 350–2), was by the 1880s offering a substantial list of local novels in volume, including works by Banks, Brierley and Waugh.[7]

Two general points remain to be made. Firstly, in the eras of both the minor and major syndicates, it is apparent that the provincial newspaper novel both reflected and contributed to a continuing sense of a broad 'Northern' cultural identity, covering the inhabitants of both Scotland and England 'beyond the Trent', in contradistinction to and often in antagonism with that of 'Southern' culture centred on the metropolis and the 'Home Counties'. Evidence includes the wide circulation enjoyed by Pae's tales, and the specific arrangements for the sharing of fiction between papers in Dundee and Sheffield, or Glasgow and Manchester. It should also be noted that Leaders, Tillotsons, or even James Henderson in his *Weekly Budget*, allowed regional novelists based in London to maintain an attachment to their roots by providing opportunities specifically to address readers in their original communities. In contrast to the focus on the industrial novel at the time of the Chartist disturbances in the mid-century, mainstream literary history of the later Victorian decades has tended to interpret provincial fiction predominantly in relation to the Southern market town, as in Trollope, Eliot, or Oliphant, or to the rural Southwest, as in Hardy or Blackmore, and largely overlooked writers like Black and MacDonald in Scotland, or Banks and Fothergill in Lancashire, though all still appear writers of considerable interest. Finally, we must note that by the 1890s there are signs even in the fiction columns of major Northern journals like the *Manchester Weekly Times*, *Liverpool Weekly Post*, or *Glasgow Weekly Herald*, as well as in Tillotsons's own lists, of a shift in the balance from regional to imperial subjects.

7.2 Composition and control

Though, as noted in Chapter 1, Norman Feltes treats it simply as an instance of the Grundyish mechanisms of control wielded by the capitalist periodical, whether *The Graphic* or the *Bolton Weekly Journal*, the case of the serialization of Hardy's *Tess* was in fact both complex and exceptional. Having already syndicated three Hardy short stories, W.F. Tillotson accepted the new novel for 1000 guineas at the end of June 1887, without sight of the manuscript, a title, or a story outline, as was his custom with well-known authors. But he died six months before the first half of the manuscript was submitted, rather later than agreed, in early September 1889, though in the meantime Hardy had given the Fiction Bureau indications of the general story line and his (frequently changing) conception of the title (Grindle and Gattrell, 1–6). The first 16 chapters, including the scenes depicting the violation of Tess and her irregular baptism of the bastard child, seem to have been already in proof before William Brimelow, now in charge at Bolton and rather more strait-laced than his former partner, realized the controversial nature of the material and asked Hardy to reconsider. Hardy refused. Tillotsons stated that they could not then carry the story, but would pay for it as contracted. Hardy then proposed that the contract be cancelled, and a seemingly amicable agreement was reached before the end of September.[8] Hardy immediately agreed to produce a short story – 'The Melancholy Hussar' – for the Fiction Bureau, and by February the following year had signed a new agreement for a short novel – eventually to become *The Well-Beloved* – for which he provided the Bolton firm with a prospectus for publicity purposes, outlining the story and affirming that there was nothing there that would 'offend the most fastidious taste' (cited in Purdy, 94–5).

On the cancellation of the contract with Tillotsons, *Tess* seems to have been offered more or less simultaneously to three of the more conservative metropolitan periodicals: the short-lived *Murray's Magazine* attached to a publishing house which had regarded fiction with disdain throughout most of the Victorian period; *Macmillan's*; and the weekly *The Graphic* (Grindle and Gattrell, 6–15). Edward Arnold at *Murray's* and Mowbray Morris, the editor of *Macmillan's* who had forced Hardy to tone down the description of the affair between Miss Damson and the doctor in his previous novel *The Woodlanders*, both refused *Tess* firmly on moral grounds after seeing the manuscript. Arthur Locker of *The Graphic*, who had taken *The Mayor of Casterbridge* in early 1886, and recently arranged for Hardy to write a series of short tales (*A Group of Noble Dames*) for his paper's 1890 Christmas number, accepted it without hesitation sight unseen. At the same time Locker arranged for subsidiary serial rights to be sold on to a number of provincial newspapers through the agency of A.P. Watt (see the discussion of belt-and-braces syndicates in Chapter 4). *The Graphic* had always been rather more circumspect in its menu of fiction than its rival *The Illustrated London News*, and there had been a public clash with Wilkie Collins over the *Law and the Lady* in early 1875, shortly after the paper began to carry serials. The terms of Collins's agreement explicitly denied the right of the journal to alter the text submitted by the author, so, after the editor had bowdlerized a paragraph describing a sexual advance, Collins through his solicitor forced *The Graphic* to print the original version; in doing so the editor at the same time expressed his strong disapproval of the tenor of the novel as a whole (Peters, 371). Hardy had no such contractual protection and when Locker insisted on extensive revisions to the treatment of sexual issues in *A Group of Noble Dames*, the author seems to have offered little resistance. Further, seemingly without any prompting from *The Graphic*, Hardy set about refashioning *Tess* so that it would be acceptable to the London paper. As a result, when *Tess of the D'Urbervilles* finally appeared as a weekly serial in the second half of 1891, both the violation and baptism scenes had been entirely excised, along with a host of other minor changes. Perhaps the most curious was in the church-going scene in chapter 20, where Angel was made to carry Tess and the other two farm girls through the flooded lane not in his arms but in a wheelbarrow. (We should note that the serial running simultaneously in the rival *Illustrated London News*, Hall Caine's Moroccan romance *The Scapegoat*, featured a number of pictures of loosely-attired harem girls, and ended with the dramatic rescue of the heroine from imminent rape by the evil Sultan.)

Hardy's own actions in the matter were obviously far from consistent, wavering between firm insistence on the artistic integrity of his writing, and meek compliance with editorial demands occasionally verging on the absurd. A similar ambivalence can indeed be seen as early in his career as 1874, when *Far From the Madding Crowd* was appearing in *Cornhill*. When the editor Leslie Stephen requested permission for cuts to avoid offending prudish readers, Hardy replied:

> . . . I am willing, and indeed anxious, to give up any points which may be desirable in a story when read as a whole, for the sake of others which shall please those who read it in Numbers. Perhaps I may have higher aims some day, and be a great stickler for the proper artistic balance of the completed work, but for the present circumstances lead me to wish merely to be considered a good hand at a serial.
>
> ([18 February?], Hardy, *Letters*, 1:28)

In the case of *Tess*, Hardy compensated for his capitulation in a number of ways. He wrote a bitter attack on the 'respectable magazines and select libraries' which were responsible for 'the charlatanry pervading so much of English fiction', as part of a symposium on 'Candour in Fiction' in the *New Review* of January 1890 (18); he quickly issued the two major scenes cut from *Tess* as independent sketches in journals whose editors enjoyed taking risks, W.E. Henley's *National Observer* (1888–97) and Frank Harris's *The Fortnightly Review*; and, when the novel appeared in three volumes in December 1891, he was able not only 'to piece the trunk and limbs of the novel together' (as he put it in a brief 'Explanatory Note' which also gave fair warning that it contained material 'addressed to adult readers') but also to add the provocative sub-title 'A Pure Woman'.

Tess proved extremely popular in volume form, selling 20 000 copies in little over a year in Britain alone (Grindle and Gattrell, 15–17), and thus, as Keating has suggested (262–3), encouraged greater sexual frankness among other novelists of naturalist bent such as George Gissing.

A further reason for recounting this incident in some detail here, is that it is one which, because of the status of the writer and work involved, has received a good deal of attention, and which has thus served to give a misleading impression of the otherwise generally overlooked role in literary history of the fiction syndication agency as represented by Tillotsons. Though they seem to converge in the *Tess* incident, the ideological positions of *The Graphic* and *Bolton Weekly Journal* were in fact far apart. Indeed, Hardy himself, in his strictures on 'Candour in Fiction', had suggested that one way to effect the emancipation of the serial novel was to issue it not in 'respectable' periodicals but 'as a *feuilleton* in newspapers' (20–1). The Tillotsons's records suggest that the cancellation of the contract for *Tess* was unique, and that requests for revisions to manuscripts on moral grounds were extremely rare. We should recall that the American newspapers often rejected the material offered by the British fiction syndicators on account of its 'immoral' tendencies. In general terms, the authorized or unauthorized bowdlerization of serials due to the fear of the adverse reaction of readers to sexual content seems to have been a regular practice in the late nineteenth century mainly in metropolitan monthly miscellanies and 'class' weeklies, that is, in the periodicals specifically aimed at bourgeois readers – the 'Philistines' in Matthew Arnold's terms (*Culture*, ch. 3). However, even here there was considerable variation in the extent to which particular journals attempted to target a 'family' audience. Among the monthlies, *Belgravia* and *Temple Bar* tended to retain a bohemian edge, while *Good Words* or *The Argosy* were considerably more staid, with *Cornhill* occupying the middle ground. Similarly Edmund Yates's *World*, which launched an attack on *The Graphic* over its stance regarding Collins's *Law and the Lady* (Peters, 371), and which went on to serialize the same author's tale of a virtuous prostitute in *The Fallen Leaves*, was noticeably more fast and fashionable than its rival Society journal *The Whitehall Review*, just as *The Illustrated London News* seems to have been less concerned about Mrs Grundy than *The Graphic*. In addition, particularly in the last decades of the century, the weeklies targeting a lower-middle-class family audience, including both the older penny miscellanies, like the *Family Journal* or *Bow Bells*, and the new maga-zine-papers, like *Tit-Bits* or the *Weekly Telegraph*, also became careful to avoid impropriety.

On the other hand, if, along with the metropolitan journals di-rected particularly towards working-class subscribers, such as *The People* and *Lloyd's Weekly*, the provincial syndicators, and the jour-nals they served, were less likely to tamper with texts to avoid giving offence to prudish readers, they seem at the same time to have been far more likely to do so to by adding a veneer of sensa-tionalism, by deleting material perceived as tedious, or simply by making pragmatic changes according to pressures of space. The following list provides typical examples of such tampering, repre-senting a wide range of journals, periods, and motives:

- The Dundee *People's Journal* purchased serial reprint rights to David Pae's 'Lucy, the Factory Girl' in 1863 on the condition that 'we shall be at liberty to curtail it and alter the title or the headings of the chapters as we may think expedient' (see Chapter 2)
- Mayne Reid complained bitterly to W.E. Adams in 1880 about unauthorized cuts in the Prologue to *No Quarter!* serialized in the *Newcastle Weekly Chronicle*, demanding 'for what reason, and by whose authority, these omissions have been made' (10 April 1880, Pollard 'Novels', 83)[9]
- In 1882, prior to the publication of Collins's, *Heart and Science* in *England*, the editor Rowland Twinker wrote to A.P. Watt with the following request: 'Will you please suggest to Mr Collins that the first chapter should be if possible a specially startling one. I mean rather sensational in order to attract the masses.' (24 May, A.P. Watt Archive)
- In 1882 Besant's *All Sorts and Conditions of Men* ran throughout in the *Glasgow Weekly Mail* as 'All Sorts of Men', while in 1891 Braddon's, *Gerard: or, the World the Flesh and the Devil* ran in the Dundee *People's Friend* as 'The Fate Reader', the intended title of the opening chapter.
- A note appended to the 'Christmas Stories' on Tillotsons's backlist for c.1884 informed potential customers that '[a]lthough these Stories were originally written for publication at Christmas time, yet the reference to Christmas can easily be eliminated' (ZBEN, 4/5)
- Following the success of Oppenheim's *John Martin, Postmaster* as a prize mystery story in the *Chicago Record*, and, on learning that the author's new story 'is not of the kind that makes it

practicable to give prizes for solution of a mystery', Victor Lawson asked C.D. Leng whether it would be possible 'to modify Mr. Oppenheim's story so as to make it of this kind?' (TLS, 12 April 1895, Outgoing, VFL)

- In mid-1889 *Lloyd's Weekly* agreed to take William Black's *Donald Ross of Heimra*, to commence at the beginning of 1891, but when Black submitted the first third of the manuscript in mid-1890, the proprietor complained that the work contained too much Scots vernacular and not enough incident and refused to publish (Wilson, 5.9)

- In general, though copy was provided by authors to syndicators in a previously agreed number of parts, subscribing journals sometimes squeezed or stretched the period of serialization by doubling-up or dividing parts according to their own requirements without consulting the author. (For examples, see the syndication details for Braddon and Collins in Tables A.4 and A.5)

In the case of initial syndication, time constraints meant that proofs were normally sent to the author by the syndicator but not by the individual subscribing journals – even when stereo plates were not employed and the work was entirely re-set (Farmer and Law). Indeed, authors often seem to have remained unaware of precisely which or indeed how many papers belonged to the 'coterie' carrying their work, doubtlessly happily so in many cases. They seem even less likely to have been aware of later reprints in minor journals. In theory, the opportunities for making unauthorized and unrecognized emendations to the text were virtually infinite. In practice, most subscribing papers were doubtless content to receive their week's supply of fiction early from the syndicator, to set up or clamp in the columns of type as early as possible in the week, and work around them. Though the time and expense necessary to carry out a collation of all the different newspaper versions of even a single widely syndicated novel would be exorbitant, a complete collation of two different serial versions of a Collins's novel revealed relatively few textual variations of any note, and almost none that could not be accounted for as slips by the compositor (Farmer and Law). However, such slips – like the entire chapters omitted from Braddon's work in the Cardiff *Weekly Mail* – could sometimes be of considerable significance.

Collins, of course, attempted to maintain control as far as possible by inserting a clause in each of his agreements with Tillotsons explicitly excluding unauthorized alterations to his texts, just as he had with *The Graphic*, though it is uncertain how much weight this carried with the syndicating journals. There were even extreme cases where editors seem to have entirely disregarded any claims by authors to control over their work once serial copyright had been sold. Around 1896, Tillotsons purchased for £125 the British and Colonial serial rights to Rita's new novel *The Sinner* without time restrictions. Around the turn of the century, the Glasgow publishers of the cheap weekly miscellany *The Red Letter* purchased second serial rights from the Fiction Bureau, and issued the work in instalments. However, the work was announced as a 'Great New Serial by "Rita"', and the title, the names of all the characters, and even the setting had been completely changed – the events now took place in north Wales instead of the original southwest Ireland. According to her account published over thirty years later, on writing to the editor of the journal in question the author was informed that 'the liberties taken with [her] story were quite permissible. It was the custom in editorial offices to change, cut, or *omit* anything in a serial story that they deemed unsuitable for their class of readers!' (Rita, 117–19, 162–4). With the support of Besant's Society of Authors, Rita brought a successful action against the publishers and thus established the precedent that the assignation of the serial copyright of an imaginative work did not permit the assignee to make alterations which might affect the credit or reputation of the author, without his or her knowledge and consent. In her 'Prefatory Note' to *The Silent Woman* (1904), Rita went on to raise her voice more generally against newspaper fiction as 'false to art, and degrading to the authors who write it'.

Apart from such legal constraints, the only other recourse open to writers wishing to assert control over their serials, was to revise them extensively before publication in volume, in order to restore specific passages emended by or for editors and to diminish the general influence of the mode of initial publication. Well-known cases in point are Elizabeth Gaskell's *North and South* – where, in the final stages of the narrative, five chapters were expanded considerably and two entirely new ones added to the book, in order to counteract the severe shortage of space experienced during its composition as a serial for *Household Words* – and, of course, Hardy's *Tess*. On the other hand, the labour required could be considerable and the financial reward negligible. Moreover, given that the volume edition normally appeared shortly before the appearance of the final serial instalment, the practical difficulties involved could sometimes be insurmountable, especially for authors who wrote close to the serial deadlines. There was also the psychological difficulty of resuming the wheel so soon after turning off the final number of the serial, to borrow Dickens's metaphor (to Wilkie Collins, 23 June 1861, *Letters*, 9:428). This could be too much even for artists as dedicated as Meredith, who could not bring himself to rework *Evan Harrington* despite the problems he encountered in producing the 'thin' instalments for *Once a Week* (see Vann, 9). Or even for Dickens himself, whose only significant changes for the volume edition of *Hard Times*, for all his complaints about the lack of elbow-room during the composition of the serial, were in the form of the added chapter, part, and sub-titles. For the later regular newspaper novelists, who tended to be both considerably more prolific and less painstaking than Meredith and Dickens, and for whom the rhythm of the weekly number quickly became second nature, the likelihood of returning to make major revisions for volume publication seems to have become increasingly remote. In general, extensive changes at the macroscopic level – to names, chapter divisions, and titles, notably – seem to have been far more commonplace than intensive revisions at the microscopic level of style and rhythm. The newspaper novels of Braddon and Collins can serve as examples.

Changes to chapter titles, and emendations immediately around a part break, such as the replacement of pronouns by proper names or expansions to establish more definitely a character's identity on first appearance, are among the most apparent revisions. Braddon probably gave more time to her first story for Tillotsons, *Taken at the Flood*, which reveals 11 chapters retitled out of 58 – 'Bad News from Demerara' to 'Gott Lenkt' for chapter 8, or 'A Bitter Blow' to 'Passion's Passing Bell' for chapter 30, for example – and a similar order of textual changes around part and chapter breaks, including two paragraphs entirely cut. Changes in chapter partitions often serve to illustrate how Braddon geared her narratives specifically to the psychological demands of weekly serialization. For example, *The One Thing Needful* had 25 chapters in serial, but this was reduced to 22 in volume, the three extra units being subsumed within adjacent chapters. The first serial instalment concluded with the hunchback Lord Lashmar standing before a crowd of onlookers on the balcony of a burning building which he had climbed to rescue a child, whose father, Lashmar's enemy, had perished in the same attempt. The newspaper reader thus had to wait in suspense until the following week to find out if Lashmar escaped with the child. There the descent was dealt with in the opening sentence: 'Five, ten minutes of supreme anxiety, and all was over.' In the book this mechanism of suspense is avoided as the rescue and escape are described seamlessly within the same chapter (ch. 3)

Changes of narrative content and style are largely restricted to changes of nomenclature. Among the earlier novels, there are a number of cases where characters are redrawn simply by being renamed. For example, in *A Strange World*, the amateur sleuth Humphrey Clissold becomes the more heroic Maurice Clissold, while the professional police investigator Paufoot is further diminished to Smelt. More telling are those many cases among the later newspaper novels where the title itself was changed significantly for the book version – indeed, the practice was so common that we must suspect that one motive at least must have been the attempt to pass off old work for new. *Gerard*, *The Venetians*, *London Pride*, and *In High Places* ran respectively in the weeklies under the more dramatic titles 'The World, the Flesh, and the Devil', 'All in Honour', 'When the World was Younger', and 'George Nameless', although continuity was preserved through the use of subtitles. There were cases, however, where the transformation was total. *Rough Justice* appeared in serial at first as 'Shadowed Lives', though here the change was due to legal pressure on the basis that the title was already copyright, a not uncommon occurrence in the later Victorian decades, as the number of novels issued rose rapidly and the title itself took on the value of a commodity.[10] *Under Love's Rule* started out unrecognizably as 'The Little Auntie', a title almost diametrically opposite in connotation and tone, while 'Whose Was the Hand?' was reborn as *One Life, One Love*. Here it seems likely that Braddon decided during the course of composition that the rhetorical appeal of the serial title was inappropriate to the narrative as it developed. Although a murder is central to the plot, the form is by no means that of a whodunit, and instead the psychological detail of the growth of obsession forms the central interest.

This brief account is inevitably based only on a cursory examination of the texts of the 27 newspaper novels in serial and volume form, but it does seem sufficient to support the contention that Braddon had little time or inclination to revise these works at all extensively before volume publication.

In general Collins also spent little time revising the text of his last novels between the newspaper and volume editions (Law, 'Wilkie'). *The Evil Genius* and *The Legacy of Cain*, for example, gain little more than chapter headings in volume, as there were no changes even in the chapter breaks. The one notable exception is the anti-vivisection novel *Heart and Science*, on which he placed such great hopes for the revival of his fading literary reputation. It was the only novel of the 1880s for which he wrote a preface. There he informed reviewers ('Readers in Particular') that the work had been 'subjected to careful revision, and I hope to consequent improvement, in its present form of publication'. This is undoubtedly true, for as has been shown elsewhere (Farmer and Law), the text was revised in around seven hundred places in total. Interesting minor changes again include those affecting nomenclature: in the triple-decker version, the cat 'Snooks' loses her name and much of her prominence; the independent lady's maid 'Jane' is Frenchified as 'Marceline'; the medical adviser Mr Null receives his negative name much earlier on; and the hero Doctor Ovid Vere is promoted to Mr Ovid Vere, surgeon, above the vivisector Doctor Benjulia. The biggest changes include: a lengthy inserted passage that adds complexity to the character of the monomaniac scientist Mrs Gallilee, by allowing her an internal life and memories of her youth; a series of revisions to render more consistent the character of the governess Miss Minerva, who had began the serial as an unmitigated villain but underwent conversion less than half way through; and a general toning down of the immediacy of the description of cruelty to animals, perhaps in part to keep a promise made to Frances Power Cobbe, the anti-vivisectionist who had sent Collins pamphlets on the subject (to Cobbe, 23 June, 21 November 1882, Collins, *Letters*, 2:446–7, 451). But there are also many substantial changes which can be characterized simply as deletions to trim the fat and additions to sharpen the focus. At the same time, a collation of the texts of the newspaper and magazine serializations in the light of letters written during the course of composition, indicates that Collins originally composed the work in weekly parts, and, that, despite a number of changes around the part breaks, *Heart and Science* as a book still bears traces of its origin as a newspaper novel.

In summary, the most consistent pressures exerted on the later Victorian novelist by the mode of initial publication in newspapers were generic. In other words, the extent to which novelists internalized the constraints of the weekly number was in the end just as significant as the explicit acts of tampering by editors, whether to remove impropriety or to add zest. There were obviously major modernizing authors who had the economic or ideological resources to reject the aesthetic demands of the serial market to a very large extent, like Henry James, who we shall discuss shortly, or Gissing, who in 1889 found the thought of writing for a newspaper syndicate 'too ignoble' (Gissing, 75), and whose thoroughgoing disdain of the modern trade of letters is recorded powerfully in both *New Grub Street* (1891) and *The Private Papers of Henry Ryecroft* (1903). Less dedicated modernizers like Grant Allen proved that even rebellion against the market could have a market value in the volatile conditions of the 1890s. As we saw in Chapter 4, Allen won a *Tit-Bits* prize competition in 1890 and his detective fiction was being sold to the Northern Newspaper Syndicate at the time of his death in 1899, but in the middle of the decade both the scandal and the profits generated by his controversial 'New Woman' novel, *The Woman Who Did* (1895), encouraged him briefly to renounce serial publication altogether. In the preface to his next novel, *The British Barbarians*, he proclaimed the concept of the 'hill-top' novel ('one which raises a protest in favour of purity'), announcing: 'I will willingly forgo the serial publication of my novels, and forfeit three-quarters of the amount I might otherwise earn, for the sake of uttering the truth that is in me, boldly and openly, to a perverse generation.' Hardy's experience remains of particular interest in part because it dramatizes starkly the tension between rebellion and complicity. The cases of Mary Braddon and Walter Besant offer interesting variations on the same theme.

7.3 Commodification: Braddon and Besant

In the 1860s there is a sharp cleavage in Braddon's fiction between penny-dreadfuls appearing in *The Halfpenny Journal* and novels issued in the middle-brow monthlies *Temple Bar* and *Belgravia*, which the blanket term 'sensation' and the fact that both types of journal were owned by Maxwell often serve to disguise (Carnell, ch. 4). While this balancing act obviously allowed Braddon's early writings to reach a very wide audience and reap a substantial financial harvest, it inevitably incurred the displeasure of the London literary establishment, who found it difficult to 'place' the author. Particular provocations were the use of multiple pseudonyms and titles to disguise parallel composition and publication, and attempts to pad out stories written as penny-dreadful serials to triple-decker length for volume publication (Wolff, *Sensational*, ch. 4). Throughout the decade we can see her attempting not only to meet the exigencies of her commercial taskmaster Maxwell, but also to placate the god of letters in the person of the elder statesman of Victorian fiction, Sir Edward Bulwer-Lytton. From 1862 until his death in 1873, Braddon wrote a series of long letters to Bulwer-Lytton as a 'devoted disciple', which have been transcribed and edited by Robert Lee Wolff. Bulwer-Lytton seems often to have urged her to write less and more carefully and in December 1862 Braddon attempted to justify herself:

> I have never written a line that has not been written against time – sometimes with the printer waiting outside the door. I have written as conscientiously as I could; but more with a view to the interests of my publishers than with any great regard to my own reputation. The curse of serial writing and hand to mouth composition has set its seal upon me, and I have had to write a lot of things together.
>
> (Wolff, 'Devoted', 11)

When the editorship of *Belgravia* gave her a greater degree of independence concerning form and theme, she used the magazine as a forum not only for justifying sensationalism in fiction (Robinson), but also to carry out experiments in social and historical narrative influenced by contemporary French models and relatively untouched by melodrama (Carnell, ch. 4).

Composed from the early 1870s, all of Braddon's newspaper novels, however, contain marked sensational elements in the form of mystery, crime, and impropriety. That this was specifically in order to appeal to the debased taste of the provincial newspaper reader is unlikely, since these factors were precisely what most library subscribers were looking for when they borrowed a new Braddon. What does seem certain, however, is that during Braddon's engagement to Tillotsons, many of the novels which were written not for the provincial syndicates but for metropolitan literary journals (not only *Belgravia*, but also, from the late 1870s, the weeklies *All the Year Round*, *The World*, and *The Whitehall Review*) were significantly less sensational. Important examples are: *Joshua Haggard's Daughter* (1876), *Vixen* (1879), *The Story of Barbara* (1880), *The Golden Calf* (1883), *Ishmael* (1884), and *Mohawks* (1886). This dichotomy is particularly apparent on the many occasions when Braddon produced two novels in a year. For example: in 1876 Tillotsons got the satirical *Dead Men's Shoes* while *Belgravia* had the tragedy *Joshua Haggard's Daughter*, which, unusually, Braddon spent over a year composing and revised extensively before volume publication; in 1884, the newspapers had the Devonshire detective story *Wyllard's Weird* rather than the *Ishmael*, an epic of the Paris Commune; and in 1886 the novelettes *One Thing Needful* and *Cut by the County* instead of the historical *Mohawks*. Placating the god of letters thus implied not only an avoidance of melodrama in favor of domestic realism or Zolaesque naturalism, but also a preference for historical or foreign settings and themes.

In this sense her characteristic mode of composition was to work alternately, both in series and in parallel, on 'serious' and 'popular' works. Figure 7.1, representing a segment from the mid-1870s shortly after Braddon's engagement to Tillotsons, illustrates the basic pattern.[11] However, the cleavage between the two modes is less sharp than had been the case in the 1860s. Between *Hostages to Fortune* and *Dead Men's Shoes* it is difficult to distinguish which is the heavyweight. And Braddon often veered towards the sensational even when she was attempting to write 'seriously'. In *The Golden Calf*, which reveals the influence of Zola's *L'Assommoir*, there is a detailed examination of the effects on an unstable marriage of the husband's mental degeneration accompanying his growing addiction to alcohol. But towards the end of the process Braddon incongruously has the deranged husband burn down the house and end his own life, while the wife is rescued from the encroaching flames by her admirer who has disguised himself as a hermit to remain near her. Conversely, we can occasionally trace naturalist tendencies in novels for Tillotsons, such as *The Cloven Foot* with its scenes in the bohemian world of the Paris theatre (see Wolff, *Sensational*, 289–91).

Contemporary critics also were by no means certain to evaluate Braddon's 'serious' efforts above her 'popular' ones. Even those London journals which had complained loudest at the impropriety and triviality of her early works, often saw things differently by the 1870s. With the first novel she wrote for Tillotsons, *Taken at the Flood*, the *Athenaeum* was grateful that Braddon had returned 'to her best style' after a period devoted to more ponderous and painstaking fiction (2 May 1874, 592). The same journal again bemoaned the defects of her 'later manner', as seen in the sentimental novel *Asphodel*

Figure 7.1 Braddon's pattern of dual composition

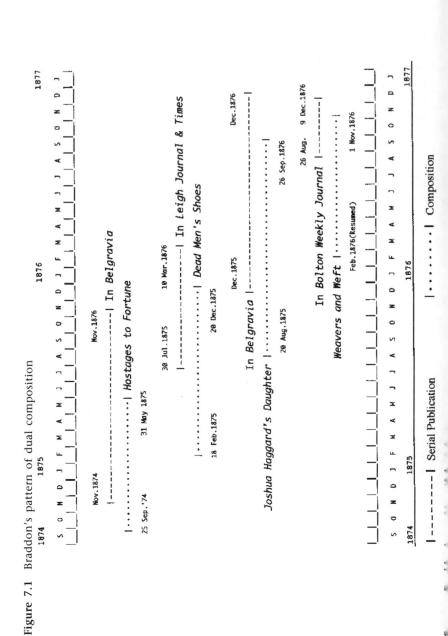

which was not built 'upon intricacy of plot, upon crime or mystery' (26 February 1881, 245–6), while *The Spectator* was far more enthusiastic about *Wyllard's Weird* than *Ishmael* (2 May 1885, 581–2). Braddon herself, not surprisingly, defended her greater labours on the 'serious' works. When, in a 1911 interview she was asked to name her favourites among her own novels, *Lady Audley's Secret* headed the list, but none of the other choices were sensational and most were the carefully researched and revised historical works (Holland, 708). And, among the few modern critics who have commented on Braddon's works written from the 1870s onwards, Wolff comes to a similar conclusion, in regarding *Joshua Haggard's Daughter* and *Ishmael* as among her finest efforts (*Sensational*, 270–7, 304–15). For the present writer, however, the later works most worthy of attention are those in which the sensation pattern laid down by Braddon in the 1860s remains apparent: the facade of respectability of the country house ruptured by the emergence of guilty secrets and suppressed passions. An economical way to pursue the ideological orientation of Braddon's work in the newspaper novels is to survey the treatment of the contrasting pairs of heroines often featured, in terms of transgression versus submission, or the erotic against the angelic.

Three of the more complex of the sensation novels written for Tillotsons can illustrate the main variations: the heroic failure of transgression, the timid triumph of submission, or radical ambivalence. After a series of insipid female leads in domestic romances – Clarissa Lovel of *The Lovels of Arden* (1871), for example – in *Taken At the Flood* Braddon reverted to the pattern of *Lady Audley's Secret* and *Aurora Floyd*, with the heroine as glamorous criminal. Sylvia Carew is a Pre-Raphaelite beauty condemned to the role of an impoverished schoolmaster's daughter. She constantly flouts respectable opinion, is suspected of murder, attempts bigamy, and is finally rewarded not with union with her lover but with death by typhoid. But Braddon is in large part sympathetic to her heroine's frustrations and admires her will-power and courage. She devotes a good deal of space to evoking Sylvia's alternating moods of ambition and listlessness, and her overwhelming feelings of constraint and claustrophobia, as she marries to be free of her domineering father only to find she is an even closer prisoner as the wife of an elderly man in declining health. In contrast, the minor heroine, the passive and long-suffering ward Esther Rochdale, may at last and by default win the hand of the handsome hero, but in the process she gains little sympathy or even sustained attention from the narrator.[12]

In *Phantom Fortune* the contrast is between the Maulevrier sisters Lady Lesbia and Lady Mary, the former glamorous and desperate for fast and fashionable cosmopolitan society, the latter unpretentious and unwilling to leave her home among the valleys and hills of the English Lake District. But Lesbia's Parisian costumes and coquetry are shown to be cold and heartless, while the tomboyish Mary exudes a warm, tweedy eroticism, and it is the latter who succeeds in the marriage market. Mary wins the kindly and handsome heir Lord Hartfield, and is allowed to keep her country haven, while Lesbia has to make do with the paunchy city financier Mr Goodward, and ends up a social outcast after allowing herself to be kidnapped and all but seduced by an adventuring scoundrel from the Caribbean. Here Braddon extends little sympathy to the transgressor.

In *An Open Verdict*, two young women are again given almost equal attention, but here the weighting of sympathy is more finely balanced. Beatrix Harefield is a detached and alabaster beauty, a wealthy heiress deprived of human warmth by a strict and jealous father. Her sole friend from childhood has been the rosy and impetuous Bella Scratchell, whose poverty forces her to earn money as a morning governess and companion. Both are attracted by the hero, the grave young socialist clergyman Cyril, but when Beatrix's father dies in suspicious circumstances, Bella's jealous actions bring suspicion of murder on Beatrix. Beatrix recoils into saint-like self-sacrifice, and Bella into greed and sensuality. The latter's profligacy leads to her death in a riding accident, while the former's patient service is finally rewarded by reconciliation with Cyril. Despite their dichotomies, both women are presented as at once victims and victors, and fairly share authorial sympathy, in marked contrast to the noble hero who hardly escapes the charge of being a bloodless prig.

A number of general points can be made on the basis of this brief and doubtless reductive survey. Firstly, the best of Braddon's newspaper novels are complex not only in their plotting but also in their social and cultural symbolism. Secondly, they remain ideologically challenging to mid-Victorian social and sexual proprieties, but less uniformly and aggressively so than in her sensation novels of the 1860s. Finally, Braddon's transgressive heroines in the 1870s and 1880s are rather more introspective than those of the early 1860s. Being allowed more fully to enter the consciousness of such female protagonists perhaps encouraged in Braddon's readers a greater degree of empathy with their gestures of defiance and understanding of the causes. This shift produces a sharper focus on the material determinants of the subjection of women, which goes together with the author's growing awareness of the claims of naturalism as a literary mode.

Walter Besant did not publish any fiction until he was in his mid-thirties, but, as Table A.6 shows, thereafter produced a full-length novel every year until his death. This was in addition to at least a dozen volumes of tales and novellas, scholarly writings on French literature towards the beginning of his career and on the history of London towards the end, plus series of works in connection with his roles both as Secretary of the Palestine Exploration Fund from 1868 and as chief organizer of the Society of Authors from 1884. Though his earliest stories were written alone, for an entire decade until the premature death from cancer of his collaborator James Rice (1843–82), all his fiction was produced in tandem. From the beginning the pattern seems to have been for Rice to draft a detailed outline of the narrative content, while Besant, who wrote with re-markable facility, would be primarily responsible for the literary form (*DNB*, 20:154).[13] Whether written alone or in collaboration, his fictional works were produced almost without exception for initial periodical publication. The bulk of his shorter tales were written as Christmas stories for *Once a Week*, *All the Year Round*, or *Arrowsmith's Annual*, while, as Table A.6 again shows, all but one of his full-length novels appeared as serials in a variety of periodicals.

Though a handful were syndicated in the provincial newspapers, and rather more were carried by monthly miscellanies like *Belgravia* or *Longman's*, the most typical venue was in the London class weeklies. Besant's flexibility and fluency seem to have been admirably suited to the constraints of serial publication. There is no evidence of him failing to meet a deadline or over-running his allotted space, in the way that Collins and Braddon sometimes did.[14] Whether writing in longer monthly or shorter weekly instalments, he seems to have felt little desire or necessity to revise his novels at all ex-tensively prior to publication in volume.[15] Writing shortly before his death in 1901, Besant cheerfully accepted that authors produc-ing serials for, say, *The Illustrated London News* did so on the firm condition that 'the story was to run for 26 weeks. This meant an average length of so many columns. Translated into numbers, it meant about 6000 words for each instalment.' He mocked the idea that the serialist wrote in chains and claimed that he 'never felt, recognized, or understood that there was the least necessity for ending an instalment with an incident' (*Autobiography*, 191–2).

Moreover, perhaps partly due to the influence, in turn, of his partner Rice and his agent Watt, both of whom held detailed knowledge of the London periodical market,[16] Besant seems frequently to have shaped his serial stories specifically according to the nature of the subscribing journal and the class of readership it targeted. Virtually all of the novels appearing in sixpenny pictorial weeklies (*The Graphic*, *The Illustrated London News*, and *The Lady's Pictorial*) were historical romances which could at the same time easily avoid contentious issues and take advantage of lavish illustration, while those written for Edmund Yates's *World* or *Time*, for Tillotsons, or for *Chamber's Journal* generally had contemporary settings and allowed themselves greater leeway for satire and critique. In fact, although nearly all of the early novels written with Rice had contemporary themes, writing solo during the 1880s and 1890s Besant generally fell into the pattern of alternating period and modern settings. Unlike that of Braddon, however, his output was throughout limited to a regular annual novel, though on the occasions when works happened to be serialized simultaneously, he reacted vigorously to accusations that he was engaged in composing two novels at once.[17] In more than one sense, then, Besant's reputation in the London literary world of the last two decades of the nineteenth century was of one who had been quick to master the art of 'writing by numbers.' This facility can obviously be seen as a mark of the author's confidence in his relationship to the bourgeois reading public, a confidence inconceivable to Gissing, Hardy, Moore, or James (Goode, 'Art', 243–6).

Although Besant explores a wide range of settings both historical and contemporary and employs a number of styles from the satirical to the allegorical, his narratives reveal a marked resistance to the modernizing modes of naturalism, impressionism, and aestheticism, and a strong underlying pull towards the tradition of the romance, and repeatedly find their resolution in marriage vows. At the same time, despite the various public causes for which he was an enthusiastic crusader – whether to improve financial arrangements for authors or leisure facilities in the East End – the cast of his mind was undoubtedly conservative. For, though Besant was preoccupied with both the early manifestations of the 'New Woman' phenomenon and the cultural conditions of the working-class, he remained a committed anti-feminist and anti-socialist. On occasion the articulation of such views forms the central theme of his novels, as in *The Revolt of Man* (1882), a fantasy on a future England where social, religious and political institutions are dominated by women, at least until a revolt led by Edward, Earl of Chester, restores the male to his rightful superiority, or in *The Ivory Gate* (1892), Besant's working of the Jekyll and Hyde motif, in which a sober Tory solicitor is converted into a fanatical socialist through the effects of brain disease. Here, however, I would like to look briefly at the way in which these themes are refracted in two of Besant's earliest solo works, *All Sorts and Conditions of Men* (1882), and *Dorothy Forster* (1884), both first published in the newspapers.

All Sorts and Conditions of Men, perhaps still the author's best-known work, appeared, of course, in both the London monthly *Belgravia* and in a series of provincial weeklies including the *Sheffield Weekly Telegraph*. The Prologue introduces both Angela, the heiress to the Messenger fortune which derives from an East End brewery, about to leave Newnham College, Cambridge with a degree in Political Economy, and Harry, the adopted son of Lord Jocelyn Le Breton, who has just been informed that his natural father was a common soldier from the East End by the name of Goslett. Both vow independently to give up the pursuit of leisure and marriage, to return to their roots in Stepney, hide their true identities, and take up a life of labour, respectively as a dressmaker and a cabinet maker. There they happen to meet and fall in love, in a common lodging house inhabited by a string of misfits with hopes of advancement. These include the Davenants, an elderly couple from New Hampshire attempting to establish their claim to an English title, and Daniel Fagg, an Australian scholar attempting to publish a book establishing his claim to have discovered an original alphabet. Harry assists Angela in her project of establishing a dress-making workshop where the girls will enjoy the fruits of their own sweatless labour, Angela encourages Harry to dream of building a People's Palace of Delight where the East Enders will learn to employ their leisure in a cultivated manner, and both assist the misfits briefly to fulfil their various fantasies. All of this is finally achieved, of course, only with the clandestine help of Angela's millions. The efforts of the East Enders to solve their own problems, whether the spiritual solution offered by the Salvation Army or the political one suggested by the socialist militants, are shown to be narrow and crooked, but they are eventually taught by Harry to 'find the swells their real friends' (ch. 41). The novel concludes by evoking the image of the earthly paradise with Harry and Angela united as the People's Palace opens its doors.[18]

Dorothy Forster was serialized in *The Graphic* in the second half of 1884, and recounts the involvement of the ancient Forster family of Northumberland in the Jacobite rebellion of 1715. It is one of three historical romances published by Besant during the 1880s in which the narration is performed obliquely by a female character in the story, in this case, the Dorothy of the title, daughter of the Sheriff of the County and the niece of the Bishop of Durham.[19] Apparently the author's favourite amongst his own novels, it is based to some extent on fact, and when published in volume was dedicated to Besant's wife, who claimed descent from the Forster family (*Autobiography*, 205–6). A beautiful young girl at the commencement of the story, Dorothy Forster reveals herself at once as a devout member of the English Church, proud of her noble birth, but also a believer in the folk myths prevalent in the North Country, and the protector of her 'gypsy' servant maid who dabbles in witchcraft. Like Dorothy herself, the English rebel leaders reveal a consistent hatred of the Whigs and the Hanoverian succession and a desire for the return of the House of Stuart, but they are also shown to be divided by religion, misled by Celtic fanatics, and half-hearted in the act of rebellion. The Jacobite rising itself occurs, as it were, off-stage, while the central interest of the drama lies rather in the complex emotional relationship of Dorothy to the three men devoted to her. These are: her brother Tom, a hard-drinking sportsman with no intellectual pretensions, who wastes his own life and the family fortune; the Earl of Derwentwater, a refined Catholic raised in France with the exiled Pretender, whose love of Dorothy is thwarted by religious scruples; and Antony Hilyard of Oxford, her brother's faithful tutor and bailiff, a mercurial character by turns a devout and learned scholar and a drunken actor and satirist, who has long felt an undeclared passion for his master's sister. All three become involved in the rebellion for a variety of complex motives, Tom as General, the Earl as figurehead, and Hilyard as mere camp-follower. After its failure, both Tom and the Earl are arrested: the latter is beheaded, but Tom flees into permanent exile due to the bravery and resourcefulness of his sister and Hilyard, who has escaped unscathed. He is made Canon of Durham for his loyalty and lives out his life in devoted service to Dorothy. He once declares his love, but Dorothy chooses to remain in saint-like self-renunciation. Both, however, along with the author, seem to share a happy vision of a future Imperial England, a reward for its return to loyalty to 'the teaching of the pure gospel and the Articles of the Church of England' (ch. 21).

The ideological continuities underlying these two superficially very different novels can best be suggested with reference to Besant's lecture on the 'Art of Fiction', delivered at the Royal Institute in April 1884, and printed as a pamphlet by Chatto and Windus the same year. Although evidently written hastily and without due regard for consistency, this piece is nevertheless revealing. In large part because of the response it elicited from Henry James under the same title, the essay remains Besant's best-known contribution to the theory of the novel. As Mark Spilka (101–2) has shown succinctly, Besant's lecture is most appropriately read as part of a wider debate in the 1880s on the future of the novel, whose most distinguished participants were Stevenson and James, but where the extreme positions were represented by Andrew Lang's defence of the romance and William Dean Howells's support of naturalism. Besant begins by defending, against the 'general – the Philistine – view' (Besant, *Art*, 6), the equality of status of the Novel with the Fine Arts of Music, Painting, and Poetry, with which James could not but agree. However, as a corollary, Besant goes on to echo the aims of the Society of Authors not only in appealing for existing members of the profession to club together to advance their interests, but also in laying down the laws governing the Art for the benefit of new entrants, which James could only see as a series of petty prohibitions drawn from the well of Philistinism itself. He was thus stimulated to articulate an increasingly unrestrained defence of the freedom of the artist.

Besant sees the novel as the highest expression of the individualism underlying the bourgeois social ideal, demanding from the writer and recreating in the reader that 'modern Sympathy' which includes 'not only the power to pity the sufferings of others, but also that of understanding their very souls' (11–12). As Spilka suggests (112), the image James offers of experience is far more passive and alienated, 'an immense sensibility, a kind of huge spider-web, of the finest silken threads, suspended in the chamber of consciousness and catching every air-borne particle in its tissue' (James, 'Art', 509). Besant forbids writers to go beyond their own social experience ('a young lady brought up in a quiet country village should avoid descriptions of garrison life; a writer whose friends and personal experiences belong to what we call the lower middle class should carefully avoid introducing his characters into Society,' 15). James finds this 'rather chilling' and is prompted to celebrate the power of the artistic imagination to transform the most fleeting impressions into experience, and encourages the writer to become 'one of the people on whom nothing is lost' (508–10). Besant attacks the school 'which pretends that there is no need for a story' and insists on 'strong ones, with incident in them, and merriment and pathos, laughter and tears, and the excitement of wondering what will happen next' (27–8), to which James retorts that story and treatment are inseparable, and that adventures can be psychological as well as physical (516–18). Above all, Besant finds it 'a great cause for congratulation', and even a source of Imperial strength, that:

> . . .the modern English novel, whatever form it takes, almost always starts with a conscious moral purpose. When it does not, so much are we accustomed to expect it, that one feels as if there has been a debasement of the Art. It is, fortunately, not possible in this country for any man to defile and defame humanity and still be called an artist; the development of modern sympathy, the growing reverence for the individual, the ever-widening love of things beautiful and the appreciation of lives made beautiful by devotion and self-denial, the sense of personal responsibility among the English-speaking races, the deep-seated religion of our people, even in a time of doubt, are all forces which act strongly upon the artist as well as upon his readers, and lend to his work, whether he will or not, a moral purpose so clearly marked that it has become practically a law of English Fiction. We must acknowledge that this is a truly admirable thing, and a great cause for congratulation.
>
> (24)

James implies that Besant views Art through 'rose-coloured window panes' and that his principle of selection comes down to 'picking a bouquet for Mrs. Grundy':

> The essence of moral energy is to survey the whole field, and I should directly reverse Mr. Besant's remark and say not that the English novel has a purpose, but that it has a diffidence. To what degree a purpose in a work of art is a source of corruption I

shall not attempt to inquire; the one that seems to me least dangerous is the purpose of making a perfect work. As for our novel, I may say, lastly, on this score, that, as we find it in England to-day, it strikes me as addressed in a large degree to 'young people,' and that this in itself constitutes a presumption that it will be rather shy. There are certain things which it is generally agreed not to discuss, not even to mention, before young people. That is very well, but the absence of discussion is not a symptom of the moral passion. The purpose of the English novel – 'a truly admirable thing, and a great cause for congratulation' – strikes me, therefore, as rather negative.

(519–20)

George Moore makes a similar point in his diatribe against Mudie's policy of 'selection' for his library in the pamphlet *Literature at Nurse, or Circulating Morals*. There Moore attempts to show that many of the fashionable sensation novels promoted by Mudie are far more salacious that his own *A Mummer's Wife* (1885), which has been judged 'an immoral publication which the library would not be justified in circulating' (5). He records Charles Edward Mudie, the personification of 'the British Matron' (16), as stating that 'he did not keep naturalistic literature – that he did not consider it "proper"' (18). Hardy would say much the same thing as Moore in 'Candour in Fiction' in 1890, perhaps in part in response to Besant's rather smug contribution to the same symposium. In this way, the issue of 'candour' in contemporary fiction is inextricably interwoven with wider issues of narrative form, mode of publication, and perceived audience (see Hiley). The argument between Besant and James thus points towards a yawning divide opening up in the late Victorian literary world.

Unlike Besant, of course, James preferred the wide-open spaces of the high-brow monthlies, the *Atlantic* or *Macmillan's*, to the narrow confines of the weekly newspapers. Under financial pressure in the middle of his career, he had resorted to selling a story or two for syndicate use to S.S. McClure or to Charles Dana of the New York *Sun* ('horresco referens!', he wrote defensively to a friend). He also employed Watt as agent for a few years from 1888, particularly to handle serial rights in Britain (Johanningsmeier, 61–2, 170–1; Anesko, 86–7, 128–30). However, the receipt of a family legacy in 1893 removed the need for such sordid transactions. Thus near the end of his life he could look back on the 'vales of Arcady' traversed by Thackeray, Trollope, or Eliot in their 'sovereign periodical appearances', and contrast them with the 'bristling mazes' facing the present generation of writers 'smothered in quantity and number': 'My claim for our old privilege is that we did then, with our pace of dignity, proceed from vale to vale' (James, *Notes*, 19–21).

By the late 1880s, the aging middle-brow monthly miscellanies with their circulations draining away, the class weeklies, their status threatened by the growth of the mass-market magazines led by *Tit-Bits* and the *Strand*, and the circulating libraries, in defensive mood as the economic rationale of the triple-decker finally disintegrated, together acted as a reactionary brake on the emergence of experiment in narrative. While the provincial syndicates had permitted a range of narrative modes and themes, the shift of the balance of power back to the metropolitan press encouraged a considerable narrowing and hardening of the dominant modes of serial fiction. Besant's career as a novelist, as indeed that of A.P. Watt as a literary agent, seems to have developed to a considerable degree in complicity with these pressures. In turn, and by reaction, they can be seen as contributing to the emergence of the coterie magazines in which many of the early English modernizing experiments were thus carried out – notably John Lane's *Yellow Book* (1894–97) and Arthur Symons's *Savoy* (1896) – confirming Regenia Gagnier's insistence on 'the concrete embeddedness of Aestheticism in a late-Victorian market economy' (11). The material developments in the serial publication of fiction in the last decades of the nineteenth century should thus be understood as among the major factors influencing the specific, and distinctly limited, forms of modernism appearing in Britain, and the breadth of the chasm opening up there between 'popular' and 'serious' culture.

Appendix: Serialization Tables

Table A.1 Early serial fiction in provincial newspapers

Author	Serial	Agent	Author	Serial	Agent
North Briton (Edinburgh) (Founded 1855; bi-weekly)			Glasgow Times (Founded 1855; weekly)		
Serials from early issues			Before 1858 No fiction until Jun. 1858.		
1855†					
Unsigned (D. Pae)	'Jessie Melville'				
1856					
Unsigned	'Jeanie Gordon'				
1857					
Unsigned	'Lady Alice Glendenning'				
AO 'Jessie Melville' (D. Pae)	'Clara Howard'				
1858			**1858**		
Unsigned	'Mary Maxwell'		Unsigned	'Grace Gray'	
Unsigned	'Esther Lyman'		Unsigned (D. Pae)	'Lucy, the Factory Girl'	+EG
Unsigned (D. Pae)	'Lucy, the Factory Girl'	+EG			
1859			**1859**		
Walter Scott	'Guy Mannering'		Unsigned	'Danby Davenport'	
Unsigned	'Ralph Darrell'	+EG	Unsigned	'Ralph Darrell's Will'	+EG
Unsigned	'Mary Barry'	+EG	Unsigned	'Mary, the Child of Poverty'	+EG
Unsigned	'Helen Graham'		Unsigned	'Garibaldi, the Hero of Italy'	+EG
Unsigned	'Garibaldi, the Hero of Italy'	+EG	Unsigned (D. Pae)	'The Heiress of Wellwood'	+EG
AO 'Jessie Melville' (D. Pae)	'The Heiress of Wellwood'	−EG			
1860			**1860**		
AO 'Lucy' (D. Pae)	'The Heir of Douglas'	+EG	Unsigned	'The Candidate's Wife'	
Unsigned	'The Ruined Cottage'		Unsigned (D. Pae)	'The Heir of Douglas'	+EG

Attribution	Title	
AO 'Jessie Melville' (D. Pae)	'The Diamond Hunter'	
Unsigned	'Family Secrets'	
1861		
Unsigned (D. Pae)	'Nelly Preston'	
Unsigned (D. Pae)	'Mina'	
Unsigned (D. Pae)	'The Lost Child'	+EG
Unsigned	'Margaret Somerville'	
1862		
Unsigned (D. Pae)	'Flora the Orphan'	
Unsigned (D. Pae)	'Norah Cushaleen'	
Unsigned (D. Pae)	'Adam Wilkie'	
Unsigned (D. Pae)	'Biddy Macarthy'	
AO 'Willie Baxter'	'Mysie Hyslope'	
1863		
Unsigned (D. Pae)	'Basil Hamilton'	
Unsigned	'Constance Marden'	
AO 'Jessie Melville' (D. Pae)	'Very Hard Times'	+EG
Unsigned	'Blanche de Cressy'	
Unsigned	'Lizzie Gray'	
1864		
Unsigned	"Tis Forty Years Since'	
AO 'Lucy' (D. Pae)	'Captain Wilde's Gang'	
Unsigned	'Margaret and Madeline'	
Unsigned	'Effie Baird'	
AO "Tis Forty Years Since'	'Deacon Brodie'	

(Dundee) People's Journal (founded 1858; weekly)

1858–62 Tales in 1–4 pts, mainly competition stories, local, anonymous.

Attribution	Title	
1863		
Unsigned (D. Pae)	'The Factory Girl'	
1864		
AO 'Greensleeves'	'The Legacy'	
AO 'The Factory Girl' (D. Pae)	'Mary Paterson'	+DS

Attribution	Title	
1861		
Unsigned	'Maggie Burns'	
AO 'Lucy' (D. Pae)	'Caroline Frazer'	+EG
1862		
Unsigned	'Fanny the Fortune Teller'	
Unsigned	'The Kentucky Pioneer'	
Unsigned (David Pae?)	'The Forged Will'	
Unsigned	'The Abducted Bride'	
1863		
Unsigned (D. Pae)	'Agnes Hardcastle'	
1864		
Unsigned	'Magdalene'	
Unsigned	'Old Israel'	
Fenton Farrel	'Jeanie Cameron'	
Unsigned	'Madeline Lennox'	+EG
Unsigned	'The Ladies of the Monastery'	

Sheffield Daily Telegraph (founded 1855; fiction in Sat. edn)

Before 1864 No fiction before W.C. Leng took over the paper in 1864

Attribution	Title
1864	
M. Bouilly	'Popular Stories'

	Left column			Right column	
1865			**1865**		
Unsigned (D. Pae)	'The Gipsy's Prophecy'	+DS	Unsigned (D. Pae)	'The Heir of Douglas'	+DS
Unsigned (D. Pae)	'Eustace the Outcast'		Unsigned (D. Pae)	'The Fatal Error'	
			Unsigned (Reuben Hallam)	'Wadsley Jack'	
1866			**1866**		
Unsigned (D. Pae)	'Effie Seaton'	+DS	AO 'The Fatal Error' (D. Pae)	'Eustace, the Outcast'	+DS
Unsigned (D. Pae)	'The Haunted Castle'	+DS	Reuben Hallam	'Wadsley Jack's Married Life'	
1867			**1867**		
Unsigned (D. Pae)	'George Dalton'	+DS	AO 'Eustace the Outcast' (D. Pae)	'Effie Seaton'	+DS
Unsigned (D. Pae)	'The Laird of Birkencleuch'	+DS	'A Private Soldier'	'Tales of the Barrack Room'	
			Unsigned (D. Pae)	'The Haunted Castle'	+DS
1868			**1868**		
Unsigned	'Agnes Glen'		AO 'The Fatal Error' (D. Pae)	'Lucy the Factory Girl'	
Unsigned (D. Pae)	'Jeannie Sinclair'	+DS	Byron Webber	'Tried and Acquitted'	
1869			**1869**		
Unsigned (D. Pae)	'Cast on the World'	+DS	AO 'The Fatal Error' (D. Pae)	'Jeannie Sinclair'	+DS
Unsigned (D. Pae)	'Clanranald'				
1870			**1870**		
Unsigned (D. Pae)	'Isaac Barton's Crime'		AO 'Lucy' (D. Pae)	'Cast on the World'	+DS
1871			**1871**		
Unsigned	'The Abbot of Aberbrothock'		AO 'Eustace the Outcast' (D. Pae)	'Very Hard Times'	
Unsigned (D. Pae)	'Helen Moir'				
Unsigned (D. Pae)	'The Foster Brother'				
1872			**1872**		
AO 'The Foster Brother' (D. Pae)	'Annabel, or the Temptation'	+DS	Unsigned (D. Pae)	'The Captain's Bride'	
1873			**1873**		
Unsigned	'The Rival Clansmen'		AO 'Grace Hamilton' (R.B. Bannister)	'Tontine'	
M.E. Braddon	'Taken at the Flood'	*T	AO 'Eustace the Outcast' (D. Pae)	'Annabel, or the Temptation'	+DS
Unsigned	'Jessie, the Key-Keeper's Daughter'		M.E. Braddon	'Taken at the Flood'	*T
AO 'The Foster Brother' (D. Pae)	'Mayhew, the Millspinner'				

Year	Author	Title	
1874	'Johnny Geddes'	'The Adventures of a Scottish Packman'	
	Unsigned (D. Pae)	'Victor Moredant'	
	Unsigned	'The Ploughman Student'	
	Unsigned	'Harold the Outlaw'	+DS

Sheffield Independent (founded in 1819; daily from 1861; fiction in Sat. edn)

Before Jan. 1866 No fiction.

Year	Author	Title	
1866	Unsigned (R.E. Leader)	'Judith Lee'	
	John Thomas	'The Story of Birley Vale Collieries'	
1867	AO 'Kate Brownville' (W.C. Hepburn)	'A Trade Dispute and What Became of It'	
	Daniel A. McKinlay	'Saint Olave's Chase'	
	James Pitt	'Lost and Won'	
1868	AO 'Kate Brownville' (W.C. Hepburn)	'The Dervishes of Wimpole Manor'	
	Geo. Manville Fenn	'Hard Pressed'	
1870	Unsigned	'Lost, Stolen, or Strayed'	
1871	Geo. Manville Fenn	'Under the Yellow Flag'	
	W.C. Hepburn	'The Heir of Dean Hall'	
	Unsigned	'Fortune's Fool'	
1872	J. Riding Ware	'The Grey Lady'	
	Geo. Manville Fenn	'A Ray of Light'	

Bolton Weekly Journal (founded 1871)

Serial novels from first issue.

Year	Author	Title	
1874	M.E. Braddon	'A Strange World'	*T
	Frederick Talbot	'Lottie's Fortune'	
	Unsigned (D. Pae)	'Victor Moredant'	+DS
1873	Dr Maurice Davies	'Sixty Per Cent'	*Ld
	Mrs Geo. Skelton	'Donna'	
	Unsigned	'The Recluse of the Old Water Tower'	
	Perrin Browne	'On this Side of the Grave'	
1874	Unsigned	'The Peasants' War'	*Ld
	Unsigned	'Sam Holberry, the Chartist'	
	J.S. Borlase	'The Adventures of a Mounted Trooper'	
	AO 'Gerald Fitzgerald'	'Boughton Manor'	
	R.D. Dowling	'The Loss of the Dream'	*Ld
	Florence Marryat	'Fighting the Air'	*T
1875	Geo. Manville Fenn	'Under Wild Skies'	*Ld
	Blanchard Jerrold	'Black-Eyed Susan's Boys'	*T
	Mortimer Collins	'A Fight with Fortune'	
	E. Owens Blackburne	'A Woman Scorned'	*Ld

Bolton Weekly Guardian (founded 1859)

No fiction before Oct. 1873, when Supplement first issued.

(Plymouth) Western Daily Mercury (founded 1860; fiction in Sat. edn)

Year	Author	Title	
1871	Unsigned (D. Pae)	'Jessie Melville'	
1872	AO 'Jessie Melville' (D. Pae)	'The Haunted Castle'	
	Unsigned (D. Pae)	'Biddy McCarthy'	
1873	AO 'Jessie Melville' (D. Pae)	'Effie Seaton'	*T
	M.E. Braddon	'Taken at the Flood'	*Ld
	AO 'Fortune's Fool'	'Ninety-Eight'	
1874	M.E. Braddon	'A Strange World'	*T
	J.E. Muddock	'The Great White Hand'	*T
	Unsigned	'The Peasant's War'	*Ld
	Dr Maurice Davies	'Sixty Per Cent'	*Ld
	J.J.G. Bradley (J.S. Borlase)	'May Mortimer's Mistake'	*T
	Florence Marryat	'Fighting the Air'	*T
1875	M.E. Braddon	'Dead Men's Shoes'	*T
	Unsigned (J. Bradbury)	'Grace Barton'	*T
	Mayne Reid	'A Brother's Revenge'	*T
	Frank Lee Benedict	'Madame'	*T
	B.L. Farjeon	'At the Sign of the Silver Flagon'	*T
1876	M.E. Braddon	'Weavers and Weft'	*T
	Mary Cecil Hay	'The Arundel Motto'	*T
	Dora Russell	'Footprints in the Snow'	*T
	Florence Marryat	'Her Father's Name'	*T

(Plymouth) Western Weekly News (founded 1861)

Year	Author	Title	
1873	Unsigned (D. Pae)	'Lucy the Factory Girl'	
1874	AO 'Lucy the Factory Girl' (D. Pae)	'Very Hard Times'	
	Unsigned	'The Secret Marriage'	*Ld
	Unsigned	'The Stolen Will'	*Ld
	Ernest King	'The Coquette'	
1875	Geo. Manville Fenn	'Under Wild Skies'	*Ld
	Alphonse Daudet	'Born to Trouble'	?
1876	AO 'Grace Barton' (J. Bradbury)	'Fatal Trust'	
	Unsigned (D. Pae)	'Flora the Orphan'	
	Unsigned	'The Two Lads'	

1860–70 Mainly short tales (1–3 parts), often signed, some local, some from metropolitan journals, some translated from French or German. Even in early 1870s serials only occasional.

1861–70 From at least 1864, regular complete tales (1–4 pts), some initialled, but most anonymous, many local but some adapted from French or German. Even in early 1870s serials only occasional.

1871

| M.A. Paull | 'Lady Ingaret' | |
| M.A. Paull | 'Phantoms of Waterloo' | |

1873

| Selwyn Eyre | 'The Artiste's Picture' | |
| M.E. Braddon | 'Taken at the Flood' | *T |

1874

| M.E. Braddon | 'A Strange World' | *T |
| Florence Marryat | 'Fighting the Air' | *T |

(Cardiff) Weekly Mail (founded 1870)

Serials from first issue.

1870

Arthur Sketchley	'Married in Haste'
AO 'Light and Shade'	'Profit and Loss'
Unsigned	'Moved by Two Passions'
Countess von Bothmer	'Cruel as the Grave'

1871

| Unsigned | 'The Mystery of Paul Wakenden' |
| Carl Morganwg | 'Gwendoline Margrave' |

1872

| Francis Vacher | 'Disappearances Extraordinary' |

1873

| M.E. Braddon | 'Taken at the Flood' | *T |

1871

| Unsigned | 'A Secret of Long Ago' | |

1873

Annie Thomas	'That Old Love Again'	
AO 'Adele Dorevant'	'Janet MacGregor'	*T
Selwyn Eyre	'First-Foot'	

1874

Emma Hall	'Nigh Unto Death'	
Selwyn Eyre	'The Lawyer's Prediction'	*T
Sidney Shelley	'Shaugh Bridge'	*T
Mrs S.R. Townshend-Mayer	'Nora's Dowry'	

(Dublin) Penny Despatch (founded 1861; weekly)

Before 1872 From late 1860s, no serials, but generally one complete tale per issue, anonymous, with no provenance, occasionally local.

1872

Unsigned	'A Bone of Contention'	
Unsigned	'Hilary'	
Unsigned	'The Sister's Crime'	

1873

Unsigned	'Helena MacDonald'	
Unsigned	'Lady Darville'	
M.E. Braddon	'Taken at the Flood'	*T
AO 'Fortune's Fool'	'Ninety-Eight'	*Ld
R.D. Dowling	'The Loss of the Dream'	*Ld

1874		*T	**1874**		
M.E. Braddon	'A Strange World'	*T	M.E. Braddon	'A Strange World'	*T
Florence Marryat	'Fighting the Air'		E. Owens Blackburne	'Refining Fire'	*T
			Sidney Fitzerin	'The Last Tenants of Castle Gerald'	
			R.B. Curtis	'Macmahon'	
			Florence Marryat	'Fighting the Air'	*T
1875		*Ld	**1875**		
M.M. Eckmann-Chatrian	'The Blacksmith of Felsenbourg'		E. Owens Blackburne	'A Woman Scorned'	*Ld
Mrs Dank	'The Roll Call'	?	E. Owens Blackburne	'Aunt Delia's Heir'	*T
Alphonse Daudet	'Born to Trouble'	?	Frank Lee Benedict	'Madame'	*T
Geo. Manville Fenn	'Under Wild Skies'	*Ld	Selwyn Eyre	'A Woman's Shadow'	*T
			Geo. Manville Fenn	'Under Wild Skies'	*Ld

Newcastle Weekly Chronicle (founded 1864)

1864–72 Occasional short serials (eg Thomas Doubleday's 'The Countess', in 13 pts in 1871), but principally tales (1–3 parts), either from metropolitan/overseas journals, translated from French/German, or 'Original Local Tales' (eg J.G. Grant's 'Sybil of Tynemouth' in 3 pts in 1869)

1873		*T
M.E. Braddon	'Taken at the Flood'	

Portsmouth Times (founded 1850)

No fiction preceding or following Braddon's Taken at the Flood'

1873		*T
M.E. Braddon	'Taken at the Flood'	

AO = 'By the author of'   *T = Syndicated by Tillotsons   *Ld = Probably syndicated by Leaders   ? = Unknown
+DS = Proto-syndicate: Dundee *People's Journal* & *Sheffield Daily Telegraph* +EG = Proto-syndicate: Edinburgh *North Briton & Glasgow Times*
† Years are those of commencement but not necessarily of completion; data not complete for all years, due to gaps in runs consulted

Sources: Original journals; Ferguson; *NPD*; Wolff, *Waterloo*.

Table A.2 Serial fiction* in the *Bolton Weekly Journal*, † 1871–99

Author[1]	Short Title[2]	Dates[3]	Length[4]	To[5]	By[6]	Conract[7]
1871						
Unsigned (D. Pae)	'Jessie Melville'	11.04.71–04.05.72	(55 pts)	?	NS	?
1872						
Unsigned (D. Pae)	'The Haunted Castle'	27.04.72–26.10.72	(27 pts)	?	NS	?
Unsigned (D. Pae)	'Biddy McCarthy'	12.10.72–05.07.73	(39 pts)	?	NS	?
1873						
Unsigned (D. Pae)	'Effie Seaton'	14.06.73–06.12.73	(26 pts)	?	NS	?
M.E. Braddon	'Taken at the Flood'	30.08.73–18.04.74	160 th.	£450	?	S
Unsigned	'Ninety-Eight'	29.11.73–28.03.74	(18 pts)	?	NS	?
1874						
Dr Maurice Davies	'Sixty per Cent'	14.03.74–16.05.74	(10 pts)	?	NS	?
M.E. Braddon	'A Strange World'	18.04.74–05.12.74	160 th.	£600	?	S
Unsigned	'The Peasant's War'	04.07.74–05.09.74	(10 pts)	?	NS	?
J.J.G. Bradley (J.S. Borlase)	'May Mortimer's Mistake'	12.09.74–05.12.74	45 th.	£20	?	?
Florence Marryat	'Fighting the Air'	07.11.74–29.05.75	156 th.	£360	£492	UK–US
J.E. Muddock	'The Great White Hand'	12.12.74–10.07.75	(31 pts)	£10	NS	Single use
1875						
B.L. Farjeon	'At the Sign of the Silver Flagon'	30.01.75–29.05.75	82 th.	£100	£233	UK
Blanchard Jerrold	'Black-eyed Susan's Boys'	05.06.75–31.07.75	30 th.	£100	?	?
Unsigned (J. Bradbury)	'Grace Barton'	05.06.75–30.10.75	(22 pts)	£10	?	?
M.E. Braddon	'Dead Men's Shoes'	31.07.75–11.03.76	160 th.	£450	£770	S
Mayne Reid	'A Brother's Revenge'	16.10.75–15.04.76	150 th.	£200	£202	S–Y1
Frank Lee Benedict	'Madame'	30.10.75–01.07.76	160 th.	£50	£70	?

Year / Author	Title	Dates	th./pts	Price		Code
1876						
Florence Marryat	'Her Father's Name'	04.03.76–02.09.76	148 th.	£210	£325	S–US
Mary Cecil Hay	'The Arundel Motto'	24.06.76–17.02.77	140 th.	50gns	?	S
M.E. Braddon	'Weavers and Weft'	26.08.76–09.12.76	(16 pts)	£300	?	S
Dora Russell	'Footprints in the Snow'	25.11.76–19.05.77	150 th.	£250	?	S–B
1877						
M.E. Braddon	'An Open Verdict'	05.05.77–15.12.77	160 th.	£500	?	S
J.E. Muddock	'The Crimson Star'	11.08.77–18.05.78	(41 pts)	£55	?	?
Joseph Hatton	'Cruel London'	24.11.77–25.05.78	150 th.	£250	?	S–US
1878						
Dora Russell	'Beneath the Wave'	11.05.78–19.10.78	150 th.	£250	?	S–B
Frederick Talbot	'One of the Firm'	01.06.78–17.08.78	40 th.	£25	£37	A–PC1st
C.E. Broad	'A Woman's Will'	07.09.78–16.11.78	64 th.	£15	?	A–PC2nd
F.W. Robinson	'Coward Conscience'	05.10.78–12.04.79	156 th.	£300	£500	UK
Jessie Fothergill	'The Lasses of Leverhouse'	16.11.78–08.03.79	(17 pts)	£10	?	A–PC3rd
1879						
Geo. Manville Fenn	'Hard to Win'	08.03.79–06.09.79	146 th.	£150	£240	S
Mrs G. Linnaeus Banks	'Under the Scars'	05.04.79–04.10.79	150 th.	150gns	£192	UK–Y3
Wilkie Collins	'Jezebel's Daughter'	13.09.79–31.01.80	110 th.	£500	£900	UK–N12
Joseph Hatton	'The Three Recruits'	27.09.79–20.03.80	112 th.	£150	£273	S–US
1880						
M.E. Braddon	'Just as I am'	07.02.80–18.09.80	160 th.	£500	?	S
Dora Russell	'Quite True'	13.03.80–21.08.80	130 th.	£250	?	S–B
Eliza Lynn Linton	'My Love!'	25.09.80–05.03.81	194 th.	£300	?	UK
B.L. Farjeon	'No. 119 Great Porter Square'	02.10.80–26.03.81	146 th.	£300	?	UK–US–Col
1881						
W. Harrison Ainsworth	'Stanley Brereton'	26.02.81–06.08.81	148 th.	£130	?	S–US–Col

Author	Title	Dates	Weeks	Price		Code
Hon. Lewis Wingfield	'The Haven of Unrest'	12.03.81–20.08.81	144 th.	£100	?	S
James Payn	'For Cash Only'	13.08.81–11.03.82	150 th.	£512	?	S-Col
Robert Buchanan	'The Martyrdom of Madeline'	27.08.81–18.03.82	116 th.	£200	?	S-B
1882						
Dora Russell	'Croesus' Widow'	04.02.82–01.07.82	156 th.	£250	?	S-B
Henry W. Lucy	'Gideon Fleyce'	17.06.82–16.12.82	156 th.	£200	£310	S
Hawley Smart	'At Fault'	12.08.82–20.01.83	140 th.	£200	£249	S
W Clark Russell	'A Sea Queen'	25.11.82–16.06.83	156 th.	£175	£192	S
1883						
Mrs Oliphant	'Sir Tom'	20.01.83–14.07.83	150 th.	£500	£578	S-US
Adeline Sergeant	'Jacobi's Wife'	16.06.83–15.01.84	200 th.	£85	?	A-2nd
B.L. Farjeon	'The Sacred Nugget'	08.09.83–23.02.84	144 th.	£300	?	S
1884						
Charles Reade	'Love and Money'	23.02.84–05.07.84	110 th.	£500	£807	2nd-UK-US
Compton Reade	'Under Which King?'	28.06.84–03.01.85	168 th.	£75	£118	S
Hawley Smart	'Tie and Trick'	12.07.84–10.01.85	140 th.	£205	£203	S
1885						
Dora Russell	'James Daunton's Fate'	10.01.85–28.02.85	44 th.	£50	?	A
Justin McCarthy	'Camiola'	14.03.85–05.09.85	156 th.	£500	£605	S-US
M.E. Braddon	'Cut by the County'	20.06.85–15.08.85	63 th.	£250	?	S-US
B.L. Farjeon	'Aunt Parker'	05.09.85–13.02.86	144 th.	£300	?	S-US
Wilkie Collins	'The Evil Genius'	26.12.85–01.05.86	105 th.	£1300	£1446	S-US-Y2
1886						
Mrs Oliphant	'The Son of His Father'	17.04.86–23.10.86	156 th.	£625	£583	S-US-Col-B
Lady M. Majendie	'On the Scent'	04.09.86–27.11.86	60 th.	£30	?	A
William Black	'Sabina Zembra'	09.10.86–02.04.87	156 th.	£1200	£1039	S-US-Y2

Author	Title	Dates	Length	Price		Code
1887						
M.E. Braddon	'Like and Unlike'	26.03.87–24.09.87	160 th.	£1 200	?	S–Y7
Walter Besant	'Herr Paulus'	10.09.87–03.03.88	156 th.	£1 300	?	S–US–Con
1888						
Bret Harte	'The Argonauts of North Liberty'	07.01.88–11.02.88	31 th.	£455	?	S–US–B
Wilkie Collins	'The Legacy of Cain'	18.02.88–07.07.88	100 th.	£1 080	?	S–US–Con–Y2
H. Rider Haggard	'Colonel Quarritch VC'	22.06.88–17.11.88	132 th.	£800	?	S
Katherine S. MacQuoid	'Miss Eyon of Eyon Court'	17.11.88–05.01.89	44 th.	£180	?	A
1889						
S. Baring Gould	'The Pennycomequicks'	26.01.89–29.06.89	156 th.	£1 000	?	A
Hall Caine	'The Bondman'	08.06.89–30.11.89	144 th.	£400	?	S–US
J. Fitzgerald Molloy	'How Came He Dead?'	30.11.89–04.01.90	70 th.	£200	?	A
1890						
J. Monk Foster	'For Love of a Lancashire Lass'	01.03.90–23.08.90	(26 pts)	(£63P)	?	CW
William Black	'Stand Fast, Craig Royston!'	30.08.90–21.02.91	156 th.	£1 100	?	S–Con–Y2
J. Monk Foster	'Slaves of Fate'	08.11.90–18.04.91	(24 pts)	(£78P)	?	CW
1891						
J. Monk Foster	'A Miner's Million'	19.09.91–02.04.92	150 th.	£87	?	A
1892						
J. Monk Foster	'A Crimson Fortune'	02.04.92–03.09.92	(23 pts)	(£84P)	?	CW
Mrs Oliphant	'The Sorceress'	10.09.92–04.03.93	156 th.	£750	?	A
1893						
M.E. Braddon	'The Venetians'	11.03.93–12.08.93	160 th.	£110	?	2nd
William Henry Moyes	'The Mormon's Daughter'	27.05.93–22.07.93	35 th.	2gns	?	S
William Henry Moyes	'When Least Expected'	05.08.93–30.09.93	50 th.	2gns	?	S
Edmund Downey	'Behind the Door'	19.08.93–21.10.93	80 th.	(£85P)	?	S–US–Col
Mary Albert	'The Luckiest Man in the World'	07.10.93–13.01.94	75 th.	£28	?	A

Author	Title	Dates		Price	?	A
Keith Fleming	'The Sins of the Fathers'	28.10.93–27.01.94	65 th.	£10	?	A
1894						
J. Monk Foster	'The White Gipsy'	20.01.94–19.05.94	(18 pts)	(£73P)	?	CW
Adeline Sergeant	'Marjory's Mistake'	27.01.94–28.07.94	(27 pts)	(£150P)	?	CW
J. Fitzgerald Molloy	'On Wheels of Fire'	26.05.94–22.09.94	80 th.	£175	?	US-Con
Mrs Hungerford	'The Red House Mystery'	29.09.94–05.01.95	78 th.	(£300P)	?	A
J. Monk Foster	'Judith Saxon'	24.11.94–06.04.95	(20 pts)	(£81P)	?	CW
1895						
A.W. Marchmont	'Sir Jaffrey's Wife'	12.01.95–20.04.95	75 th.	£105	?	S–US-Con
Ernest Glanville	'The Golden Rock'	27.04.95–31.08.95	80 th.	£10	?	S–Con
Maggie Swan	'Life's Blindfold Game'	06.07.95–21.09.95	65 th.	£30	?	A
Annie Thomas	'A Lover of the Day'	19.10.95–01.02.96	(16 pts)	(£20E)	?	?
Dora Russell	'A Strange Message'	19.10.95–28.03.96	(24 pts)	(£360P)	?	CW
1896						
Bessie Temple	'Liz, A Transvaal Heroine'	08.02.96–18.04.96	80 th.	£15	?	S–B
John K. Leys	'The Broken Fetter'	18.04.96–25.07.96	60 th.	£60	?	S–Con
John Strange Winter	'The Colonel's Daughter'	16.05.96–01.08.96	80 th.	£275	?	S
G.A. Henty	'The Queen's Cup'	01.08.96–12.12.96	100 th.	£300	?	A
R.J. Charlton	'The Honourable Jim'	05.09.96–16.01.97	100 th.	£30	?	S
1897						
Florence Marryat	'In the Name of Liberty'	09.01.97–27.03.97	60 th.	£100	?	A
Mary H. Tennyson	'Within Her Grasp'	23.01.97–03.07.97	150 th.	£50	?	S–Con
J. Monk Foster	'The Watchman of Orsden Moss'	08.05.97–18.09.97	(20 pts)	(£85E)	?	CW
Ernest Glanville	'The Lover's Quest'	10.07.97–30.10.97	85 th.	£35	?	S–US-Con
J. Fitzgerald Molloy	'The Mystery of Redcliffe Hall'	25.09.97–01.01.98	(15 pts)	(£140E)	?	?
Mrs George Corbett	'The Star of Yukon'	06.11.97–08.01.98	50 th.	£50	?	S–Con

1898

				To	By	
A.W. Marchmont	'In the Grip of Hate'	22.01.98–30.04.98	75 th.	£110	£180	S–US–Con
E.W. Hornung	'Young Blood'	22.01.98–07.05.98	80 th.	£200	£194	S–Con
Walter Wood	'Through Battle to Promotion'	07.05.98–23.07.98	65 th.	145gns	?	S–B
William Le Queux	'The Bond of Black'	14.05.98–22.10.98	65 th.	£180	?	S–Con
Ernest Glanville	'His Enemy's Daughter'	06.08.98–12.11.98	75 th.	£30	?	S–US–Con
William Black	'Wild Eelin'	05.11.98–22.04.99	140 th.	£570	£538	S–Con–Y2
J. Monk Foster	'The Cotton King'	19.11.98–30.03.99	(20 pts)	(£85E)	?	CW

1899

Iza DuFus Hardy	'MacGilleroy's Millions'	08.04.99–22.07.99	80 th.	(£80P)	?	A
Mary Angela Dickens	'On the Edge of a Precipice'	29.04.99–15.07.99	60 th.	£85	?	S–Con
John W. Mayall	'Bitter Blood'	05.08.99–11.11.99	80 th.	£35	?	S–Con
J. Monk Foster	'The Forge of Life'	26.08.99–06.01.00	(20 pts)	(£90P)	?	CW
Fergus Hume	'The Lady from Nowhere'	16.11.99–10.02.00	65 th.	£110	?	A

* Serial Fiction = Of at least six instalments.

† *Bolton Weekly Journal* = Until 20 May 1893 under that title, thereafter *Bolton Journal and Guardian*.

1 Author = Standardized to form most frequently occurring.

2 Dates = Of first and last instalments, in British style (DD.MM.YY)

3 Short Title = Sub-titles, if any, omitted.

4 Length = estimate of word count (Notebook A, TURNER), or when unavailable or clearly erroneous, number of weekly instalments (averaging around 5,000 words):

   th. = thousand words;   pts = instalments.

5 To = Payment to author (Notebook A, TURNER, or ZBEN, 1/2–6):

   (£nP) = Proportionate sum based on length, in case of payment for plural works;

   (£nE) = Estimate based on author's stories of similar length/period, if data unavailable.

6 By = Receipts (to nearest £) within 12 months of first appearance (ZBEN, 1/2–6) – incomplete due to gaps in record and to cases of combined payments for more than one story

   NS = Not syndicated by Tillotsons.

[7] Contract = Details summarized in Notebook A or B, TURNER:

S = Simple serial/newspaper rights
Ƀ = Book publication excluded

Con = Serial rights in Continental Europe
Nn = Limit to number of newspapers

A = Absolute copyright
UK = Serial rights in Gt. Britain & Ireland
US = Advance sheets/serial rights in USA
2nd = Second serial rights
PC = Winner of 1878 Prize Competition

B = Book copyright
U̶S̶ = Serial publication in USA excluded
Col = Serial rights in British Colonies
Yn = Time limit in years
CW = Writer under contract to Tillotsons

Sources: Bolton Weekly Journal; or as noted.

Table 4.3 Serial fiction* in the Melbourne *Age*, 1872–99

Author⁻	Short title†	Dates†	British serialization‡	Agent**
M.E. Braddon	'To the Bitter End'	20.04.72–11.01.73	*Belgravia*	John Maxwell
Anthony Trollope	'Harry Heathcote of Gangoil'	15.11.73–03.01.74	*The Graphic*	?
Edmund Yates	'The Impending Sword'	21.02.74–26.09.74	*The Home Journal*	?
Miss (Anne) Thackeray	'Miss Angel'	13.02.75–07.08.75	*Cornhill*	?
J.P. (James Payn)	'Halves'	14.08.75–25.12.75	?	?
Wilkie Collins	'The Two Destinies'	19.02.76–14.10.76	*Temple Bar*	H. Biers
B.L. Farjeon	'Shadows on the Snow'	16.12.76–10.02.77	*Tinsley's Magazine*	?
(John Habberton)	'Helen's Babies'	05.05.77–16.06.77	?	?
Mrs (Annie) Edwards	'A Blue Stocking'	01.09.77–01.12.77	*Temple Bar*	?
Wilkie Collins	'My Lady's Money'	08.12.77–16.03.78	*The Illustrated London News*	H. Biers
M.E. Braddon	'The Cloven Foot'	28.12.78–?08.11.79	*Newcastle Weekly Chronicle*, etc (Tillotsons)	John Maxwell
Ivan Tourguenieff	'Spring Floods'	03.01.80–20.03.80	?	?
M.E. Braddon	'Just as I am'	27.03.80–01.01.81	*Bolton Weekly Journal*	John Maxwell
E. Lynn Linton	'My Love!'	01.01.81–22.10.81	*Bolton Weekly Journal*	Tillotsons ?
John Saunders	'Victor or Victim?'	26.10.81–07.12.81	*Leigh Journal and Times*	Tillotsons ?
A.C. (Ada Cambridge)	'A Girl's Ideal'	10.12.81–?14.01.82	*Australian*	
Mrs (Loisa) Parr	'Robin'	25.01.82–07.10.82	*Temple Bar*	?
David Christie Murray	'A Model Father'	10.06.82–26.08.82	?	?
W. Clark Russell	'A Sea Queen'	06.06.83–13.10.83	*Bolton Weekly Journal*, etc (Tillotsons)	Tillotsons
Unsignec	'The Bread Winners'	10.11.83–08.03.84	USA	
Jessie Fothergill	'Peril'	05.01.84–29.11.84	*Temple Bar*	?
M.E. Braddon	'Ishmael'	22.03.84–14.03.85	*The Whitehall Review*	Tillotsons
Robert Buchanan	'Matt'	18.04.85–06.06.85	*The Graphic*	Watt
Geo. Manville Fenn	'The Master of the Ceremonies'	11.07.85–20.03.86	*Bolton Weekly Journal*, etc (Tillotsons)	Tillotsons
M.E. Bracdon	'The One Thing Needful'	24.04.86–18.09.86	*Sheffield Weekly Independent*, etc (Leaders)	Leaders/ Tillotsons
Unsigned (Edmund Gosse)	'The Unequal Yoke'	16.10.86–27.11.86	*The English Illustrated Magazine*	?
H. Rider Haggard	'Allan Quartermain'	01.01.87–16.07.87	*Longman's Magazine*	Watt
Robert Buchanan	'A Hero in Spite of Himself'	09.07.87–24.09.87	*Sheffield Weekly Telegraph*, etc (W.C. Leng nad Co.)	W.C. Leng and Co.

Author	Title	Dates	Publication	Rights
Walter Besant	'Herr Paulus'	22.10.87–?16.06.88	Leigh Journal & Times, etc (Tillotsons)	Tillotsons
A.C. (Ada Cambridge)	'A Black Sheep'	07.07.88–05.01.89	AUSTRALIAN	
M.E. Braddon	'The Day Will Come'	12.01.89–27.07.89	Sheffield Weekly Telegraph, etc (W.C. Leng and Co.)	W.C. Leng and Co.
A.C. (Ada Cambridge)	'A Woman's Friendship'	31.08.89–26.10.89	AUSTRALIAN	
M.E. Braddon	'Whose was the Hand?'	11.01.90–14.06.90	Pictorial World	W.C. Leng and Co./Tillotsons
William Black	'Stand Fast, Craig Royston'	12.07.90–03.01.91	Bolton Weekly Journal, etc (Tillotsons)	Tillotsons
Margaret Oliphant	'The Heir Presumptive and the Heir Apparent'	10.01.91–04.07.91	London Society & Newcastle Weekly Chronicle etc (Tillotsons)	Tillotsons
W.E. Norris	'Miss Wentworth's Idea'	11.07.91–30.10.91	?	?
Mrs (Annie) Alexander	'Mammon'	10.10.91–30.01.92	?	?
Mark Twain	'The American Claimant'	16.01.92–16.04.92	USA	McClure
Antarlo (Catherine Martin)	'The Silent Sea'	02.04.92–14.01.93	AUSTRALIAN	
Edmund Mitchell	'The Temple of Death'	21.01.93–03.06.93	?	?
W. Clark Russell	'The Emigrant Ship'	03.06.93–04.11.93	?	?
Margaret Oliphant	'That House in Bloomsbury'	11.11.93–10.02.94	The Young Woman	Tillotsons
M.E. Braddon	'Thou Art the Man'	06.01.94–07.07.94	Sheffield Weekly Telegraph etc (W.C. Leng and Co.)	W.C. Leng and Co./Tillotsons
Henry Herman	'The Sword of Fate'	07.07.94–03.11.94	?	?
Bret Harte	'Clarence'	03.11.94–12.01.95	?	Watt ?
A. Conan Doyle	'The Stark Munro Letters'	05.01.95–05.06.95	?	?
Dora Russell	'The Drift of Fate'	09.02.95–27.07.95	?	?
Mrs (Rosa) Campbell Praed	'Mrs Tregaskiss'	20.07.95–11.01.96	Liverpool Weekly Post, etc (Tillotsons)	Tillotsons
Walter Besant	'The Master Craftsman'	11.01.96–30.05.96	?	?
Ian Maclaren (John Watson)	'Kate Carnegie'	30.05.96–28.11.96	Chamber's Journal	Tillotsons
E. Phillips Oppenheim	'Till the Day of Judgment'	28.11.96–20.02.97	Sheffield Weekly Telegraph, etc (W.C. Leng and Co.)	Watt ?
E. Phillips Oppenheim	'A Daughter of Astrea'	20.02.97–27.03.97	Sheffield Weekly Telegraph, etc (W.C. Leng and Co.)	W.C. Leng and Co.
Guy Boothby	'The Lust of Hate'	03.04.97–24.07.97	?	Watt ?
F. Marion Crawford	'Corleone'	24.07.97–19.02.98	?	Watt ?
William Black	'Wild Eelin'	19.02.98–22.10.98	Bolton Weekly Journal, etc (Tillotsons)	Tillotsons
F. Frankfort Moore	'A Whirlwind Harvest'	22.10.98–04.02.99	?	Tillotsons
E. Phillips Oppenheim	'The Man and His Kingdom'	04.02.99–17.06.99	Sheffield Weekly Telegraph, etc (W.C. Leng and Co.)	W.C. Leng and Co.

C.J. Cutcliffe Hyne	'The Lost Continent'	22.07.99–30.12.99	?	Pinker ?
George Horton	'A Fair Brigand'	30.08.99–08.11.99	?	?
Walter Besant	'The Fourth Generation'	15.11.99–14.02.00	?	Tillotsons

* Includes serials issued in six instalments or more.   † Based on Morrison 'Newspaper', App. 1.
‡ Based on Johnson-Woods, *VFRG*, Houghton, *Wellesley*, Sutherland, *Stanford*, or original journals.
** Based on BERG, Johanningsmeier, WILSON, VFL, TURNER, PEMBROKE, ZBEN.

Sources: As noted.

Table A.4 Syndication of the novels of M.E. Braddon

Book title Serial Title (if different)	Syndicator Payment to author	First Weekly Serialization Parts Pub. dates	Other weekly serializations traced Parts Pub. dates	Overseas serializations traced* Pub. dates	1st vol. edn No. of vols Pub. Date
Taken at the Flood	Tillotsons £450	(Plymouth) *Western Daily Mercury* 33 pts 30 Aug. 1873–11 Apr. 1874	(34 pts) 30 Aug. 1873–18 Apr. 1874: *Bolton Weekly Journal*, (Dundee) *People's Journal*, *Sheffield Daily Telegraph, Newcastle Weekly Chronicle*, (Dublin) *Penny Despatch, Portsmouth Times*, (Cardiff) *Weekly Mail, Farnworth Journal & Observer, Tyldesley Weekly Journal* (pts 23–34 only) 31 Jan.–18 Apr. 1874: *Leigh Weekly Journal, Eccles & Patricroft Journal*	(New York) *Harper's Weekly*, 13 Sept. 1873–23 May 1874 (Melbourne) *Leader*, 25 Oct. 1873–18 July 1874 *Canadian Illustrated News, Calcutta Englishman*, U	Maxwell 3 vols [Apr.] 1874
A Strange World	Tillotsons £600	(Dublin) *Penny Despatch* 31 pts 18 Apr.–28 Nov. 1874 (omitting 14 Nov.)	(33 pts) 18 Apr.–5 Dec. 1874: *Bolton Weekly Journal, Tyldesley Weekly Journal, Sheffield Daily Telegraph, Western Daily Mercury* (Plymouth), *Newcastle Weekly Chronicle*, (Cardiff) *Weekly Mail* (33 pts) 22 Apr.–9 Dec. 1874: (Dundee) *People's Friend*	(New York) *Harper's Weekly*, 13 May 1874–9 Jan. 1875	Maxwell 3 vols [Feb.] 1875
Dead Men's Shoes	Tillotsons £450	*Leigh Journal & Times* 33 parts 30 July 1875–10 Mar. 1876	(33 pts) 31 July 1875–11 Mar. 1876: *Bolton Weekly Journal, Sheffield Daily Telegraph* (33 pts) 4 Aug. 1875–15 Mar. 1876: (Dundee) *People's Friend* (37 pts) 31 Jul. 1875–8 Apr. 1876: *Western Daily Mercury* (Plymouth)	(New York) *Harper's Weekly*, 31 July 1875–Apr. 22 1876	Maxwell 3 vols [Feb.] 1876

Title	Publisher/terms	Serialisation	Other serialisations	Overseas serialisations	Book publication
Weavers and Weft 'Weavers and Weft: or, in Love's Net' / 'or, "Love that hath us in his Net"'	Tillotsons £300	As 'Weavers and Weft: or, in Love's Net': *Bolton Weekly Journal* 16 pts 26 Aug.–9 Dec. 1876	As 'Weavers and Weft: or, in Love's Net': Same dates & parts: *Sheffield Daily Telegraph* 1876: (16 pts) 30 Aug.–13 Dec. 1876: (Dundee) *People's Friend*	As 'Weavers and Weft: or, "Love that hath us in his Net"': (New York) *Harper's Weekly*, 9 Sept. 1876–6 Jan. 1877	Maxwell 3 vols (as *Weavers and Weft, & other tales*) [? Mar.] 1877
An Oper Verdict	Tillotsons £500	*Leigh Journal & Times* 33 pts 4 May–14 Dec. 1877	(33 pts) 5 May–15 Dec. 1877: *Bolton Weekly Journal*, *Sheffield Daily Telegraph*, *Hereford Times*, (Dundee) *People's Journal* (40 pts) 12 May–2 Feb. 1878: *Bath Herald*	(Melbourne) *Leader*, 14 July 1877–9 Mar. 1878 (Sydney) *Town & Country Journal*, 3 Apr.–18 Dec. 1880 (New York) *Harper's Weekly*, 19 May 1877–9 Feb. 1878	Maxwell 3 vols [Jan.] 1878
The Clown Foot	Tillotsons £400	*Newcastle Weekly Chronicle* 24 pts 5 Oct. 1878–15 Mar. 1879	Same dates & parts: *Leicester Chronicle* (24 pts) 30 Nov. 1878–10 May 1879: (Cardiff) *Weekly Mail* (25 pts) 9 Oct. 1878–26 Mar. 1879: *Hereford Times*, (Dundee) *People's Friend* (31 pts) 12 Oct. 1878–10 May 1879: *Bath Herald* (Not in Tillotsons's 'Lancashire Journals')	*Brisbane Courier*, 7 Dec. 1878–79 Aug. 1879 (Melbourne) *Age*, 28 Dec. 1878–8 Nov. 1879 (Sydney) *Town & Country Journal*, 8 Feb.–1 Nov. 1880	J & R Maxwell 3 vols [(? Sep.) 1879]
Just as I am	Tillotsons £500	*Newcastle Weekly Chronicle* 32 pts 7 Feb.–11 Sept. 1880	Same dates & parts: *Sheffield Daily Telegraph* (33 pts) 7 Feb.–18 Sept. 1880: *Bolton Weekly Journal*, (Dundee) *People's Journal* (33 pts) 14 Feb.–25 Sept. 1880: *Bath Herald*	(Melbourne) *Age*, 27 Mar. 1880–1 Jan. 1881	J & R Maxwell 3 vols [(? Oct.) 1880]

Phantom Fortune	Tillotsons £750	*Leigh Journal & Times* 27 pts 9 Mar.–7 Sept. 1883	(25 pts) 24 Mar.–8 Sept. 1883: *Liverpool Weekly Post* (26 pts) 17 Mar.–8 Sept. 1883: *Farnworth Journal & Observer* (27 pts) 14 Mar.–12 Sept. 1883: (Dundee) *People's Friend* (27 pts) 16 Mar.–14 Sept. 1883: *Nottinghamshire Guardian*	*Illustrated Sydney News*, 14 Apr. 1883–15 Mar. 1884 Four (?) US newspapers, inc. *Chicago Daily News*, U	J & R Maxwell 3 vols [Sept.] 1883
Wyllard's Weird	Tillotsons £750	*Leigh Journal & Times* 27 pts 19 Sept. 1884–20 Mar. 1885	(20 pts) 8 Nov. 1884–21 Mar. 1885: *Birmingham Weekly Mercury* (28 pts) 20 Sept. 1884–28 Mar. 1885: *Newcastle Weekly Chronicle, South London Press* (27 pts) 20 Sept. 1884–21 Mar. 1885: *Yorkshire Weekly Post, Cardiff Times* (28 pts) 24 Sept. 1884–1 Apr. 1885: (Dundee) *People's Friend*	(Melbourne) *Leader*, 1 Nov. 1884–30 May 1885 Several US newspapers, inc. *New York Mercury*, U	J & R Maxwell 3 vols [20 Mar. 1885]
Cut by the County	Tillotsons £250	*Leigh Journal & Times* 6 pts 3 July–7 Aug. 1885	Same dates & parts *Bolton Weekly Journal* (9 pts) 20 June–15 Aug. 1885: *Birmingham Weekly Mercury* (9 pts) 27 June–22 Aug. 1885: *Leicester Chronicle* (9 pts) 25 July–19 Sept. 1885: *Glasgow Weekly Mail* (9 pts) 3 Sept.–31 Oct. 1885: *Cardiff Times*	Several US newspapers, U	J & R Maxwell (3rd vol. of *The One Thing Needful*) [15 Aug. 1886]
The One Thing Needful	Leaders for Tillotsons £500	*Sheffield Weekly Independent* 20 pts 27 Mar.–7 Aug. 1886	Same date & parts: *Yorkshire Weekly Post* (18 pts) 18 Sept. 1886–15 Jan. 1887: (Cardiff) *Weekly Mail* (Not in Tillotsons's 'Lancashire Journals')	(Melbourne) *Age*, 24 Apr.–18 Sep. 1886 *Chicago Weekly News*, U	J & R Maxwell 3 vols (inc. *Cut by the County*) [15 Aug. 1886]

Title					
Like and Unlike	Tillotsons £1200	*Leigh Journal & Times* 27 pts 25 Mar.–23 Sept. 1887	(27 pts) 26 Mar.–24 Sept. 1887: *Bolton Weekly Journal; South London Press* (27 pts) 30 Mar.–28 Sept. 1887: (Dundee) *People's Friend* (30 pts) 7 May–26 Nov. 1887: *Burnley Express*		Spencer Blackett 3 vols [24 Sept. 1887]
The Fatal Three	W.C. Leng and Co. £1250	(Sheffield) *Weekly Telegraph* 24 pts 14 Jan.–23 June 1888	Same dates & parts: *Nottinghamshire Guardian, Yorkshire Weekly Post* (24 pts) 18 Jan.–27 June 1888: (Dundee) *People's Friend*	(Brisbane) *Queenslander,* 7 Jan.–14 July 1888 (Melbourne) *Leader,* 28 Jan.–4 Aug. 1888	Simpkin, Marshall 3 vols [(? June) 1888]
The Day Will Come	W.C. Leng and Co. £1250 (Queensland serial rights to Tillotsons, £10)	(Sheffield) *Weekly Telegraph* 25 pts 12 Jan.–29 June 1889	(26 pts) 14 Jan.–8 July 1889: (Also appeared in 10 monthly parts in *London Society,* Feb.–Nov. 1888)	(Melbourne) *Age,* 12 Jan.–27 July 1889	Simpkin, Marshall 3 vols [1889]
One Life, One Love 'Whose was the Hand?'	W.C. Leng and Co. £1250 (Col. serial rights to Tillotsons, £50)	(London) *Pictorial World* 24 pts 2 Jan.–12 June 1890	(Dundee) *People's Friend* (23 pts) 11 Jan.–14 June 1890: (Sheffield) *Weekly Telegraph* (24 pts) 11 Jan.–21 June 1890:	(Melbourne) *Age,* 11 Jan.–14 June 1890 (Sydney) *Town & Country Journal,* 1 Feb.–20 Sept. 1890 *Chicago Daily News,* U	Simpkin, Marshall 3 vols 1890
Gerard: or, The World, the Flesh, and the Devil 'The World, the Flesh, and the Devil'/'The Fate Reader'	W.C. Leng and Co. Unknown	As 'The World, the Flesh, and the Devil': (Sheffield) *Weekly Telegraph* 22 pts 10 Jan.–6 June 1891	*Glasgow Weekly Mail* As 'The World, the Flesh and the Devil': Same dates & part: (Belfast) *Weekly Northern Whig* As 'The Fate Reader': (24 pts) 5 Jan.–15 June 1891: (Dundee) *People's Friend*	As 'The World, the Flesh, and the Devil': (Melbourne) *Leader,* 24 Jan.–4 July 1891	Simpkin, Marshall 3 vols 1891
The Venetians 'The Venetians: or, All in Honour'	W.C. Leng and Co. Unknown (2nd serial rights to Tillotsons, £110)	(Sheffield) *Weekly Telegraph* 23 pts 9 Jan.–11 June 1892	(23 pts) 10 Mar.–11 Aug. 1893: *Leigh Journal & Times, Eccles Patricroft Journal* (23 pts) 11 Mar.–12 Aug. 1893: *Bolton Weekly Journal*		Simpkin, Marshall 3 vols 1892

All Along the River	Tillotsons (Serial rights from W.C. Leng and Co., £500)	Newcastle Weekly Chronicle 20 pts 21 Jan.–3 June 1893	(19 pts) 8 June–12 Oct. 1893: Ripon Observer (21 pts) 21 Jan.–10 June 1893: Birmingham Weekly Mercury (Not in Tillotsons's 'Lancashire Journals')	(Melbourne) Leader, 4 Feb.–29 July 1893	Simpkin, Marshall 3 vols (final vol. short stories) 1893
Thou Art the Man	W.C. Leng and Co. Unknown (2nd serial rights to Tillotsons, £350)	(Sheffield) Weekly Telegraph? 23 pts 6 Jan.–9 June 1894		(Melbourne) Age, 6 Jan.–7 July 1894	Simpkin, Marshall 3 vols [1894]
Sons of Fire	W.C. Leng and Co. Unknown (2nd serial rights to Tillotsons, £350)	(Sheffield) Weekly Telegraph? 23 pts 5 Jan.–8 June 1895		(Melbourne) Leader, 3 Feb.–14 Sept. 1895	Simpkin, Marshall 3 vols [1895]
London Pride: or, When the World was Younger 'When the World was Younger: A Tale of Merry England'	Tillotsons (Serial rights from W.C. Leng and Co., £850)	Birmingham Weekly Mercury 26 pts 5 Oct. 1895–28 Mar. 1896			Simpkin, Marshall 1 vol. 1896
Under Love's Rule 'The Little Auntie'	Tillotsons (Serial rights from W.C. Leng and Co., £450)	Newcastle Weekly Chronicle 10 pts 10 Oct.–12 Dec. 1896			Simpkin, Marshall 1 vol. 1897
Rough Justice 'Shadowed Lives'/ 'A Shadowed Life'	W.C. Leng and Co. Unknown	(Sheffield) Weekly Telegraph 19 pts 16 Jan.–22 May 1897	(Possibly serialized in Britain exclusively in the Sheffield Weekly Telegraph)		Simpkin, Marshall 1 vol. 1898

				Australian appearances*	
In High Places 'George Nameless: A Romance of Life in High Places'	Hutchinson £1000	(Sheffield) *Weekly Telegraph* 23 pts 29 Oct. 1898–1 Apr. 1899	(Issued previously in 12 monthly parts in (London) *Lady's Realm*, Nov. 1897–Oct. 1898)	Melbourne *Argus*, U	Hutchinson 1 vol. 1898
During Her Majesty's Pleasure	W.C. Leng and Co. Unknown (Australian serial rights to Tillotsons, £30)	(Sheffield) *Weekly Telegraph* 11 pts 12 Jan.–23 Mar. 1901		?	Hurst & Blackett 1 vol. 1908
The Conflict	Watt £420	(London) *The People* 29 pts 7 Sept. 1902–22 Mar. 1903	(Possibly serialized in single papers in Scotland and Ireland, U)	?	Simpkin, Marshall 1 vol. 1903
The Rose of Life	Watt £450	(London) *Tit-Bits* 18 pts 18 June–15 Oct. 1904		?	Hutchinson 1 vol. 1905
Dead Love Has Chains 'Alias Jane Brown'	Northern Newspaper Syndicate £125	Untraced c. Jan.–June 1906	(British and Colonial serial rights for two years transferred by letter of A.P. Watt on 2 Dec. 1905, Folder 85.10, Wilson)	?	Hurst & Blackett 1 vol. 1907

* Australian appearances based on Johnson-Woods   U = Unconfirmed
Sources: Original journals, Wilson, Zben; or as noted.

Table A.5 Syndication of the Novels of Wilkie Collins

Title	Syndicator Payment	1st UK serialization Parts/dates	Other UK weekly locations traced	UK monthly serialization	Overseas serializations traced*	1st vol. Ed. Vols/date
Jezebel's Daughter	Tillotsons £500	*Bolton Weekly Journal* 21 pts 13 Sept. 1879-31 Jan. 1880	Same dates & parts: *Farnworth Journal & Observer, Glasgow Weekly Mail, Newcastle Weekly Chronicle,* (Plymouth) *Western Weekly Mercury* (21 pts) 20 Sept. 1879 –7 Feb. 1880: *Bath Herald*	None	None	Chatto & Windus 3 vols [Mar.] 1880
The Black Robe	Leaders Unknown	*Sheffield Independent* 26 pts 2 Oct. 1880-26 Mar. 1881	Same dates & parts: (Cardiff) *Weekly Mail, Glasgow Weekly Herald, South London Press*	None	(New York) *Frank Leslie's Magazine,* U (Melbourne) *Leader,* 13 Nov. 1880–7 May 1881 *Canadian Monthly,* Nov. 1880–June 1881	Chatto & Windus 3 vols [Apr.] 1881
Heart and Science	Watt £973	*Manchester Weekly Times* 26 pts 22 July 1882-13 Jan. 1883	(27 pts) 28 July 1882–26 Jan. 1883: *Nottinghamshire Guardian* (28 pts) 22 July 1882–27 Jan. 1883: *Aberdeen Weekly Journal, Bath Observer, Bristol Observer,* (Cardiff) *Weekly Times, Liverpool Weekly Post,* (Edinburgh) *Scottish Reformer* (29 pts) 22 July 1882–3 Feb. 1883: *Weekly Irish Times* (30 pts) 22 July 1882–17 Feb. 1883 omitting 6 Jan.: (London) *England Nottinghamshire Evening Post, Moray & Nairn Weekly Journal,* U	*Belgravia* 11 pts Aug. 1882–June 1883	(New York) *Frank Leslie's Magazine,* U Australian weekly, U	Chatto & Windus 3 vols [Apr.] 1883

'*I Say No*'	Watt £1 600 (?)	*Manchester Weekly Post* (31 pts) 15 Dec. 1883–12 July 1884: 30 pts 22 Dec. 1883–12 July 1884	(31 pts) (Cardiff) *Weekly Times, Glasgow Weekly Herald, Leicester Chronicle Supp., Newcastle Weekly Chronicle* (31 pts) 16 Dec. 1883–13 July 1884: (London) *The People* (31 pts) 12 July 1884–7 Feb. 1885: *Bradford Citizen* (32 pts) 15 Dec. 1883–19 July 1884: *Belfast Weekly News*	*London Society* 12 pts Jan.–Dec. 1884	(New York) *Harper's Weekly*, 22 Dec. 1883–12 July 1884	Chatto & Windus 3 vols [Oct.] 1884
The Evil Genius	Tillotsons £1 300	*Farnworth Weekly Journal & Observer* 20 pts 12 Dec. 1885–24 Apr. 1886	(21 pts) 11 Dec. 1885–30 Apr. 1886: *Eccles & Patricroft Journal, Leigh Journal & Times, Pendlebury & Swinton Journal, Tyldesley Weekly Journal* (21 pts) 12 Dec. 1885–1 May 1886: *Bolton Weekly Journal* (27 pts) 31 Oct. 1885–1 May 1886: (Cardiff) *Weekly Times, Leicester Chronicle, Sheffield Weekly Independent, South London Press, Newcastle Weekly Chronicle, Yorkshire Weekly Post* (27 pts) 6 Nov. 1885–7 May 1886: *Nottinghamshire Guardian*	None	*Sydney Mail*, 26 Dec. 1885–26 June 1886 Eight US newspapers, inc. *Chicago Daily News*, U	Chatto & Windus 3 vols [Sept.] 1886
The Legacy of Cain	Tillotsons £1 080	*Leigh Journal & Times* 20 pts 17 Feb.–29 June 1888	(20 pts) 18 Feb.–30 June 1888: *Bolton Weekly Journal* (21 pts) 17 Feb.–6 July 1888: *Eccles & Patricroft Journal* (21 pts) 18 Feb.–7 July 1888: (Cardiff) *Weekly Times, Farnworth Weekly Journal, Nottinghamshire Weekly Journal, Sheffield Weekly Independent Guardian, Sheffield Weekly Independent* (31pts, daily) 30 Dec. 1889–18 Feb. 1890: *Staffordshire Sentinel Tyldesley Weekly Journal, Pendlebury & Swinton Journal*, U	None	At least two newspapers in USA, U	Chatto & Windus 3 vols [Nov.] 1888

| *Blind Love* | Watt £1 000 (?) | *The Illustrated London News* 26 pts 6 July–28 Dec. 1889 | Same dates & parts: *Newcastle Weekly Chronicle* (26 pts) 12 Oct. 1889–5 Apr. 1890: *Penny Illustrated Paper* | None | *New York World*, 30 June–29 Dec. 1889 | Chatto & Windus 3 vols [Jan.] 1890 |

* Australian appearances based on Johnson-Woods   U = Unconfirmed

Sources: Law, 'Wilkie'; Farmer and Law; or as noted.

Table A.6 Serial publication of the novels of Walter Besant

Title	1st UK serialization	Overseas serializations traced*	Notes	1st UK edn in vol.
Ready Money Mortiboy	Once a Week 6 Jan.–29 June 1872		With James Rice	Tinsley, 3 vols, 1872
My Little Girl	Once a Week 7 Dec. 72–31 May 1873		With James Rice	Tinsley, 3 vols, 1873
With Harp and Crown	Tinsley's Magazine Jan.–Dec. 1875		With James Rice	Tinsley, 3 vols, 1875
This Son of Vulcan	London Society July 1875–Oct. 1876		With James Rice	Sampson Low 3 vols, 1876
The Golden Butterfly	The World 5 Jan.–18 Oct. 1876		With James Rice	Tinsley, 3 vols, 1876
By Celia's Arbour	The Graphic 1 Sept. 77–23 Mar. 1878	Sydney Mail 8 Sept. 1877–29 June 1878	With James Rice	Sampson Low 3 vols, 1878
The Monks of Thelema	The World 15 Jan.–2 Oct. 1878	Melbourne Leader, 23 Mar.–19 Oct. 1878 Canadian Monthly, U	With James Rice	Chatto & Windus, 3 vols, 1878
The Seamy Side	Time Apr. 1879–Apr. 1880		With James Rice	Chatto & Windus, 3 vols, 1880
The Chaplain of the Fleet	The Graphic 4 Dec. 1880–11 June 1881	Australian, 27 Nov. 1880–28 May 1881	With James Rice	Chatto & Windus, 3 vols, 1881
All Sorts and Conditions of Men	Belgravia Jan.–Dec. 1882		Also in: Birmingham Weekly Post, Leicester Chronicle, Sheffield Weekly Telegraph (7 Jan.–1 July 1882), Glasgow Weekly Mail (14 Jan.–15 July 1882), Liverpool Weekly Post (7 Jan.–12 Aug. 1882)	Chatto & Windus, 3 vols, 1882

The Revolt of Man	Not serialized		Published anonymously	Blackwoods, 1882
All in a Garden Fair	Good Words Jan.–Dec. 1883			Chatto & Windus, 3 vols, 1883
Dorothy Forster	The Graphic 12 Jan.– 12 July 1884	Sydney Mail, 26 Jan.–18 Oct. 1884		Chatto & Windus, 3 vols, 1884
Children of Gibeon	Longman's Magazine Jan.–Dec. 1886	Australian, 8 May–11 Dec. 1886	This and following serial appearances arranged by A.P. Watt, as Besant's literary agent	Chatto & Windus, 3 vols, 1886
The World Went Very Well Then	The Illustrated London News 3 July–25 Dec. 1886	Sydney Mail, 17 July 1886–26 Feb. 1887	Also in: Sheffield Weekly Telegraph (10 Jul.–24 Dec. 1886), Glasgow Weekly Herald (3 July–25 Dec. 1886)	Chatto & Windus, 3 vols, 1887
Herr Paulus	Leigh Journal & Times 9 Sept. 1887–2 Mar. 1888	Melbourne Age, 22 Oct. 1887–16 June 1888	Syndicated by Tillotsons (with illustrated stereos); also in: Bolton Weekly Journal, Nottinghamshire Guardian, Sheffield Weekly Independent, (Plymouth) Western Weekly Mercury (10 Sept. 1887–3 Mar. 1888), Burnley Express (12 Nov. 1887–, U)	Chatto & Windus, 3 vols, 1888
For Faith and Freedom	The Illustrated London News 7 July–29 Dec. 1888	Australian, 7 July 1888–5 Jan. 1889		Chatto & Windus, 3 vols, 1888
The Bell of St. Paul's	Longman's Magazine Jan.–Dec. 1889	Melbourne Leader, 5 Jan.–26 Oct. 1889		Chatto & Windus, 3 vols, 1889
Armorel of Lyonesse	The Illustrated London News 4 Jan.–28 June 1890			Chatto & Windus, 3 vols, 1890
St. Katherine's by the Tower	Thee Graphic 3 Jan.–27 June 1891	Sydney Mail, 3 Jan–27 June 1891	Also in Birmingham Weekly Post, Liverpool Weekly Courier (3 Jan. 1891–U)	Chatto & Windus, 3 vols, 1891

Title	Serial publication	Book publication	Notes
The Ivory Gate	*Chambers's Journal* 2 Jan.–24 Sept. 1892	*Melbourne Leader,* 13 Feb.–29 Oct. 1892	Chatto & Windus, 3 vols, 1892
The Rebel Queen	*The Illustrated London News* 7 Jan.–24 June 1893		Chatto & Windus, 3 vols, 1893
Beyond the Dreams of Avarice	*Tit-Bits* 7 July–15 Dec. 1894	*Harpers Weekly,* U	Chatto & Windus, 1895
The Master Craftsman	*Chambers's Journal* 4 Jan.–27 June. 1896	*Melbourne Age,* 11 Jan.–30 May 1896 *Montreal Gazette,* U *Pittsburg Times,* U *Providence Journal,* U	Serial rights to Tillotsons; UK serial rights sold on to *Chambers's*	Chatto & Windus, 2 vols 1896
The City of Refuge	*The Pall Mall Magazine* Mar.–Oct. 1896		Chatto & Windus, 3 vols, 1896
A Fountain Sealed	*The Illustrated London News* 2 Jan.–27 Mar. 1897		Chatto & Windus, 1897
The Changeling	*Chapman's Magazine* Mar.–Oct. 1898		Chapman & Hall, 1898
The Orange Girl	*The Lady's Pictorial* 7 Jan.–24 June 1899	*Australian,* 7 Jan.–1 July 1899	Chatto & Windus, 1899
The Alabaster Box	*The Leisure Hour* 25 Oct. 1899–24 Mar. 1900		Thomas Burleigh, 1900
The Fourth Generation	Untraced (Agreement specifies publication between 31 Oct. 1899–91 Mar. 1900)	*Melbourne Age,* 15 Nov. 99–14 Feb. 1900	As short story 'To the Third and Fourth Generation' in *Humanitarian* (July–Sept. 1893), *Harper's Magazine* (Aug. 1893); serial rights of extended version to Tillotsons in 1899	Chatto & Windus, 1900

The Lady of Lynn	*Queen* 5 Jan.–29 June 1901		Chatto & Windus, 1901
No Other Way	*The Lady's Realm* Nov. 1901–Oct. 1902	Also in Sheffield *Weekly Telegraph* (14 Dec. 1901–17 May 1902)	Chatto & Windus, 1902

* Australian appearances based on Johnson-Woods   U = Unconfirmed
Sources: BERG; WILSON; TURNER; Houghton, *Wellesley*; *VFRG*; original journals; or as noted.

Notes

Chapter 1: Serial Fiction

1 John Cooke's edition of the British Novelists in 6d weekly numbers from the 1790s was one of the most worthy results.

2 We should note that at that time the largest provincial paper, Isaac Thompson's *Newcastle Journal* (1737–88), probably had a circulation only a little over two thousand copies (Cranfield, *Press*, 184; Williams, *English*, ch. 3).

3 Among the notable examples offered are *Parker's Penny Post* or John Applebee's *Original Weekly Journal* in London around 1730, and the *Sussex Weekly Advertiser* or *Cambridge Journal* in the provinces around 1750. Wiles's research thus shows that Pollard was mistaken in suggesting that serial stories then functioned merely as 'a cheap method of filling out a paper', and that, after 1725, there was 'no space to waste on serial stories' ('Serial', 254–5).

4 The former path was taken in the provinces by Isaac Thompson of the *Newcastle Journal* with his *Newcastle General Magazine* (1747–60), probably the most successful miscellany outside London. The latter path was taken by Robert Walker's *London and Country Journal*, which from 1739 was issued in distinct editions for the metropolitan and provincial markets, both of which included literary supplements in the form of fascicles.

5 As Table 1.1 indicates, in 1757 the minimum newspaper stamp was set at 1d, and the tax on advertisements doubled to 2s and applied to periodicals published at intervals of more than a week. As Cranfield shows (*Development*, 237–41, 272–3) this hit provincial publishers especially hard.

6 Even the crude measure of literacy represented by the percentage of newly-weds signing the marriage register was not included in the returns of the Registrar-General until 1839, when they showed 66.3% for males and 50.5% for females. Equivalent figures for 1861, 1881 and 1900 were 75.4/65.3%, 86.5/82.3%, and 97.2/96.8% (cited in Porter, 147). Altick's conclusions, however, seem generally to be supported by the detailed statistical research on occupational literacy in various industrial districts reported in Vincent, ch. 4. See also Webb, ch. 1.

7 In order to outlaw, for example, the issuing from 1816 of a 2d unstamped edition of Cobbett's *Political Register*, which excluded the news material itself but retained the political commentary (see Altick, *English*, 324–6).

8 It should be remembered, of course, that new books were normally sold at a significant discount from the advertised retail price to cash and bulk purchasers, particularly between the 1852 collapse of the Booksellers' Association with its restrictions on underselling and the introduction of the Net Book Agreement in 1900 (Barnes).

9 On the extensive provision of Gothic fiction material to circulating libraries, especially in the provinces, around this period by the Minerva Press, see Blakey, ch. 6.

10 Early examples of series of non-copyright fiction were Whittingham's Pocket Novelists, which were priced from as little as 2s a 16mo volume, or the even cheaper productions of John Limbird, both produced in the 1820s.

11 For a detailed analysis of the reprint history of a single Victorian novel handled by Chatto and Windus in the last decades of the century, see Eliot 'His Generation', on Besant's *All Sorts and Conditions of Men*.

12 Though *Life in London* was much more lavishly illustrated and the instalments sold at 3s each – see Sutherland, *Victorian Fiction*, 88–9.

13 More generally on the limited nature of the boom in instalment fiction, see Sutherland, *Victorian Fiction*, ch. 4. On the influence of the agreement concerning *Pickwick* between Chapman and Hall and Dickens on later contracts for publication of fiction in independent numbers, see Harvey, 13.

14 Following Sutherland (*Victorian Fiction*, 104, 108–13), we should also note here the compromise evolved by Blackwoods in the 1870s, of issuing novels of exceptional length by major writers in eight 5s bound monthly parts equivalent to half a standard volume. Possibly based on a proposal by Bulwer-Lytton in 1849 that was not then taken up, the procedure was first put into practice by G.H. Lewes and John Blackwood for George Eliot's *Middlemarch* (1871–2) where the parts were initially issued bimonthly (Sutherland, *Victorian Novelists*, 188–205; Sutherland, *Victorium Fiction*, 107–13; Martin, ch. 5). It was subsequently employed by the same publisher for Eliot's *Daniel Deronda* (1876), as also by Chapman and Hall for Trollope's *The Prime Minister* (1875–76).

15 Among them, John Limbird's *Mirror of Literature* (1822–49) and John Clements's *The Romancist, and Novelist's Library* (1839–46), both at 2d a week, stand out as worthy and long-running examples.

16 Subsequent serials featured in *The Sunday Times* were: Ainsworth's *Old Saint Paul's* (1841) and *The Lancashire Witches* (1848), for each of which the author was paid £1000 according to Boase (1:31), although Hobson *et al.* (39) give £500 as the figure for *Old St. Paul's*; Richard Brinsley Peake's *Cartouche* (1842); Lady Blessington's *Strathern* (1843); G.P.R. James's *The Smugglers* (1844) and *The Step-Mother* (1845); James Sheridan Knowles's *Fortescue* (1846); and Rede's *The Man in Possession* (1847; broken off by the author's death from apoplexy).

17 Other examples in *The Illustrated London News* include: Mrs (Catherine) Crowe's *Gerald Gage; or, the Secret* (10 January–14 March 1846); Camilla Toulmin's *Gold; or, The Half-Brothers* (4 July–14 November 1846); and former basket-maker Thomas Miller's *Fred Holdsworth; or, Love and Pride* (19 October 1850–11 January 1851).

18 Further examples include Marryat's *Joseph Rushmore* (under the title 'The Poacher', 13 December 1840–23 May 1841) in the 6d Tory Sunday paper *The Era* (1838–1939) edited by Leitch Ritchie (see Vann, 108), or R.S. Surtees's *Hawbuck Grange* (as 'Sporting Sketches') in the sporting Sunday paper *Bell's Life in London*, 25 October 1846–27 June 1847. Andrews

(2:255–6) also notes appearances at this time of tales by the Baroness de Calabrella in the *Court Journal* (1829–1925), and sketches by Mrs S.C. (Anna Maria) Hall and Thackeray in another new Tory weekly, *Britannia* (1839–56). Herbert Ingram (1811–60), proprietor of *The Illustrated London News*, even attempted an experiment in publishing a daily serial on the French model in his *London Telegraph*, priced cheaply at 3d but running only for five months from February 1848 (Herd, 158). Serials can also be found occasionally in the provincial press around this period, including the semi-autobiographical novel of industrial life, 'Sunshine and Shadow' by Thomas Martin Wheeler, former Secretary to the National Charter Association, in the Leeds *Northern Star* from 31 March 1849 to 5 January 1850.

19 The sales of *The Sunday Times*, for example, had dropped back to below 10 000 by the early 1850s (*RN51–53*, 13).

20 Examples include the three anonymous lives of Jack Sheppard dating from 1840 in the Barry Ono Collection at the British Library – see James and Smith. Turpin had featured in Ainsworth's *Rookwood* in 1834.

21 Other 'Salisbury Square' publishers included John Clements, W.M. Clark, John Dicks, and George Vickers (Summers; James, *Fiction*, App. 3).

22 For example, in evidence to the Select Committee on Newspaper Stamps, Samuel Bucknall, a Gloucestershire newspaper proprietor, described the Salisbury Square publications *en masse* as 'the foulest filth of all literary matter' (Minutes of Evidence, Q1265, *RSC51*, 205–6).

23 In their instructive material they can also be seen as imitating the utilitarian and evangelical weeklies emerging in the early 1830s, as discussed later in the chapter.

24 According to claims on the front page of the first and last issues of the year, the circulation of *The News of the World* doubled during the course of 1845 from 17 500 to 35 000.

25 In 1855, the circulations of *The London Journal*, *Family Herald*, and *Reynolds's Miscellany* were reported by Charles Knight to have been respectively, 450 000, 300 000, and 200 000 (cited in Altick, *English*, 394). Around the same period *Lloyd's Weekly Newspaper*, *The Weekly Times*, and *Reynolds's Weekly Newspaper* had reached sales of 96 000, 75 000, and 49 000 respectively, although *The News of the World* remained ahead with 110 000 (Altick, *English*, 394).

26 As early as 1851, in evidence to the Select Committee on Newspaper Stamps, the Manchester bookseller and newsagent Abel Heywood had noted that *The Family Herald* differed from *The London Journal* and *Reynolds's Miscellany* in being addressed 'to the fairer sex in large measure' (Minutes of Evidence, Q2502, *RSC51*, 377).

27 Though John Dicks (1818–81) only seems to have formally become a partner of George Reynolds in 1863, he was by then already playing a dominant role in their joint ventures. He had taken over the publishing of both Reynolds's novels in volume and *Reynolds's Miscellany* in 1848, shortly before *Reynolds's Weekly Newspaper* was founded. See *DLB*, 106:126–8.

28 In his scathing critique in the *Quarterly Review* in 1863 (499), H.L. Mansel used the term 'the Newspaper Novel' to describe the fashion for sensation

fiction, indicating that material more appropriate to the popular Sunday journals was finding its way into middle-class fiction. In *Temple Bar* in 1870, Alfred Austin further characterized 'The Sensational School' as 'that one touch of anything but nature that makes the kitchen and the drawing-room kin' (424). Hughes *Maniac* (9–18), Vicinus, Flint (277–8), Pykett (ch. 11), and Cvetkovich (15–19) have all addressed this general issue in a variety of contexts. See also Altick, *Presence*, 78–88, and the discussion in Chapter 7 of E.S. Dallas's review of *Great Expectations*.

29 Though his work on popular Victorian literature in *Victorian Wallflowers* and *Old Gods Falling* is now unduly neglected, Malcolm Elwin was mistaken in ignoring the rise of the literary weekly and in assuming that the decline of the monthly miscellany entailed the decline of the serial story both as a literary form and as a source of income to novelists. See, for example, Elwin, *Old*, 42–3.

30 See Sutherland *'Cornhill's'* and *Victorian Novelists*, 189–90. The prices indicated also included the purchase of the right of initial volume publication by the house of Smith, Elder.

31 Most notably three novels by Trollope, beginning with *The Belton Estate* (1865–6), and five by Meredith including *Beauchamp's Career* (1874–5); at those periods both novelists were involved in the running of the review.

32 *Temple Bar* was founded by John Maxwell, but was purchased by Bentley from its second owner George Sala in January 1866. In 1868 it incorporated *Bentley's Miscellany*, recently bought back from Harrison Ainsworth and Chapman and Hall, to whom it had been sold in 1854.

33 There were also new monthly magazines which combined serial fiction with 'Society' news, like *London Society*, or with 'home' interests, like *The St. James's Magazine*.

34 This point was made strongly by the educationalist W.E. Hickson in his evidence to the Select Committee on the Newspaper Stamp of 1851 (Minutes of Evidence, Q3248–3251, *RSC51*, 478). See also: Altick, *English*, ch. 14; and Bennett, 225–57.

35 *Once a Week*, the weekly miscellany which Bradbury and Evans founded when Dickens dropped *Household Words*, was markedly different. It was stylishly illustrated and priced at 3d, though it also came to rely heavily on serial fiction, beginning with Meredith's *Evan Harrington* in 1860. Its initial circulation was over 20 000 but soon declined sharply (Altick, *English*, 395). It was afterwards sold to James Rice, then George Manville Fenn. See Elwell.

36 Notably, Dickens's own *Hard Times* (1854), Gaskell's *North and South* (1854–55), and Collins's *Dead Secret* (1857), each in around 20 parts.

37 These were Collins's *The Woman in White* (1859–60), *No Name* (1862–63), and *The Moonstone* (1868), Reade's *Hard Cash* (1863), Bulwer-Lytton's *A Strange Story* (1861–62), and Dickens's own *Great Expectations* (1860–61).

38 It should also be noted that in the 1850s and 1860s many of the upmarket weekly miscellanies – including *Chambers's Journal*, *Good Words*, *The Family Herald*, *Cassell's Magazine*, and both of Dickens's weekly journals – were also reissued in separate covers as monthlies, presumably with

the sensibilities or the purchasing patterns of the bourgeois family in mind. There was also a premium to be paid – penny and twopenny weeklies typically reappeared as monthlies at 6d and 11d respectively.

39 The records of the North of Scotland Newspaper and Printing Company offer a good example for our purposes, since its *Aberdeen Weekly Journal* featured regular serial fiction. Producing Tory papers in a staunchly Liberal region from 1876, the Company rarely turned a profit during the first quarter of a century of its existence, and only did so when advertising revenue was considerably in excess of income from newspaper sales. 'The mainstay of the business . . . is its advertising connection. Only by adequate extension of that connection can ends be made to meet', wrote manager Archibald Gillies in a report dated 16 August 1878 (Minute Book of Directors, 1876–82, AJR).

40 For example: the series of detective stories in the *Strand* featuring Conan Doyle's Sherlock Holmes or Arthur Morrison's Martin Hewitt; Robert Barr's 'Luke Sharp' sketches or Margaret Westrup's 'Billy Stories' in the *The Idler*; and Kipling's 'Stalky & Co.' in *The Pall Mall Magazine*.

41 Although the category of 'Class Papers and Periodicals' was employed by *NPD* as early as 1879, the pairing of 'classes' and 'masses' seems to have been popularized by Gladstone in an article in the *Pall Mall Gazette* of 3 May 1886, 11–12. William Westall (80), for example, used both terms in his discussion of newspaper fiction in 1890.

42 In the *NPD* of 1870 (192), T. Tather of Hull was advertising 'Newscolumn stereotyping machines' for sale at that price.

43 Comparative newspaper circulations in London and Paris were outlined in an article on 'Taxes on Newspapers' in the *Working Man's Friend* (an unstamped radical paper) of 27 July 1833, cited in Cranfield, *Press*, 139. Similar figures contrasting the circulation of stamped newspapers in Britain and unstamped papers in the USA were presented by Bulwer-Lytton during the parliamentary debate on an unsuccessful motion to repeal the stamp in June 1832 (cited in Collet, 48–52).

44 The term 'feuilleton' was often used to described the serial fiction beginning to appear in British newspapers. See, for example, the 1857 *NPD* description of the *Grimsby Advertiser* (1854–77) as 'with feuilletons' (45). In the 1870s *The World* used the term in the heading for its section devoted to fiction in serial.

45 This is in contrast to Japan, where the newspaper novel has also predominantly been issued in the national daily press. There the *feuilleton* originated in the last decades of the nineteenth century, in part under French influence, but even today all four of Japan's large general-interest national dailies carry a column devoted to the *shimbun shôsetsu* (newspaper novel). See Honda, Preface.

46 The same assumption was made in the *Pall Mall Gazette* which suggested 'Mr. W.F. Tillotson . . . first acclimatized in this country the American system of "syndicating" fiction' (20 February 1882, 6).

Chapter 2: Before Tillotsons

1 No first-hand evidence of the agreement seems to have survived. Among the papers at Bolton, the Fiction Bureau accounts only go back to November 1874, while the surviving correspondence between John Maxwell and W.F. Tillotson begins only in 1879. However, the trade journal the *Newsvendor* of August 1873 (3) mentions the transaction, giving the names (slightly inaccurately in some cases) of the subscribing journals, the information presumably being supplied by Maxwell himself.

2 See, for example: the description of fiction syndication in the article on the 1880 edition of *NPD* in the *Quarterly Review* (Review, 533–4); H.A. Boswell's comments in *About Newspapers* (40); and the remarks of William Westall, himself an experienced newspaper novelist, in his 1890 essay on 'Newspaper Fiction' (77).

3 Not to mention the many cases of reprinted serials in eighteenth-century newspapers, or the few examples of original novels appearing in metropolitan weeklies around the 1840s (see Chapter 1).

4 In this the *People's Journal* was perhaps following the lead of John Cassell's weekly the *Working-Man's Friend* (1850–53), which from March 1850 issued monthly supplements featuring contributions by readers, with cash or books as prizes. According to Nowell-Smith (*House*, 22–3), over 600 entries were received within the first year.

5 Andrew Stewart, sub-editor of the *People's Friend* under David Pae and then editor in his own right, in an essay appended to Pae's *Eustace the Outcast* published in 1884 by John Leng and Co. to mark Pae's death, lists 43 serial novels by Pae in probable order of publication. Donaldson (163–4) reproduces Stewart's list, adding two further serials traced, plus an additional listing of those novels, ten in all, which appeared in volume form. Further, I have come across two serials ('Caroline Frazer; or, the Witch of the Eccleston Moor' aka 'The Lost Child', *Glasgow Times*/Edinburgh *North Briton*, 1861, and 'The Rose of Glenlee', *Hamilton Advertiser*, 1864–65) plus one volume edition (*Clara Howard: the Captain's Bride*, London: 1856; held in the Bodleian Library), none of which appears in Donaldson.

6 The only examples I have discovered where Pae's serials were signed are a number of cases in the *Middlesbrough Gazette* in the early 1880s, shortly before his death.

7 Like 'The Lost Child' and 'Caroline Frazer', both of which carry the subtitle 'The Witch of Eccleston Moor' (see note 5) 'Mary Barry' and 'Mary, the Child of Poverty' prove to be the same tale.

8 The novel was issued in a single volume as *Lucy, the Factory Girl: or, the Secrets of the Tontine Close* (as in the *Glasgow Times*) from Thomas Grant in Edinburgh in 1860, a copy being held in the British Library. The National Library of Scotland holds an undated edition from W. and W. Lindsay in Aberdeen, entitled *The Factory Girl: or, The Dark Places of Glasgow* (as in the *People's Journal*), assigned in the catalogue to c.1855, but this must be incorrect as the title page continues 'by the author of "Eustace the Outcast"', a later work according to Andrew Stewart, which seems to have first appeared in the *People's Journal* in 1866.

9 For example, some of the earliest complete stories found in the weekly edition of the Plymouth *Western Daily Mercury* were signed by 'The Editor', while, as shown below, the first serial to appear in the *Sheffield Independent* was written by one of the proprietors. Sinclair (181–4) reported that the first serial story to appear in the *Glasgow Weekly Herald*, 'Love and Treason' in 1869, was by William Freeland, one of the editors, and that three further serial tales were later contributed by another staff member, T.G. Smith.

10 A further case of a similar nature is recorded, involving Charles Reade, perhaps the most litigious of Victorian novelists. Published in instalments in the *Pall Mall Gazette* at the end of November 1874, 'A Hero and a Martyr', his biographical sketch of James Lambert (a Glaswegian reputed to have lost his sight saving people from drowning in the Clyde and for whom Reade was trying to raise subscriptions) was reprinted without permission in a number of provincial papers. Reade took legal action against the *Glasgow Herald* only, however, because, besides pirating the article, the Scottish paper cast doubts on its veracity, and refused an offer from the author to forego proceedings if £50 were paid into the Lambert Fund (Elwin, *Charles*, 276–80; Copinger, 1904, 248–9).

11 The appropriate entries in *NPD* for 1855 and 1856 indicate that just over half of the 113 newly established provincial journals were based on sheets printed in London, but a random sampling of other new journals not so designated suggests that the actual percentage was significantly higher. Turner ('Syndication', 15) reaches a similar conclusion. The Provincial Newspaper Society, founded in 1836, which fought consistently against the expansion of the provincial press by opposing in turn the repeal of each of the 'taxes against knowledge', refused to admit as members proprietors whose publications depended on partly printed sheets (Lee, 53).

12 John Bennett's 'Broadfields Manor: A Tale of Modern Times', in six parts, June–November 1854, was the first such story. Up until the end of 1856 there were four others in from two to five parts (one again by John Bennett, two by his wife Mary Bennett, and the anonymous 'Love or Money', in 10 chapters and five parts, July–December 1856, omitting November), plus at least half-a-dozen complete tales.

13 'The Indian Girl: A Tale of Louisiana' (unsigned) ran from 15 September to 20 October 1855.

14 All known subscribers to Dorrington's sheets seem to have dropped them in November or December 1855, when most switched to unillustrated sheets, suggesting that the supply ceased around this time; journals using the monthly higher-quality illustrated sheets ceased to receive them from January 1857.

15 The *Alnwick Mercury* featured fiction regularly until it shifted to weekly publication in January 1865, though usually in the form of complete tales. Some were local smuggling yarns like the unsigned 'The Wrecker's Daughter' (November 1860), a few were reprinted from metropolitan journals like *Good Words*, though the most common source was John Mackay Wilson's *Tales of the Borders*.

16 In addition to those from Eglington and Cassell, advertisements for

such services occur in the *NPD* by the following companies from the years specified: the London and Provincial Newspaper Co., operated by John Tallis of Water Street, the Strand (1861); Joseph Bruton of Crane Court, Fleet Street (1863); and C.W. Allen and Co., of Snow Hill, Birmingham (1867).

17   This was one of a number of new projects undertaken shortly before the founder John Cassell's death, and after he had got into serious financial difficulties in the mid-1850s when the firm had in effect been taken over by the printers Petter and Galpin (Nowell-Smith, *House*, chs 4–5).

18   In 1875, Cassell's General Press was still claiming to supply more than a hundred 'county newspapers' in this way (*NPD*, 1875, 202); according to Nowell-Smith (*House*, 78) this line of Cassell's business in fact continued until the 1920s.

19   While it is easy to see from internal evidence when a number of papers use common partly printed sheets, there is often difficulty in identifying the source, since local editors were anxious not to reveal the fact of their dependence to their subscribers, and central suppliers were happy to comply by avoiding direct acknowledgement of provenance on the sheets themselves. In the case of Cassell, however, identification is made simple by the fact that prominent notices of the firm's recent publications were included in the advertising material forming part of the news sheets distributed to country papers.

20   For example, J.M. Philp's short tale 'Three Christmas Days' appeared in the 1865 Christmas issue of the *Todmorden Advertiser*, *Sittingbourne Gazette* and *Yarmouth Chronicle* (which seems to have switched from Cassell's to Eglington's sheets in February 1865).

21   For example, judging by common evidence in the *Alcester Chronicle*, *Andover Chronicle*, and *Campden Herald*, Cassell's sheets featured the following 52–week sequence of unsigned serials in 1878: 'The Strange Claimant; or, Twice Wed' (22 parts); 'The White Slave; a Few Scenes from a True History' (5 parts); and 'Trials and Triumphs: A Story of Life' (25 parts). The general pattern from 1875 was for the serial instalment to be accompanied by a single short complete tale, so that an entire page was devoted to fiction.

22   Henderson went on to build up a substantial periodical empire, centred on the *Budget*, but later including cheap children's adventure story papers like the *Young Folks Paper*, which carried several of Stevenson's tales in the 1880s, cheap illustrated journals such as the *Penny Pictorial News*, plus a number of comic papers like *Comic-Life*.

23   Exceptionally, Henderson also began to publish serial fiction regularly in *The South London Press: a Family Local Paper and Literary Magazine*, the local twopenny weekly paper he started in 1865. As well as duplicating serials carried in the *Weekly Budget*, this included a number of local stories such as 'Money's Worth', an 'Original Novel of South London Interest' by Tom Hood in 1869, or the anonymous 'Crystal Palace Belle' the following year. It should also be noted that Henderson attempted a brief and unsuccessful experiment in publishing serial fiction daily in one of the first halfpenny metropolitan evening papers, his *Evening Mercury* which appeared only from 1–13 October 1868 (Herd, 176).

24 Wilson (*Stereotyping*, 84–5) notes that Cassell's General Press developed its own technique for attaching the stereo plate to the block on which it was mounted to achieve the height of the surrounding type.

25 In the run of the *Sheffield Times* seen at the British Library Newspaper Library, supplements are not available for many issues, and the only fiction I have been able to find in the paper throughout the 1860s is a single long serial novel, 'The Stolen Will: A Tale of Domestic Life', running for almost a year from December 1868. The same story appeared in the *Bolton Weekly Guardian* in 1874.

26 On the transfer of ownership of the *Sheffield Times* from Samuel to Mary Harrison and finally to Leader and Sons, see the appropriate entries in *NPD*, 1871–74; on the sale of Harrison's syndication business, see Wilson, *Stereotyping*, 23.

27 In the run of the *Telegraph* inspected at the British Library Newspaper Library, a significant number of the volumes were missing, unfit for use, or lacked the weekly supplement in which serial fiction appeared. However, some attempt has been made to circumvent the last-mentioned problem by referring to announcements of publication in other editions of the paper.

28 Interestingly, regular advertisements for the Dundee weeklies appeared in the columns of the *Sheffield Daily Telegraph* from 1870. They were addressed 'To Scotchmen in Sheffield', and gave details of a local newsagent where the periodicals were available. Later the *People's Friend* also claimed many subscribers in Ireland and the Colonies (*How a Newspaper*, 55).

29 Support for the idea that these appearances were arranged by the Leng brothers rather than by Pae personally might be provided by the fact that stories by writers other than Pae first published in the *People's Journal* or *People's Friend*, can be found in northern English papers from at least the 1880s. The writers involved included Andrew Stewart and David Pae, Jr, while among the journals concerned were the *Staffordshire Sentinel* and *Burnley Express*, as well as the *Sheffield Weekly Telegraph* itself. For example, Stewart's 'One False Step' appeared in all three journals between 1887 and 1890, after its first appearance in the *People's Friend* in 1886.

30 The popularity of Pae's serials probably helps to explain the doubling of the circulation of the *Northern Daily Telegraph* from 20 000 to 40 000 between 1887 and 1888 (Lee, 292).

31 See the brief bibliography of R.E. Leader's writings compiled by Addy (218–19). *Judith Lee* was also published in volume form by Leader and Sons in Sheffield in 1866.

Chapter 3: Tillotsons

1 In addition to the four papers listed in Table 2.1, which started up in 1873–74, in this period the 'Lancashire Journals' included the *Pendlebury and Swinton Journal*, founded in 1875.

2 The term 'Fiction Bureau' appears first to have been employed sometime in 1886, when it appeared on a new style of headed stationery.

The heading ran, rather inaccurately in terms of the year of establishment, 'From TILLOTSON & SON'S FICTION BUREAU./Established 1871./For Supplying the Works of Popular Novelists to the Newspaper Press'. At the foot appeared a list of services offered and distinguished authors represented. Up to that time, correspondence concerning the syndication operation was written on paper headed 'The Bolton Evening News etc'. At some point in the early 1890s the notepaper heading changed to 'TILLOTSONS' NEWSPAPER LITERATURE/For Supplying the Newspaper Press with special Articles and the Works of Popular Novelists'.

3   There is still no comprehensive account of Maxwell's life, and, particularly in the early years, his business dealings remain obscure and his character has been variously interpreted. The discussion in Wolff, *Sensational*, 97–101, can be supplemented with the following accounts: Escott, 268–9; Liveing, 33; Maxwell, 157–61; Rita, 43–7; Sala, chs 29–36; Straus, 154; Tinsley, 1:61–3; *VFRG*, 19/20, *passim*; and Yates, vol. II. See also Carnell, ch. 3, and Law, 'Engaged', 1–3.

4   This hypothesis might be supported by the following evidence: the participation in the coterie for *Taken at the Flood* of untypical papers like the *Portsmouth Times* and the Dublin *Penny Despatch*, which seem to reflect John Maxwell's rather than W.F. Tillotson's sphere of influence; the lack of reference to any leading role played by the Bolton firm in the early account in the *Newsvendor* of August 1873; and the following passage in a later but generally reliable account: 'A combination of six [sic.] newspapers was formed and resulted in a commission to Miss Braddon, who thus wrote "Taken at the Flood" – the first story of any great writer published serially in newspapers. The first experiment, however, proved the absolute necessity of one firm alone assuming financial responsibility when commissioning an author, and thus grew and developed the Syndicate.' (*Progress*, 100).

5   Judging from the trade ledgers (ZBEN, 1/2), Tillotsons appear first to have offered complete tales to their subscribers at Christmas 1878. The provenance of the many anonymous short stories that appeared in the *Bolton Weekly Journal* in 1871–72, especially at the Christmas season, is unknown; it seems possible that some at least might have been provided by Harrison.

6   As Table A.1 shows, both journals belonged to Tillotsons's earliest coteries but also, for example, ran George Manville Fenn's *Under Wild Skies* in 1875, which appeared simultaneously in the *Sheffield Independent* and thus seems likely to have been syndicated by Leaders. R.D. Dowling's 'The Loss of the Dream' (1873–74) and E. Owens Blackburne's 'A Woman Scorned' (1875) are other likely examples of serials syndicated by Leaders around this time.

7   Notebook A, 124 (TURNER) reveals that the work was in fact by one J. Bradbury, whose fiction was also used by the *Bolton Guardian*, where Bradbury's *Fatal Trust; or, The Great Earl of Derby* appeared in 1876.

8   I have been able to locate no data corresponding to this period, though in 1883 the Lancashire Journals Series was claiming *in toto* an annual circulation in excess of four and a half million copies, that is, around 87 000 per week (*Sell's*, 1883–84, 201). See Table 5.1.

9 Though the trade ledgers at Bolton (ZBEN, 1/2) do not record the papers subscribing to specific serials, and thus of the sums they paid to Tillotsons, information is available from other sources. The *Aberdeen Journal* Records, for example, reveal that, in the late 1870s and still with a relatively small circulation, that paper agreed to pay Tillotsons £15 for Dora Russell's *The Vicar's Governess*, and £20 for B.L. Farjeon's *No. 119 Great Porter Square* (15 March 1878 and 27 February 1880, Minute Book of Finance Committee 1877–1883, AJR). At the other end of the scale, in 1881 Collins's *Heart and Science* was worth £100 to the *Manchester Weekly Times* with its large regional circulation, while the *Aberdeen Weekly Journal* paid only £50. Here the syndicator was A.P. Watt, but other letters in the same archive suggest that Tillotsons were commanding similar sums (Collins Acc., BERG).

10 The earliest stories available in stereo on Tillotsons's later backlists (see that of c.1884 held at Bolton, ZBEN, 4/5) date from 1876.

11 Braddon's *Like and Unlike*, Besant's *Herr Paulus*, and Collins's *The Legacy of Cain*, available in turn from March 1887, September 1887, and February 1888 (Tables A.4–6), appear to be among the first sequence of illustrated serials offered by Tillotsons.

12 For example, a Tillotsons's advertisement in *The Stationer* in 1875 (5 June, 402) offered 'to supply newspapers at a comparatively nominal price with copy in reprint' of a number of novels, including Braddon's *Dead Men's Shoes*.

13 Elizabeth Morrison (personal communication) has located a copy of a Tillotsons's advertisement from 1896, for Bessie Temple's 'Liz: A Transvaal Heroine' which contains a short extract from the opening of the novel as well as information on the author and the length and price of the serial. The first surviving programme may be that of 1894 held among the Tillotsons's materials at the Bodleian (TURNER), though an example for 1881–82 was clearly referred to in a note in the *Academy* (749, 9 July 1881, 28), which mentions works by James Payn, Robert Buchanan, John Saunders ready in August 1881, by William Westall in October, and by Dora Russell and Charles Gibbon in February the following year. The earliest surviving example of the backlist catalogue is almost certainly that of c.1884 held at Bolton (ZBEN, 4/5).

14 Referred to in ALS from John Maxwell to W.F. Tillotson of 21 January 1879, the first of their surviving correspondence at Bolton, ZBEN, 4/3. This call mark refers to a file consisting principally of letters from Maxwell to Tillotson from 1879 to 1887, but also including telegrams and postcards, a few documents from outside this period, occasional letters from Braddon herself, Tillotson or third parties, and some attached printed papers, altogether totaling nearly 200 unnumbered items. Unless otherwise stated, references to ZBEN, 4/3, indicate ALSs from Maxwell to Tillotson.

15 For example, in the case of four novels by G.A. Henty in the 1890s, where volume rights were sold on to Chatto and Windus – see Newbolt, 580–5.

16 The first such example was the agreement for Marryat's *Fighting the Air* of 18 July 1874; other early cases include Farjeon's *No. 119 Great Porter Square* and Ainsworth's *Stanley Brereton*.

17 See ALSs of 11 October, 27 and 29 December 1882, and 1 January 1883, and the attached printed circular headed 'Author's Advance Proofs of Fiction for the United States of America' and dated 30 December 1882 (ZBEN, 4/3). More generally on the role of Tillotsons in the development of fiction syndication in the United States, see Johanningsmeier, ch. 2.

18 Notebook A, 119, TURNER, however, records that Tillotsons paid McClure around £430 'for Newsp. copyright outside America' for 'The Outlaws of Tunstall Forest', presumably in 1888, when the story appeared in, for example, the *Staffordshire Sentinel*.

19 Held among the Victor Fremont Lawson papers at the Newberry Library, Chicago. The correspondence in question is to be found mainly under the headings 'Chicago Daily News – Incoming Letters' (10 965 letters/26 boxes) and 'Outgoing Correspondence – Regular Series 1882–1925' (64 vols/34 boxes).

20 For an early and detailed account of the rise of the Colonial press, see Andrews, vol. II, chs 9, 17; see also the recent essays in Vann and VanArsdel, *Periodicals*.

21 Article VII of the Berne Convention gave authors and publishers the right to prohibit the reproduction or translation in other signatory countries of any article not pertaining to news and current affairs published in newspapers or magazines in any signatory country. The Paris amendments of 1896 removed the obligation of authors and publishers to expressly state such prohibition in the case of serial stories. See Briggs, parts III and V.

22 W.F. Tillotson wrote to Charles Reade, for example, on a number of occasions, obtained an interview in 1878, and offered £640 for a novel in 26 instalments, then a record for the Bureau. But at that time Reade was reluctant to undertake a new novel due to failing health and the poor reception of his recent work. He finally agreed in 1883 to sell second serial rights to *A Perilous Secret* for £500, which started its run as 'Love and Money' in the *Bolton Weekly Journal* and other papers in February 1884, shortly before his death (Elwin, *Charles*, 291–304; Table A.2). Tillotson must even have written to Gladstone requesting a contribution, based on the rumour that the latter wrote fiction under an assumed name; Gladstone replied politely that the rumour was unfounded (December 1879, ZBEN, 4/6).

23 On 29 June 1887, Hardy signed an agreement to sell for 1000 guineas serial rights/American advance sheets of an unnamed novel (*Tess of the D'Urbervilles*) in 24 instalments/c.120 000 words to begin around October 1889, but the contract was eventually cancelled (see Chapter 7). In 1892 Tillotsons paid £525 for the same rights to the shorter novel *The Pursuit of the Well-Beloved*. Hardy also sold serial rights to five short stories to Tillotsons ('The Benighted Travellers' for £24 10s in 1881, 'A Mere Interlude' for £80 in 1885, 'Alicia's Diary' for £70 in 1887, 'The Melancholy Hussar' for £50 in 1890, and 'A Changed Man' for £60 in 1900 – the last being for American rights only).

24 Five ALSs and five telegrams within a single week in November 1884 during the negotiations over 'Cut by the Country' was probably the most concentrated burst.

25 In fact, Maxwell's interpretation of British copyright law proved extreme. In 1886 the house of Maxwell issued a Mayne Reid novel in volume without authorization, on the grounds that no British copyright existed since serialization of the work in the United States had concluded in advance of that in the United Kingdom. Reid's widow and his British publishers successfully sought an injunction against infringement of copyright by Maxwells, upheld on appeal, on the ground that the first part of the novel had been first published in England (Briggs, 498–9).

26 See ALSs to W.F. Tillotson from John Maxwell (30 January 1886) and John Maxwell, Jr (27, 30 January and 4 February 1886), all ZBEN, 4/3.

27 See TLS, 10 March 1887, C.D. Leng to John Maxwell, forwarded to W.F. Tillotson: 'For what sum would Miss Braddon engage to write us a story and sell us the entire serial rights? Would she give us the first refusal of her next three stories, and at what price?' (ZBEN, 4/3).

28 For example, Henderson's *Penny Pictorial News* of 20 December 1886 carried Foster's 'The Moss-Pit Mystery'. His first story to be accepted by Tillotsons was the same tale (under the title 'The Black Moss Mystery') which appeared in the *Bolton Weekly Journal* at Christmas 1888.

29 Tillotsons were not the only publishers to anticipate Mudie's announcement by reducing the length of their serials; *The Graphic* and *The Illustrated London News*, for example, switched from a general pattern of two longer serials per year to three or four shorter ones in 1893 and 1894 respectively.

30 See the discussion in Griest (204–8) of the resistance to the demise of the triple-decker novel by Braddon (whose *Sons of Fire* was one of only 50 or so novels to appear in that format in 1895).

31 Certainly Tillotsons's New York office had been closed down well before 1921 – see TLS from Tillotsons to A.P. Watt and Co. of 12 February 1921 (WILSON, 442.8).

Chapter 4: Rivals of Tillotsons

1 Rice in fact died of throat cancer in April 1882 after a protracted illness, and *All Sorts and Conditions of Men* was thus Besant's solo effort, though all the serial appearances, including that in *Belgravia*, recorded the work as by Besant and Rice (see Eliot, 'His Generation', 27–30). Besant's Preface to the volume edition of the novel of February 1883 says of Rice: 'Almost the last act of his in our partnership was the arrangement, with certain country papers and elsewhere, for the serial publication of this novel.'

2 All but *No Quarter!* appeared in the *Sheffield Independent*. Other appearances located are: *Gwen Wynn* in the *Leeds Mercury* Weekly Supplement, *Birmingham Weekly Post*, and *Western Daily Mercury*; *The Flag of Distress* in the *Newcastle Courant*, after its first serial run in *Chamber's Journal* in 1875 (Reid, 217); *The Free Lances* again in the *Newcastle Courant*, plus the *Manchester Weekly Post* and *Dublin Weekly Freeman*, after its first serial run in the *New York Ledger* in 1869 (Pollard, 'Novels', 83); and *No Quarter!* in the *Newcastle Weekly Chronicle* and *Manchester Weekly Post*.

3 J.E. Muddock (who wrote thrillers as 'Dick Donovan' in the 1890s) represents another early case of self-syndication. According to his own account (107–10), he sold *The Great White Hand*, a tale of the Indian Mutiny published in volume only in 1896, independently to a wide range of country papers from the early 1870s, including the *Dundee Weekly News* (1855–). Tillotsons's *Bolton Weekly Journal* also paid £10 to reprint the serial from December 1874. Muddock claimed to have made a total of £1500 from serialization of the work. Muddock was a friend of Reid's and had previously discussed the idea with him, as well as with Wilkie Collins; the dates suggest that he preceded Reid in putting the idea into practice. He states that he published a number of later novels in this way, without giving details. In addition to 'The Crimson Star' sold to Tillotsons in 1877 (*The Star of Fortune* in volume in 1894), a number of other works not handled by the Bolton firm have been located in provincial weeklies, including 'The Mystery of Jasper Janin' in the *Sheffield Telegraph* in 1878.

4 In addition to Wilkie Collins's *Black Robe* noted above, other works which appear to have been syndicated by Leaders in the later 1870s include Frederick Talbot's *Closed at Dusk* (1877), Roger Frith's *Spoiling the Egyptians* (1877), Sarah Stredder's *Saved from the Wreck* (1878), and Geo. Manville Fenn's *The Foundry Belle* (1878). Simultaneously with their appearance in the *Sheffield Independent*, these have been located in the *Birmingham Weekly Post* (1869–) and the *Western Weekly Mercury*.

5 An early indication of the Agency's activities is found in a letter to the *Newsvendor* in December 1873 (199) replying to the article 'Provincial Newspapers' in the previous issue (discussed in Chapter 2), where it was stated that partly printed newspapers were in decline and were now only offered by Eglingtons and Cassell. The manager claimed his new agency was in fact 'doing a large and increasing business' of the kind referred to. *NCBEL* (3:1762) mentions a volume published in 1898 to celebrate the Agency's silver anniversary, but I have been unable to locate a copy, none being found in the major British copyright collections.

6 This appearance seems not to have been previously recorded (see Hamer, App. 2). Based on a personal communication from John Palmer, a railway periodical enthusiast, now deceased but then on the British Library staff, Colby suggests that *Ayala's Angel* started to appear in a journal entitled *The Train*, which 'ceased publication before the novel could complete its run' ('Tale', 13n8). This might be the penny paper listed in Wolff *Waterloo* as *The Train: A Weekly Topical and Popular Journal for the Travelling Public*, running from April 1884 to January 1886, though I have been unable to locate a copy. However, the journal is not mentioned in the article on the subject by Palmer (with Harold Paar), which lists two others with the same title but with publication dates too early for our purposes. The novel appeared as a triple-decker from Chapman and Hall in June 1881.

7 Central News itself seems to have dealt in fiction also from the mid-1880s, judging by letters from manager John Moore to A.P. Watt, arranging purchase of serial rights to Bret Harte's 'Struck at Devil's Creek', where

he confessed 'this class of business is to some extent new to us' (ALS, 15 March 1886, Harte Acc., BERG).

8 The Tory *Aberdeen Journal* took the daily London letter from Saunders's Central News on a trial basis in autumn 1879, but promptly switched to take 'nightly Conservative sketches of Parliament during the Session' from the Central Press (Minutes of Finance Committee, 12 September 1879 and 23 January 1880, AJR), though no evidence exists of them receiving fiction from the Tory agency.

9 As early as 1884, an agent associated with the *Detroit Free Press* wrote to a number of well-known British novelists attempting to set up an international syndicate to carry their work in newspapers around the English-speaking world (ALSs from Robert Dennis to M.E. Braddon and Wilkie Collins, both of 15 December 1884, ZBEN, 4/3 and PEMBROKE).

10 See, for example, TLSs from Watt to the Northern Newspaper Syndicate of 16 January 1901 concerning Besant's short story 'Kerb and Gutter' (WILSON, 442.08), and of 2 December 1905 confirming terms for M.E. Braddon's *Dead Love Has Chains* (under the title 'Alias Jane Brown', WILSON, 85.10).

11 This is suggested by the case of Arnold Bennett whose work was handled by all three syndicators after the turn of the century; see Bennett, *Letters*, 1:36–134.

12 For brief accounts of Watt's beginnings, see Hepburn, 51–5; Bonham-Carter, 168–9; Doran, ch. 12; Mumby and Norrie, 247; Nicoll; Gillies; Rubinstein; and Zinkhan, 165–7. General correspondence to and from Watt is located: in the Berg Collection at the New York Public Library (the 16 surviving volumes of the 26-volume Letterbook containing copies of Watts outgoing business letters from 1879 to 1891, plus files of correspondence from clients covering a similar period); in client files from around 1885 onwards in the A.P. Watt archive in the Wilson Library, University of North Carolina, Chapel Hill; and reprinted in the *Collection of Letters Addressed to A.P. Watt*, 1893 onwards. The manuscript letters from Wilkie Collins to Watt from late 1881 to the author's death in 1889 are now held in three bound volumes at Pembroke College, Cambridge.

13 Correspondence at PEMBROKE shows that Watt was still using stationery headed 'Advertising Agent', and listing clients such as *Blackwoods*, as late as April 1884. (The outgoing correspondence in the BERG Letterbooks is in the form of copies on India paper which carry no letter heading.)

14 Although the earliest volume of Watt's Letterbooks, covering the period up to around October 1879, is unfortunately lacking (BERG), there seems to be no documentary evidence to support the contention that Watt began to acquire client-authors as early as 1875, discussed by Hepburn, 52–3, and accepted by Rubinstein and Bonham-Carter, 168–9. In an interview in the *Bookman* of October 1892 (reprinted in *Collection*, 1893, 65–79), Watt recalled that he began to sell stories for MacDonald 'some fourteen years ago' (66), while MacDonald himself, penning a recommendatory letter for Watt in June 1892, wrote: 'I cannot tell how many years have passed, but they must be more than ten, since first

you took the weight of business off my shoulders' (*Collection*, 43).

15 None seem to have been taken up by the Bolton firm. Simon Eliot notes a similar offer in February 1881 ('Unequal', 86).

16 In 1884, for example, Watt offered the *Aberdeen Journal* for £25 each the serial rights to any of a list of half a dozen novels recently published by Chatto and Windas (ALS, 21 August, Letterbook, 7:969, BERG).

17 Further, on 11 November 1880, Watt wrote to William Black offering £1200 for a new novel to appear from Chatto and Windus in 1882 in both *Belgravia* and in three volumes, but allowing freedom for simultaneous serialization in country papers (Letterbook, 3:126, BERG); Black refused the offer, however.

18 The payments from *Frank Leslie's* and *Belgravia* (which gave Collins £1 per page in monthly instalments totalling £308) are recorded in various ALSs from Collins to Andrew Chatto, 23 August 1882–83 July 1883, PARRISH. For details of the payments negotiated with British newspapers, which ranged from £30 from the *Cardiff Weekly Times* to £100 from the *Liverpool Weekly Post* (probably reduced to £95 for providing proofs), see Law 'Wilkie', 265n. Collins complained bitterly about the quality of the proofs pulled by the Liverpool paper and later persuaded *Belgravia* to provide the service (see Chapter 6). As was his standard practice, Watt simply took a commission on the sums he negotiated. On 31 August 1882, for example, Collins wrote to Watt acknowledging the receipt of £199. 10s, the first of three instalments of newspaper subscriptions for the right to publish *Heart and Science* periodically, less commission of 10 per cent (ALS, PEMBROKE). Chatto and Windus paid £600 for a seven-year lease on the volume rights (Weedon, 181).

19 As Table 4.1 shows, from the end of 1884, *The People* was to carry Zola's *Germinal: or, Master and Man*, translated by Albert D. Vandam (then Paris correspondent of the *Globe*, the London evening paper under the same ownership) prior to the novel's appearance in volume form from Vizetelly. Clearly the scandalous image of Zola's writings in Britain in the 1880s offered a popular as well as a bohemian attraction. It was three years later that Vizetelly was prosecuted for obscenity for issuing Zola's *La Terre* in English translation.

20 For details of the payments from British newspapers, which ranged from £25 from the *Belfast Weekly News* to £100 from the *Glasgow Weekly Herald*, see Law 'Wilkie', 265n. The single letter in the Watt files concerning serialization in *The People* gives no indication of the payment (ALS from the *Globe* office, 29 October 1883, Collins Acc., BERG), though £100 seems a likely figure. A letter to Watt suggests that Collins received three payments of £300 from Kelly's (ALS, 3 April 1884, PEMBROKE). Chatto and Windus paid £500 for a seven year lease on the volume rights (Weedon, 181).

21 Though the relevant Watt Letterbooks are lacking at the BERG (vols 20–4, December 1889–February 1891), four letters from the end of January 1891 in a file at the WILSON (10.7) prove that this was the case. Like Besant's *The World Went Very Well Then*, Black's *Wolfenburg*, and Crockett's *The Grey Man*, *Tess* was also serialized simultaneously in Australia in the *Sydney Mail*, under the title 'A Daughter of the D'Urbervilles' as in

the provincial papers (Johnson-Woods; Grindle and Gattrell, 1–25). The appearance in the *Birmingham Weekly Post*, which seems not to have been previously noted, was found by John Stock Clarke in the course of research into the serialization of Oliphant's fiction (personal communication); as in *The Graphic* and *Nottinghamshire Guardian*, the novel ran there from 4 July-26 December 1891. The serialization of *Tess* is discussed further in Chapter 7.

22 The uncertainty of Watt's touch is indicated, for example, by the more than a dozen ALSs that he sent offering *Heart and Science* to smaller Welsh and English local papers, with no tradition of carrying serial fiction, in late March and early April 1882 (Letterbook 2, BERG). Similarly proprietors of major provincial journals were often annoyed by Watt's ignorance of the large circulation areas they claimed.

23 For accounts of the setting-up of the Society of Authors and its relations to the production of late Victorian fiction, see: Besant, *Society*; Bonham-Carter, ch. 6; Colby, 'Authorship' and 'Harnessing'; and Goode, 'Decadent', 116–21.

24 In *The Society of Authors: a Record of Its Action from Its Foundation*, initially delivered as an address to the Annual General Meeting of the Society in December 1892, Besant described the Author's Syndicate, together with the Author's Club (for gentlemen) and the Writer's Club (for ladies) as 'off-sets, independent branches of our work, not controlled by the Committee' (32).

25 Under pressure from Besant, Colles cut the commission taken for administrative expenses from 25% to 10% and finally to 5% ('On Syndicating', *The Author*, 15 May 1890, 10; Colby, 'Tale', 10). The agent John Chartres acted as the Syndicate's New York representative from the early 1890s (Johanningsmeier, 97).

26 At the end of the decade, Besant asserted that the Literary Agent had 'become almost indispensable for the author of every kind, but especially for the novelist', adding that '[s]ome of us wanted him to become a part of the Society of Authors, but at the time the Society was not strong enough to make that a safe position. He is, therefore, independent' (Besant, *Pen*, 215 & 220). Slightly later (*Autobiography*, 204–5) Besant paid warm tribute to Watt for his services.

27 See: on Gissing, Korg, 194, 213; on Wells, MacKenzie and MacKenzie, 113–15, 133; and on Bennett, Drabble, 84–5.

28 Other London local papers were also carrying serial fiction by this stage: the *South Eastern Herald*, for example, was accepting material from A.P. Watt in the early 1880s (ALS to Watt of 29 June 1882, MacDonald Acc., BERG).

29 Unaccountably, Caine (376–7) later claimed that he received a total of only £150 for the publication of the novel, including the three-volume edition from Chatto and Windus.

Chapter 5: Readership

1   See *RN37–50*, *RN51–53* and *RN54*. It remained possible, of course, for a newspaper to temporarily inflate the returns by stamping sheets in advance.

2   The newspaper stamp in fact remained as an optional postal charge from 1855 to 1870, and these returns are also available. Alvar Ellegard has attempted to manipulate the figures statistically in order to estimate actual circulations during this period, but whatever the value of his results, they are of little use for our purposes as few weekly journals and almost no provincial papers are included.

3   The main directories are *NPD*, *Sell's*, *Deacon's*, and *May's*. *Deacon's* made the biggest effort to provide circulation data, distinguishing between audited and unaudited figures from 1880:

> In our Edition of last year we introduced that which many thought would be an unreliable and hazardous feature – the giving of the Circulations of the various newspapers wherever we could induce the publications to supply them. It seemed to us a very strange circumstance, that whilst in the Newspaper guides of the Continent and America it is always possible to get a statement of the circulation of a newspaper, no attempt had hitherto been made to supply this most vital information to the English Advertisers.
>
> (Preface, 1881)

Nevertheless, figures were provided for less than a tenth of the journals listed.

4   For example, the *NPD* for 1874 (3) stated that the *Bolton Weekly Journal* circulated 'in Bolton and the townships of the Bolton Union, with a population of 250,000' (the population of the town of Bolton itself was then around 82 000), while an advertisement in *Sell's* 1885 (343) for Tillotsons's papers proudly claimed that '16,000 of these Papers are Printed and folded per Hour by our "Victory" machines'.

5   For example, an *NPD* advertisement showed the combined weekly totals of the *Liverpool Daily Post*, *Weekly Post* and (evening) *Echo* rising from 428 605 in 1882 to 1 028 502 in 1892 (*NPD*, 1893, 276). Even the detailed Aberdeen Journals Records give no precise circulation figures for specific papers, and always conflate the income from sales of the *Weekly Journal* with its daily counterpart, and often with the *Evening Express*. As an example of a dispute over claimed circulation, Brown (26n) cites that in Leeds between the Tory *Daily News* and the radical *Express* reflected in their respective advertisements in *NPD*, 1894, 275.

6   Though we should note the articles by Leigh and Haslam published just after the turn of the century on reading habits in proletarian districts of Lancashire, based on informal surveys of local newsagents.

7   Exceptionally, Feargus O'Connor's Chartist weekly the (Leeds) *Northern Star* (1837?–1852), despite its price of $4\frac{1}{2}$d, attracted a large proletarian readership and sold well over 10 000 copies an issue between 1838 and

1842, and even briefly touched a peak of over 50 000 in April 1839 (Cranfield, *Press*, 194–7).

8 ALSs to A.P. Watt from Alexander Ireland of the *Weekly Times* (27 February 1882) and James H. Stoddard of the *Herald* (5 July 1883), both Collins Acc., BERG.

9 In 1888 an informed commentator, H.A. Boswell, described the *People's Friend* as 'the most widely read of all the publications issued from Mr. Leng's Dundee Printing Works' (79).

10 The following instances are not untypical. At the head of the third part of Pae's 'Lucy, the Factory Girl' in the *Glasgow Times* (15 December 1858), there appeared a digest of the previous instalment '[f]or the benefit of those among our readers who were unsuccessful in purchasing copies of our last week's issue.... Today, we are better able to meet the extraordinary demand.' Similarly there was an announcement at the head of the second instalment of Braddon's *London Pride* in the *Birmingham Weekly Mercury*: 'In consequence of the Great Demand for the *Weekly Mercury* last week, which we were not able to supply after Saturday, we herewith print a comprehensive *resumé* of the first instalment which appeared in last week's issue' (12 October 1894, 2). Here a notice that back numbers were available followed every instalment. More unusually, when Tillotsons themselves started two further Lancashire Journals in January 1874, both were able to take up the serialization of Braddon's *Taken at the Flood* from the 23rd episode (out of 34), by including a huge 10-column synopsis of the story thus far.

11 Yates's novel, written hastily during a lecture tour of the US from September 1872, was also serialized in the New York *Fireside Companion* (10 February–28 April 1873), and appeared in volume from W.F. Gill in Boston in 1876 as *Going to the Bad* (Edwards, 126n, 215)

12 In the case of the newspaper novel, there was understandably no equivalent of the running commentary on monthly serials in progress which Hughes and Lund have traced so effectively in the review columns of the metropolitan weekly press.

13 The Plymouth *Mercury* remained a regular member of Tillotsons's syndicates until 1880, just after the creation of the *Weekly Mercury*, the last novel it took from the Bolton firm at that time being Collins's *Jezebel's Daughter*. One of the first of the new 'inferior' tales to appear was David Pae's 'Annabel; or the Temptation' from 1881. Interestingly, the proprietors must again have decide to retarget the readership of the journal in 1887, when the name was changed to the *Western Weekly Mercury*, and material from Tillotsons reappeared, beginning with Besant's *Herr Paulus*.

14 The recent work of Eddie Cass on the literary content of Victorian newspapers in Lancashire offers a further model.

15 There is evidence for this not only in the composition of the syndicates for Braddon's and Collins's novels for Tillotsons recorded in Tables A.4 and A.5, but also in Turner ('Syndication', App. 3) where there is a complete listing of the journals subscribing to the 1909 Tillotsons's fiction programme.

16 Note in W.F. Tillotson's hand on printed circular advertising the stereotype edition of Braddon's novels, accompanying proofs sent to John Maxwell, 16 February [1886], ZBEN, 4/3.

17 By the turn of the century, announcements in *NPD* aimed at potential advertisers were claiming proudly of the *Sheffield Evening Telegraph* also that it contained 'no politics'.

18 A notice in *NPD* for 1920 (538) claimed brazenly that the *Weekly Telegraph*'s 'circulation has been built up without the aid of coupon-cutting prize competitions' (538).

19 Many of the subscribing newspapers, like the (Dublin) *Penny Despatch* with Braddon's *Taken at the Flood*, claimed that syndicated stories were 'specially written for' their journal (Announcement, 9 August 1873, 4). It is unusual to find acknowledgements to the syndicating agency such as the phrase 'Copyrighted by Tillotson & Sons [sic]', in the *Ripon Observer*'s serialization of Braddon's *All Along the River* (8 June 1893, 2). Probably the Cardiff *Weekly Mail* was unique in prefacing each instalment of *Taken at the Flood* with a list of all the coterie members (for example, 30 August 1873, 2).

Chapter 6: Authorship

1 However, as noted in Chapter 5, Yates's 'A Bad Lot' appeared in the *Birmingham Morning News* in 1873, while the Tillotsons records show that Yates signed an agreement to write a novel for the Fiction Bureau on 27 January 1875, though the contract seems not to have been fulfilled (ZBEN, 4/4).

2 Other early examples of metropolitan journalists serving as occasional novelists for their own periodicals include Charles Mackay for *Robin Goodfellow*, or Robert Brough for *The Welcome Guest*.

3 Other regular newspaper novelists with early experience in the Provincial press include Charles Gibbon, George Manville Fenn, William Clark Russell, and Justin McCarthy. Those with early metropolitan newspaper experience would include F.W. Robinson and Richard Dowling.

4 In analysing the bio-bibliographical information concerning the 878 Victorian novelists listed in his own *Stanford Companion*, John Sutherland (*Victorian Fiction*, 159–64) records that 82 out of 566 male writers (14.5%) also had careers as professional journalists, compared to only 9 out of 312 female writers (2.9%).

5 The *Glasgow Times* offered £1 per week for 'Lucy' which ran for 21 weeks; the bi-weekly *North Briton* offered 1 guinea per week for 'Heiress', which ran to 60 parts; and John Leng put up the simple sum of 10 guineas (see Chapter 2).

6 As cited in the Tauchnitz collection, the letter continues, ' . . .[name omitted] gets £1500 from a syndicate of this sort. The papers are always situated far apart so as not to interfere with each others' circulation'. Since Tillotsons, though generous, were not paying rates anything like as high as this until the mid-1880s, it seems likely that Payn was referring to Joyce Muddock's claim to have made precisely that sum by syndicating *The Great White Hand* himself, as noted in Chapter 4.

7 As in the case of Hall Caine's *The Bondmen*, for example, for which the author received £400 for serial rights from Tillotsons in 1889, and where he was persuaded to accept an advance of £300 against royalties from Heinemann for the three-volume edition, though he had originally asked for £400 for absolute copyright (Keating, 18–20).

8 Indeed, elsewhere Oliphant complained with equal bitterness that women authors earned more: 'Mrs Craik, a great deal more, George Elliot [sic.] of course ten times and Miss Braddon's books go on selling as well as ever now they say' (Oliphant, *Complete*, 157). Generally on Oliphant's struggles in the fiction market, see Colby and Colby.

9 Anesko, App. B, shows that even as selective a periodical contributor as Henry James earned considerably more literary income from serial rights than book sales throughout the 1880s and 1890s.

10 Michael Turner's detailed description of Tillotsons's agreements with authors ('Tillotson's') is of limited use for our purposes, as he did not have access to information about the earliest agreements (ZBEN, 4/4), spends only a couple of paragraphs (357–8) discussing those surviving from the 1880s, and instead concentrates on those from the 1890s onwards.

11 Several of Hay's novels of the 1870s were first issued in serial in *The Family Herald* as by 'Markham Howard', including *Old Myddleton's Money* (2 February – 12 September 1874). W.F. Tillotson finally conceded, although in this case the fault seems strictly to have been the author's (six ALSs, 9 November to 6 December 1883; ZBEN, 4/3; see Law, 'Engaged', 15–19).

12 For example, Dickens had spoken out against the absence of copyright protection for foreign authors on his first visit to the States in 1842, and was involved briefly in the first, short-lived Society of British Authors in 1843 (Bonham-Carter, ch. 4). Collins's anger at the lack of international copyright in the USA is reflected in his 1880 pamphlet *Considerations on the Copyright Question*, reprinted in *The Author* of June 1890 as 'Thou Shalt not Steal'.

13 See Chapter 3. Collins was well informed on the legal issues involved, as illustrated by a lengthy letter to his solicitor William Tindell of 16 July 1874 (MITCHELL).

14 Interestingly, despite this experience, Watt ran into trouble in 1892 when Harpers in New York, to whom he had sold American serial rights to Besant's *Rebel Queen*, threatened to take legal action because their copyright was being infringed by the circulation of the serial in the US edition of the *Illustrated London News*, to which Watt had sold British serial rights (WILSON, 6.3).

15 Though, as Simon Eliot has noted ('Unequal' 73), Besant himself often ignored his own advice as to the inadvisability of selling copyrights outright to publishers.

16 See, for example, the two-part prefaces to *Armadale* (1866) and *Heart and Science* (1883), and the discussion in Lonoff, 55–66.

17 W.F. Tillotson stipulated that, if the new novel were to be of a length with *The Evil Genius*, it should be divided into 20 parts (thus earning £1000 at £50 per instalment, against the £1300 paid for 26 parts). He

explained to Watt that six of the eight US newspapers taking *The Evil Genius* had refused *The Legacy of Cain*, largely because the numbers of the earlier novel had averaged less than 4000 words (TLSs, 20 and 23 November 1886, Collins Acc., BERG), though Tillotson's circular to the American newspapers guaranteed 5500 words, as Victor Lawson in Chicago had insisted to Tillotson (TLS, 31 December 1885, Outgoing, VFL).

18 See the many letters of friendship received by W.F. Tillotson from his authors (ZBEN, 4/6), and the moving letters of condolence sent to his widow in early 1889 (WFT). Ouida and Collins seem to have be among the few well-known Tillotsons's authors who did not write at the time of his death.

19 Collins suggested to Chatto that they cease to address each other as 'mister' in a letter of 19 March 1883 (ALS, PARRISH), and did the same with Watt on 23 October 1885 (Collins, *Letters*, 2:486–7). Collins wrote pointedly to W.F. Tillotson in 1883: 'My literary arrangements are all now made for me – with my approval, of course – by my friend and representative Mr A.P. Watt' (letter copied by Watt, 17 April, PEMBROKE).

20 See, for example, the opening of the letter from W.F. Tillotson to A.P. Watt at the early stages of the negotiations for *The Evil Genius*: 'Mr Collins wrote me that you were his Literary Representative, and I have manifested every disposition to treat with you. Why should I not? Why should I write Mr. Collins?' (ALS, 17 November 1884, Collins Acc., BERG).

21 See, for example, the postscript to the letter from W.F. Tillotson to A.P. Watt of 19 May 1885: 'P.S. Is it true that the "Leicester Mercury" paid £40 last year for Wilkie Collins Story, and that there was to be no other publication so near as Nottingham and counties immediately surrounding Leicester. We have asked £50 which is declined on above grounds' (ALS, Collins Acc., BERG).

22 W.F. Tillotson is quoted in John Maxwell's reply of 24 October 1885: 'I sent Mr. Watts' letter to you that you might see the quest for a Braddon and protect yourself and me from his interference. I have neither desire nor intention to assist a "parasite", but I must get an outlet as you well know' (ZBEN, 4/3). The same terms of disparagement was later used of the literary agent by both Ouida, as we have seen, and by the publisher William Heinemann in a letter to the *Athenaeum* of November 1893 (cited in Hepburn, 1–2).

23 As early as 1863, she claimed almost to have 'earned enough money to keep me and mother for the rest of our lives' (letter to Bulwer-Lytton, 13 April, reprinted in Wolff 'Devoted', 13).

24 Reproduced in Wolff (*Sensational*, Plate 25). See also Charles Reade's conclusion that 'her taskmaster drove her too hard' in his 1874 notebook (cited in Wolff, *Sensational*, 79–83).

25 The entries for Braddon's *Phantom Fortune* and *Just as I Am* in Tillotsons's printed backlist of c.1884, and those alone, are erased in ink by hand in the copy surviving at Bolton (ZBEN, 4/5). For Collins's accusations to Watt, see, for example, ALS of 9 March 1889 noting '[s]mart practice on the part of the late Mr Tillotson' (PEMBROKE).

26 Still in 1907 only six out of fifty-seven writers on the Council were women (Colby, 'What', 72).

27 *The World* first responded to Ouida's outburst on 27 May 1891 (25) in 'What the World Says', when, after listing a dozen major authors who had paid tribute to Watt's competence, it commented 'The public can judge between the wail of Weeder on the one hand and the hearty testimonials of these well-known English authors on the other.'

28 At the same time, I am aware of empirical and theoretical flaws in Tuchman's case, such as its exclusive reliance on data from the Macmillan archives and the *DNB* (App. A), or its assumption that the 'High-Culture Novel' at the end of the century was unambiguously realist in orientation (ch. 4). See the caveats in the generally positive reviews of Tuchman by Cogan, Gallagher, and Mukerji.

Chapter 7: Genre

1 Due allowance being made for complete changes of title between serial and volume publication, and non-submission to the copyright libraries by publishers in the provinces and/or of cheap fiction.

2 Phillips notes that, in the 1860s, the standard length of the instalments in a novel issued in *All the Year Round* and *Cornhill*, were respectively 'from 4000 to 6000 words, or rather less than half a sheet' and 'one [sheet] or a little more'; at the same time he points out that, taking up two sheets, the independent monthly number could go be as much as double the word-count of an instalment in *Cornhill* (86).

3 See the discussion of Dickens's use of monthly and weekly serials in Fielding's two articles in the *Dickensian* of 1858, and in Coolidge (who uses the terms 'fat' and 'thin' instalments).

4 Though Pae, like most writers in the penny journals, retains a preference for the virtuous heroine, and in no sense prepares the way for the likes of Braddon's Lady Audley or Collins's Lydia Gwilt.

5 We should perhaps note here cases where fiction with a local theme was produced for a provincial paper by an author with no local connection. Examples include 'Hard Pressed: a Tale of the Sheffield Flood' (1868) written for the *Sheffield Independent* by the Londoner George Manville Fenn; or the various local tales published by the widely travelled James Skipp Borlase, including 'Force and Fraud; or the Luddites in Leicester' in the *Leicester Chronicle* (1884) and the 'The Lancashire Mill Girl' in the *Liverpool Weekly Post* (1894).

6 Though Gibbon and Buchanan were born on the Isle of Man and in Staffordshire respectively, both were brought up in Glasgow, and retained a sense of their Scottish 'roots' even after embarking on literary careers based in London. On Buchanan, see *DLB*, 18: 18–22.

7 The banquet given in honour of Harrison Ainsworth in Manchester Town Hall on 15 September 1881, at which the title of 'The Lancashire Novelist' was conferred on the author, reflected a growing regional literary consciousness (Ellis, 2:317–36). Fothergill, Banks, Waugh, Heywood and Alexander Ireland of the *Manchester Times* are among the guests listed by Ellis. Edmund Yates was perhaps the only metropolitan journalist present, and wrote a warm tribute appearing in *The World* on 21 September.

8 A note in red ink at the bottom of the contract records that the agreement was cancelled in accordance with the author's letter of 24 September
   1889 (f.395/1, BODLEIAN). The agreement stipulated that the opening
   instalments be submitted by 13 June 1889, with publication commenc-
   ing around the first Saturday in October 1889.

9 The nature of the cuts is unclear though Reid was to some extend mol-
   lified by the reply he must have received (see letter to W.E. Adams, 13
   April 1880, Pollard, 'Novels', 84). Given the virulence of the attack on
   Disraeli which survived (*Newcastle Weekly Chronicle*, 13 April 1880, 6),
   it is possible that the editor removed even stronger remarks, as likely
   to attract an action for libel.

10 A similar incident had occurred in 1881, with Braddon's *The Story of
   Barbara*, which began to run in *The World* under the title 'Splendid
   Misery', but an action was brought by John Dicks whose journal *Every
   Week* was already running a serial under the same title (Copinger, 1904,
   247; Wolff, *Sensational*, 491–2).

11 During the period of her engagement to W.C. Leng and Co., of course,
   Braddon's output declined to a single novel per year, and the pattern
   of dual composition finally ceased.

12 In a rare modern instance of extended discussion of the novel, Rachel
   Anderson (*Purple*, 85–91) seems entirely to misread the narratorial tone
   in judging the moral of the story to be 'the sin, and the foolishness, of
   marrying, not for love, but for material gain'.

13 That this method was congenial to Besant is suggested by the speed
   and facility with which, on Wilkie Collins's incapacitation and death
   in 1889, he completed from the author's detailed working notes the
   novel *Blind Love*, then running in *The Illustrated London News* (Peters,
   ch. 24).

14 For example, in both cases due to illness, Collins was late with the
   monthly instalments of *The Two Destinies* for *Temple Bar* in 1876 (Peters, 380), while Braddon failed to complete *Bound to John Company* for
   Belgravia and it was finished by another hand (Wolff, *Sensational*, 228–9).
   As regards over-running, Collins finally produced 32 weekly instalments
   of *The Moonstone* for *All the Year Round*, although he had originally
   planned for only 26 (Peters, 291), while Braddon's *Wyllard's Wierd* ran
   to 27 parts instead of the 24–6 originally agreed with Tillotsons (15
   February 1884, ZBEN, 4/3; Table A.4).

15 Though no scholarly editions of Besant's work exist, a rapid survey of
   first periodical and volume editions available at the British Library of
   works written during the 1880s came up with few changes in chapter
   numbers or titles. In the case of *All Sorts and Conditions of Men* and
   Dorothy Forster, the two examples discussed below, there were no changes
   at all to the number or titles of chapters between the serial versions
   traced and the three-volume editions. However, there is evidence in
   the Watt archives of Besant significantly expanding the length of some
   of the serials written after 1895 before volume publication (for example, TLS Watt to Chatto, 13 October 1899, WILSON, 44:5).

16 Simon Eliot ('Unequal') has shown that business arrangements for the
   partnership were undertaken almost entirely by Rice, who may thus be

regarded as Besant's 'first literary agent and mentor on the business of publishing' (93). Eliot also suggests that Rice's touch was less sure in the book market than in that for periodicals, and that he may frequently have been out-manoeuvred by Andrew Chatto, who acted as principal volume publisher for Besant from the late 1870s onwards.

17 See the Prefaces to *The World Went Very Well Then* (1887) – 'I cannot, as a matter of fact, write two novels at once, and I should be very much afraid to try such an experiment.' – and *The City of Refuge* (1897) – 'Again, if the matter concerns anybody, I might mention that it would be to me, and I believe to everybody, utterly impossible to write two novels at the same time.'

18 This brief description of *All Sorts and Conditions of Men* is indebted to the more detailed analyses found in Goode, 'Art', 246–57, Eliot, 'His Generation', 30–6, and Feltes, *Literary*, 71–8.

19 The other works being *The Chaplain of the Fleet* (1881; with Rice), set in eighteenth-century London, and *For Faith and Freedom* (1888), concerning the Monmouth rebellion.

Works Cited

Unpublished sources

A.P. Watt and Company Records (#11036), General and Literary Manuscripts, Southern Historical Collection, Wilson Library, The University of North Carolina at Chapel Hill.

A.P. Watt Archive, Berg Collection, New York Public Library.

Aberdeen Journals Records (Ms 2770), Department of Special Collections and Archives, University of Aberdeen Library.

Bolton Evening News Archive (ZBEN), Bolton Central Library, Greater Manchester.

John Leng Collection, Local Studies Department, Dundee Central Library.

Leader Collection, Archives Section, Sheffield Central Library.

Letters from Wilkie Collins to A.P. Watt, 1881–89 (LCII 2840–2), Pembroke College Library, University of Cambridge.

Letters from Wilkie Collins to William Tindell (#891117), Mitchell Library, Glasgow.

Morris L. Parrish Collection, Princeton University Library, New Jersey.

Records of the Pae Family of Newport on Tay, in the possession of Mr and Mrs A.J. Cooke, c/o Archive and Record Centre, Dundee.

Tillotsons's Fiction Bureau Agreement Books, 1880–87 and 1890–94 (Ms.Eng.Misc.f.395/1–2), Bodleian Library, Oxford.

Tillotsons's Fiction Bureau Records, in the care of Michael L. Turner, Head of Conservation, Bodleian Library, Oxford.

Victor Fremont Lawson papers, Newberry Library, Chicago.

W.F. Tillotson Papers, held in the *Bolton Evening News* Offices, Newspaper House, Churchgate, Bolton, Greater Manchester.

Wolff Collection, Harry Ransom Humanities Research Center, The University of Texas at Austin.

Contemporary sources

(For reasons of space, single references to items in contemporary newspapers are cited fully in the text but not included in the list of Works Cited.)

Addy, S.O. 'Robert Eadon Leader, President of this Society, An Appreciation.' In *Transactions of the Hunter Archaeological Society*, 2 (1924) 213–19.

Allen, Grant. *The British Barbarians*. London: John Lane, 1895.

Andrews, Alexander. *The History of British Journalism*, 2 vols. London: Bentley, 1859.

Arnold, Matthew. *Culture and Anarchy*. London: Smith, Elder, 1869.

Arnold, Matthew. 'Copyright.' In *Fortnightly Review*, NS 27 (Mar. 1880) 319–34.

Arnold, Matthew. 'Up to Easter.' In *Nineteenth Century*, 123 (May 1887) 628–43.

Arnold, Thomas. *Christian Life, Its Course, Its Hindrances, and Its Helps: Sermons Preached Mostly in the Chapel of Rugby School.* 4th edn. London: B. Fellowes, 1845.

[Austin, Alfred.] 'The Sensational School.' In *Temple Bar*, 29 (June 1870) 410–24.

Bennett, E. Arnold. *Journalism for Women: a Practical Guide.* London: John Lane, 1898.

Bennett, E. Arnold. *How to Become an Author.* London: Pearson, 1903.

[Bennett, E. Arnold.] *Letters of Arnold Bennett*, ed. James Hepburn, 4 vols. London: Oxford University Press, 1966–70.

Besant, Walter. *All Sorts and Conditions of Men*, 3 vols. London: Chatto and Windus, 1883.

Besant, Walter. *The Art of Fiction.* London: Chatto and Windus, 1884.

Besant, Walter. *Dorothy Forster*, 3 vols. London: Chatto and Windus, 1884.

Besant, Walter. *The World Went Very Well Then*, 3 vols. London: Chatto and Windus, 1887.

Besant, Walter. Contribution to Symposium on 'Candour in English Fiction.' In *New Review*, 2:1 (Jan. 1890) 1–7.

Besant, Walter. 'The Place of Fiction in Newspapers.' In *Sell's Dictionary of the World's Press* (1893) 17–22.

Besant, Walter. *The Society of Authors: a Record of Its Actions from Its Foundations.* London: Society of Authors, 1893.

Besant, Walter. *The City of Refuge*, 3 vols. London: Chatto and Windus, 1896.

Besant, Walter. *The Pen and the Book.* London: Thomas Burleigh, 1898.

Besant, Walter. *Autobiography.* London: Hutchinson, 1902.

Boase, Frederic. *Modern English Biography*, 6 vols. Truro: privately printed, 1892–1928.

[Boswell, H.A.] *About Newspapers: Chiefly English and Scottish.* Edinburgh: privately printed, 1888.

Braddon, M.E. *The One Thing Needful*, 3 vols. London: J. and R. Maxwell, 1886.

Briggs, William. *The Law of International Copyright.* London: Stevens and Haynes, 1906.

Caine, Hall. *My Story.* London: William Heinemann, 1908.

Collection of Letters Addressed to A.P. Watt by Various People. London: The Literary Agency, 1893.

Colles, W.M. 'The Authors' Syndicate.' In *The Author* (Apr. 1892) 349–50.

Collet, Collet Dobson. *History of the Taxes on Knowledge*, 2 vols. London: T. Fisher Unwin, 1899.

Collins, Wilkie. *Considerations on the Copyright Question Addressed to an American Friend.* London: Trübner, 1880.

Collins, Wilkie. 'The Unknown Public.' In *Household Words*, 18 (21 Aug. 1858) 217–22.

Collins, Wilkie. *Jezebel's Daughter*, 3 vols. London: Chatto and Windus, 1880.

Collins, Wilkie. *Heart and Science: a Story of the Present Time*, 3 vols. London: Chatto and Windus, 1883.

[Collins, Wilkie.] *The Letters of Wilkie Collins*, eds William Baker and William M. Clarke, 2 vols. London: Macmillan, 1999.

[Conrad, Joseph.] *The Collected Letters of Joseph Conrad*, eds Frederick R.

Karl and Laurence Davies, 5 vols. Cambridge: Cambridge University Press, 1983–96.

Copinger, W.A. *The Law of Copyright in Works of Literature and Art*, 4th edn, ed. J.M. Easton. London: Stevens and Haynes, 1904.

Copinger, W.A. *The Law of Copyright in Works of Literature and Art*, 5th edn, ed. J.M. Easton. London: Stevens and Haynes, 1915.

Der Verlag Bernhard Tauchnitz, 1837–1912. Leipzig: Tauchnitz, 1912.

[Dickens, Charles.] *Letters of Charles Dickens*, eds Madeline House, Graham Storey, and Kathleen Tillotson, 10 vols. Oxford: Clarendon Press, 1965–99.

Disraeli, Benjamin. *Sybil, or The Two Nations*, 3 vols. London: Colburn, 1845.

Dowell, Stephen. *A History of Taxation and Taxes in England: from the Earliest Times to the Present Day*, 4 vols, 2nd edn. London: Longmans Green, 1888.

Downey, Edmund. *Twenty Years Ago: a Book of Anecdote Illustrating Literary Life in London*. London: Hurst and Blackett, 1905.

Ellis, S.M. *William Harrison Ainsworth and His Friends*, 2 vols. London: John Lane, 1911.

Escott, T.H.S. *Platform, Press, Politics, and Play*. Bristol: Arrowsmith [1895].

Fox Bourne, R.H. *English Newspapers: Chapters in the History of Journalism*, 2 vols. London: Chatto and Windus, 1887.

Friedrichs, Hulda. *The Life of George Newnes, Bart*. London: Hodder and Stoughton, 1911.

[Gissing, George.] *The Letters of George Gissing to Eduard Bertz, 1887–1903*, ed. Arthur C. Young. London: Constable, 1961.

Hardy, Thomas. Contribution to Symposium on 'Candour in English Fiction.' In *New Review*, 2:1 (Jan. 1890) 15–21.

Hardy, Thomas. *Tess of the D'Urbervilles: a Pure Woman*, 3 vols. London: Osgood, McIlvaine, 1891.

[Hardy, Thomas.] *The Collected Letters of Thomas Hardy*, eds Richard Little Purdy and Michael Millgate, 7 vols. Oxford: Clarendon Press, 1978–88.

Haslam, James. *The Press and the People: an Estimate of Reading in Working Class Districts*. London: Manchester City News, 1906.

Holland, C. 'Fifty Years of Novel Writing: Miss Braddon at Home.' In *Pall Mall Magazine* (Nov. 1911) 707–9.

How a Newspaper Is Printed. Dundee: John Leng and Co. [1891].

How We Publish Our Papers. Sheffield: Wm. Leng and Co. [1893].

Hunt, William. *Then and Now: or, Fifty Years of Newspaper Work*. Hull: Hamilton, Adams, 1887.

James, Henry. 'The Art of Fiction.' In *Longman's Magazine*, 4:23 (Sept. 1884) 502–21.

James, Henry. *Notes of a Son and Brother*. New York: Scribner, 1914.

Jay, Harriet. *Robert Buchanan*. London: T. Fisher Unwin: 1903.

Leader, J.D. *Seventy-Three Years of Progress: a History of the Sheffield Independent from 1819 to 1892*. Sheffield: Leader and Sons, 1892.

Leigh, J.G. 'What Do the Masses Read?'. In *Economic Review*, 14 (Apr. 1904) 166–77.

Linton, Eliza Lynn. *My Literary Life*. London: Hodder and Stoughton, 1899.

Low, Sidney J. 'Newspaper Copyright.' In *National Review*, 19:113 (1892) 648–66.

[Mansel, H.L.] 'Sensation Novels.' In *Quarterly Review*, 133:226 (Apr. 1863) 481–514.

Moore, George. *Literature at Nurse, or Circulating Morals*. London: Vizetelly, 1885.

Muddock, J.E.P. ('Dick Donovan'). *Pages from an Adventurous Life*. London: T. Werner Laurie, 1907.

Murray, David Christie. *Recollections*. London: John Long: 1908.

Nicoll, W. Robertson. 'A.P. Watt, the Great Napoleon of the Realm of Print.' In *British Weekly*, 57 (12 Nov. 1914) 127.

Norrie, William. *Edinburgh Newspapers Past and Present*. Earlston: Waverley, 1891.

Oliphant, Margaret. 'Sensation Novels.' In *Blackwood's Edinburgh Magazine*, 91 (May 1862) 564–84.

Oliphant, Margaret. 'Novels.' In *Blackwood's Edinburgh Magazine*, 102 (Sept. 1867) 257–80.

Oliphant, Margaret. *Autobiography and Letters*, ed. Mrs Harry Coghill. Edinburgh: Blackwood, 1899.

Oliphant, Margaret. *The Autobiography of Margaret Oliphant: the Complete Text*, ed. Elisabeth Jay. Oxford: Oxford University Press, 1990.

[Pae, David.] *Lucy, the Factory Girl: or, the Secrets of the Tontine Close*. Edinburgh: Thomas Grant, 1860.

Pascoe, Charles E. 'The Story of the English Magazines.' In *Atlantic Monthly*, 54 (Sept. 1884) 364–74.

Payn, James. *Some Literary Recollections*. London: Smith, Elder, 1884.

Phillips, Walter C. *Dickens, Reade, and Collins: Sensation Novelists*. 1919; New York: Russell and Russell, 1962.

Porter, G.R. *The Progress of the Nation in Its Various Social and Economic Relations from the Beginning of the Nineteenth Century*. 1836; revised by F.W. Hirst, London: Methuen, 1912.

Progress of British Newspapers in the Nineteenth Century, Illustrated. London: Simpkin, Marshall, Hamilton, Kent [1901].

[Rae, W. Fraser.] 'Sensation Novelists: Miss Braddon.' In *North British Review*, 43 (1865) 180–205.

Reid, Elizabeth, with C.H. Coe. *Captain Mayne Reid: His Life and Adventures*. London: Greening and Co., 1900.

Report from the Select Committee on Newspaper Stamps. House of Commons Papers, 17:558, 1851.

Report of the Executive Committee of the Society of Authors (Incorporated). Society of Authors, Jan. 1890.

A Return of the Number of Newspaper Stamps, 1837–50. House of Commons Papers, 28:42, 1852.

A Return of the Number of Newspaper Stamps, 1851–3. House of Commons Papers, 39:117, 1854.

A Return of the Number of Newspaper Stamps, 1854. House of Commons Papers, 40:497, 1855.

Review of *The Newspaper Press Directory and Advertiser's Guide, Thirty-fifth Annual Issue*, London, 1880. In *Quarterly Review*, 150 (Oct. 1880) 498–537.

'Rita' [Mrs Desmond Humphries]. *Recollections of a Literary Life*. London: Andrew Melrose, 1936.

'Rita'. *The Silent Woman*. London: Hutchinson, 1904.

Roebuck, John Arthur. *Life and Letters*, Ed. R.E. Leader. London: Edward Arnold, 1897.

Sala, George Augustus. *Life and Adventures of George Augustus Sala*, 2 vols. London: Cassells, 1895.

Sheffield Daily Telegraph 1855–1925: a Record of Seventy Years. Sheffield: W.C. Leng and Co. [1925].

Sinclair, Alexander. *Fifty Years of Newspaper Life, 1845–1895*. Glasgow: privately printed [1895].

Smith, Laura Alex. 'Women's Work in the London and Provincial Press.' In *Mitchell's Newspaper Press Directory* (1897) 14–15.

Sprigge, S. Squire. *The Society of French Authors: Its Foundations and Its History*. London: Incorporated Society of Authors, 1889.

Tinsley, William. *Random Recollections of an Old Publisher*, 2 vols. London: Simpkin, Marshall, Hamilton, Kent, 1900.

Westall, William. 'Newspaper Fiction.' In *Lippincott's Monthly Magazine*, 45 (Jan. 1890) 77–88.

Whyte, Frederic. *William Heinemann, a Memoir*. London: Jonathan Cape, 1928.

Wilson, Frederick J.F. *Stereotyping and Electrotyping*. London: Wyman and Sons [1880].

[Wise, J.R.] 'Belles Lettres.' In *Westminster Review*, NS 30 (July 1866) 268–80.

Yates, Edmund. *Edmund Yates: His Recollections and Experiences*, 2 vols. London: Bentley, 1884.

Modern sources

Altick, Richard D. *The English Common Reader: a Social History of the Mass Reading Public, 1800–1900*. Chicago, Ill.: University of Chicago Press, 1957.

Altick, Richard D. *The Presence of the Present: Topics of the Day in the Victorian Novel*. Colombus, Ohio: Ohio State University Press, 1991.

Anderson, R.A. *Education and Opportunity in Victorian Scotland*. Oxford: Clarendon Press, 1983.

Anderson, Rachel. *The Purple Heart Throbs: the Sub-literature of Love*. London: Hodder and Stoughton, 1974.

Anesko, Michael. *'Friction with the Market': Henry James and the Profession of Authorship*. New York: Oxford University Press, 1986.

Barnes, James J. *Free Trade in Books: a Study of the London Book Trade Since 1800*. Oxford: Clarendon Press, 1964.

Bellanger, Claude, Jacques Godechot, Pierre Guiral and Fernand Terrou. *Histoire Générale de la Presse Française*, 4 vols. Paris: Presses Universitaires de France, 1969–75.

Bennet, Scott. 'Revolutions in Thought: Serial Publication and the Mass market for Reading.' In J. Shattock and M. Wolff (eds), *The Victorian Periodical Press: Samplings and Soundings*, Leicester: Leicester University Press, 1982, pp. 225–57.

Berridge, V.S. 'Popular Journalism and Working Class Attitudes, 1854–86: a Study of *Reynolds's Newspaper*, *Lloyd's Weekly Newspaper* and the *Weekly*

Times.' Unpublished PhD Dissertation, University of London, 1976.

Berridge, Virginia. 'Popular Sunday Papers and Mid-Victorian Society.' In George Boyce, James Curran and Pauline Wingate (eds), *Newspaper History: from the Seventeenth Century to the Present Day*, London: Constable, 1978, pp. 247–64.

Berridge, Virginia. 'Content Analysis and Historical Research on Newspapers.' In Michael Harris and Alan Lee (eds), *The Press in English Society from the Seventeenth to Nineteenth Centuries*, London: Associated University Presses, 1986, pp. 201–18.

Blakey, Dorothy. *The Minerva Press 1790–1820*. London: Oxford University Press for The Bibliographical Society, 1939.

Bonham-Carter, Victor. *Authors by Profession: Volume 1, From the Introduction of Printing until the Copyright Act 1911*. London: Society of Authors, 1978.

Boyce, George, James Curran and Pauline Wingate (eds). *Newspaper History: from the Seventeenth Century to the Present Day*. London: Constable, 1978.

Brake, Laurel. *Subjugated Knowledges: Journalism, Gender, and Literature in the Nineteenth Century*. New York: New York University Press, 1994.

Brake, Laurel, Aled Jones and Lionel Madden (eds). *Investigating Victorian Journalism*. London: Macmillan, 1990.

Brantlinger, Patrick. 'What is "Sensational" about the "Sensation Novel"?.' In *Nineteenth Century Fiction*, 37:1 (June 1982) 1–28.

Brown, Lucy. *Victorian News and Newspapers*. Oxford: Clarendon Press, 1985.

Carnell, Jennifer. *The Literary Lives of Mary Elizabeth Braddon*. Hastings, E. Sussex: Sensation Press, 2000.

Cass, Eddie, Alan Fowler and Terry Wyke. 'The Remarkable Rise and Long Decline of *The Cotton Factory Times*.' In *Media History*, 4:2 (Dec. 1998) 141–60.

Cass, Edward Fletcher. '*The Cotton Factory Times*, 1885–1937: a Family Newspaper and the Lancashire Cotton Community.' Unpublished PhD dissertation, Edge Hill University College, University of Lancaster, 1996.

Clarke, William M. *The Secret Life of Wilkie Collins*. London: Allison and Busby, 1988.

Cogan, Frances B. Review of *Edging Women Out*, by Gaye Tuchman with Nina E. Fortin. In *Annals of the American Academy of Political and Social Science*, 509 (May 1990) 181–2.

Colby, Robert A. 'Goose Quill and Blue Pencil: the Victorian Novelist as Editor.' In J.H. Wiener (ed.), *Innovators and Preachers: The role of the Editor in Victorian England*, Westport, Conn.: Greenwood Press, 1985, pp. 203–29.

Colby, Robert A. 'Tale Bearing in the 1890s: *The Author* and Fiction Syndication'. In *Victorian Periodicals Review*, 18:1 (spring 1985) 2–16.

Colby, Robert A. '"What Fools Authors Be!" The Authors' Syndicate, 1890–1920.' In *Library Chronicle of the University of Texas 35* (1986) 60–87.

Colby, Robert A. 'Harnessing Pegasus: Walter Besant, *The Author* and the Profession of Letters.' In *Victorian Periodicals Review*, 23:3 (autumn 1990) 111–20.

Colby, Robert A. 'Authorship and the Book Trade.' In J. Don Vann and Rosemary T. VanArsdel (eds), *Victorian Periodicals and Victorian Society*, Aldershot: Scolar Press, 1994, pp. 143–61.

Colby, Vineta and Robert A. Colby. *The Equivocal Virtue: Mrs. Oliphant and the Victorian Literary Market Place*. [Hamden, Conn.]: Archon Books, 1966.

Coleman, D.C. *The British Paper Industry, 1495–1860: a Study in Industrial Growth.* Oxford: Clarendon Press, 1958.

Collie, Michael. *George Meredith: a Bibliography.* Toronto: University of Toronto Press, 1974.

Coolidge, Archibald Cary. *Charles Dickens as Serial Novelist.* Ames: Iowa State University Press, 1967.

Cowan, R.M.W. *The Newspaper in Scotland: a Study of Its First Expansion 1815–1860.* Glasgow: George Outram, 1946.

Craig, David. *Scottish Literature and the Scottish People 1680–1830.* London: Chatto and Windus, 1961.

Cranfield, G.A. *The Development of the Provincial Newspaper 1700–1760.* Oxford: Oxford University Press, 1962.

Cranfield, G.A. *The Press and Society: from Caxton to Northcliffe.* London: Longman, 1978.

Cross, Nigel. *The Common Writer: Life in Nineteenth-Century Grub Street.* Cambridge: Cambridge University Press, 1985.

Cvetkovich, Ann. *Mixed Feelings: Feminism, Mass Culture, and Victorian Sensationalism.* Brunswick, N.J.: Rutgers University Press, 1992.

Dalziel, Margaret. *Popular Fiction 100 years Ago: an Unexplored Tract of Literary History.* London: Cohen and West, 1957.

Donaldson, William. *Popular Literature in Victorian Scotland: Language, Fiction and the Press.* Aberdeen: Aberdeen University Press, 1986.

Dooley, Allan C. *Author and Printer in Victorian England.* Charlottesville, Va.: University Press of Virginia, 1992.

Doran, George H. *Chronicles of Barabbas, 1884–1934.* London: Methuen, 1935.

Drabble, Margaret. *Arnold Bennett: a Biography.* London: Weidenfeld and Nicolson, 1974.

Edwards, P.D. *Dickens's 'Young Men': George Augustus Sala, Edmund Yates and the World of Victorian Journalism.* Aldershot: Ashgate Press, 1997.

Eliot, Simon. '"His Generation Read His Stories": Walter Besant, Chatto and Windus and *All Sorts and Conditions of Men.'* In *Publishing History*, 21 (1987) 25–67.

Eliot, Simon. 'Unequal Partnerships: Besant, Rice, and Chatto, 1876–82.' In *Publishing History*, 26 (1989) 73–109.

Eliot, Simon. *Leading the Literary Life: Walter Besant and the Professionalisation of Literature 1870–1901.* University Park, Pa.: Pennsylvania State University Press, forthcoming.

Ellegard, Alvar. 'The Readership of the Periodical Press in Mid-Victorian Britain.' In *Victorian Periodicals Newsletter*, 13 (1971) 5–22.

Elwell, Stephen. 'Editors and Social Change: a Case Study of *Once a Week* (1859–90).' In J.H. Wiener (ed.), *Innovators and Preachers: the Role of the Editor in Victorian England*, Westport, Conn.: Greenwood Press, 1985, pp. 23–42.

Elwin, Malcolm. *Charles Reade.* London: Jonathan Cape, 1931.

Elwin, Malcolm. *Victorian Wallflowers: a Panoramic Survey of the Popular Literary Periodicals.* London: Jonathan Cape, 1934.

Elwin, Malcolm. *Old Gods Falling.* London: Collins, 1939.

Engel, Elliot and Margaret F. King. *The Victorian Novel Before Victoria: British Fiction During the Reign of William IV, 1830–37.* London: Macmillan, 1984.

Farmer, Steve and Graham Law. '"Belt-and-Braces" Serialization: the Case of *Heart and Science.*' In *Wilkie Collins Society Journal*, NS 2 (1999) 61–71.

Feather, John. *The Provincial Book Trade in Eighteenth-century England.* Cambridge: Cambridge University Press, 1985.

Feather, John. *A History of British Publishing.* London: Routledge, 1988.

Feltes, N.N. *Modes of Production of Victorian Novels.* Chicago, Ill.: University of Chicago Press, 1986.

Feltes, N.N. *Literary Capital and the Late Victorian Novel.* Madison, Wis.: University of Wisconsin Press, 1993.

Ferguson, Joan P.S. *Directory of Scottish Newspapers.* Edinburgh: National Library of Scotland, 1984.

Fielding, K.J. 'The Monthly Serialization of Dickens's Novels.' In *Dickensian*, 54:1 (Jan. 1958) 4–11.

Fielding, K.J. 'The Weekly Serialization of Dickens's Novels.' In *Dickensian*, 54:3 (Sept. 1958) 134–41.

Flint, Kate. *The Woman Reader, 1837–1914.* Oxford: Clarendon Press, 1993.

Gagnier, Regenia. *Idylls of the Marketplace: Oscar Wilde and the Victorian Public.* Stanford, Cal.: Stanford University Press, 1986.

Gallagher, Catherine. Review of *Edging Women Out*, by Gaye Tuchman with Nina E. Fortin. In *Comparative Literature*, 44:3 (summer 1992) 322–4.

Gasson, Andrew. *Wilkie Collins: an Illustrated Guide.* Oxford: Oxford University Press, 1998.

Gettmann, Royal A. *A Victorian Publisher: a Study of the Bentley Papers.* Cambridge: Cambridge University Press, 1960.

Gillies, Mary Ann. 'A. P. Watt, Literary Agent.' In *Publishing Research Quarterly*, 9 (spring 1993) 20–33.

Goode, John. 'The Art of Fiction: Walter Besant and Henry James.' In D. Howard, J. Lucas and J. Goode (eds), *Tradition and Tolerance in Nineteenth Century Fiction*, London: Routledge and Kegan Paul, 1966, 243–81.

Goode, John. 'The Decadent Writer as Producer.' In Ian Fletcher (ed.), *Decadence and the 1890s*, London: Edward Arnold, 1979, pp. 109–29.

Griest, Guinevere L. *Mudie's Circulating Library and the Victorian Novel.* Bloomington, Ind.: Indiana University Press, 1970.

Griffiths, Dennis (ed.). *Encyclopaedia of the British Press, 1422–1992.* London: Macmillan, 1992.

Grindle, Juliet, and Simon Gatrell (eds). Thomas Hardy, *Tess of the D'Urbervilles.* Oxford: Clarendon Press, 1983.

Guthrie, Diana. 'The First Fifty Years of the Sheffield Daily Telegraph: an Experiment in Provincial Journalism'. Unpublished MA dissertation. University of Sheffield: 1970.

Haining, Peter (ed.). *The Penny Dreadful: Or, Strange, Horrid and Sensational Tales!.* London: Victor Gollancz, 1975.

Hamer, Mary. *Writing by Numbers: Trollope's Serial Fiction.* Cambridge: Cambridge University Press, 1987.

Harden, Edgar F. *The Emergence of Thackeray's Serial Fiction.* London: Prior, 1979.

Harris, Michael, and Alan Lee (eds). *The Press in English Society from the Seventeenth to Nineteenth Centuries.* London: Associated University Presses, 1986.

Harvey, John. *Victorian Novelists and Their Illustrators.* New York: New York University Press, 1971.

Hepburn, James. *The Author's Empty Purse and the Rise of the Literary Agent.* Oxford: Oxford University Press, 1968.

Herd, Harold. *The March of Journalism: the Story of the British Press from 1622 to the Present Day.* London: Allen and Unwin, 1952.

Hilley, Nicholas. '"Can't You Find Me Something Nasty?": Circulating Libraries and Literary Censorship in Britain from the 1890s to the 1910s.' In Robin Myers and Michael Harris, (eds). *Censorship and the Control of Print in England and France, 1600–1910,* Winchester: St. Paul's Bibliographies, 1992, pp. 123–47.

Hobson, Harold, Phillip Knightley, and Leonal Russell. *The Pearl of Days: an Intimate Memoir of the Sunday Times, 1822–1972.* London: Hamish Hamilton, 1972.

Honda, Yasuo. *Shimbun shôsetsu no tanjo.* [The Birth of the Newspaper Novel.] Tokyo: Heibonsha, 1998.

Houghton, Walter E. (ed.). *The Wellesley Index to Victorian Periodicals,* 5 vols. Toronto: University of Toronto Press, 1966–89.

Hughes, Linda K. and Michael Lund. *The Victorian Serial.* Charlottesville, Va.: University Press of Virginia, 1991.

Hughes, Winifred. *The Maniac in the Cellar: Sensation Novels of the 1860s.* Princeton, NJ: Princeton University Press, 1980.

[Huxley, Leonard.] *The House of Smith, Elder.* London: privately printed by William Clowes, 1923.

Jackson, Kate. 'The "Tit-Bits" Phenomenon: George Newnes, New Journalism and the Periodical Text.' In *Victorian Periodicals Review,* 30:3 (autumn 1997) 201–26.

James, Elizabeth and Helen R. Smith. *Penny Dreadfuls and Boys's Adventures: the Barry Ono Collection of Victorian Popular Literature in the British Library.* London: The British Library, 1988.

James, Louis. *Fiction for the Working Man 1830–1850.* London: Oxford University Press, 1963.

James, Louis (ed.). *Print and the People, 1819–51.* London: Allen Lane, 1976.

James, Louis. 'The Trouble with Betsy: Periodicals and the Common Reader in Mid-Nineteenth-Century England.' In J. Shattock and M. Wolff (eds), *The Victorian Periodical Press: Samplings and Soundings,* Leicester: Leicester University Press, 1982, pp. 349–66.

Johanningsmeier, Charles. *Fiction and the American Literary Marketplace: the Role of Newspaper Syndicates in America, 1860–1900.* Cambridge: Cambridge University Press, 1997.

Johnson-Woods, Toni. *Index to Fiction Serials in Australian Periodicals.* Canberra: Mulini Press, forthcoming.

Jones, Aled. 'Tillotson's Fiction Bureau: The Manchester Manuscripts.' In *Victorian Periodicals Review,* 17:1/2 (spring/summer 1984) 43–9.

Jones, Aled. 'The New Journalism in Wales.' In J.H. Wiener (ed.), *Papers for the Millions: the New Journalism in Britain,* Westport, Conn.: Greenwood Press, 1988, pp. 165–81.

Jones, Aled. *Powers of the Press: Newspapers, Power, and the Public in Nineteenth-Century England.* Aldershot: Scolar Press, 1996.

Keating, P.J. *The Haunted Study: a Social History of the English Novel 1875–1914.* London: Secker and Warburg, 1989.

Korg, Jacob. *George Gissing: a Critical Biography*. London: Methuen, 1965.

Law, Graham. 'Wilkie in the Weeklies: the Serialization and Syndication of Collins's Late Novels.' In *Victorian Periodicals Review*, 30:3 (autumn 1997) 244–69.

Law, Graham. 'Last Things: Materials Relating to Collins in the Watt Collection at Chapel Hill.' In *Wilkie Collins Society Journal*, NS 1 (1998) 50–8.

Law, Graham. '"Engaged to Messrs. Tillotson and Son": Letters from John Maxwell, 1882–8.' In *Humanitas* (Waseda University Law Society) 37 (1999) 1–42.

Lee, Alan J. *The Origins of the Popular Press in England 1855–1914*. London: Croom Helm, 1976.

Liveing, Edward. *Adventure in Publishing: the House of Ward Lock, 1854–1954*. London: Ward Lock, 1954.

Lonoff, Sue. *Wilkie Collins and His Victorian Readers: a Study in the Rhetoric of Authorship*. New York: A.M.S. Press, 1982.

Lyon, Peter. *Success Story: the Life and Times of S.S. McClure*. New York: Scribner, 1963.

MacKenzie, Norman and Jeanne MacKenzie. *The Life of H.G. Wells: the Time Traveller*. London: Hogarth Press, 1987.

March, Kenneth Geoffrey. 'The Life and Career of Sir William Christopher Leng 1825–1902: a Study of the Ideas and Influence of a Prominent Victorian Journalist.' Unpublished MA dissertation. University of Sheffield: 1966.

Martin, Carol A. *George Eliot's Serial Fiction*. Columbus, Ohio: Ohio State University Press, 1994.

Maxwell, W.B. *Time Gathered*. London: Hutchinson, 1937.

Mayo, Robert Donald. *The English Novel in the Magazines, 1740–1815*. Evanston, NJ: Northwestern University Press, 1962.

Mitchell, Sally. *The Fallen Angel: Chastity, Class and Women's Reading*. Bowling Green, Ohio: Bowling Green University Popular Press, 1981.

Morison, Stanley. *The English Newspaper: Some Account of the Physical Development of Journals Printed in London between 1622 and the Present Day*. Cambridge: Cambridge University Press, 1932.

Morrison, Elizabeth. 'Newspaper and Novelists in Late Colonial Australia: Serial Fiction in the Melbourne *Age*, 1872–1899.' Unpublished MA dissertation. Monash University: 1983.

Morrison, Elizabeth. 'Serial Fiction in Australian Colonial Newspapers.' In John O. Jordan and Robert L. Patten (eds), *Literature in the Marketplace: Nineteenth-century British Publishing and Reading Practices*, Cambridge: Cambridge University Press, 1995, pp. 306–24.

Mukerji, Chandra. Review of *Edging Women Out*, by Gaye Tuchman with Nina E. Fortin. In *Comparative Sociology*, 19:4 (July 1990) 511–13.

Mumby, Frank Arthur. *The House of Routledge, 1834–1934*. London: Routledge, 1934.

Mumby, Frank Arthur and Ian Norrie. *Publishing and Bookselling*. London: Jonathan Cape, 1974.

Nelson, Claudia. *Fatherhood in Victorian Periodicals, 1850–1910*. Athens, Ga.: University of Georgia Press, 1995.

Nevett, T.R. 'The Development of Commercial Advertising, 1800–1914.' Unpublished PhD dissertation. University of London: 1979.

Nevett, Terry. 'Advertising and Editorial Integrity in the Nineteenth Century.' In George Boyce, James Curran and Pauline Wingate (eds), *Newspaper History: from the Seventeenth Century to the Present Day*, London: Constable, 1978, pp. 149–67.

Newbolt, Peter. *G.A. Henty 1832–1902: a Bibliographical Study*. Aldershot: Scolar Press, 1996.

Nowell-Smith, Simon. *The House of Cassell, 1848–1958*. London: Cassell and Co., 1958.

Nowell-Smith, Simon. *International Copyright Law and the Publisher in the Reign of Queen Victoria*. Oxford: Clarendon Press, 1968.

Palmer, John E.C. and Harold W. Paar. 'Transport.' In J. Don Vann and Rosemary T. VanArsdel (eds), *Victorian Periodicals and Victorian Society*, Aldershot: Scolar Press, 1994, pp. 179–98.

Patten, Robert L. *Charles Dickens and His Publishers*. Oxford: Clarendon Press, 1978.

Peters, Catherine. *The King of Inventors: a Life of Wilkie Collins*. London: Secker and Warburg, 1991.

Plant, Marjorie. *The English Book Trade: an Economic History of the Making and Sale of Books*. London: Allen and Unwin, 1939; 1974.

Pollard, Graham. 'Serial Fiction.' In John Carter (ed.), *New Paths in Book Collecting*, London: Constable and Co., 1934, pp. 247–77.

Pollard, Graham. 'Novels in Newspapers: Some Unpublished Letters of Captain Mayne Reid.' In *Review of English Studies*, 18:69 (Jan. 1942) 72–85.

Purdy, Richard Little. *Thomas Hardy: a Bibliographical Study*. London: Oxford University Press, 1954.

Pykett, Lyn. *The "Improper" Feminine: the Women's Sensation Novel and the New Woman Writing*. London: Routledge, 1992.

Queffélec, Lise. *Le Roman-Feuilleton Français au XIXe siècle*. Paris: Presses Universitaires de France, 1989.

Raven, James. 'Serial Advertisement in 18th-century Britain and Ireland.' In Robin Myers and Michael Harris, (eds). *Serials and Their Readers, 1620–1914*, Winchester: St Paul's Bibliographies, 1993, pp. 103–22.

Read, Donald. *Press and People 1790–1850: Opinion in Three English Cities*. London: Edward Arnold, 1961.

Robinson, Solveig C. 'Editing *Belgravia*: M.E. Braddon's Defense of "Light Literature".' In *Victorian Periodicals Review*, 28:2 (spring 1995) 109–22.

Rubinstein, Hilary. 'A.P. Watt: The First Hundred Years.' In *The Bookseller*, 3619 (3 May 1975) 2354–8.

Sadleir, Michael. *Trollope: a Bibliography*. London: Constable, 1928.

Sadleir, Michael. *Things Past*. London: Constable, 1944.

Saunders, David. *Authorship and Copyright*. London: Routledge, 1992.

Saunders, J.W. *The Profession of English Letters*. London: Routledge and Kegan Paul, 1964.

Saunders, L.J. *Scottish Democracy 1815–40*. Edinburgh: Oliver and Boyd, 1950.

Schmidt, B.Q. 'Novelists, Publishers and Fiction in Middle-class Magazines, 1860–1880.' In *Victorian Periodicals Review*, 17:4 (winter 1984) 142–53.

Shattock, J. and M. Wolff (eds). *The Victorian Periodical Press: Samplings and Soundings*. Leicester: Leicester University Press, 1982.

Shillingsburg, Peter L. *Pegasus in Harness: Victorian Publishing and W.M. Thackeray*. Charlottesville, Va.: University Press of Virginia, 1992.

Singleton, Frank. *Tillotsons 1850–1950*. Bolton: Tillotson and Son, 1950.

Spilka, Mark. 'Henry James and Walter Besant: "The Art of Fiction" Controversy'. In *Novel*, 6:2 (winter 1973) 101–19.

Srebrnik, Patricia. *Alexander Strahan, Victorian Publisher*. Ann Arbor, Mich.: University of Michigan Press, 1986.

Straus, Ralph. *Sala: the Portrait of an Eminent Victorian*. London: Constable, 1942.

Sullivan, Alvin. *British Literary Magazines*, 4 vols. Westport, Conn.: Greenwood Press, 1984.

Summers, Montague. *A Gothic Bibliography*. London: Fortune Press [1941].

Sussex, Lucy and John Burrows. 'Whodunit?: Literary Forensics and the Crime Writing of James Skipp Borlase and Mary Fortune.' In *Bibliographical Society of Australia and New Zealand Bulletin*, 21: 2 (2nd quarter, 1997) 73–105.

Sutherland, J.A. *Victorian Novelists and Publishers*. London: Athlone Press, 1976.

Sutherland, J.A. '*Cornhill*'s Sales and Payments: The First Decade'. In *Victorian Periodicals Review*, 19:3 (autumn 1986) 106–8.

Sutherland, J.A. *Victorian Fiction: Writers, Publishers, Readers*. London: Macmillan, 1995.

Sutherland, John. *The Stanford Companion to Victorian Fiction*. Stanford, Cal.: Stanford University Press, 1989.

Terry, R.C. *Victorian Popular Fiction 1860–1880*. London: Macmillan, 1983.

Topp, Chester W. *Victorian Yellowbacks and Paperbacks, 1849–1905*, 2 vols. Denver, Colo.: Hermitage Antiquarian Bookshop, 1993–95.

Tredrey, F.D. *The House of Blackwood 1804–1954*. Edinburgh: William Blackwood, 1954.

Tuchman, Gaye, with Nina E. Fortin. *Edging Women Out: Victorian Novelists, Publishers, and Social Change*. New Haven, Conn.: Yale University Press, 1989.

Turner, E.S. *Boys will be Boys*, 2nd edn. London: Michael Joseph, 1957.

Turner, Michael L. 'The Syndication of Fiction in Provincial Newspapers, 1870–1939: The Example of the Tillotson "Fiction Bureau"'. Unpublished BLitt dissertation. Oxford University: 1968.

Turner, Michael L. *Index and Guide to the Lists of Publications of Richard Bentley and Son, 1829–1898*. Bishop's Stortford: Chadwyck-Healey, 1975.

Turner, Michael L. 'Tillotson's Fiction Bureau: Agreements with Authors'. In *Studies in the Book Trade: In Honour of Graham Pollard*, Oxford: Oxford Bibliographical Society, 1975, pp. 351–78.

Turner, Michael L. 'Reading for the Masses: Aspects of the Syndication of Fiction in Great Britain'. In Richard G. Langdon (ed.), *Book Selling and Book Buying: Aspects of the Nineteenth-Century British and American Book Trade*, Chicago, Ill.: American Library Assocation, 1978, pp. 52–72.

Vann, J. Don, and Rosemary T. VanArsdel (eds). *Periodicals of Queen Victoria's Empire: an Exploration*. Toronto: University of Toronto Press, 1996.

Vann, J. Don, and Rosemary T. VanArsdel (eds). *Victorian Periodicals and Victorian Society*. Aldershot: Scolar Press, 1994.

Vann, J.D. *Victorian Novels in Serial*. New York: Modern Language Association of America, 1985.

Vicinus, Martha. '"Helpless and Unfriended": Nineteenth-century Domestic Melodrama.' In *New Literary History*, 13 (1981) 127–43.

Victorian Fiction Research Guide 9 (1983). Indexes to Fiction in *Pall Mall Magazine* (1893–1914). Ed. Sue Thomas.

Victorian Fiction Research Guide 11 (1986). Margaret Oliphant (1828–1897): a Bibliography. Ed. John Stock Clarke.

Victorian Fiction Research Guide 14 (n.d.). Indexes to Fiction in *Belgravia*. Eds P.D. Edwards, I.G. Sibley and Margaret Versteeg.

Victorian Fiction Research Guide 17 (1989). Indexes to Fiction in *Chambers's Journal* 1854–1910. Ed. Sue Thomas.

Victorian Fiction Research Guide 19/20 (1993). Letters of George Augustus Sala to Edmund Yates. Ed. Judy McKenzie.

Victorian Fiction Research Guide 23 (1996). Indexes to Fiction in *The Idler* (1892–1911). Eds William B. Thesing and Becky Lewis.

Vincent, David. *Literacy and Popular Culture: England 1750–1914*. Cambridge: Cambridge University Press, 1989.

Wadsworth, A.P. 'Newspaper Circulations 1800–1954'. In *Transactions of the Manchester Statistical Society* (Session 1954–55, 1955) 1–41.

Walbank, Felix Alan. *Queens of the Circulating Library: Selections from Victorian Lady Novelists, 1850–1900*. London: Evans Bros, 1950.

Watson, Elmo Scott. *A History of Newspaper Syndicates in the United States, 1865–1935*. Chicago, Ill.: privately printed, 1936.

Webb, R.K. *The British Working Class Reader, 1790–1848: Literacy and Social Tension*. London: Allen and Unwin, [1955].

Weber, Gary. 'Henry Labouchere, *Truth* and the New Journalism'. In *Victorian Periodicals Review*, 26:1 (spring 1993) 36–43.

Weedon, Alexis. 'Watch This Space: Wilkie Collins and New Strategies in Victorian Publishing in the 1890s'. In Ruth Robbins and Julian Wolfreys (eds). *Victorian Identities: Social and Cultural Formations in Nineteenth-Century Literature*, London: Macmillan, 1996, pp. 163–83.

Whiting, John Roland. *Ernest E. Taylor, Valiant for Truth*. London: Bannisdale Press, 1958.

Wiener, J.H. *The War of the Unstamped: the Movement to Repeal the British Newspaper Tax, 1830–1836*. Ithaca, NY: Cornell University Press, 1969.

Wiener, J.H. 'Edmund Yates: The Gossip as Editor'. In J.H. Wiener (ed.), *Innovators and Preachers: the Role of the Editor in Victorian England*, Westport, Conn.: Greenwood Press, 1985, pp. 259–73.

Wiener, J.H. (ed.). *Innovators and Preachers: the Role of the Editor in Victorian England*. Westport, Conn.: Greenwood Press, 1985.

Wiener, J.H. 'How New was the New Journalism?'. In J.H. Wiener (ed.), *Papers for the Millions: the New Journalism in Britain*, Westport, Conn.: Greenwood Press, 1988, pp. 165–81.

Wiener, J.H. (ed.). *Papers for the Millions: the New Journalism in Britain*. Westport, Conn.: Greenwood Press, 1988.

Wiles, R.M. *Serial Publication in England before 1750*. Cambridge: Cambridge University Press, 1957.

Wiles, R.M. *Freshest Advices: Early Provincial Newspapers in England*. Columbus, Ohio: Ohio State University Press, 1965.

Williams, Keith. *The English Newspaper*. London: Springwood Books, 1977.

Williams, Raymond. *Communications*. Harmondsworth: Penguin Books, 1962.

Wilson, Charles. *First with the News: the History of W.H. Smith, 1792–1972*. London: W.H. Smith, 1985.

Wolff, Michael, John S. North and Dorothy Deering (eds). *The Waterloo Directory of Victorian Periodicals, 1824–1900*. Waterloo, Ontario: Wilfred Laurier University Press for the University of Waterloo, 1977.

Wolff, Robert Lee. 'Devoted Disciple: The Letters of Mary Elizabeth Braddon to Sir Edward Bulwer-Lytton, 1862–1873'. In *Harvard Library Bulletin*, 22:1–2 (1974) 5–35, 129–61.

Wolff, Robert Lee. *Sensational Victorian: the Life and Fiction of Mary Elizabeth Braddon*. New York: Garland, 1979.

Zinkhan, Elaine. 'Early British Publication of *While the Billy Boils*: the A.P. Watt Connection'. In *Bibliographical Society of Australia and New Zealand Bulletin*, 21:3 (3rd quarter, 1997) 165–82.

Index

* Page numbers in italics indicate references in the Notes.
* Material in the Preface, Acknowledgements and Appendix is not indexed.
* Place of publication of periodicals is London unless otherwise indicated in the title or in parenthesis.

290   *Index*